Keyboarding
for
Canadian Colleges

3rd Edition

Sandra D. Ubelacker, B.A., M.A., Ph.D.
Professor
Department of Secondary Education
University of Alberta

Melvin R. Delaney, B.Ed., M.Ed.
Dean of Business and Applied Arts
Lethbridge Community College
(Former Chairperson, Secretarial Science Department)
Red Deer College

Donna J. Allan, B.Ed., M.Ed., Ph.D.
President
Lethbridge Community College
(Former Chairperson, Secretarial Science Department)
Red Deer College

Career Course

Copp Clark Pitman Ltd.
A Longman Company
Toronto

ISBN 0-7730-4965-7

Editing/Jennie Bedford
Typesetting/Compeer Typographical Services Ltd.
Printing and Binding/John Deyell Co.

Canadian Cataloguing in Publication Data

Ubelacker, Sandra D.
    Keyboarding for Canadian colleges : career course

3rd ed.
ISBN 0-7730-4965-7

1. Electronic data processing-Keyboarding
2. Typewriting.   I. Delaney, Melvin R.
II. Allan, Donna J.   III. Title.

Z49.U24   652.3'024   C90-093371-2
1990

Disclaimer

An honest attempt has been made to secure permission for and acknowledge contributions of all material used. If there are errors or omissions, these are wholly unintentional and the publisher will be grateful to learn of them.

Copp Clark Pitman Ltd.
2775 Matheson Boulevard East
Mississauga, Ontario   L4W 4P7

Printed and bound in Canada

3 4 5   4965-7   94   93

Contents

Foreword

Keyboarding for Canadian Colleges, 3rd Edition is a revision of the well-known text *Keyboarding for Canadian Colleges, 2nd Edition.*

The excellent features of both the first and the second edition, however, are maintained in this third edition.

- **The alpha-numeric approach** in teaching the keyboard, introduced by Ubelacker, Delaney, and Allan in the first edition, helps students develop proficient keyboarding skills on the entire keyboard. The development of these skills is particularly relevant in meeting the increasing demand for speed and accuracy in keyboarding, which is prevalent today.
- **Practical exercises and applications** incorporate business vocabulary and realistic business situations.
- **Unarranged and handwritten material** are included in wide variety to encourage the development of problem solving and thinking skills.
- **English language skills** are stressed throughout.

When the authors were writing *Keyboarding for Canadian Colleges, 2nd Edition,* they responded to business educators' criticisms of current keyboarding texts by including many of their recommendations. It was natural then when work began on the revision of the text to survey users so that their comments and ideas could be incorporated in the 3rd edition.

The changes in *Keyboarding for Canadian Colleges, 3rd Edition* are listed below:

- more handwritten material and timed writings
- new instructions encouraging use of automatic options on typewriters and computers
- updated content of production exercises dealing with information processing and technology, computers, etc.
- new graphs, charts, tables in production exercises.
- new terminology — information processing terms, information technology terms, computer terms, etc.
- updated legal section in the *Career Course*
- updated Dasmund project in the *Career Course*
- new mini projects at the end of Units V, VI, and VII
- new number pad drills
- additional number practice drills
- new material on in-text references, endnotes, and footnotes
- new methods for setting margins and correcting errors

We hope that you will find *Keyboarding for Canadian Colleges, 3rd Edition* a comprehensive and up-to-date text that will meet your students' needs in helping to develop the skills suitable for use in today and tomorrow's market-place.

The Publisher

Acknowledgments

To the many people who have taken valuable time out from their busy schedules to complete or participate in the review survey for *Keyboarding for Canadian Colleges, 3rd Edition*, the authors and publisher would like to extend their sincere appreciation. Without your constructive criticism there would not have been the regional input that is necessary to produce a truly Canadian keyboarding program.

The following business educators were asked for detailed reviews of draft material and deserve a special note of thanks:

- Jane Parmeter, Kwantlen College, Surrey, B.C.
- Keyboarding Instructors, Vancouver Vocational Institute, Vancouver, B.C.
- Elsie Swartz, Humber College, Toronto, Ontario
- Keyboarding Instructors, Centennial College, Toronto, Ontario
- Pat Hudson, Humber College, Toronto, Ontario
- Doreen Wilgoss, Mohawk College, Hamilton, Ontario

Introduction

You are ready to begin *Keyboarding for Canadian Colleges, 3rd Edition*. After completing the study program, you will be able to key by touch and apply your skill to personal and business applications such as formatting and keying letters, tables, forms, reports, and completing a series of simulated secretarial tasks.

Organization of the text

Keyboarding for Canadian Colleges, 3rd Edition, is organized into eight units of twenty lessons each. Each unit deals with specific topics: Unit I introduces the keyboard and centering; Unit II, tabulation; Unit III, letters; Unit IV, reports; Unit V, additional letters; Unit VI, additional tabulation; Unit VII, additional reports; and Unit VIII, Dasmund Project. There is a Mini Project at the end of Units V, VI, and VII which will challenge you to use your decision-making skills. Numbers are presented as a logical extension of the second-row keys introduction in a lesson. Beginning with lesson two, you will practise numbers daily through drill material and apply number-keying skill in the production exercises. Special symbols such as editors' marks are introduced as they are needed. In each unit, lessons are planned with directed drill material, production practice, and applications in spelling. English usage, word division, capitalization, metric usage, number keying, and punctuation. The last lesson of each unit is a test to assess your progress. A pre-test and post-test are provided in the instructor's manual and will be supplied by your instructor.

Drill Material

Each unit has analytical practice and graduated speed practice drills. Analytical practice provides additional reinforcement for the alphabetic and number keys that may be causing errors. Graduated speed practice provides timed, short-drill material for either speed or accuracy development. Specific practice goals should be set each day for all types of drills (for a complete listing see the index under *Drills*). Drills should be timed and you should continually measure your progress. You should set your own individual goals with the assistance of your instructor or according to the marginal instructions. Number pad drills are available at the end of the text, in the Consolidated Drills section.

Timed Writings

Each lesson has a timed writing with the difficulty specified in terms of syllabic intensity (SI). The material is more difficult to key as the SI increases. A record of gross words per minute (GWPM) and the number of errors for your best timing should be kept on your Record Sheet (found in the Workbook). The best timing is the one keyed with the highest GWPM and with the number of errors below the maximum set by your instructor. If you are working without an instructor, refer to the timed writing objective given on each unit objective page. Additional timed writings are available at the end of the text, in the Consolidated Drills section.

Production Material

Editors' marks are introduced as they are needed for production exercises. Material is presented in arranged, handwritten, and unarranged format. The number of words in each production exercise is given in the Workbook. The word count is the number of keyed words in the production exercises. Allowance has not been made for the use of service mechanisms (setting tabs, enter/return key, etc.). Production exercises should be timed and the word count should be used as a guide in assessing production skill. A production word count, which makes allowance for the use of service mechanisms, is given for each unit test and will be supplied by your instructor.

Pica or Elite or 15-Pitch

To determine the pitch of your typewriter or printer, key 12 ds and compare the following:

Pica type: ppppppppppp

Elite type: ddddddddddd

15-Pitch: ddddddddddd

Alternatively, take a full sheet of letter-size paper and place the left edge at zero on the appropriate scale on the front of the typewriter or printer to measure the width of the paper. Pica type measures 85 spaces, elite type measures 102 spaces, and 15-pitch measures 127 spaces. If your typewriter or printer has more than one pitch available, select the one desired and reset your margins accordingly.

The spacing in this text is shown in elite or pica. Use the margin signal allowance to make the appropriate adjustments desired.

Workbooks Lessons 1-160

The Workbooks provide forms and letterhead paper for the production exercises, additional drills for each unit, the timing Record Sheet, composition, French-keying drills, and timed writings.

Illustrations of a typewriter and computer hardware components are provided to assist you in identifying the parts of the equipment you are using.

You are now ready to start lesson one. Follow the instructions and read the explanations carefully as you progress through *Keyboarding for Canadian Colleges, 3rd Edition.*

Instructions

The marginal instructions should be used as guidelines. Instructors should time as many drills as possible. If you are on individual progress, you should follow the instructions after the word "*or*" and provide variety by periodically timing yourself.

Four types of technique reminders are also found in the margins. **SC** or *stop check* is a reminder to you about good office and general keyboarding practices. **SP** indicates a difficult word that should be carefully checked for correct spelling. **P** is a new editors (proofreaders') mark that you will likely encounter in keying reports or edited copy. Finally, a ☛ is a reminder to use accepted metric notation.

INDEX

Unit I

Objectives

1 The student will begin to develop correct keyboarding technique.

2 The student will learn the correct use of a standard keyboard and service mechanisms.

3 The student will learn to key the alphabetic and numeric keyboard by touch.

4 The student will learn to format material on a page using horizontal centering, spread centering, block centering, and vertical centering.

5 The student will work toward developing a minimum speed of 20 words per minute with four or fewer errors on a two-minute timing.

Timing 10 — Three- or Five-Minute Timing

	1	CW	3

What ever happened to the paperless office that was
predicted for the 1990's? In fact, since the opposite seems
to be happening in so many firms, what happened to the
dreams of the office systems planners? The unfulfilled
promises have lead to a lot of skepticism on the part of
both employers and employees. The increased usage of paper
remains at approximately 3.2% annually.

While word processing and electronic mail capabilities
have allowed easy storage and direct communication from the
office equipment, an exponential growth of paper usage has
been associated with facsimile equipment (growth sometimes
as high as 22% per year) and with specialized graphics,
computer aided design, and computer aided manufacturing (up
to 20% per year). New ways of putting images on paper
require new paper designs and the pulp and paper industry
responds to each newly found need.

Certainly, less paper is being used from the corrections and retyping found in the use of manual typewriters
(and even electrics) of yesteryear but paper usage is still
increasing due to other needs in the office. On the other
hand, the advances in electronic document technology continue to become more dependable. New developments in optical disk storage, which is easily retrieved and read on
screen, could be the breakthrough which helps to lead closer
to the dream of a "paperless" office.

Line	1	CW	3
	11	11	3
	23	23	7
	34	34	11
	45	45	15
	56	56	18
	68	68	22
	76	76	25
	12	88	29
	24	100	33
	35	111	37
	46	122	40
	57	133	44
	69	145	48
	80	156	52
	91	167	56
	98	174	58
	11	185	62
	23	197	66
	34	208	69
	46	220	73
	57	231	77
	69	243	81
	80	254	85
	92	266	89
	100	274	91

SI = 1.39

• • • • 1 • • • • 2 • • • • 3 • • • • 4 • • • • 5 • • • • 6 • • • • 7 • • • • 8 • • • • 9 • • • •10 • • •11 • • • •12 **1 min**

1   2   3   4 **3 min**

1

A/S/D/F J/K/L/;

Are you ready to begin?

Your Work Station

1. Is your keyboard even with the front of your desk?
2. Is your desk clear except for the instruction book on the right side of your machine?
3. Is your instruction book standing upright?

SC

Did you set the line space regulator for single spacing? The line space regulator is usually located on the left side of the carriage behind the cylinder.

Your Typewriter

1. Is the paper guide set so the left edge of the paper is at 0 on the margin scale?
2. Is the line space regulator set for single spacing?
3. Are your margins set at 30 and 75?
4. Can you identify and use the paper bail and the paper release?
5. Can you insert a piece of paper in your typewriter?
6. Is your typewriter plugged in?

 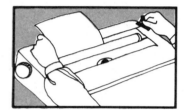

Your Computer

1. Is your computer plugged in OR Is the network ready?
2. Is your computer turned *on*?
3. Is your monitor turned *on*?
4. Is the word processing program loaded?
5. Is your formatted data disk loaded?
6. Is your monitor displaying a screen ready for word processing?
7. Is the paper in the printer aligned so the left edge of each sheet of paper is at 0 on the margin scale?

Your Posture

1. Are you sitting erect?
2. Are you sitting approximately a handspan from the edge of the machine?
3. Is your body centered opposite the **J** key?
4. Are your feet flat on the floor?
5. Are your hands relaxed at the sides of your body?

Timing 9 — Three- or Five-Minute Timing

For many years the office worker has been familiar with	12	12	4
electronic mail. A more recent development is the technol-	24	24	8
ogy for voice mail. Although voice mail has been available	35	35	11
for a number of years, it is only fairly recently that it	47	47	15
has become cost effective enough to bring it onstream in	58	58	19
many smaller firms. We are starting to see systems being	69	69	23
advertised for under $1,000.00.	76	76	25
Voice mail is being integrated into the microcomputer	11	87	29
office systems, as well. The larger, more expensive systems	23	99	33
handling numerous telephone lines and solely voice messaging	35	111	37
are now downsized to smaller micro systems. These latter	47	123	41
systems provide a host of other features, such as call-	58	134	44
forwarding with screening, call screening, sales pros-	69	145	48
pecting, and follow-up calls.	74	150	50
A further development allows these digital voice sys-	11	161	53
tems to be converted into digital pulses, and then stored on	23	173	57
a disk instead of the cassette tapes normally used in other	35	185	61
systems. The user initiates this process by entering an	46	196	65
access code into a telephone, and then dictating material	58	208	69
which may be accessed at the machine used for transcription	70	220	73
or word processing. One special advantage of the digitized	81	231	77
voice is the ability to insert dictated material without	93	243	81
taping over that which was already dictated.	102	252	84

SI = 1.35

• • • • 1 • • • • 2 • • • • 3 • • • • 4 • • • • 5 • • • • 6 • • • • 7 • • • • 8 • • • • 9 • • • • 10 • • • • 11 • • • • 12 **1 min**

1   2   3   4 **3 min**

Are you ready to begin?

Your Hands

1. Place the fingers of your left hand on **A S D F**.
2. Place the fingers of your right hand on **J K L ;**.
3. Curve your fingers slightly so that you will key using the ends of your fingers.
4. Place your fingers slightly *above* the keys.
5. Keep your elbows relaxed at your side and your hands parallel with the slant of the keyboard.
6. Keep the palms of your hands above the keyboard.

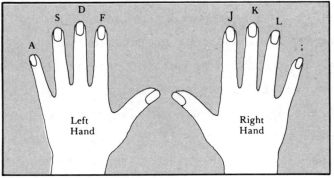

The Space Bar

1. Strike the space bar with your right thumb.
   - Do not rest your thumb on the space bar.
   - Do not hold the space bar down.
2. Keep your right hand, wrists, and other fingers as motionless as possible when striking the space bar.

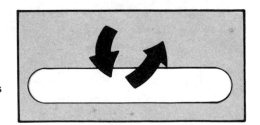

Space Bar Drill

(space) once once twice twice once twice once

Practice

Timing 8 — Three- or Five-Minute Timing

"Would you please FAX that to me today?" That request | 12 | 12 | 4
is becoming nearly as common in the modern office as asking | 23 | 23 | 7
for a telephone call. The number of facsimile machines now | 35 | 35 | 11
in use in our country is growing by leaps and bounds. It is | 47 | 47 | 15
anticipated that by the year 2000 nearly every business in | 59 | 59 | 19
the country will have its own facsimile number. | 69 | 69 | 23

Facsimile machines are able to send and receive quality | 12 | 81 | 27
copies of any kind of document, including detailed graphs or | 24 | 93 | 31
pictures. Now that the problems of high cost and poor | 35 | 104 | 34
quality have been overcome, fax is one of the fastest | 45 | 114 | 38
growing categories of office equipment. Since fax operates | 57 | 126 | 42
over the telephone system, the cost of transmitting a letter | 69 | 138 | 46
or other document within a local dialing area is limited | 80 | 149 | 49
only to the basic monthly telephone fee, the depreciation of | 92 | 161 | 53
the fax machine, and the price of the fax paper. | 102 | 171 | 57

A facsimile machine is not just a glorified office | 12 | 183 | 61
copier! It has become an integral part of the existing | 23 | 194 | 64
office databases and networked telecommunication systems. | 34 | 205 | 68
The fax copies can be stored electronically for future | 45 | 216 | 72
recall, allowing writers of reports to access a data picture | 56 | 227 | 75
whenever it is needed to bring clarity to a report. The | 68 | 239 | 79
microcomputer-based facsimile systems allow for copies to be | 80 | 251 | 83
communicated between microcomputers or between them and | 91 | 262 | 87
other facsimile machines. The technology is rapidly | 101 | 272 | 90
expanding as additional software comes on the market. | 112 | 283 | 94

SI = 1.46

• • • • 1 • • • • 2 • • • • 3 • • • • 4 • • • • 5 • • • 6 • • • • 7 • • • • 8 • • • • 9 • • • •10 • • • •11 • • • •12   1 min
　　　　1　　　　　　　2　　　　　　　3　　　　　　　4   3 min

Some electronic typewriters and word processing software have automatic word wrap as a default. This can be used in Unit III, Letters.

The Return or Enter Key

1. Anchor index finger over **J** key.
2. Reach with the small or semicolon finger of your right hand to the return or enter key.
3. Strike the return or enter key and return your finger to home row.
4. The return should be completed with one continuous motion.

Return or Enter Key Drill

(space) once once twice twice *(return)*
once twice twice once *(return)*

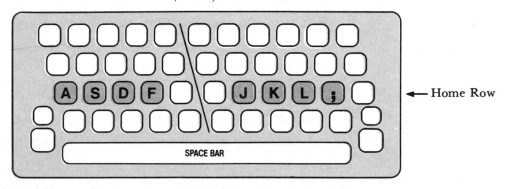

← Home Row

SPACE BAR

Double-space before each new line to be practised. This will make it easier to assess your progress. To double-space return twice. This leaves only one blank line between keyed lines.

Practice

Individualized Instructions
Follow directions in margin.
40-space line
Spacing: 1 (single spacing)

The F and J Keys

```
1 fff jjj fff jjj fff fff jjj jjj fj fj fj
2 fff jjj fff jjj fff fff jjj jjj fj fj fj
3 fjf fjf jfj jfj fff jjj fj fj jf jf fjfj
4 fjf fjf jfj jfj fff jjj fj fj jf jf fjfj
```

Place fingers lightly above home row keys. Use index finger of left hand to key **f** and index finger of right hand to key **j**. Use a quick stroke with the side of your right thumb on the space bar. Key each line once.

The D and L Keys

```
5 ddd lll ddd lll dld dld ddd lll dld ldld
6 ddd lll ddd lll dld dld ddd lll dld ldld
7 dld dld ldl ldl ddd lll ld ld ld dl dl d
8 dld dld ldl ldl ddd lll ld ld ld dl dl d
```

Keep fingers lightly above home row keys. Use the middle finger of left hand to key **d** and ring finger of right hand to key **l**. Try to bounce off each key. Key each line once.

Timing 7 — Three- or Five-Minute Timing

				1	CW	3

Ergonomics is the science that strives to match the needs of people in the workplace with their surroundings in order to help increase comfort and performance. It has too long been considered by some employers to be only a term used by salesmen to help sell their products and services. It is important to note that in the modern office, ergonomically designed machines and surroundings are not a frill.

Attention to ergonomics has been a positive productivity enhancer for many firms. The increased use of VDTs brought about many complaints of stress, muscle and joint strain, and visual fatigue. Improvements to the design of offices and the furniture and equipment placed in them has given the office worker the desired results. More recent attention is being given to the area of acoustics and their effect upon office productivity.

Two main reasons to consider ergonomic issues are being proposed by leading office furniture systems manufacturers. One is that dollars spent on improving office ergonomics will easily be regained in office productivity, with figures as high as 25 per cent being quoted. The second reason is that, following the lead of some European countries, legislation may force companies in our country to provide safe and comfortable work surroundings. Many firms are rising to the occasion without governmental intervention.

1	CW	3
11	11	3
23	23	7
34	34	11
46	46	15
57	57	19
69	69	23
81	81	27
11	92	30
23	104	34
34	115	38
46	127	42
57	138	46
69	150	50
80	161	53
87	168	56
12	180	60
24	192	64
35	203	67
47	215	71
58	226	75
70	238	79
82	250	83
94	262	87
103	271	90

SI = 1.37

• • • • 1 • • • • 2 • • • • 3 • • • • 4 • • • • 5 • • • • 6 • • • • 7 • • • • 8 • • • • 9 • • • 10 • • • • 11 • • • • 12 1 min

1   2   3   4 3 min

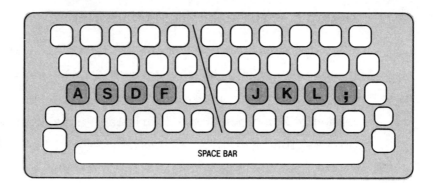

The S and K Keys

₉ sss kkk sss kkk sks sks sss kkk sk sk ks

₁₀ sss kkk sss kkk sks sks sss kkk sk sk ks

₁₁ sks sks ksk ksk sss kkk ksk ksk sk ks sk

₁₂ sks sks ksk ksk sss kkk ksk ksk sk ks sk

Use ring finger of left hand to key **s** and middle finger of right hand to key **k**. Remember to keep your fingers lightly above home row keys. Key each line once.

The A and ; Keys

₁₃ aaa aaa ;;; ;;; aaa ;;; a;a a;a ;a; aa;;

₁₄ aaa aaa ;;; ;;; aaa ;;; a;a a;a ;a; aa;;

₁₅ a;a a;a ;a; ;a; aaa ;;; ;a; a;a aaa a;;a

₁₆ a;a a;a ;a; ;a; aaa ;;; ;a; a;a aaa a;;a

Use little fingers to key **a** and **;**. Keep other fingers above home row while you bounce off these new keys. Key each line once.

Drill on New Keys

₁₇ aaa sss kkk ask ask lll aaa ddd lad lads

₁₈ fff aaa ddd fad fad fff lll ask flask as

₁₉ ask a sad lad; ask a sad lad; ask a lass

₂₀ add a salad; add a fad; as a lass; alas;

₂₁ dad adds; a lad adds; a lass adds; alas;

₂₂ dad falls; a sad lad falls; a lass falls

Key two 1-min timings on each line *or* repeat each line three times.

Spacing Reminder: Semicolons

- One space follows a semicolon.
- No space before a semicolon.

Timing 6 — Three- or Five-Minute Timing

	The Canadian Government is interested in the welfare	11	11	3

The Canadian Government is interested in the welfare
and safety of all of the workers in the nation. To that
end, in October, 1988, new legislation came into effect,
commonly known as WHMIS (Workplace Hazardous Materials
Information System). By that date, all employers in the
nation had to have a system in place wherein all hazardous
materials were both properly labelled and placed on stan-
darized inventories.

The first step of the process was to identify all
hazardous materials and establish an inventory control system for all such materials. This inventory was to be comprehensive and updated annually. Secondly, there was to be
an assurance that all the materials would be stored safely
in accordance with the recommendations of the supplier.

In addition to the above, on an annual basis (or more
often as deemed necessary), surplus or outdated stock of
hazardous materials must be disposed of in accordance with
proper waste management procedures. Another part of the
program is to assure that standardized labelling of all
hazardous materials is used throughout every firm. More
information on this program is available at your closest
federal office.

Line	1	CW	3
	11	11	3
	22	22	7
	34	34	11
	44	44	14
	56	56	18
	67	67	22
	79	79	26
	83	83	27
	11	94	31
	22	105	35
	34	117	39
	46	129	43
	57	140	46
	59	142	47
	12	154	51
	23	165	55
	34	176	58
	46	188	62
	56	198	66
	68	210	70
	79	221	73
	82	224	74

SI = 1.50

• • • • 1 • • • • 2 • • • • 3 • • • • 4 • • • • 5 • • • • 6 • • • • 7 • • • • 8 • • • • 9 • • • • 10 • • • • 11 • • • • 12   1 min

1   2   3   4   3 min

2

E/U/3/7

Individualized Instructions
Follow directions in margin.
40-space line
Spacing : 1

SC

Is your work station organized before you start?

Key two 1-min timings on each line *or* repeat each line three times.

Use **D** finger. Keep other fingers above home row. Key each line twice.

Use **J** finger. Keep other fingers above home row. Key each line twice.

Key two 1-min timings on each line *or* repeat each line three times.

Use **D** finger. Keep other fingers above home row. Key each line twice.

When a new key is introduced, glance at your keys and visually follow the reach path as your finger makes the reach. Then keep your eyes on the copy. If necessary, refer to the keyboard chart to review a reach path. *Beware* – keywatching is habit forming!

Review of the Home Row Keys

1 sss aaa lll ddd salad salad; ff kk flask

2 add a flask; ask all sad lads; a sad ad;

Reach to the E Key

3 ddd ded ddd ded ded eee ddd ded ded dd e

4 ded ded eee edd dee dee eed eed de de ed

Reach to the U Key

5 jjj juj jjj juj juj ju ju jjj uuu juj uu

6 juj juj uuu juu uju jjj uuu juj uj uj ju

Drill on E and U Keys

7 sue use duel fuel dude feud luke fuse us

8 feed full duds dual duke suede sulk leaf

Reach to the 3 Key

9 ded de3 de3 ded de3 de3 ded de3 de3 e3ed

10 ded d3d ded d3d e3e e3e d3d d3d de3 33ed

Timing 5 — Three- or Five-Minute Timing

1 CW 3

The telephone has become commonplace in every office in | 12 | 12 | 4
our country. Many improvements have been made in the recent | 24 | 24 | 8
past, allowing digital data to be transmitted between compu- | 36 | 36 | 12
ters and telephones. Even voice signals have been digitized | 48 | 48 | 16
to allow the storage and playback of voice messages. It has | 60 | 60 | 20
been demonstrated that voice signals can be added to switch- | 72 | 72 | 24
ing capabilities of office switchboards. However, this is a | 84 | 84 | 28
mere beginning. | 87 | 87 | 29

The telephone has become commonplace in every office in	12	12	4
our country. Many improvements have been made in the recent	24	24	8
past, allowing digital data to be transmitted between compu-	36	36	12
ters and telephones. Even voice signals have been digitized	48	48	16
to allow the storage and playback of voice messages. It has	60	60	20
been demonstrated that voice signals can be added to switch-	72	72	24
ing capabilities of office switchboards. However, this is a	84	84	28
mere beginning.	87	87	29
Technology which has been developed by Northern Telecom	12	99	33
for the 1990's show that the telephone goes beyond transmit-	24	111	37
ting voice to send us data, text and video at the same time.	36	123	41
In fact, the business customers are being asked to use their	48	135	45
imaginations in considering applications for the new techno-	60	147	49
logy. Telephones made to this new standard will use digital	72	159	53
signals which are transmitted at speeds of up to two million	84	171	57
bits per second. Most modems in use in the 1980's worked at	96	183	61
speeds up to 2400 bits per second.	103	190	63
A display screen is standard on the new telephones. To	12	202	67
give an example of its use, an incoming call can display the	24	214	71
identity of the caller before the call is picked up. As the	36	226	75
call is being answered, the customer's file can be retrieved	48	238	79
with all supporting documentation ready for use. This could	60	250	83
include past orders, method of payment, credit rating, along	72	262	87
with any other information that is programmed into the unit.	84	274	91
In another setting, one or more persons talking on the tele-	96	286	95
phone could have access to the same data from data files. A	108	298	99
further advantage is the tracing of unwanted calls!	118	308	102

SI = 1.34

```
• • • • 1 • • • • 2 • • • • 3 • • • • 4 • • • • 5 • • • • 6 • • • • 7 • • • • 8 • • • • 9 • • • •10• • • •11• • • •12   1 min
        1                 2                 3                 4   3 min
```

Reach to the 7 Key

11 juj ju7 ju7 j7j ju7 ju7 ju7j 77j u7j 777
12 juj j7j j7j juj j7j j7j u7u u7u j7j j77j

Line Indicators

Five strokes equals one word. Therefore, there are eight words in a 40-stroke line. A line indicator is shown at the bottom of drill lines and timings. In order to calculate the number of words completed in any line read vertically down from the last character to the line indicator. In the first example, 11 words have been completed. In the second example, 15 words have been completed.

Example 1

juj ju7 ju7 j7j ju7 ju7 ju7j 77j u7j 777
juj j7j j7j j7

· · · · 1 · · · · 2 · · · · 3 · · · · 4 · · · · 5 · · · · 6 · · · · 7 · · · · 8

Example 2

alas a dull duke sees all deals as fakes
a duke leads a duel; a fluke deal;

· · · · 1 · · · · 2 · · · · 3 · · · · 4 · · · · 5 · · · · 6 · · · · 7 · · · · 8

Drill on 3 and 7 Keys

13 7 lads fall; 33 salads; 37 fads; 77 elk;
14 ask 73 lads; add 737 sleds; use 337 ads;

Drill on New Keys

15 alas a dull duke sees all deals as fakes
16 a duke leads a duel; a fluke deal; a fad
17 3 sad lads see 73 elk fed sea kale feed;
18 dull lasses use 737 ladles as dusk falls

Key one 1-min timing on each line *or* repeat each line twice.

SC
Are your fingers in the curved-hand position?

Drill on Common-Letter Combinations

19 us use used uses a as ask asks asked all
20 dead lead seas seal leaf fake sake lakes

· · · · 1 · · · · 2 · · · · 3 · · · · 4 · · · · 5 · · · · 6 · · · · 7 · · · · 8

Timing 4 — Three- or Five-Minute Timing

When one desires to purchase a personal computer, there | 12 | 12 | 4
are important considerations to be made. You need to try to | 24 | 24 | 8
ascertain which machine is most likely to be compatible with | 36 | 36 | 12
the software packages in use today and in the future. There | 48 | 48 | 16
is also a need to consider the type of service available and | 60 | 60 | 20
the reliability of that service when it is needed. The per- | 72 | 72 | 24
formance, memory, and speed are important factors in select- | 84 | 84 | 28
ing your personal computer as well as an ability to add that | 96 | 96 | 32
new feature which is just around the corner. The price, al- | 108 | 108 | 36
though it needs to figure into the total purchase, should be | 120 | 120 | 40
only one of the factors that should be considered carefully. | 132 | 132 | 44

Remember that the true cost of a personal computer will | 12 | 144 | 48
involve more than the purchase price. In fact, the purchase | 24 | 156 | 52
price may be one of the minor costs if they are figured over | 36 | 168 | 56
a longer period of time. Sometimes a "clone" without needed | 48 | 180 | 60
service and reliability can bring out hidden costs in a very | 60 | 192 | 64
big hurry! Offices or homes without people who can trouble- | 72 | 204 | 68
shoot problems in these machines are not suited to computers | 84 | 216 | 72
of this type. | 86 | 218 | 73

If yours is mainly an office application, your personal | 12 | 230 | 77
computer should likely have a hard disk drive. Availability | 24 | 242 | 81
of expansion slots or drive bays will help keep your machine | 36 | 254 | 85
from becoming outdated as quickly. Additional software fea- | 48 | 266 | 89
tures can be added as they come available only if your mach- | 60 | 278 | 93
ine has the built-in capacity for expandability. Still more | 72 | 290 | 97
consideration should be given to the possibility of connect- | 84 | 302 | 101
ing the computer into communications systems. One should be | 96 | 314 | 105
sure that the decisions made regarding choosing the personal | 108 | 326 | 109
computer are the best possible at a given point in time. | 119 | 337 | 112

SI = 1.38

• • • • 1 • • • • 2 • • • • 3 • • • • 4 • • • • 5 • • • • 6 • • • • 7 • • • • 8 • • • • 9 • • • •10• • • •11• • • •12 **1 min**

1　　　　　　　2　　　　　　　3　　　　　　4 **3 min**

H/R/4/.

SC
Are your feet flat on the floor and is one foot slightly ahead of the other for balance and good posture?

Key two 1-min timings on each line *or* repeat each line three times.

Use **J** finger. Keep other fingers above home row. Key each line twice.

Use **F** finger. Keep other fingers above home row. Key each line twice.

Key two 1-min timings on each line *or* repeat each line three times.

Use **F** finger. Keep other fingers above home row. Key each line twice.

Use **L** finger. Keep **J** finger anchored above **J** key. Key each line twice.

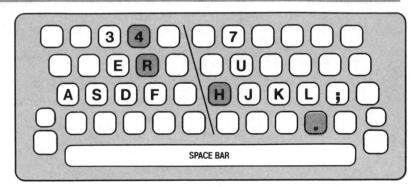

Review

1 a fuel leads as a deal; dad uses 3 sleds
2 ask a duke; sue a dude; use a jell ladle

Reach to the H Key

3 jhj jhj jjj jhj jhj hhh jjj jh hj jhj hh
4 jhj hhj jhj hhh jjj hh jj jh hj hj jh hj

Reach to the R Key

5 fff frf fff frf frf fr rf frf rrr ff rrf
6 frf rrr frf frr rrf rrf rrr fr rf rr rfr

Drill on H and R Keys

7 hard hurl husk rear rude half dear refer
8 rehash hall she herself ruler read herds

Reach to the 4 Key

9 frf fr4 fr4 frf fr4 fr4 f4f f4f fr4 f44f
10 f4f f4f fff 444 f4f r4r r4r f4f f4r f44f

Reach to the . Key

11 111 1.1 1.1 111 1.1 111 ... 1.1 1.1 ..1.
12 1.1 1.1 ... 1.1 ..1 1.1 .1. .1. 1.1 1.1.

· · · · 1 · · · · 2 · · · · 3 · · · · 4 · · · · 5 · · · · 6 · · · · 7 · · · · 8

Timing 3 — Three- or Five-Minute Timing

It has been said that the 1990's is the period when one will finally see the predominant usage of one main operating system for both microcomputers and mainframes. Such predictions were being made throughout the 1970's and 1980's as an urgent plea was being made to process data which was already in existence but on different machines and stored in different software formats.

The new operating system includes common communications as well as applications, programming interfaces, and instant user access. The main feature of the updated operating system is that applications software will work on every machine in the entire line of computer products. This capability is what brings new meaning to the phrase, "user friendly." One does not have to remember important changes in software when moving from one machine to another.

Microcomputers using the universal operating system can run the majority of the programs which previously could only be run on mainframe computers. The majority of this load is transferred to the microcomputers, leaving the mainframes to support many more terminal users. The software programs run considerably more slowly on the micros than on the mainframe but the task can be accomplished without tying up the costly larger machines. At last, through the computer linkages, an accurate business report can be output which meets the needs of management.

1	CW	3
12	12	4
24	24	8
36	36	12
48	48	16
60	60	20
72	72	24
76	76	25
12	88	29
24	100	33
36	112	37
48	124	41
60	136	45
72	148	49
84	160	53
91	167	56
12	179	60
24	191	64
36	203	68
48	215	72
60	227	76
72	239	80
84	251	84
96	263	88
108	275	92
110	277	92

SI = 1.38

• • • • 1 • • • • 2 • • • • 3 • • • • 4 • • • • 5 • • • • 6 • • • • 7 • • • • 8 • • • • 9 • • • •10 • • • •11 • • • • 12 1 min
     1   2   3   4 3 min

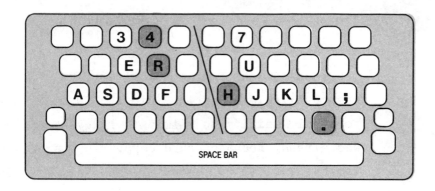

Drill on 4 and . Keys

13 434 jars. 4 herds. 34 deer. 47 sheds.

14 44 shares. 474 rakes. 47 rear rudders.

Drill on New Keys

15 she has had a red rash. her rash heals.

16 she has fear. she has had hard hurdles.

17 he uses rural halls. he read all rules.

18 a duke has 4 rakes; 34 ladles; 3 shares.

Drill on Common-Letter Combinations

19 he she shed sheds her hers herself heard

20 rule ruler rulers refer referee referees

21 ha has had hard harder haul hauls hauler

22 re red reds redder read reads reader are

• • • • • 1 • • • • 2 • • • • 3 • • • • 4 • • • • 5 • • • • 6 • • • 7 • • • • 8

Spacing Reminder: Periods

- Two spaces follow a period at the end of a sentence.
- One space follows a period at the end of an abbreviation as the period is part of the word.
- No space before a period.

Key two 1-min timings on each line *or* repeat each line three times.

Key one 1-min timing on each line *or* repeat each line twice.

Key one 1-min timing on each line *or* repeat each line twice.

SC

Did you use your paper release when removing the paper from your typewriter? OR Did you save this lesson as a file on your data disk?

Timing 2 — Three- or Five-Minute Timing

1	CW	3

Optical character recognition machines (OCR) are becoming more commonplace in today's office. Although OCR's have been available since the late 1960's, they were known mainly for their ability to eliminate rekeying of information which was already found on hard copy. In its original format, OCR took typewritten or computer-generated text and digitized it so that a computer could read it and process it further.

OCR has now made a strong showing in the modern offices in our country. Prices have dropped and improved technology has encouraged the development of new OCR applications. New desktop OCR devices can also accept photographs, signatures, charts, and other images and turn them into digitized format that is readable by the computer. These latter applications are called image processing. Image processing is a separate process from that of the original OCR, limited by definition to text, although both processes are most often found in the same machine.

When first introduced in the early 1980's, common desktop readers could recognize only two or three standard typefaces and graphics were simply beyond their capabilities. A new wave of scanners incorporate both text and graphics at a rate of speed and accuracy that is astounding. Images being processed simultaneously with OCR characters have given many offices the chance to enter the world of modern data entry.

1 (col)	CW	3 (col)
12	12	4
24	24	8
36	36	12
48	48	16
60	60	20
72	72	24
83	83	28
12	95	32
24	107	36
36	119	40
48	131	44
60	143	48
72	155	52
84	167	56
96	179	60
108	191	64
110	193	64
12	205	68
24	217	72
36	229	76
48	241	80
60	253	84
72	265	88
83	276	92

• • • • 1 • • • • 2 • • • • 3 • • • • 4 • • • • 5 • • • • 6 • • • • 7 • • • • 8 • • • • 9 • • • •10 • • • •11 • • • •12   1 min

1   2   3   4   3 min

4 Review/Setting Margins

40-space line
Spacing: 1

Key two 1-min timings on each line *or* repeat each line three times.

SC

Is your line space regulator set for the spacing as directed?

Key two 1-min timings on each line *or* repeat each line three times.

Letter Review Practice

1 a fake suede sale; use faded jade flasks
2 a salad fed elk feels full; a jell flask
3 use 4 jade shades; rake a dead red leaf.
4 7 hard jade flasks fell; use 4 red jars.
5 a sad elf jerks lake reeds; he has duds.
6 a fake elf jeers a duke; she has a duel.
7 she heard 3 rude jeers afar; she sulked.

Number Review Practice

8 73 elk; 3 sea salads; 7 lads feed seals;
9 33 sales; 7 lasses; 37 flakes; 373 fads;
10 47 shares. 43 rural hares. 74 hurdles.
11 47 jars; 44 rulers; herd 477 elk; use 47
12 734 deer; 433 jars; 473 lakes; 747 hues.
13 74 jars; 733 herds; 44 shades; 73 halls.
14 747 dukes; 434 elk; 373 deer; 737 rakes.

· · · · 1 · · · · 2 · · · · 3 · · · · 4 · · · · 5 · · · · 6 · · · · 7 · · · · 8

Timed Writings

One word consists of five strokes including letters and numbers (characters) and spaces. Timed writings are based on the *gross words per minute* (GWPM). For example, eight words completed in 30 seconds (30 s) is the equivalent of 16 wpm. For each timing, the line indicator, marked in five-stroke groups, is found at the bottom of the exercise.

Thirty-Second Timings

Timing

Key two 30-s timings on each line *or* repeat each line three times. Try to increase your speed on each successive try.

30 s

15 alas; a rude elf has half a real saddle. |16
16 here a sad hare feels he has a head rash |16
17 real sad lads heard all hard rules read. |16
18 a seal refreshes herself as flakes fall. |16
19 a sad lad heralds a duke. hear a ruler. |16

· · · · 2 · · · · 4 · · · · 6 · · · · 8 · · · · 10 · · · · 12 · · · · 14 · · · · 16   30 s
1   2   3   4   5   6   7   8   60 s

Timing 1 — Three- or Five-Minute Timing

If one desires up-to-date facts that are available only	12	12	4

If one desires up-to-date facts that are available only
in the office, and at the same time, your job takes you outside the office regularly, then consider purchasing a laptop
computer. Laptop computers have become another of society's
fads similar to the colored telephone! It seems that almost
every time that we turn around, we find someone else who has
a use for one. At one stage, it was usually a national ball
team executive who used one, or someone who worked for auto-
motive manufacturers, or your local insurance salesperson.

The great demand for the laptop computer has forced the
computer manufacturers to listen to their clients and try to
meet their demands. Sales staff and consultants need compu-
ting power in their hands on a regular basis if they perform
at their maximum potential. Hooked to telecommunications, a
laptop computer can place an organization's entire databases
and processing power within easy reach of an executive whose
job it is to access and process new data which is needed for
a new sale or a new project.

To illustrate the usefulness of the laptop computer for
the insurance industry, consider that most brochures are becoming obsolete since information is changing so quickly. A
laptop computer hooked to the nearest telephone jack applies
the newest insurance rates and services to the client's particular case, and calculates a quick adjustment as every new
change is entered. The most useful models for these type of
sales situations have a built-in hard disk so that it stores
most of the data needed for detailed problems. Typically, a
gasplasma screen gives the clear visibility over wide angles
so that it can be read by three people at the same time, one
of the main considerations for this type of sales setting in
a typical home.

Column 1	CW	3
12	12	4
24	24	8
36	36	12
48	48	16
60	60	20
72	72	24
84	84	28
96	96	32
107	107	36
12	119	40
24	131	44
36	143	48
48	155	52
60	167	56
72	179	60
84	191	64
96	203	68
101	208	69
12	220	73
24	232	77
36	244	81
48	256	85
60	268	89
72	280	93
84	292	97
96	304	101
108	316	105
120	328	109
132	340	113
144	352	117
147	355	118

SI = 1.50

· · · · 1 · · · · 2 · · · · 3 · · · · 4 · · · · 5 · · · · 6 · · · · 7 · · · · 8 · · · · 9 · · · ·10 · · · ·11 · · · ·12   1 min
1   2   3   4   3 min

Keep as many fingers as possible anchored above the home row keys at all times. If you need assistance to remember a certain reach, glance at the reach path once; then keep your eyes on the book to complete the drill. Key each line as your instructor directs *or* repeat each line twice.

SC

Are you striking the return or enter key by touch so that your eyes do not leave the copy?

Review

20 fff jjj fjf fjf jfj jfj fj fj jf jf fjfj
21 ddd lll dld dld ldl ldl ld ld ld dl dl d
22 sss kkk sks sks ksk ksk ksk ksk sk ks sk
23 aaa ;;; a;a a;a ;a; ;a; ;a; a;a aaa a;;a
24 ded ded eee edd dee dee eed eed de de ed
25 juj juj uuu juu uju jjj uuu juj uj uj ju
26 ded d3d ded d3d e3e e3e d3d d3d de3 33ed
27 juj j7j j7j juj j7j j7j u7u u7u j7j j77j
28 jjj hhh jhj hhj jhj hh jj jh hj hj jh hj
29 fff frf rrr frr rrf rrf rrr fr rf rr rfr
30 frf fr4 fr4 frf fr4 fr4 f4f f4f fr4 f44f
31 lll 1.1 ... 1.1 ..1 1.1 .1. .1. 1.1 1.1.

• • • • 1 • • • • 2 • • • • 3 • • • • 4 • • • • 5 • • • • 6 • • • • 7 • • • • 8

Setting Margins

Know Your Typewriter

1. Locate the print indicator, the alignment scale, and the paper guide.
2. Locate the margin stops on your machine.

Steps for Setting Margins

1. If the paper guide is at 0, the center point of the paper is 50 (elite — 12 pitch) or 42 (pica — 10 pitch).
2. Half of the keyed line should be to the right of the center point and half to the left of the center point.
3. Calculate the margin settings.

Margin Signal Allowance

After the margin signal, make a decision to end your line near the right margin preferably without dividing words. For your typewriter, determine how many spaces you can key between the margin signal and the right margin. Know your typewriter.

40-stroke line (12-pitch)

Left Margin	Center Point	Right Margin
30	▲ 50	75

$$\begin{array}{r} 50 \\ -20 \\ \hline 30 \end{array} \qquad \begin{array}{r} 50 \\ +20 \\ \hline 70+5^* \end{array}$$

40-stroke line (10-pitch)

Left Margin	Center Point	Right Margin
22	▲ 42	67

$$\begin{array}{r} 42 \\ -20 \\ \hline 22 \end{array} \qquad \begin{array}{r} 42 \\ +20 \\ \hline 62+5^* \end{array}$$

SC

Did you allow five spaces for the margin signal allowance if you are using a typewriter?

*Add five strokes to the right margin for margin signal allowance.

4. Set the margin stops for the line length desired.
   • Set your new left margin first.
   • Set your new right margin.

70 WPM

Each diagonal (/) represents one-quarter minute. Do **not** key the diagonal.

A fund has been set up to build a new gym and swimming pool. The boys and girls in this/part of town will make good usage of these once they are built. Three of our schools can/make use of the complex during the school year. A number of club members have spoken/for space in evenings on a regular basis and the local town leagues have asked for it also./

Very Easy
SI = 1.18

Because of the late frost this spring, many of these gardens had to be replanted. There/is still a good chance that rows of tomatoes and corn will be ready before fall. Summer/days have been long and hot; this is just what was needed to make the plants mature at/their best rate. Unless something else happens to prevent us, our deliveries will be made./

Easy
SI = 1.29

The young writer sat down to write about the incident before she had developed the main/plot of the story. This accident had been imprinted vividly on her mind and she did want/this account to be complete. Even as she recorded the events, an anticipation arose of/the possibilities for the story. Each word was chosen to give particular color and form./

Average
SI = 1.56

• • • •1• • • •2• • • •3• • • •4• • • •5• • • •6• • • •7• • • •8• • • •9• • • •10• • • •11• • • •12

Know your Computer and Software

The word processing program loaded in your computer will have a set line length which is called the line-length default. It will also have a type-pitch default which is usually 10 pitch (pica). The margin- and type-pitch defaults can be changed at any time. Read the software manual or ask your instructor how to reset the margins and the pitch.

Keep your line-length default for the drill lines throughout this text. This provides drill and practice of the return/enter key. The resetting of margins will be necessary in the production exercises.

One-Minute Timings

Each diagonal (/) represents one-quarter minute. Do **not** key the diagonal.

The construction industry has shown a great deal of interest in our city in/the past two years. Many commercial projects have been registered with city/hall and already machines are beginning to excavate for basements. Project/foremen are on the jobs and they have indicated that hiring is now assured./

Average SI = 1.57

65 WPM

The price of gas and oil has been on the rise for some time. As the needs of all of/us are seen to be greater, the use of gas and oil will soon exhaust the limited/supply. It is now clear that the world must turn to other basic sources to get the/energy to maintain our way of life. Some have turned to the sun and sea for help./

Very Easy SI = 1.17

We would be glad to help the ball club to buy their new uniforms. Our firm makes/a point of helping out any worthwhile cause to make our town a better place and/one of which pride is worthy. Our ball club has many fine people involved that go/ to a great deal of trouble to see that good sportsmanship will be the accepted aim./

Easy SI = 1.23

Anthony wants to buy a new house but mortgage money has been hard to get this year./ It has been our experience that some extra investment is common near the end of/the year and this usually means that mortgage money is released sometime after the/middle of February. In the meantime, there is little he can do but wait and save./

Average SI = 1.40

• • • • 1 • • • • 2 • • • • 3 • • • • 4 • • • • 5 • • • • 6 • • • • 7 • • • • 8 • • • • 9 • • • •10 • • • •11 • • • 12

5

G/I/C/8

40-space line
Spacing: 1

SC

Do you keep your eyes on the copy except for establishing new stroke reaches?

Key two 1-min timings on each line *or* repeat each line three times.

Use **F** finger. Keep other fingers above home row. Key each line twice.

Use **K** finger. Keep other fingers above home row. Key each line twice.

Key two 1-min timings on each line *or* repeat each line three times.

Use **D** finger. Keep **F** finger anchored above **F** key. Key each line twice.

Use **K** finger. Keep **J** finger anchored above **J** key. Key each line twice.

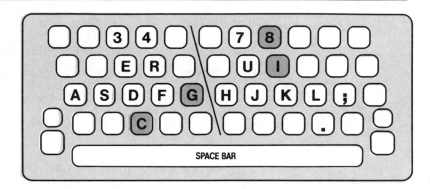

Review

1 a dear lass refuses her used red rulers.

2 she sells suede dresses; she sells furs.

Reach to the G Key

3 fff fgf fgf fff ggg fgf fgf fg fg fgf gf

4 fgf fgf fg gf fggf fgf fff ggg fg gf ggf

Reach to the I Key

5 kkk kik kik kkk iii kik kik ki ki kik ik

6 kik kik ki ik kiik kik kkk iii ki ik iik

Drill on G and I Keys

7 girl grid laughs jig sigh high hid grill

8 guide fridge jug idea disguise glass ail

Reach to the C Key

9 ddd dcd dcd ddd ccc dcd dcd dc dc dcd cd

10 dcd dcd dc cd dccd dcd ddd ccc dc cd dcd

Reach to the 8 Key

11 kkk kik ki8 ki8 k8k ki8 k8k k8k kkk 88kk

12 k8k k8i k8i k8k k88k kkk 888 8k k8 k8 8i

• • • • 1 • • • • 2 • • • • 3 • • • • 4 • • • • 5 • • • • 6 • • • • 7 • • • • 8

Each diagonal (/) represents one-quarter minute. Do **not** key the diagonal.

55 WPM

Unless we hear from you in the near future, we will have the account/closed. You have been a valued friend of ours for a number of years./ It is with a great deal of regret that the outstanding debt has made/us choose this as the last course. We hope you plan to make this right./

It is time that we considered bidding on additional new cars for our/expanded business. The last three reports from your office have shown/that we can wait no longer. If we delay a month longer, we will need/to pay a higher price and risk an additional loss in municipal sales./

The contract has been awarded for building the huge arena in Parkvue/Place. The residents of that community have spent a great deal of time/and energy trying to convince their local and provincial government./ Even as late as this spring, one could not guess that it would come./

60 WPM

The last raise in the tax rate occurred in May of last year. You will find/that the new tax rate just struck will give us enough cash to do the road work/in front of your land. Much of the survey work was done last year but we /could not order the rest done until this year. You will no doubt agree now./

It seems that there must have been some error in reading our water meter the/last time. Since the bill appeared too high when we received it, we found /the one from last month. This latter bill was compared to the earlier one,/a present read-ing was taken, and the result was obvious. Please alter it./

• • • • 1 • • • • 2 • • • • 3 • • • • 4 • • • • 5 • • • • 6 • • • • 7 • • • • 8 • • • • 9 • • • • 10 • • • • 11 • • • • 12

Very Easy
SI = 1.14

Easy
SI = 1.21

Average
SI = 1.41

Very Easy
SI = 1.10

Easy
SI = 1.30

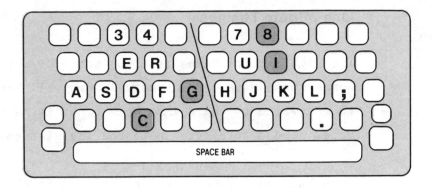

Drill on C and 8 Keys

13 8 cars; 8 cards; 8 cases; 8 high chairs.

14 a child has his cheese cake hurled high.

Drill on New Keys

15 if a high glass is ideal as a juice jug.

16 8 clear clues; 38 curled cigars; 84 jugs

17 a cheerful girl guide greased a red car.

18 a clerk giggled as a cigar case clicked.

· · · · 1 · · · · 2 · · · · 3 · · · · 4 · · · · 5 · · · · 6 · · · · 7 · · · · 8

Drill on Common-Letter Combinations

19 grease grass grace grade grill grid grad

20 glares giggle glass glad glaciers glides

21 chide chill cheese cheerful ached church

Letter Review Practice

22 a dear judicial clerk failed his grades.

23 graceful sails jerk ahead as she huddles

· · · · 1 · · · · 2 · · · · 3 · · · · 4 · · · · 5 · · · · 6 · · · · 7 · · · · 8

24 she jigs as a used fiddle creaks a reel.

25 a cheerful girl asked if a judge laughed

· · · · 1 · · · · 2 · · · · 3 · · · · 4 · · · · 5 · · · · 6 · · · · 7 · · · · 8

Number Review Practice

26 3 hills; 7 churches; 4 disks; 837 cigars

27 83 juice jugs are chilled as 74 gals jig

· · · · 1 · · · · 2 · · · · 3 · · · · 4 · · · · 5 · · · · 6 · · · · 7 · · · · 8

Key two 1-min timings on each line *or* repeat each line three times.

Key one 1-min timing on each line *or* repeat each line twice.

Key one 1-min timing on each line *or* repeat each line twice.

Key two 1-min timings on each set of lines *or* repeat each set three times. (Key lines 22 and 23, then repeat. Key lines 24 and 25, then repeat.)

SC

If you have a posture chair, does the back of the chair fit comfortably in the hollow part of your back?

Key two 1-min timings on each line *or* repeat each line three times.

Each diagonal (/) represents one-quarter minute. Do **not** key the diagonal.

The high rate of taxes is a subject of great concern in/many homes these days. Each party leader will have to be/attuned to the voice of the common home owner if he hopes/to get the votes needed to elect him to the legislature./

Easy
SI = 1.30

Average
SI = 1.56

Anne has applied to work for our firm in the capacity of/our only secretary. It will be necessary for her to get/another reference before she is interviewed for the job./ She refers to previous work with you. Please telephone./

50 WPM

Very Easy
SI = 1.11

A few of us will be there by three. We hope to have socials of/this make-up again. A good time is planned but our hopes will/dim if they cannot get time off while everyone is here. Efforts/should be made to help them get the time off to come this time./

Easy
SI = 1.28

We purchased a set of table and chairs at your shop at least a/month ago and you promised delivery within two weeks. You went/to phone your factory and they assured you that the set was in/stock. You said it would arrive at our home well before June./

Average
SI = 1.41

The directors of this company will meet next week to produce an/operating budget which will reflect the cut-backs. Three staff/members have been assigned to get all reports ready to present/them to the directors. All of the men and women are to attend./

• • • • 1 • • • • 2 • • • • 3 • • • • 4 • • • • 5 • • • • 6 • • • • 7 • • • • 8 • • • • 9 • • • •10 • • • •11 • • • 12

40-space line
Spacing: 1

SC

Are you striking the space bar with a quick bounce of the right thumb?

Key two 30-s timings on each line *or* key each line twice.

Use **F** finger. Keep other fingers above home row. Key each line twice.

Use **F** finger. Keep other fingers above home row. Key each line twice.

Key two 1-min timings on each line *or* repeat each line three times.

Use **L** finger. Keep **J** finger anchored above **J** key. Key each line twice.

Use **L** finger. Keep **J** finger anchored above **J** key. Key each line twice.

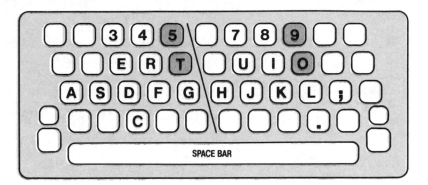

Review

1 a gruff judge glared as a child laughed.
2 she uses garlic juice if all else fails.

Reach to the T Key

3 ftf ftf ftt ftt ttt fff ft ft ftf ftf tf
4 ftf ttf fff ttt ftf tft ft tf ttf fft tf

Reach to the 5 Key

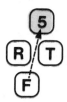

5 fff ftf f5f fff f5f ff 55 f5f f5 5f f55f
6 f5f f5f 5f5 ff 55 ft f5 ft5 5f 55f 5tf 5

Drill on T and 5 Keys

7 5 tarts; 5 teas; 5 tests; 5 cake treats.
8 these tired teachers talk at their desk.

Reach to the O Key

9 lll lol lol ooo lol lo ol lol ll oo lool
10 lol ool lo lo oll lool lo ool llo lol ol

Reach to the 9 Key

11 lll lo9 191 191 9ol 191 lll 999 lo9 99ol
12 191 lo9 lll 999 191 o9o 191 1199 9911 19

· · · · · 1 · · · · 2 · · · · 3 · · · · 4 · · · · 5 · · · · 6 · · · · 7 · · · · 8

Easy
SI = 1.34

Thank you for the information you sent us a/week ago. These results will be used to get/the reports ready for the annual meeting of/our company. We hope that you plan to come./

Average
SI = 1.41

For the past three weeks, we have been on/holidays in north-ern Canada. It was thrilling/to observe the many species of birds that/are never seen in the confines of villages./

40 WPM

Very Easy
SI = 1.09

In this case, I will tell all of you what I had in/mind when the surprise was planned. Both Jack and/Beth were flying to visit us last week. Since it/was to be a surprise, I had to make sure you came./

Easy
SI = 1.24

Now that you have been in this course for a spell,/give us a number of comments on how you would make/any changes in your beginning approach. It can be/a help to new students to see comments from others./

Average
SI = 1.59

Bill is interested in the next civic election for/the hospi-tal board. He feels that it is the time/to apply for better facilities. The government is/placing health on a very high priority next season,/

45 WPM

Very Easy
SI = 1.19

It has been almost four years since we went to that lake/for a swim. The sandy wide beach there stretches a great way/to the east from the park. In fact, the fun we had /that summer makes me long to return for relaxing holidays./

• • • • 1 • • • • 2 • • • • 3 • • • • 4 • • • • 5 • • • • 6 • • • • 7 • • • • 8 • • • • 9 • • •10• • • •11• • • •12

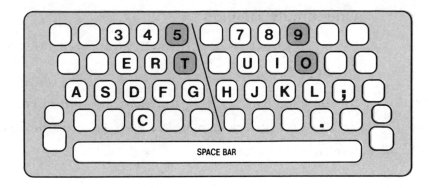

Key two 1-min timings on each line *or* repeat each line three times.

Drill on O and 9 Keys

13 9 oaks; 9 oats; 9 oars; 9 other colours.

14 our 9 orchards ought to test that offer.

Key one 1-min timing on each line *or* repeat each line twice.

Drill on New Keys

15 our old colored outfit has odd oil odors

16 5 tickets; 9 tacks; 59 tigers; 95 trees.

17 the three teachers are tired of a tease;

18 5 orioles; 95 hares; 59 outraged otters.

Sp

colour or *color*
Know the preference in your part of Canada and be consistent.

Drill on Common-Letter Combinations

19 of off offer offers offered offset lofts

20 their there therefore these this thought

21 or ore order oral orator orchard ordeals

22 true trust truth trace trick trial trait

Key one 1-min timing on each line *or* repeat each line twice.

SC

Are you reading under-scored letters as a group?

Letter Review Practice

23 the girls used dark colored offset jars.

24 the official task of the judges is hard.

Key two 1-min timings on this set of lines *or* repeat this set of lines three times. Every alphabetic character introduced to date is included in these lines.

Number Review Practice

25 37 clerks; 48 tills; 59 cashiers; 9 hats

26 83 girls take 49 jars to get 57 cheeses.

Key two 1-min timings on each line *or* repeat each line three times. All number keys introduced to date are included in these lines.

One-Minute Timings

(Very Easy 1.0 to 1.19   Easy 1.20 to 1.39   Average 1.40 to 1.59)

25 WPM

It is time for us to plan most /of our work. At first glance it /looks like we can still get it /done before they come next week./

Very Easy
SI = 1.00

As this is your second course, /you should be able to address a /letter at a fast rate. You are /required to set it up very well./

Easy
SI = 1.22

We are ready to take delivery /on those items which you carry in /stock. We are prepared to assess /quotations after seeing them./

Average
SI = 1.52

30 WPM

All of the cheques were signed by the /next day. We hope the cheque has come /by now and that the bills are marked /paid. A complaint form has been mailed. /

Very Easy
SI = 1.03

The lady tried to return the lamps to /our store last winter. She showed that /the bases were chipped and scratched /but her earlier report is still filed./

Easy
SI = 1.25

The bank has just advised us to check /over our records. The savings account /shows a negative balance, indicating /that we have now overdrawn our account./

Average
SI = 1.48

35 WPM

Call your friend by phone and see if he can /come to see us a week from today. We might /be able to employ him now since a man left us /just when we had a lot of work to process. /

Very Easy
SI = 1.10

• • • • 1 • • • • 2 • • • • 3 • • • • 4 • • • • 5 • • • • 6 • • • • 7 • • • • 8 • • • • 9 • • • • 10 • • • • 11 • • • • 12

7

40-space line
Spacing: 1

SC

Is your book propped at an angle for easy reading?

Key two 30-s timings on each line *or* key each line twice.

Use **S** finger. Keep **F** finger anchored above **F** key. Key each line twice.

Use **J** finger. Keep other fingers above home row. Key each line twice.

Key two 1-min timings on each line *or* repeat each line three times.

Use **S** finger. Keep **F** finger anchored above **F** key. Key each line twice.

Use **K** finger. Keep other fingers above home row. Key each line twice.

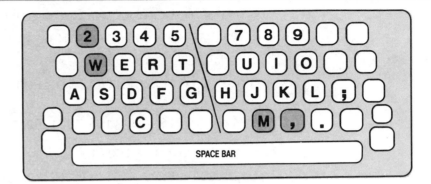

Review

1 just three clocks caused good old fights
2 let us regard this cute kite joke of his

Reach to the W Key

3 sss sws sws sss sws sws www sws sw ws sw
4 sws sws sss sws sww wws sw sw swws sws w

Reach to the M Key

5 jjj jmj jmj jjj mmm jmj jmj jm mj jmj jm
6 jmj jmj jmmj jm jm mj jmmj jm jm mj jmmj

Drill on W and M Keys

7 we woke them well ahead of time to walk.
8 the major goes west where he sows wheat.

Reach to the 2 Key

9 sss sw2 sw2 sss s2s sw2 s2s s2s s2 2s 2s
10 s2s sw2 s2s s2s s2 22s s2s 222 s2s s2 2s

Reach to the , Key

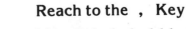

11 kkk k,k k,k kkk k,k ,,, k,k k, ,k k,k ,k
12 k,k k,k kkk k,k ,,, k,k ,k k ,,k k,, ,k

· · · · · 1 · · · · 2 · · · · 3 · · · · 4 · · · · 5 · · · · 6 · · · · 7 · · · · 8

DRILL TO CONCENTRATE ON MIDDLE ROW

465 654 464 564 4465 6546 5465 4675 6424 6358 4168 6545 4674
566 435 474 568 4654 6455 6445 6254 4624 6364 4645 5645 6445

DRILL TO CONCENTRATE ON TOP ROW

798 787 987 779 4985 7948 7957 7599 9875 8975 5798 8976 9879
858 947 795 897 7958 9759 9576 8795 7987 8979 9587 7984 5987

DRILL TO CONCENTRATE ON BOTTOM ROW

123 434 132 126 1325 4125 6321 4216 3213 4125 4315 2313 2424
342 432 216 432 4166 1321 6213 6432 4135 6432 4321 4132 4613

MORE DECIMAL DRILLS

126.20 928.07 420.12 4957.10 1580.28 4168.45 6375.45 6247.15
360.18 630.81 427.46 3641.74 6847.01 5090.64 2348.47 2134.50

604.80 642.30 127.09 4108.07 4135.97 6312.87 4871.08 3480.02
907.47 301.58 431.57 1205.88 4354.80 2080.87 4089.89 3041.60

Key two 1-min timings on each line *or* repeat each line three times. Leave one space after a comma.

Drill on 2 and , Keys

13 82 homes, 22 molds, 2 mothers, 272 memos
14 2 whales, 232 walks, 29 shows, 252 worms

Drill on New Keys

Key one 1-min timing on each line *or* repeat each line twice.

15 we used 2 good jams to make milk shakes.
16 her mother wears warm wool waist jackets
17 252 farmers take time while wheat grows.
18 the waiter carried water, toast, coffee.
• • • • 1 • • • • 2 • • • • 3 • • • • 4 • • • • 5 • • • • 6 • • • • 7 • • • • 8

Drill on Common-Letter Combinations

Key two 30-s timings on each line *or* key each line twice.

19 we wee were wear wears were wed weigh we
20 who whose where wherefore what which who
21 ow owe owes shower tower grow low tow ow

Letter Review Practice

Key two 1-min timings on this set of lines *or* repeat this set of lines three times. Every alphabetic character introduced to date is included in these lines.

22 aged cars meet few jeers; his luck holds
23 a mower faces a rough task; a milk juice

24 thick cheese could grow mould if it jars
25 come, use a light jigsaw for those desks
• • • • 1 • • • • 2 • • • • 3 • • • • 4 • • • • 5 • • • • 6 • • • • 7 • • • • 8

Number Review Practice

Key two 1-min timings on each line *or* repeat each line three times. All number keys introduced to date are included in these lines.

26 27 watches; 89 towers; 53 whales; 4 tows
27 248 games; 925 homes; 72 mills; 39 times
• • • • 1 • • • • 2 • • • • 3 • • • • 4 • • • • 5 • • • • 6 • • • • 7 • • • • 8

Spacing Reminder: Commas

- One space follows a comma.
- No space before a comma.

REVIEW (2, 3, 4, 5, 6, 8, 9)

5 64 86 96 52 658 468 496 9364 4682 6328 6395 6938 8284 6394
9 39 94 59 58 293 395 593 5823 9356 9543 3495 6594 3965 4939

1, 4, 7 KEY DRILL

4 47 74 41 14 474 414 471 4774 4117 4714 4771 1177 4174 4174
1 14 41 74 17 471 117 741 1744 7177 4117 7171 1747 4741 1177

REVIEW (1, 2, 3, 4, 5, 6, 7, 8, 9)

4 28 64 84 51 894 594 928 4681 4683 2852 4688 4381 8334 8387
8 92 13 79 91 939 497 381 1985 5826 7684 1728 9238 4819 3948

0 (ZERO) KEY DRILL

0 40 50 60 06 050 060 040 0650 5060 5080 1060 7090 0807 3020
0 70 80 90 01 030 020 203 2090 0803 5070 4003 3010 3081 7020

REVIEW (1, 2, 3, 4, 5, 6, 7, 8, 9, 0)

0 40 60 08 03 219 608 803 3089 4320 8038 6108 8030 0830 5710
9 03 80 90 38 130 083 820 2100 0730 7108 9003 4180 0384 0730

DECIMAL KEY DRILL (Use the ring finger, keeping the index finger over the 4 key)

6 63 6. 6. 3. 6.3 6.6 .36 .636 6.69 93.3 3.69 9.63 39.6 39.3
3 36 .6 .3 .9 6.9 3.6 .93 .933 69.3 9.63 39.3 9.39 3.99 3.63

REVIEW (1, 2, 3, 4, 5, 6, 7, 8, 9, 0, Decimal)

63.4 6.64 5.96 5.84 2.84 6.89 40.5 120.6 465.3 438.91 92.183
31.5 4.81 3.84 5.34 1.58 9.38 48.2 463.7 972.4 632.74 20.918

10-KEY NUMBER PAD DRILL

5642 2468 4322 2848 6481 1930 0984 5608 9648 19608 26489 061
3103 6907 6318 4607 4650 6087 9407 6302 9280 76840 30207 608

6408 6430 2187 6413 6781 9108 6430 4608 7210 40908 72507 683
6090 6408 7138 8138 4608 6480 9384 6230 8027 90871 63808 681

1069 4631 7182 2098 9438 4980 5462 3570 8404 89049 82028 431
9780 6823 4080 6430 4982 2819 9508 4680 6874 13804 73079 480

5.90 4803.83 4280.34 5207.34 4902.08 4983.74 6349.37 4903.09
4.01 8940.82 4321.07 4319.80 6581.02 6080.07 4385.05 6920.01

4.25 6902.12 2810.20 1094.03 3204.50 6083.01 4082.06 4689.21
2.05 6502.02 8213.60 4130.58 9216.27 8210.03 2010.08 4012.62

8

Review/Editing

40-space line
Spacing: 1

Key two 30-s timings on each line *or* repeat each line twice. Every alphabetic character introduced to date is included in these lines.

SC

Is your chair or table adjusted to achieve the proper slope of your arms to the keyboard?

Key two 1-min timings on each line *or* repeat each line three times. All number keys introduced to date are included in these lines.

Letter Review Practice

1 a cold jam flask grows her wild mustard.
2 come, wake us as four lads watch 2 jigs.
3 he weighed just hams for four old cooks.
4 a major ought to like whiskers cared for
5 we were awake while a loud whistle came.
6 28 modest mice might use oil as a mirror

Number Review Practice

7 27 wheels; 45 towers; 93 games; 8 homes.
8 58 meals; 29 matches; 74 masks; 3 shows.
9 73 toads; 25 tigers; 48 turtles; 9 owls.
10 23 titles; 75 ties; 49 tales; 8 tickets.
• • • • 1 • • • 2 • • • 3 • • • 4 • • • 5 • • • 6 • • • 7 • • • 8

Editing for Changes (Proofreading)

There are three types of errors in keying: *word errors*, *spacing errors*, and *punctuation errors*. The paper-bail method of editing is most accurate on a typewriter. The paper should not be taken out of your typewriter until you have read the material.

Read each line twice. First, read each word for correctness and then reread for meaning. On the paper copy in your typewriter, circle the entire word if an error has been made. If you are using a computer, read your monitor before printing the file. Circle the entire word on the printed copy if an error has been made. Only one error is charged to any one word, no matter how many errors it contains.

Use teh paper bail to prrofread your work.
Stroking Error

Read the line line above the paper bail
Repeated Word/Punctuation

Cercle the errors in the line. Turn the
Strikeover/Wrong Spacing

cylinder up and read the nex t line
Extra Spacing/Punctuation

Proofreadone line at time.
Omitted Spacing/Omitted Word

SC

Does your software have a scrolling feature? Ask your instructor or read the software manual.

Number Pad Drills

Numeric Keypad

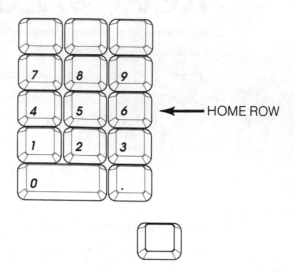

← HOME ROW

Sometimes a keyboard operator deals with so much numerical data that it can save time in the input stage if the 10-key number pad is used. A little concentrated practise can produce accurate results from the touch method. Following are drills to help learn to operate these keys by touch. The index, middle, and ring fingers should be placed just above the home row (4, 5, and 6 keys). These fingers will reach the corresponding key above and below the home row key. The thumb is used to operate the zero key at the bottom. Do the drills in order to help learn the keys gradually by touch. This will help you to use the ten-key calculator effectively, as well.

HOME ROW DRILL (4, 5, and 6 keys)

```
4  44  45  55  54  456  456  556  4456  6544  4556  6544  5645  5644  4665
5  45  56  66  64  564  554  665  4654  5456  6456  4656  4564  6546  4654
```

2, 5, 8 KEY DRILL

```
5  58  58  85  52  258  852  225  8255  5285  8822  2585  2858  2885  2288
2  28  82  52  28  825  825  825  8282  2825  8252  2288  8282  8252  2285
```

REVIEW (2, 4, 5, 6, 8)

```
4  65  85  25  28  852  258  468  6428  8462  6548  6824  6588  8246  6482
6  82  48  28  68  854  864  642  6484  5264  8682  2828  6284  6482  6426
```

3, 6, 9 KEY DRILL

```
6  63  36  69  96  639  663  366  6996  6963  3399  9636  3969  6369  6339
9  69  63  39  93  633  993  369  9693  3963  9639  6639  9336  6993  3963
```

Skill Building

Key each line once, correcting the errors as you key. Each of the lines has two errors. Capital letters cannot be keyed in this lesson.

SC

Did you read Editing for Changes on the previous page?

SC

Did you key lines 11-20 correctly? If you did, all lines will be even at the right margin.

Timing

Key three 1-min timings on each set of lines *or* key each set three times. What is your best timing for each set?

Editing Practice

11 a girl could feel at home wihh that hat.

12 3 small mice; 78 awkwardhorses; 9 c ats.

13 wear white lacecoat to a music class.

14 9 dark   swallows;   38 fish; 2 lame horses.

15 thiscake will add calories to our diet.

16 read the cards tha t just came from home .

17 do take the time look atall the ore.

18 feel freeto take as much tim as usual.

19 which cold mouthwash wash should tastesweet.

20 4 whitewhistles;   29 word games;   5 dogs.

One-Minute Timings

1 min

21 what will we do while the waiter watches | 8

22 most tame white whales make huge showers | 16

23 we will watch a cricket match or a game. | 24

• • • • 1 • • • 2 • • • 3 • • • 4 • • • 5 • • • 6 • • • 7 • • • 8

24 where messes are made, wheels are stuck. | 8

25 we might use mouth wash if we smell sour | 16

26 a word game will make his lame jaw ache. | 24

• • • • 1 • • • 2 • • • 3 • • • 4 • • • 5 • • • 6 • • • 7 • • • 8

Review

Skill Building

Keep as many fingers as possible anchored above the home row keys at all times. If you need assistance to remember a certain reach, glance at the reach path once; then keep your eyes on the book to complete the drill. Key each line as your instructor directs *or* repeat each line twice.

27 fff fgf fgf fff ggg fgf fgf fg fg fgf gf

28 kkk kik kik kkk iii kik kik ki ki kik ik

29 ddd dcd dcd ddd ccc dcd dcd dc dc dcd cd

30 kkk kik ki8 ki8 k8k ki8 k8k k8k kkk 88kk

31 ftf ftf ftt ftt ttt fff ft ft ftf ftf tf

32 fff f5f f5f fff f5f ff 55 f5f f5 5f f55f

33 lll lol lol ooo lol lo ol lol ll oo lool

34 lll 19l lo9 191 9ol 191 111 999 lo9 99ol

35 sws sws sss sws sww wws sw sw swws sws w

36 jmj jmj jmmj jm jm mj jmmj jm jm mj jmmj

37 s2s sw2 s2s s2s s2 22s s2s 222 s2s s2 2s

38 k,k k,k kkk k,k ,,, k,k ,k k, ,,k k,, ,k

Stroking Practice

Select the letter combinations giving you difficulty in the drills just completed in your lesson. Key each line twice.

4/t
46 44 tins; 14 tents; 434 tablets; 54 tests; 4 tourists; 4 toys
At least 4 540 tourists took part in Tour 4 starting Friday.

4/5
47 45 records; 5 months; 6 years; 5 645 days; 354 hours; 55 min
Sales on item 454 rose to $5 450 in 1984--an increase of 5%.

5/t
48 585 tracts; 54 tractors; 595 toys; 5 565 tools; 5 535 trains
The authors entered 515 titles in the 55th writer's contest.

5/6
49 65 motors; 156 bonds; 615 bills; 1 656 books; 5 065 students
They ordered 56 rulers, 650 pens, 56 pencils and 65 refills.

6/u
50 6 turns; 16 urns; 6 unions; 626 flutes; 266 users; 636 tubes
At least 60 of the graduate nurses of the total 166 arrived.

6/y
51 686 years; 96 youths; 66 bays; 64 boys; 626 yachts; 56 trays
66 voyages; 6 646 trays; 6 plays; 96 toys; 626 keys; 6 yells

6/7
52 7 types; 6 agents; 76 loads; 167 files; 6 756 notes; 6 calls
By June 16 or 17, we had collected $6 760 of the total debt.

7/u
53 71 tunnels; 737 turkeys; 77 lunches; 47 nurses; 78 graduates
All 7 trucks were loaded with 7 177 bags of new sugar beets.

7/8
54 87 bonds; 78 roads; 7 trucks; 8 pieces; 18 trips; 87 numbers
The bequest included: 87 cheques, 7 bonds and 8 787 shares.

8/i
55 83 ideas; 8 imports; 8 interviews; 18 invitations; 88 issues
After 8 interviews we decided to order 8 870 imported items.

8/9
56 98 units; 9 suites; 8 dinettes; 9 buffets; 8 hutches; 9 sets
Deposit these 9 twenties, 89 tens, 9 fives and 198 quarters.

9/1
57 19 labels; 9 ladders; 29 ladles; 92 ladies; 99 lakes; 9 lids
List these in the monthly ledger: $93.89, $99.19, & $19.39.

9/0
58 9 motors; 90 pieces; 909 radios; 9 209 plants; 1 090 letters
Chairs numbered 9, 80, 90, 909 and 940 will go on sale next.

0/p
59 30 packets; 20 pans; 40 pages; 10 pads; 30 parks; 60 peppers
Pupils will give planned reports on Sept. 10, 20, 25 and 30.

0/-
60 Bill: 201-0407; Azim: 708-3002; Vi: 603-0070 or 603-0073.
I can be reached at one of: 205-4050, 205-0060 or 308-1090.

• • • • 1 • • • • 2 • • • • 3 • • • • 4 • • • • 5 • • • 6 • • • 7 • • • • 8 • • • • 9 • • • •10• • • •11• • • •12

9

40-space line
Spacing: 1

SC

Is your posture showing?
The importance of good
posture cannot be over-
emphasized.

Key two 30-s timings on
each line *or* repeat each line
twice.

Use **F** finger. Keep other
fingers above home row.
Key each line twice.

Use **J** finger. Keep other
fingers above home row.
Key each line twice.

Key two 1-min timings on
each line *or* repeat each line
three times.

Use **A** finger. Keep **F**
finger anchored above **F**
key. Key each line twice.

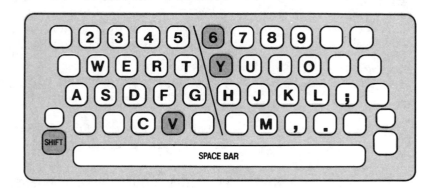

Review

1 she was glad we shared the sheet feeder.

2 we were calm as the deal was called off.

Reach to the V Key

3 fff fvf fvf fff fvf vvv fvf fv vf ffv vf

4 fvf fvf ffv fvf vfv fv vf fvvf fv fv vvf

Reach to the Y Key

5 jjj jyj jyj jjj jyj yyy jyj jyj jy yj yj

6 jyj jyj jjy jyj yjy yj jy yjjy yj jy yyj

Drill on V and Y Keys

7 very every vest yet voyage you jive levy

8 yours truly yoke view hay yam view value

Reach to the Left Shift Key

To capitalize letters on the right side of the keyboard:
1. Anchor **F** finger above **F** key.
2. Depress left shift key with **A** finger.
3. Strike the letter with required finger of right hand.
4. Release shift key and return **A** finger to home row.

9 Hay Have You Your Jay Joy James Jive Lay

10 May Kay Yam His Hers Here Kite Hive Lady

• • • • 1 • • • • 2 • • • • 3 • • • • 4 • • • • 5 • • • • 6 • • • • 7 • • • • 8

Stroking Practice

Select the letter combinations giving you difficulty in the drills just completed in your lesson. Key each line twice.

l/o 31 sold loan color float close hold loaf coal troll clock cloth
Olga sold her only foal and an old clock for eighty dollars.

m/n 32 men amount meeting many month name mention remain number man
The men hope to nominate the miners at next month's meeting.

o/p 33 power open soap phone ploy pound prose hope loop dope people
Phone the power company to report a stoppage of power there.

r/t 34 letter interest after report trust return matter part market
Try to start to write a letter while travelling on the tram.

r/u 35 rut turn under ruin run rubber ruler unfair uniform rub rust
There is rust under the trunk that could hurt or ruin a car.

s/w 36 sway saw wash sew ways wise sweet waste wash waist west show
We saw the Strawberry Roan in the show of the old wild west.

t/y 37 pretty tiny yacht youth yet toy try type tyrant truly treaty
Thirty tiny yachts were sailing yet when we saw Thunder Bay.

u/y 38 buy fully yule you youngster youth usually ugly unduly unity
It is your duty to buy young yule turkeys for your employee.

l/q 39 11 quacks; 13 quail; 141 quakes; 112 quills; 171 quick quips
Of the 1 181, 120 reported by 01:15 and only 1 161 by 01:51.

1/2 40 12 apples; 121 cherries; 212 plums; 2 121 apricots; 21 pears
The firm plans to hire 22 employees by 1991 and 122 by 1992.

2/w 41 22 whales; 202 watches; 272 wheels; 122 towers; 2 202 wagons
You wanted 2 122 wool sweaters, 12 shawls, and 22 wardrobes.

2/3 42 23 maps; 32 keys; 23 ties; 233 pans; 3 232 men; 2 303 women
We shipped 23 chairs to 3212 33 Ave. and 3 chairs to 3rd St.

3/e 43 3 beets; 313 elected; 73 electives; 353 emblems; 33 elements
Project 3133 for the Lee Co. of 33rd St. started 1990 03 31.

3/4 44 34 caps; 43 hats; 134 boots; 43 socks; 3 443 shirts; 4 belts
Credit account $4334 for White for $34.30, $43.30 and $3.43.

4/r 45 4 reels; route 434; 44 rugs; 24 ropes; 4 144 rivets; 4 racks
Another 40 rafters were ordered for delivery at 47 - 84 Ave.

• • • • 1 • • • • 2 • • • • 3 • • • • 4 • • • • 5 • • • 6 • • • 7 • • • • 8 • • • • 9 • • • • 10 • • • • 11 • • • • 12

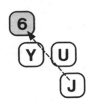

Reach to the 6 Key

11 jjj jy6 jy6 jjj j6j j6j j6j jjj jy6 j66j

12 j6j j6j jjj j6j j66 6jj j6j j6 6j jy6 j6

Drill on Left Shift Key and 6 Key

13 Yours truly; Have a vote; My vivid view;

14 6 vats; 6 vests; 66 yams; My 26 volumes;

Drill on New Keys

15 My village values volumes of good water.

16 I voice my wish to try a variety of ads.

17 Lou loves thick yogurt with yeasty cake.

18 Your yellow yams give variety to summer.

• • • • 1 • • • • 2 • • • 3 • • • 4 • • • 5 • • • 6 • • • 7 • • • 8

Drill on Common-Letter Combinations

19 very, every, lever, liver, verse, fever.

20 ye yes yet yesterday yeasts years yellow

Letter Review Practice

21 His forty cows filled 2 heavy milk jugs.

22 Our Joywer cord Levis fit Mike Hag well.

23 His few mauve jackets hid a gaudy color.

24 Hit for cover; take jugs for my wee lad.

• • • • 1 • • • • 2 • • • 3 • • • 4 • • • 5 • • • 6 • • • 7 • • • 8

Number Review Practice

25 636 eyes; 58 yams; 237 m; 293 mL; 2.46 h

26 26 vests; 786 levers; 35 livers; 49 vats

• • • • 1 • • • • 2 • • • 3 • • • 4 • • • 5 • • • 6 • • • 7 • • • 8

Use **J** finger. Keep other fingers above home row. Key each line twice.

Key two 1-min timings on each line *or* repeat each line three times.

Key two 1-min timings on each line *or* repeat each line three times.

Key two 1-min timings on each line *or* repeat each line three times.

Key two 1-min timings on each set of lines *or* repeat each set three times. Every alphabetic character introduced to date is included in these lines.

Key one 1-min timing on each line *or* key each line twice. All numbers introduced to date are included in these lines.

No period follows a metric symbol unless at the end of a sentence. Leave one space between a metric symbol and the numeral.

Stroking Practice

Select the letter combinations giving you difficulty in the drills just completed in your lesson. Key each line twice.

e/i   16 copies require receipt line credit receive provide give lien
Delia believes that receipts are required for carried items.

e/r   17 lever renew error clerk were secure are clear care early ear
Several new clerks arrived early to clear the store counter.

e/s   18 see easy selects size lease sews please season stone sincere
She selects several easy dresses and sweaters to sew for me.

e/t   19 set the seat take tear ten enter better test estate entities
Take the letter about the estate to the best lawyer in town.

e/w   20 were ewe where whet sweet whine weak stew wealthy week weigh
Where were we when the wind blew the weak white whale close?

f/g   21 fig gift flight fragile forgive glorify grief freight fringe
This gift is too fragile to fling in the fragmented freight.

f/r   22 fresh refer friend free first fever form fringe raffle frame
This is the first fresh fruit from the fat farmer's orchard.

f/t   23 fat flat float freight flaunt flute often graft soft flatter
The frightened flautist forgot to bring her flute and music.

g/h   24 high night sigh hug hang haulage hedge highest hinge freight
The freight truck lunged into the huge hedge a night before.

g/t   25 got together tough though gate gentle grant great typist tug
The girls got together and gathered twigs to graft on trees.

h/j   26 jack huge jug hat banjo joy hug jump hint joint hoist jacket
John and Joseph joined Johanna in her jeep on the road home.

i/k   27 king rink ink kitchen link like picks dike chicken sick mink
The kind king fed chicken to the kitten in the kitchen sink.

i/o   28 choice oil omit toil oriole soils boil origin notice options
This novice oil painter soiled the official original canvas.

i/u   29 illusion illuminate immune inbound until umpire unit unlined
Is it unrealistic to illustrate the unique signed bulletins?

k/l   30 like kill lack leak lick link lock look luck buckle booklets
Luke lacked the knowledge to fix the link leakage in sewers.

· · · · 1 · · · · 2 · · · · 3 · · · · 4 · · · · 5 · · · · 6 · · · · 7 · · · · 8 · · · · 9 · · · · 10 · · · · 11 · · · · 12

10

B/P/0/Right Shift

40-space line
Spacing: 1

SC

Are your fingers in the
curved-hand position?

Key two 30-s timings on
each line *or* key each line
twice.

Use **F** finger. Keep other
fingers above home row.
Key each line twice.

Use **;** finger. Keep other
fingers above home row, if
possible, but **J** finger must
be anchored above **J** key.
Key each line twice.

Key two 1-min timings on
each line *or* repeat each line
three times.

Use **;** finger, Keep **J**
finger anchored above **J**
key. Key each line twice.

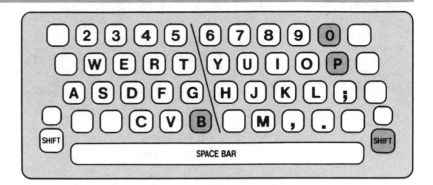

Review

1 I varied my verdict to view a live game.

2 63 vats of yeast; 6 level jars of yogurt

Reach to the B Key

3 fff fbf fbf fff fbf fb bf fbbf fbf fb bf

4 fbf fbf ffb fbb bf fb fff bbb fb bf fbbf

Reach to the P Key

5 ;;; ;p; ;p; ;;; ppp ;p; ;p; ;p p; ;p; p;

6 ;p; ;p; ;;; ppp ;p; ;pp pp; ;p; p;p ;pp;

Drill on B and P Keys

7 His pretty pet pig has a pair of apples.

8 Joy broke this old black bicycle basket.

Reach to the Right Shift Key

To capitalize letters on the left side of the keyboard:
1. Anchor **J** finger above **J** key.
2. Depress the right shift key with the **;** finger.
3. Strike the letter with the required finger of the left hand.
4. Release shift key and return **;** finger to home row.

9 Bob Barb Bart Bradley Babs Bill Berkeley

10 Trudy Tom Theresa Rob Ed Sid Ted Shirley

• • • • 1 • • • • 2 • • • • 3 • • • • 4 • • • • 5 • • • • 6 • • • • 7 • • • 8

Stroking Practice

Select the letter combinations giving you difficulty in the drills just completed in your lesson. Key each line twice.

a/e

1 fade easy have year date advise make sale same area able tea
Have all of them advise Rachael of the sale in her new area.

a/q

2 quack equals quash quadrant quarters quaint quantity equator
A quantity of quacking ducks were quarrelling by the garage.

a/s

3 as has please sales last case days cause past ask lease task
Sally has been pleased with the salary and the safer office.

a/z

4 azure amaze crazy daze faze lazy fuzzy razor glaze prize zip
We were amazed to see the azure zinnias in the prize sample.

b/g

5 beg bug gab brag burglar grub bought bargain baggage bargain
The big burglar bragged that he could grab the grey luggage.

b/n

6 been bland bin knob bland blink band nibble nobody bond born
The neighborhood band has been building a band shell for us.

b/v

7 above verb valuable bevel verbal vocabulary vestibule behave
I believe Bev invariably drinks vegetable beverages at noon.

c/d

8 dice duct cards could voiced credits iced deduct cited coded
Candy decided to credit the invoices according to new codes.

c/s

9 scale scene cities scheme scrap scissors cords select screen
The scales on each fish must be scraped with these scissors.

c/s/x

10 exacts success excuse exercise expects six extinguish exacts
I expect the exercise to be a success in extinguishing fire.

c/v

11 cave vice vacate cover civic convey convince convert coveted
A convoy of civil convicts convened in the vacant park cave.

d/e

12 decide end held dread sled slide bed dream bead dined seeded
The riders will decide which sled should lead on that slide.

d/f

13 fade defect fed friend fiddle defend defer fed field flooded
The defence was forced to defend the left field to win then.

d/k

14 dike dark ranked dusk kind knocked killed desk decks derrick
It was dusk and would be dark before the kind duke accepted.

d/s

15 sad ads advised records does asked regards address send lads
The lads said that they passed Sid's address at Shady River.

• • • • 1 • • • • 2 • • • • 3 • • • • 4 • • • • 5 • • • • 6 • • • • 7 • • • • 8 • • • • 9 • • • • 10 • • • • 11 • • • • 12

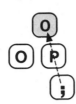

Reach to the O Key

11 ; ; ;   ;p;   ;O;   ;pp   ;O;   ;O;   ;p;   ;O O;   ;O ;O;

12 ;O;   ;O;   ; ; ;   ;O;   ;OO OO;   ;O;   ;O;   ; ;O O;O;

Drill on Right Shift and O Keys

13 20 Black Bicycles;   30 Bridal Books;   Bay;

14 40 jobs for Betty;   50 volumes for Velma;

Drill on New Keys

15 A bride bakes wheat bread for the table.

16 Pretty Pearl pours peach tea at parties.

17 20 jumpy polkas;   30 big pickles;   40 bibs

18 50 black bears;   70 parties;   0 peach pies

· · · · 1 · · · · 2 · · · · 3 · · · · 4 · · · · 5 · · · · 6 · · · · 7 · · · · 8

Drill on Common-Letter Combinations

19 bear best better belt below belief bells

20 pace paper pack packer pad page paid par

21 black blade blame blows blue bless block

22 prepaid prepare prepay prerecord presale

Letter Review Practice

23 Stacy will publish five more good jokes.

24 Hilda checks to sew brief vogue pyjamas.

25 Mob fights hurt previously cracked jaws.

26 Jay Maki weighed five old picture tubes.

· · · · 1 · · · · 2 · · · · 3 · · · · 4 · · · · 5 · · · · 6 · · · · 7 · · · · 8

Number Review Practice

27 39 pages, 84 paces, 750 papers, 26 pairs

28 29 belts;   843 bibs;   75 bibles;   60 blocks

· · · · 1 · · · · 2 · · · · 3 · · · · 4 · · · · 5 · · · · 6 · · · · 7 · · · · 8

Use ; finger. Keep J finger anchored above J key. Key each line twice.

Key two 1-min timings on each line *or* repeat each line three times.

Key two 1-min timings on each line *or* repeat each line three times.

Key two 30-s timings on each line *or* repeat each line twice.

Key two 1-min timings on each set of lines *or* repeat each set three times. Every alphabetic character introduced to date is included in these lines.

Key two 1-min timings on each line *or* repeat each line twice. All numbers introduced to date are included in these lines.

Selected Number Practice B

1

1 and 11; 81 to 171; at least 181 of 912; 131 and 141; 1 101
Invoices were mailed for: $17.11; $181.17; $101.10; $161.21.

2

2 and 22; 62 to 252; at least 292 of 822; 242 and 252; 2 029
Call these numbers: 272 2528; 272 8202; 292 8262; 282 8062.

3

3 and 33; 35 to 373; at least 303 of 833; 351 and 393; 3 053
The cost price was $73.83 bringing the net price to $131.33.

4

4 and 44; 49 to 414; at least 474 of 844; 424 and 142; 4 804
Rooms 401, 402, 404, 414, 415, and 424 are closed for today.

5

5 and 55; 52 to 454; at least 505 of 835; 575 and 105; 5 651
The numbers reported were: 5 152, 5 875, 2 545, and 15 850.

6

6 and 66; 62 to 636; at least 686 of 612; 626 and 106; 6 862
Numbers to be changed: 6 163, 6 796, 8 656, 7 606, and 636.

7

7 and 77; 73 to 717; at least 707 of 730; 737 and 977; 7 372
At least 787 of the throng of 1 770 were here by 7:00 today.

8

8 and 88; 81 to 808; at least 858 of 878; 908 and 828; 8 286
We sold 182 books, 181 binders, 808 pencils, and 158 rulers.

9

9 and 99; 95 to 494; at least 919 of 979; 904 and 939; 9 490
Remove the following files: 9892, 9169, 9075, 9395, and 90.

0

0 and 00; 40 to 300; at least 102 of 403; 906 and 907; 4 020
Phone the messages to these numbers: 304 6080 and 103 8040.

• • • • 1 • • • • 2 • • • • 3 • • • • 4 • • • • 5 • • • • 6 • • • 7 • • • • 8 • • • • 9 • • • • 10 • • • 11 • • • 12

Select the numbers giving you difficulty or causing errors in the drills just completed in your lesson. Key each line twice.

Students on individual progress should also practice the drills for the numbers indicated in point 5 in the lesson.

11

X / ' / Q / 1

SC

Is the paper guide on your typewriter or printer set at zero?

Key two 30-s timings on each line *or* repeat each line twice.

Use **S** finger. Keep **F** and **D** fingers anchored above home row. Key each line twice.

Use **;** finger. Keep other fingers above home row. Key each line twice.

If the apostrophe key is not located in this position on your keyboard, locate the appropriate key and use it.

Key two 1-min timings on each line *or* repeat each line three times.

Use **A** finger. Keep other fingers above home row. Key each line twice.

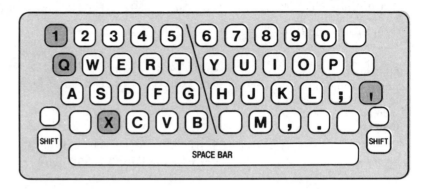

Review

1 Betty made baskets from 9 spruce boughs.
2 Pick 90 pears; pick at least 20 peaches.

Reach to the **X** Key

3 sss sxs sxs sss sxs xxx sxs sx xs sx xxs
4 sxs sxs ss sxs sx sxxs sx xs sxs sx sxsx

Reach to the **'** Key

5 ;;; ;'; ;'; ;;; ''' ;'; ;'; ;' '; ;' ;';
6 It's Max's or Mary's radio. I'll hurry.

Drill on **X** and **'** Keys

7 Pat's taxi; fix Bob's taxi axle; ax box;
8 Trixie's mixed wax; Roxy's box of phlox.

Reach to the **Q** Key

9 aaa aqa aqa aaa qqq aqa aqa qa aq aqqa q
10 aqa aqa aaa aqq qa aq qqa aaq aqa aqa qa

• • • • 1 • • • • 2 • • • • 3 • • • • 4 • • • 5 • • • • 6 • • • 7 • • • • 8

Selected Number Practice A

Select the numbers giving you difficulty or causing errors in the drills just completed in your lesson. Key each line twice.

Students on individual progress should also practice the drills for the numbers indicated in point 5 in the lesson.

1 of 11; 11 of 17; 13 of 211; 121 of 171; 141 of 311; 1 of 1
Of the 1 191, 1 012 reported by 2:15 and only 1 171 by 3:11.

2

2 of 22; 21 and 212; 212 from 2 232; 12 and 224; 92 of 2 122
Project 2 122 for the Rowe Co. of 22nd St. starts 1992 02 22.

3

3 of 33; only 313 of 3 233; 83 and 3 131 and 13 373; 3 of 33
Your invoice 231330 was in our file 133-733-3 by 1990 03 23.

4

4 of 44; 44 of 64; 43 of 414; 424 of 474; 434 of 494; 4 of 4
The list price on items 2434 and 2484 were cut 44% by today.

5

5 of 55; 51 and 515; 515 from 5 535; 15 and 554; 95 of 5 255
Of the 557 students tested on May 5 and 15, only 515 passed.

6

6 of 66; only 616 of 6 266; 86 and 6 161 and 16 676; 6 of 66
Item 1636 (606 belts at $1.66 each) are discounted by 66.6%.

7

7 of 77; 67 of 77; 73 of 717; 727 of 747; 737 of 797; 7 of 7
Payments were made: $7.70 on May 7 and $70.70 on August 27.

8

8 of 88; 81 and 818; 818 from 8 838; 18 and 884; 98 of 8 288
Item 18-188 (80 pens at $0.88) will be sold for $0.38 today.

9

9 of 99; only 919 of 9 299; 89 and 9 191 and 19 979; 9 of 99
Your invoice 891992 was in our File 199-799-9 by 1989 09 19.

0

0 of 80; 10 of 60; 30 of 600; 207 of 400; 2 070 from 103 002
The list prices on items 670 and 6707 were cut 50% by today.

• • • • 1 • • • • 2 • • • • 3 • • • • 4 • • • • 5 • • • • 6 • • • • 7 • • • • 8 • • • • 9 • • • •10 • • • •11 • • • •12

Use **A** finger. Anchor **F** finger above **F** key. Reach to the **1** key. Key each line twice.

Key two 1-min timings on each line *or* repeat each line three times.

Key two 30-s timings on each line *or* repeat each line twice.

Key two 30-s timings on each line *or* repeat each line twice.

Key two 1-min timings on each set of lines *or* repeat each set three times. Every alphabetic character introduced to date is included in these lines.

Key two 1-min timings on each line *or* repeat each line twice.

Spaces, not commas, are left between groups of 3 digits to the left and right of the decimal marker.

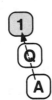

Reach to the 1 Key

11 aaa aqa aql ala ala aa ll ala lla all la
12 111 171 181 191 101 161 181 191 173 18 1

Drill on Q and 1 Keys

13 21 quills; 15 quilts; 32 quotas; 16 axes
14 121 quilts, 171 quests, 161 quarters, 13

Drill on New Keys

15 Six boxed quality red quilts; six boxes.
16 Twelve Quebec taxis required to qualify.
17 Xerxes' bride requested the pixie's sox.
18 Trixie Fox's Xmas quilt was quite heavy.

· · · · 1 · · · · 2 · · · · 3 · · · · 4 · · · · 5 · · · · 6 · · · · 7 · · · · 8

Drill on Common-Letter Combinations

19 quails quarter quack quake quality equal
20 ax axes axis taxes lax relax taxis axles
21 quick quiet quite quill quilt quits quip

Letter Review Practice

22 Every quick light fox jumped swiftly by.
23 Max drove a quick bright jalopy for Wes.

24 bluff catch dig jockey quivers map waxes
25 Days Wish Pecks Jug Bloom Quest Fear Vex

· · · · 1 · · · · 2 · · · · 3 · · · · 4 · · · · 5 · · · · 6 · · · · 7 · · · · 8

Number Review Practice

26 27 axes; 83 boxes; 649 taxis; 150 pixies
27 3 927 quotas, 84 quilts, 16 570 quarters

· · · · 1 · · · · 2 · · · · 3 · · · · 4 · · · · 5 · · · · 6 · · · · 7 · · · · 8

Spacing Reminder: The Apostrophe

• No spaces before or after the apostrophe.

Selected Letter Practice

Select the letters giving you difficulty or causing errors in the drills just completed in your lesson. Key each line twice.

Students on individual progress should also practice the drills for the letters indicated in part 5 in the instructions in the lesson.

y

eye yacht yard year yet buy sorry happy youth fairy why play
Why is Sammy playing with the yellow yo-yo while Baby yells?

A very tiny bicycle was by the hydrant near your yellow
buggy yesterday. One of the boys did try to find you to see
if the bicycle was yours. Your yard was empty so then I had
the boys put their bicycle in the faculty yard for the hour.

z

zero size snooze razor crazy blazer graze buzz zipper dozing
The zipper in this zigzag striped blazer is the issued size.

Izzy won the prize for his bronze zinnia. The zone had
some large-sized zinnias but Izzy had zealously utilized the
best-sized vase. Those other zinnias looked dazed and fuzzy
in their oversized glazed pots. Dizzy Izzy was very joyful.

• • • 1 • • • • 2 • • • • 3 • • • • 4 • • • • 5 • • • • 6 • • • • 7 • • • • 8 • • • • 9 • • • • 10 • • • 11 • • • 12

12

N/Z///?

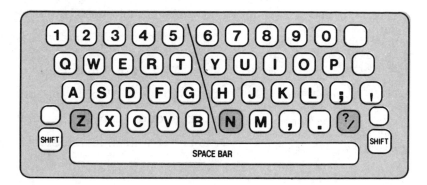

40-space line
Spacing: 1

SC

Do you keep your eyes on the copy except for establishing new stroke reaches?

Key two 30-s timings on each line *or* key each line twice.

Use **J** finger. Keep other fingers above home row. Key each line twice.

Use **A** finger. Keep other fingers above home row. Key each line twice.

Key two 1-min timings on each line *or* repeat each line three times.

Use **;** finger. Keep other fingers above home row. Key each line once.

Use **A** finger on left shift key and **;** key. Keep other fingers above home row. Key each line twice.

Review

1 Fix taxi axles with axes from old boxes.
2 Six pixies used axes to chip Xmas trees.

Reach to the N Key

3 jjj jnj jnj jjj jnj nnn jn nj jnnj jn nj
4 jnj jnj jjj nnn jnj jnnj jn nj jnnj jnjn

Reach to the Z Key

5 aaa aza aza aaa zzz aza aza az za za aza
6 aza aza azza az za aza aaa zzz az za aza

Drill on N and Z Keys

7 Zinnias and zucchini; crazy zinc zippers
8 Zany zebras were near zoology zoo zones.

Reach to the / Key

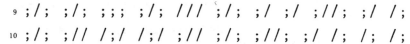

9 ;/; ;/; ;;; ;/; /// ;/; ;/ ;/ ;//; ;/ /;
10 ;/; ;// /;/ /;/ ;// ;/; ;//; ;/ /; /; /;

Reach to the ? Key

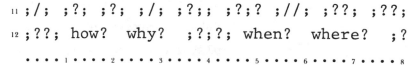

11 ;/; ;?; ;?; ;/; ;?;; ;?;? ;//; ;??; ;??;
12 ;??; how? why? ;?;?; when? where? ;?

. . . . 1 . . . 2 . . . 3 . . . 4 . . . 5 . . . 6 . . . 7 . . . 8

Selected Letter Practice

Select the letters giving you difficulty or causing errors in the drills just completed in your lesson. Key each line twice.

Students on individual progress should also practice the drills for the letters indicated in part 5 in the instructions in the lesson.

u

up snug skunk unable usually unlawful until cut push uranium
Lulu is playing loud music on a huge tuba outside the house.

    You were unfortunately and unduly misunderstood in your talk to us. Until you used the unusual example to upset the status quo, many were unable to understand the unique status of the insurance underwriter. We must discuss this further.

v

velvet very sever vision vest vehicle save void visitor give
An aviator is veering over a vacant village to visit Victor.

    Vivian drove to that village hoping to visit several of her relatives who lived by the river. She arrived very soon after Vincent, the roving aviator. Every relative was there for this visit. They gave Vivian five lovely mauve violets.

w

wage wall was way weight well what where who will wish wheel
A wild wind is howling and blowing away a new wooden wrench.

    The wheel on the new brown wooden wagon was wobbling as Wendy walked slowly through the cow meadow. She was worried that this wheel would fall off and the wagon full of walnuts would fall down. She watched for me to bring a wheelbarrow.

x

fox ax six extra relax exercise exact saxophone tax exerting
Relax while the fox and the ox mix the box of excellent wax.

    The sixteen taxi cabs have axles to fix. Those drivers can relax until the axles are fixed. An excellent job could take six extra hours. Exactly six of the taxi drivers might play saxophones while extra drivers do exhausting exercises.

• • • • 1 • • • • 2 • • • • 3 • • • • 4 • • • • 5 • • • 6 • • • 7 • • • • 8 • • • • 9 • • • •10 • • • •11 • • • •12

Drill on / and ? Keys

13 new names? necessary? neither? never?
14 2/10, n/30; 2/15; n/60; 1/20, n/90; n/45

Drill on New Keys

15 Nancy needs nine new national newspapers
16 Not now? Nine rust zinnias? No noises?
17 Won't a zany zebra doze in the new zoos?
18 zeal/zealous; size/zone; Noel's/Norma's;
• • • • 1 • • • • 2 • • • • 3 • • • • 4 • • • • 5 • • • • 6 • • • • 7 • • • • 8

Drill on Common-Letter Combinations

19 near neck neon nerve nests never neutral
20 sing wing rings swing thing being coming
21 nice night nil nine nitrogen niece nicks
22 none noon nor normal noses notice notify

Letter Review Practice

23 bank judge chime flop quest rye vex whiz
24 zebra sox equip caved many what jig flak

25 axle zest bevy wand rip jam quick if hog
26 quart zenith jumps bow relax sky gave of
• • • • 1 • • • • 2 • • • • 3 • • • • 4 • • • • 5 • • • • 6 • • • • 7 • • • • 8

Number Review Practice

27 314 nouns, 580 nails, 62 nests, 79 lions
28 948 razors 306 zones 72 zebras 150 sizes
• • • • 1 • • • • 2 • • • • 3 • • • • 4 • • • • 5 • • • • 6 • • • • 7 • • • • 8

Spacing Reminder: Diagonals and Question Marks

- No spaces before or after a diagonal.
- Two spaces after a question mark as it ends the sentence.
- No space before a question mark.

Selected Letter Practice

Select the letters giving you difficulty or causing errors in the drills just completed in your lesson. Key each line twice.

Students on individual progress should also practice the drills for the letters indicated in part 5 in the instructions in the lesson.

q

equal quarrel request quail quarter query question quit quip
A quiet queen in a quilted hat plays croquet with a quarter.

Vi Quilliam joined the queue to get her quota of queen-sized quilts. They were reduced by one quarter quite by accident after the clerk was requested to put quilts aside for quick sale. No query was made so quality wasn't questioned.

r

rate records reference regret repairs require regular result
A rhinoceros prefers a rugged river for resting and roaring.

Rory would rather repair the required radio speaker for the rancher than refund his purchase price. Regular service and proper care will keep the radio running. The rancher is going to request that Rory returns the repaired radio to me.

s

sales saws said same satisfy shares sold start system stated
Silas spills sausages and spaghetti in my steaming soup pot.

Since she sent the size six pants, her sister shipped a set of silk shirts and shorts. These were on sale this season and a supply is still on sale but all will be sold soon. We suggest you see this sale for yourself and assess offers.

t

take telephone that the them these think three time together
The train hit a trailer truck of tomatoes as its tires turn.

Today two or three term tests were written by the class of students to determine their standing. A letter grade was omitted this time but the top and bottom totals were written on the board. We think they will need to study pretty hard.

• • • • 1 • • • • 2 • • • • 3 • • • • 4 • • • • 5 • • • • 6 • • • • 7 • • • • 8 • • • • 9 • • • 10 • • • 11 • • • 12

13 Review/Tabulation

50-space line
Spacing: 1

Skill Building
Key two 1-min timings on each sentence or key each sentence twice. Every alphabetic character is included in each sentence.

Alphabetic Sentences

1 Our fire insurance policy will soon be paid and it is amazing that we get six more quick adjustments.

2 Only a queen can relax in a gown of bronze velvet; most of us prefer dark jeans when resting at home.

Key two 1-min timings on each line *or* repeat each line three times.

One-Hand Words

3 bade hill cafe hump dart poll east mill dear nylon
4 bags plum cast hulk dare look deaf yolk stab union
5 bare pill fast loom reef hull raze mink wear jolly

Key two 1-min timings on each line *or* repeat each line three times.

Alternate-Hand Words

6 am bid cut end ham then busy foam keys civic forms
7 an bib cub eke got them burn flap kept chair forks
8 do aid die fir hen town clay form lake cubic girls

· · · · 1 · · · · 2 · · · · 3 · · · · 4 · · · · 5 · · · · 6 · · · · 7 · · · · 8 · · · · 9 · · · · 10

Postal Codes

The Canadian Postal Code is called the *ANA NAN* code. The format of the postal code is: *Alpha Numeric Alpha* (Space) *Numeric Alpha Numeric.*

No other characters, periods, commas, hyphens, etc., should be included as part of the postal code. The postal code is preferred as the last line of the address.

Dasmund Enterprises Ltd.
25 York Mills Road
TORONTO, Ontario
M2P 1B5

Postal Code Drill

9 J2X 4L1 and J2X 4L1 and J2X 4L1
10 G5C 1R5 and G5C 1R5 and G5C 1R5
11 A1E 3X1 and A1E 3X1 and A1E 3X1

Key two 1-min timings on each line *or* repeat each line three times.

Timing

Key three 1-min timings on the set of three lines *or* key the set three times. Circle all errors and calculate gross words per minute (GWPM).

One-Minute Timing   1

She has had to use many more weeks at other times. | 10
Sammy will just try to jump as high as Billy does. | 20
The dear old man was nice to me when I helped him. | 30

· · · · 1 · · · · 2 · · · · 3 · · · · 4 · · · · 5 · · · · 6 · · · · 7 · · · · 8 · · · · 9 · · · · 10

Selected Letter Practice

Select the letters giving you difficulty or causing errors in the drills just completed in your lesson. Key each line twice.

Students on individual progress should also practice the drills for the letters indicated in part 5 in the instructions in the lesson.

m

man me may meet member maim mammal memento memorial maxim am
My motorcycle might smoke if it misses motor oil on Tuesday.

Her mother was in a good mood when she made milk shakes from ice cream, milk, jam and marshmallows. Mary might come home and be mad because she missed the meal her mother meant to be a complete surprise. It seems that Mary had a mishap.

n

name net now notes nation nine non notion nuns nylon sunning
A green plane landed in an unusual pond near the news stand.

Notice has been given that the Queen will not visit our nation next year as planned. Instead, she plans now to find time in the fall to open some provincial government sessions in: Manitoba, Saskatchewan, Newfoundland and New Brunswick.

o

of oil on one only or over ozone opinion option orator orlon
Open the portholes in the boat so you can hear the foghorns.

The old officer often wore his coat outdoors when walking in the orchard. He loved to go outside and took all opportunities to walk in the woods and look at the colors. He soon will find too much snow and it will force work indoors.

p

pie paper past people pipe plus pauper pulpit pep purple pop
A plump portly porcupine has plenty of sharp pointed quills.

Penny was happy to pay a top price for the pretty pearl and opal ring. Her pal spoke to her previously at the party about the Peoples' ad printed in the paper. Penny phoned up at once but she was not happy until the parcel was pocketed.

• • • • 1 • • • • 2 • • • • 3 • • • • 4 • • • • 5 • • • • 6 • • • • 7 • • • • 8 • • • • 9 • • • •10 • • • •11 • • • •12

Skill Building

Select a sentence that you think you can key in the time indicated by your instructor. If you complete the line within the time limit, try the next line. If not, try again or adjust your goal. Students on individual progress should key each line twice, as quickly as possible.

Graduated Speed Drills

		15s	12s	10s
1	I am here.	8	10	12
2	A man came.	9	11	13
3	It would do.	10	12	14
4	I go to town.	10	13	16
5	Please buy it.	11	14	17
6	She might know.	12	15	18
7	Make a new copy.	13	16	19
8	The dog is there.	14	17	20
9	The order is here.	14	18	22
10	The bus is due now.	15	19	23
11	She can read a form.	16	20	24
12	Len will fix the tow.	17	21	25
13	Ruth is not down here.	18	22	26
14	There were no new maps.	18	23	28
15	A cub will rush from me.	19	24	29
16	Pay the woman for a disk.	20	25	30

· · · · 1 · · · · 2 · · · · 3 · · · · 4 · · · · 5

Review

Key two 30-s timings on each line *or* key each line twice.

V fvf fvf ffv fvf vfv fv vf fvvf fv fv vvf fvvf vffv

Y jyj jyj jjy jyj yjy yj jy yjjy yj jy yyj jyyj yjjy

6 j6j j6j jjj j6j j66 6jj j6j j6 6j jy6 j6 6jj6 j66j

B fff fbf fbf fff fbf fb bf fbbf fbf fb bf fbbf bffb

P ;p; ;p; ;;; ppp ;p; ;pp pp; ;p; p;p ;pp; ;pp; p;;p

O ;o; ;o; ;;; ;o; ;oo oo; ;o; ;o; ;;o o;o; ;oo; o;;o

X sxs sxs ss sxs sx sxxs sx xs sxs sx sxsx xssx sxxs

Q aqa aqa aaa aqq qa aq qqa aaq aqa aqa qa aqqa qaaq

N jnj jnj jjj nnn jnj jnnj jn nj jnnj jnjn njjn jnnj

Z aza aza azza az za aza aaa zzz az za aza azza zaaz

· · · · 1 · · · · 2 · · · · 3 · · · · 4 · · · · 5 · · · · 6 · · · · 7 · · · · 8 · · · · 9 · · · · 10

Tabulation

Tabulation means that the print indicator or cursor will stop at the point(s) where you have set *tab stops*. This allows you to set up material in columns and to indent for paragraphs. For tabulation, you need to know how to use the:
• tab key   • tab clear key or option   • tab set key or option

Selected Letter Practice

Select the letters giving you difficulty or causing errors in the drills just completed in your lesson. Key each line twice.

Students on individual progress should also practice the drills for the letters indicated in part 5 in the instructions in the lesson.

i

ice icicle if into inch incident infinite inhibits initiated
Cindy likes licking ice cream before going swimming with us.

Irving is icing a nice big cake. He likes to stir some
ingredients himself. This time he is trying to surprise his
friends by writing interesting items on the sides of a cake.
The top will look like a field of tiny mauve and white iris.

j

job just judge joint jet jeans jam jack joyful juice journal
Jan wore pyjamas just to play joyous jingles on a new banjo.

A jolly jet pilot adjusted his jacket before journeying
across the airport to jump into his jet. It was going to be
a joyous occasion when he met his jubilant juvenile son. He
would be wearing his jade-green jacket to join that jubilee.

k

key kind king know kick kegs back knuckle knocked kick kiosk
Keep the kegs of sour pumpkin pickles to make a quick snack.

Kelly knew that the knife was kept in the kitchen sink.
Quickly he stuck the knife in his back pocket and walked out
to the pumpkin patch. This pumpkin would make good pie. He
cut the thick stem and packed the pumpkin in a wicker basket.

l

lad last level local labelling legally logical parallel well
Plenty of clean laundry is on this long yellow clothes line.

Lovely Lily walked slowly through the tall plants. The
yellow flowers bloomed beside the lettuce and broccoli. She
slipped and fell on a peel that had been left by some little
child. Lily was unhurt but the flowers looked like a salad.

• • • • 1 • • • • 2 • • • • 3 • • • • 4 • • • • 5 • • • 6 • • • 7 • • • • 8 • • • • 9 • • • • 10 • • • • 11 • • • • 12

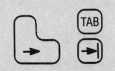

SC

Electronic typewriters and computers using word processing software frequently have preset tabs. To reset or clear these tabs, ask your instructor or read the software manual.

Tab Key

1. Locate your tab key.
2. Depress the tab key. This will move the print indicator or cursor to any previously set tab.

Tab Clear Key or Option

To clear tab stops:
1. Depress the tab key to locate previously set tab stops.
2. Depress the tab clear key or option to clear the tab stop.
3. Repeat steps 1 and 2 until each tab stop is cleared.

To clear all tabs:
1. Move the print indicator to the extreme right margin.
2. Depress the tab clear key and hold.
3. Return.
4. Release the tab clear key.
Some machines have a total clear key which, when depressed, will clear all previously set tab stops.

Tab Set Key or Option

1. Move your print indicator to the position where you would like to set a tab stop.
2. Depress the tab set key or option.
3. Repeat steps 1 and 2 to set each tab stop.

Production Practice

P

The symbol **DS** means double space. Return twice, leaving one blank space between lines.

Production 1

Set tab stops at 10 spaces, 20 spaces, 30 spaces, and 40 spaces from your left margin. Beginning at the left margin, key the following words.

DS↓

one	two	three	four	five
six	seven	eight	nine	ten
↑ Left Margin	↑ Tab Stop	↑ Tab Stop	↑ Tab Stop	↑ Tab Stop

SC

Did you remember to clear all previously set tabs?

P

The symbol ≡ means use a capital letter.

Production 2

Set your left margin at 30. Set tab stops at 50 and 65. Key the following words.

DS

length	metre	m
volume	litre	l
mass	gram	g
time	second	s
temperature	celsius	c

Selected Letter Practice

Select the letters giving you difficulty or causing errors in the drills just completed in your lesson. Key each line twice.

Students on individual progress should also practice the drills for the letters indicated in part 5 in the instructions in the lesson.

e

each ease eater effect electric element elite enter even end
An eager elephant ate eleven evergreen trees and some grass.

Ernie drives an excellent red fire engine. It has some hose, a bell and a siren. Ernie has to take the firemen who are needed to help extinguish the fire in the green house on the corner of Maple Street. The men put water on the house.

f

far feel file firm first five free from full baffle fifth if
A friendly wolf and his furry friend fished for fresh frogs.

The fat farmer failed to get off his crop of flax. The few freight cars were filled before his flax was felled. He feared a fairly famished future if he failed to sell all his flax. Finally, four freight cars removed the farmer's flax.

g

gas get good grain garage giggle grading grudge ginger given
George is wearing green goggles while working in the garden.

George has a good garage. He sells good gasoline to an angry girl. George wears gloves and goggles when he greases grinding gears. He graciously guarantees all gaskets tested in this garage. Grateful grandmothers get generous service.

h

had half hand he heavy help here high him hold hatch hunches
The red helicopter is hovering high over her handsome house.

Hannah has a habit of hanging her clothes on a hat hook here in the hall. She hates having to search through a heap of clothes for her hat. She helps keep her house organized. Her mother is happy to have her help with the harder chores.

• • • • 1 • • • • 2 • • • • 3 • • • • 4 • • • • 5 • • • • 6 • • • • 7 • • • • 8 • • • • 9 • • • • 10 • • • • 11 • • • • 12

Analytical Practice/ Paragraph Indentation

50-space line
Spacing: 1

Key two 30-s timings on each line *or* repeat each line three times.

Analyze Your Practice Needs

Key three 1-min timings on each sentence *or* repeat each sentence five times. Every alphabetic character is included in each sentence.

Circle all errors.

After Selected Letter Practice, key two 1-min timings on each sentence and determine if you have improved your accuracy.

If you have practised the necessary lines before your instructor calls time, begin keying at line **A** and key each line once.

Alternate-Hand Words

1 but ham she also flap land pays civic handy formal
2 cow hay sir body foam lamb pens coals panel handle

Alphabetic Sentences

3 Jack played squash for six long hard games when he bagged the first prize; everyone else cheered him.

4 The square vehicle won a prize as the best of many in the rod axle class; getting a prize was a joke.

• • • • 1 • • • • 2 • • • • 3 • • • • 4 • • • • 5 • • • • 6 • • • • 7 • • • • 8 • • • • 9 • • • • 10

Selected Letter Practice

1. Analyze your errors in the Alphabetic Sentences.
2. Choose the letter or letters giving you difficulty or causing errors.
3. Select the appropriate Selected Letter Practice.
4. Key each line twice.

A above accept according account act add address air
Eat an apple as you catch a train to Canada House.

B back balance bank basis because being bond both be
Ben is able to buy a big bird bath but he is busy.

C called can capital car cash certain change clients
A clever calico cat caught a clean claw in a clam.

D damage day debt decide defend deposit display dock
The dark haired doll was dropped in a dirty drain.

E each economy effect enclosed every estate exchange
Every egg will be eaten if we leave enough pepper.

• • • • 1 • • • • 2 • • • • 3 • • • • 4 • • • • 5 • • • • 6 • • • • 7 • • • • 8 • • • • 9 • • • • 10

Selected Letter Practice

Select the letters giving you difficulty or causing errors in the drills just completed in your lesson. Key each line twice.

Students on individual progress should also practice the drills for the letters indicated in part 5 in the instructions in the lesson.

a

a an at above act all age air adamant am annual area away as
A man has fallen on a banana peel; call an ambulance for me.

Anne's ability to act was acquired at an early age when she was taking dancing lessons. Anne's teacher asked her to act the part of a sad lass who was afraid. At that age Anne was unaware that one day she would have an agent and awards.

b

bad bake bath beg bib bit blow but bubble both book boat bug
A blue barge with bells, boxes and bags is in a busy harbor.

The bald baker put the bread in a brown bag before Babe began to barter for the banana buns. She bought both brands because the baker gave a big bargain. Babe said her brother will come back to buy a birthday cake in a box for her baby.

c

can calcium calculate calculus cancer carcass chance coaches
Crowds came to Chuck Church's picnic for a piece of popcorn.

A crowd came to Clarence's picnic even though the cloud cover made the day chilly. Children munched on ice-cream, a cake, celery and chunks of spicy chicken. A musician played an accordian and danced. Clarence cooked a delicious lunch.

d

dad data decade decayed deduct demand did died divide drudge
A damaged ladder drops in a deep mud puddle on a dirty road.

Dan trudged sadly down the dusty road. Today he had to do the thing he dreaded. Could he detour and hide in a deep ditch by the mud puddle? No, that was a bad idea. Besides, dad had said he had to clean the mud from the windows today.

• • • • 1 • • • • 2 • • • • 3 • • • • 4 • • • • 5 • • • • 6 • • • • 7 • • • • 8 • • • • 9 • • • • 10 • • • • 11 • • • • 12

F fact far fee few if of off file fill five fly form
Frank will try the frozen fish if the fire flames.

G gas general get guide good government grade grants
Gary is going to give the flag girls a good grade.

H had half handling have head held high home hundred
Hannah will help her haul the hunter to the hotel.

I ice idea if immediately important in inform its is
I will iron this item if it is in the bin in time.

J jackets job jewel jokes judge just joint joins jam
A jet journey to Jasper would just be a joy to me.

K keeps kept kitten kind know kitchen keys knee knew
Talk to the clerk as you take back the keen knife.

L land large lease level loan lumber local list life
Look at the little library; they loan lined forms.

M mail make may me meeting mills model much must man
Most of the map men are meeting in the dim motels.

Sp

neighbors or *neighbours*
Know the preference in your part of Canada and be consistent.

N name necessary need new nine no north number nurse
The newsstands were noisy with nineteen neighbors.

O obtain oath of offer office only oil on off out on
One noon hour Olga found the pool crowded and hot.

P page print paper pension people pipe please policy
Philip prepared the plate parcel promptly for Pam.

• • • • • 1 • • • • • 2 • • • • • 3 • • • • • 4 • • • • • 5 • • • • • 6 • • • • • 7 • • • • • 8 • • • • • 9 • • • • 10

Graduated Alphanumerical Speed Practice

Select a sentence that you think you can key in the time indicated (20 s, 15 s, and 12 s). If you complete the line within the time limit, try the next line. If not, try again or adjust your goal.

		20s	15s	12s
1	Cheque Number 1732 was cashed.	24	32	40
2	The guests arrived after 08:35.	25	33	41
3	It took Chad 35 min to go 42 km.	25	34	42
4	The first runner was in by 13:06.	26	34	43
5	Beth's old skates sold for $15.30.	26	35	44
6	Aunt Alice's number ends with 4768.	27	36	45
7	The A team had 13 girls and 17 boys.	28	37	46
8	We hope to visit him by August, 1996.	28	38	47
9	There were 7321 crafts in Sara's sale.	29	38	48
10	In 1990 the trip to Peru was cancelled.	29	39	49
11	Last month's invoice amounted to $23.60.	30	40	50
12	Sean lives 463.3 km away from Ed's house.	31	41	51
13	Toronto had 3.4 million people on July 15.	31	42	52
14	The clerk demanded $42.35 for the red coat.	32	42	53
15	Murray's house is the 24th one on 38 Avenue.	32	43	54
16	Our next meeting should start at 18:30 sharp.	33	44	55
17	Deme and Nancy shared 36 cookies and 12 tarts.	34	45	56
18	Only 24 cows and 13 horses were sold at Thurso.	34	46	57
19	The error of $92.31 was found in the last audit.	35	46	58
20	It took nearly 1.5 h to travel the 73 km to York.	35	47	59
21	On Friday, 20 clerks and 45 laborers will be paid.	36	48	60
22	Over 120 people came for the garage sale on June 4.	37	49	61
23	The score in the last game in Montreal was 26 to 17.	37	50	62
24	We had 20 cm of snow on Monday and 32 cm again today.	38	50	63
25	Aunt Ann's recipe calls for 250 mL of milk and 3 eggs.	38	51	64
26	Mae cooked a 10 kg turkey and a 2.5 kg duck on Tuesday.	39	52	65
27	Susan's sleeve length is 70 cm but Mary's is only 65 cm.	40	53	66
28	Her new chemistry class begins at 10:45 every second day.	40	54	67
29	Roy travelled an average of 90 km/h for the 85 km to Bath.	41	54	68
30	The favored Argonauts had 15 first downs and scored 36 pts.	41	55	69
31	A Tuesday serving had 4.2 mg of iron and 0.6 mg of thiamine.	42	56	70

• • • • 1 • • • • 2 • • • • 3 • • • • 4 • • • 5 • • • • 6 • • • 7 • • • • 8 • • • • 9 • • • • 10 • • • • 11 • • • • 12

Q quality equal question quote quiet quota quotation
  Their queen was quick to quote a quip in the quiz.

R rate rather realize reason record refer road rules
  Harry dared Ruth to run with rubbers on the rails.

S said sale schedule school set she size small start
  The dress shop also had shoes, shirts, and slacks.

T take tax telephone their time type two trust towns
  The time trials start in about twenty-two minutes.

U unable under units using usual up urging until use
  I must use Trudy's umbrella until you return mine.

V value vehicle very view visit volume vote everyone
  I value every vacation in the vacant valley villa.

W want was water week where will work write worn win
  Wash the wine walls with water and a wet wall mop.

X xerox laxative taxes axis pixie fox axle fix relax
  Relax on the box while I fix the axle on the taxi.

Y year yard yellow yet yes you your youth yield yarn
  A yellow yak yearns for yams, yarrow and red yarn.

Z zinc zero doze prize size zone zippers zeal zinnia
  Zealous zebras in the zoo gaze in on prized grass.

Sentence with Numbers

There are 23 new cars on lot 106, 37 on lot 215, 8
on lot 7, 19 on lot 29, 14 on lot 35, 4 on lot 86,
9 on lot 87, 16 on lot 45, and 6 on lot 109.

· · · · · 1 · · · · · 2 · · · · · 3 · · · · · 4 · · · · · 5 · · · · · 6 · · · · · 7 · · · · · 8 · · · · · 9 · · · · 10

Key three 2-min timings on the sentence *or* repeat the sentence five times. All numbers are included in the sentence.

Circle all number errors.

Graduated Alphanumerical Speed Practice

Select a sentence that you think you can key in the time indicated (20 s, 15 s, and 12 s). If you complete the line within the time limit, try the next line. If not, try again or adjust your goal.

		20s	15s	12s
1	Their invoice totalled $14.86.	18	24	30
2	Prince George is 357.5 km away.	19	25	31
3	That Easter holiday was in 1990.	19	26	32
4	It was 18:35 when father arrived.	20	26	33
5	The Spanish class begins at 08:30.	20	27	34
6	He sold the skis to her for $75.00.	21	28	35
7	Old Leopard took 45 min to do 28 km.	22	29	36
8	Walt's car is the 13th one in Lot 28.	22	30	37
9	Number 8932 won the contest for Henry.	23	30	38
10	Come to Anderson's at 38 - 42nd Street.	23	31	39
11	Ed tried to sell the fur coat for $2058.	24	32	40
12	An error of $48.92 was found on the stub.	25	33	41
13	Ship the 35 fans and 72 heaters to Barrie.	25	34	42
14	The last 36 km to Halifax took only 0.25 h.	26	34	43
15	Uncle Stuart's car took 34.85 L of gasoline.	26	35	44
16	The error of $97.83 was found by six o'clock.	27	36	45
17	Receipt Number 2381 was missing from the file.	28	37	46
18	There were 14 girls and 18 boys on the B teams.	28	38	47
19	Caitlan gave Jack 18.25 L of kerosene yesterday.	29	38	48
20	The total flight distance to Regina was 2 435 km.	29	39	49
21	The Stampeders won with 22 first downs and 48 pts.	30	40	50
22	Our vacation in August, 1989 was our most exciting.	31	41	51
23	Crystal Carpets on 23rd has over 90 carpets on sale.	31	42	52
24	It was 19:50 before any guests arrived from Hamilton.	32	42	53
25	Farm Sales had 23 tractors and 19 trucks listed today.	32	43	54
26	The family camp begins in the first week of July, 1991.	33	44	55
27	A 10 kg turkey and a 12 kg beef roast were sold at Ed's.	34	45	56
28	By '83 Canada's population had reached 25 million people.	34	46	57
29	Nearly 20 cm was cut off from the 90 cm leg of Al's pants.	35	46	58
30	On Tuesday, the firm will hire 12 assistants and 27 clerks.	35	47	59
31	The number 5768 is the last four digits for Andrew's phone.	36	48	60

• • • • 1 • • • • 2 • • • • 3 • • • • 4 • • • • 5 • • • • 6 • • • • 7 • • • • 8 • • • • 9 • • • • 10 • • • • 11 • • • • 12

Selected Number Practice

1. Analyze your errors in the Sentence with Numbers.
2. Choose the number or numbers giving you difficulty or causing errors.
3. Select the appropriate Selected Number Practice.
4. Key each line twice.

After Selected Number Practice, key two 2-min timings on the sentence and determine if you have improved your number accuracy.

```
1  1 or an 11 or 111 and 12 for a 31 by 1 among 1 121
2  by 12 since 232 by 2 and a 2 or 21 and 2 122 or 12
3  3 and 33 by 313 yet 3 131 or 3 323 by 3 but 3 or 3
4  4 but 14 and 4 141 by 44 among 41 for 4 424 and 14
5  55 or 515 by 51 but 25 at least 5 251 for 51 and 5
6  6 since 616 then 61 but 16 626 for 16 or 66 but 62
7  7 or a 71 or 7 171 and 7 for a 72 by 7 among 7 737
8  8 and 88 by 818 yet 8 181 or 8 828 by 8 but 8 or 8
9  9 but 19 and 9 191 by 9 among 949 for 9 929 and 19
0  0 or 040 by 30 but 20 at least 1 040 for 200 and 0
   • • • 1 • • • • 2 • • • • 3 • • • • 4 • • • • 5 • • • 6 • • • • 7 • • • • 8 • • • • 9 • • • 10
```

Paragraph Indentation

Set a tab stop five spaces from the left margin for paragraph indentation. Your machine or word processing program may have a preset tab. Know your machine.

Production

Production Practice

P

The symbol ¶ means start a new paragraph.

Key the following paragraph using a 50-space line.

⌐5¬ ¶ The catalogue company has billed us for items which we did not purchase. Please telephone their city office and give them the invoice numbers from our files. ¶Please provide them with any more information that they request about the shipment. Ask them to check their company files, especially the shipping department, to verify the claim. ⌐5¬¶Perhaps you should stress at this opportunity that this is the third such occurrence that I have had to investigate in less than six months.

SC

Did you indent properly? If you did, all lines will be even at the right margin.

Consolidated Drills

In order to provide for individual differences in speed and accuracy development, the skill drills have been consolidated in this section.

Students should set their own objectives in using the following drills:

Graduated Alphanumerical Speed Practice
Selected Letter Practice
Selected Number Practice
Stroking Practice
Number Pad Drills
One-Minute Timings of Graduated Difficulty
Three- or Five-Minute Timings

15 Horizontal Centering

50-space line
Spacing: 1
Key two 1-min timings on each line *or* repeat each line three times.

Skill Building

Key two 1-min timings on each line *or* repeat each line three times. Key these drills as quickly as you can.

Key two 1-min timings on each line *or* repeat each line three times. Try to increase your speed slightly on the second try.

Key one 1-min timing on each line *or* repeat each line twice.

If the shift lock key is not located in this position on your keyboard, locate the appropriate key and use it.

Key each line twice using the shift lock correctly.

One-Hand Words

1 bear pull faded moon stew link sage mono ware noun
2 wade loop tare loon feed lump aged plump wart pool

Alternate-Hand Words

3 me bug oak pep men work disk half lent firms rifle
4 od bus own pro map worn dock hams maid flair amend
5 of but and rid she also down hand make flake angle
6 or cow pan rig sir body dual held male flame audit

Common-Word Sentences

7 The food for the next big party is fit for a king.
8 The bill they received last week was already paid.
9 John will soon find some good group games to play.
10 The rich young lady rode in a brand new green car.

• • • • 1 • • • • 2 • • • • 3 • • • • 4 • • • • 5 • • • 6 • • • • 7 • • • • 8 • • • • 9 • • • • 10

Postal Codes

Set tab stops 12, 24, and 36 spaces from the left margin.

11 R1A 0V5   S4P 3K3   G9T 1W2   A1B 1Z4
12 E2K 2L6   T9A 1W7   L8M 1S9   V9Y 2R8
13 L3C 2G9   C1N 3L0   S4P 3N9   J2G 6Z1

         ↑ Tab   ↑ Tab   ↑ Tab

Shift Lock

To key a word or words in all capitals.
1. Use the **A** finger to depress the shift lock key. It is above the left shift key.
2. Key the letters desired in capitals.
3. Use either the right or left shift key to release the shift lock.

   Note: Remember to release the shift lock if some letters or special characters are not to be keyed in upper case.

14 She is a client of FOLEY, WILLIAMS AND WALKEMEYER.
15 Pick up a copy of MEMO from COPP CLARK PITMAN LTD.
16 Samuel read GRAPES OF WRATH and LORD OF THE FLIES.

Production 1

Compose and key a letter in AMS style. The letter is to be sent to the initiator of the invitation to speak to the Administrative Management Society. The letter should include: 1) thanks for the opportunity to speak at the 50th Annual Conference, 2) acknowledgment for the honorarium of $200 already received, and 3) expression of pleasure for the gracious reception received and a word about being met personally and given a special send-off at Vancouver International Airport. Prepare it for James Dasmund's signature. Use the letterhead provided in the Working Papers. Key an envelope or an envelope label.

Production 2

Key the first page of the report The Quest For Artificial Intelligence on page 384 . Use the formal footnote style and give the full footnote references at the bottom of the page.

Production 3

Key the following itinerary on a full sheet of paper. Set it up in attractive tabular form.

Peter Gallin is travelling to Chicago to attend a convention.

Tuesday, April 16. Leaves Regina Airport at 09:00, Northwest Airlines Flight 145 arriving at Chicago's O'Hare Airport at 10:00. Hotel reservation is at the Palmer House (State and Monroe Streets) where the convention of Hardware Manufacturers is taking place. The reservation has been made for an extra-large room with additional chairs so a luncheon meeting can be scheduled.

Wednesday, April 17. 09:30 convention opens. Exhibits open at 11:00 and you specifically want to visit those exhibits shown on your "Special List" in your brief case. You should arrange for a luncheon meeting in your room for Thursday with these exhibitors. *Select the menu for the luncheon meeting. Remind exhibitors about tomorrow's meeting.*

Thursday, April 18. Confirm your return reservation. Northwest Flight 211 leaves Friday at 11:30. Convention continues. Order table flowers for the luncheon today. 12:00 luncheon in your room. Present the proposal for bids on hardware items which Dasmund wishes to carry exclusively. Proposal is in brief case with copies to be handed out to those interested.

Friday, April 19. Leaves Chicago O'Hare International Airport at 11:30 on Northwest Flight 211 arriving in Regina at 13:30. Wife will meet you at the airport. *Check in at O'Hare at least 90 min before departure.*

Horizontal Centering

Horizontal centering means that half the keyed text is to the left of the center point of the paper and half to the right of the center point of the paper.

Prepare Your Machine

1. Set your margin stops at the extreme left and extreme right of your machine.
2. Clear all tab stops.

Find the Center Point

1. Insert your paper.
2. Note the print indicator at the left edge of the paper.
3. Note the print indicator at the right edge of the paper.
4. Subtract step 2 from step 3 for total number of spaces.
5. Divide your answer by two.
6. Add your answer in step 5 to step 2 and you will always have the center of your paper regardless of paper size.

Example: (Elite — 12 pitch)

Step 1	Insert paper	
Step 2	Left edge scale	0
Step 3	Right edge scale	100
Step 4	$100 - 0 =$	100
Step 5	$100 \div 2 =$	50
Step 6	$50 + 0 =$	50

The center of the paper is 50.

Example 2: (Pica — 10 pitch)

Step 1	Insert paper	
Step 2	Left edge scale	0
Step 3	Right edge scale	85
Step 4	$85 - 0 =$	85
Step 5	$85 \div 2 =$	42 (approximately)
Step 6	$42 + 0 =$	42

The center of the paper is 42.

If you are using a computer, determine the horizontal center point of the paper in your printer. This is not necessarily the center point of your monitor OR the center point between your margins.

The status line on your monitor indicates the line number and the character position of the cursor. For horizontal centering, read the character position and move the cursor to the appropriate center point.

7. Set a tab stop at the center point.
8. Adjust your paper guide or printer to align the left edge of the paper at zero.

The Backspace Method*

1. Tab or move your cursor to the center point.
2. Backspace once for every two characters or spaces in the word or phrase of the line.
   Example: Center the word CENTERING.

CE NT ER IN G

*Do not backspace for any odd letter or number left at the end of the line.

3. Key the word or line to be centered.

*Your software package may have an automatic center option. This may be used in later lessons.

Assess Your Progress

60-space line
Spacing: 1 and 2
Key two 30-s timings on each line *or* repeat each line three times.

Assess Your Speed

Set spacing at 2. Key at least one 3-min *or* 5-min timing. Circle all errors and calculate gross words per minute. Record the timing on your Progress Chart.

Double-Letter Words

1 rolls class needed attend comment setting mutually expressed
2 wells holly indeed attach million appoint assigned territory

Three- or Five-Minute Timing

	1	CW	3
The computer technology will continue to have a growing	12	12	4
impact on society in the future. It is much easier to fore-	24	24	8
tell the technical possibilities than the impact of a social	36	36	12
nature. The computer has become so much a part of our soci-	48	48	16
ety that most of our institutions are now nearly totally de-	60	60	20
pendent upon them. Industry, business, government, and edu-	72	72	24
cation use computers for both administrative and office uses	84	84	28
as well as in countless ways to reduce the amount of repeti-	96	96	32
tive tasks and thus, decrease the cost for manual labor.	107	107	36
This trend to use automation wherever possible will de-	12	119	40
crease the amount of manual labor and one direct result will	24	131	44
be shorter working hours for individuals and thus, more time	36	143	48
for leisure. When more menial and routine jobs are replaced	48	155	52
by automated machines, there is generally a need for better-	60	167	56
educated or trained personnel to fill the new employment the	72	179	60
firms need to create. How this leisure will be used is more	84	191	64
of a problem than society at first realized. Increased num-	96	203	68
bers of holidays, early retirement and a shorter week give a	108	215	72
combined social issue that needs to be resolved.	118	225	75
If recent patterns are allowed to continue, a continual	12	237	79
loss of privacy will occur. The application of law and con-	24	249	83
trols is very difficult so without a major change in a trend	36	261	87
to less privacy, it will continue to be eroded. One step to	48	273	91
favor this change is the growing interest of scientist along	60	285	95
with the man or woman on the street in taking steps to avoid	72	297	99
what looks to be the inevitable.	78	303	101

• • • • 1 • • • • 2 • • • • 3 • • • • 4 • • • • 5 • • • • 6 • • • • 7 • • • • 8 • • • • 9 • • • • 10 • • • • 11 • • • • 12 1 min

1   2   3   4 3 min

SI   1.64
AWL 4.48

Did you achieve the unit objective of 55 words per minute with 3 errors on a three-minute timing; or 50 words per minute with 4 errors or less on a five-minute timing?

Production 1

Center your name.

Center your address.

Center your city and province.

Check your work.

Production 2

Can you horizontally center the following? Use the Backspace Method.

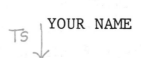

YOUR NAME

Instructions for Horizontal Centering

Move the margin stops to paper edges
Clear all tab stops
Insert your paper
Find the paper center point
Set a new tab stop at the paper center
Set the paper guide accordingly
Backspace once for every two characters or spaces
Ignore a single character left at the end of a line
Key the word or line

Production 3

Center each of the following words. Use the Backspace Method.

TS
appointment
mail
telephone
letter
business correspondence

Assess Your Improvement
Set spacing at 2. Key at least one 3-min *or* 5-min timing. Circle all errors and calculate gross words per minute. Record the timing on your Progress Chart.

1 CW 3

Many people are referring to the coming generation living in a cashless society. The computer has had a great influence on our money and banking system and it is not difficult to imagine that the time-consuming paperwork can be replaced by simple messages transmitted from a computer in one city to another some distance away. Already many accounting systems in banks are connected to a central computer that is only seconds away for information retrieval.

12	12	4
24	24	8
36	36	12
48	48	16
60	60	20
72	72	24
84	84	28
93	93	31

Heralds of the cashless society say that a machine-read credit card can be used instead of cash or cheques. Systems of this type are already underway. No paper has to be used. For a purchase of $23.10, the clerk would insert your credit card in a register and key in the correct amount. A central computer would verify that your account was in good standing and that your credit was good for this amount. Without your receiving a bill or writing a cheque, telephone bills, house payments or other charges would be made directly.

12	105	35
24	117	39
36	129	43
48	141	47
60	153	51
72	165	55
84	179	59
96	191	63
106	201	66

Salaries would be paid by means of direct transfers. A transfer of $1508.63 would be deducted from an account of an employer and added to that of the employee. General banking procedures would be much simpler and more economical because there would be less paper handled. A personal recordkeeping system would be easily maintained by checking monthly statements from the bank to verify that all charges were in order that month. The basis for this cashless system is already a reality in larger urban areas.

12	213	70
24	225	74
36	237	78
48	249	82
60	261	86
72	273	90
84	285	94
96	297	98
102	303	100

• • • • 1 • • • • 2 • • • • 3 • • • • 4 • • • • 5 • • • • 6 • • • • 7 • • • • 8 • • • • 9 • • • • 10 • • • • 11 • • • • 12 1 min
       1   2   3   4 3 min

SI 1.65
AWL 4.76

Spread Centering

One-Hand Words

1 bars plop fears null daze look draw milk stay noun
2 bare pill feast loom reef hull rate mine wear noon

Alphabetic Sentences

3 Give them six equal portions of prize pumpkin cake
  or a dish of juicy cherries when they arrive here.

4 Quite a few jokes were told about zoo animals that
  got free from very old cages and boxed each other.

• • • • 1 • • • • 2 • • • • 3 • • • • 4 • • • • 5 • • • • 6 • • • • 7 • • • • 8 • • • • 9 • • • • 10

Selected Letter Practice

1. Analyze your errors in the Alphabetic Sentences.
2. Choose the letter or letters giving you difficulty or causing errors.
3. Turn to Lesson 14 and select the appropriate Selected Letter Practice.
4. Key each line twice.

Two-Minute Timing

All timings are expressed in words per minute. Therefore, a 2-min timing would require that the total words completed be divided by two. For ease in scoring, a 2-min timing scale is added for your convenience. This scale is already shown in words per minute so it is not necessary to divide by two.

	1	2
The large grey eyes gazed up from beneath the	10	5
fringe of brown lashes. The nose and rounded pink	20	10
cheeks were flecked with freckles. I saw the tiny	30	15
mouth curve in the start of a smile. The trust of	40	20
a child of two shone from the childish face. This	50	25
life can be full of wonder for a child. I reached	60	30
out and took his hand.	64	32

• • • • 1 • • • • 2 • • • • 3 • • • • 4 • • • • 5 • • • • 6 • • • • 7 • • • • 8 • • • • 9 • • • • 10   1 min

       1   2   3   4   5   2 min

Difficulty of Keyed Material

- SI or *syllabic intensity* means the average number of speech syllables per actual word in the timing.
- AWL or *average word length* measures the stroke intensity of words. AWL shows the average number of letters in the actual words used in the timing.

Skill Building

60-space line
Spacing: 1 and 2
Key two 30-s timings on
each line *or* repeat each line
three times.

Double-Letter Words

1 tools drill tariff bottle efforts pattern kindness witnessed

2 blood feels exceed yellow running smaller employee difficult

One-Minute Timings

1. Turn to the One-Minute Timings, page 421.
2. Select the paragraph that you think you can complete in one minute.
3. Key the One-Minute Timing as a drill.
4. If you had two or more errors, practice Accuracy Improvement.
   If you had fewer than two errors, practice Speed Improvement.

Skill Building

Key two 30-s timings on
each line concentrating on
the speed *or* accuracy goal
set in your One-Minute
Timings.
Students on individual
progress should key each
line three times with their
speed *or* accuracy goal in
mind.

Word-Combination Practice

3 Hopefully you will leave enough hammers to finish his shack.

4 Try your reference issue even though helpful labels are few.

5 Report to our rooms as soon as some events seem nearly done.

6 Help prevent traffic congestion now while Earl Lane is shut.

• • • • 1 • • • • 2 • • • • 3 • • • • 4 • • • • 5 • • • • 6 • • • • 7 • • • • 8 • • • • 9 • • • •10• • • •11• • • •12

Stroking Practice

1. Turn to the Stroking Practice, page 414.
2. Key the lines selected by your instructor or the letter combinations giving you difficulty in the drills just completed.
3. Students on individual progress should select lines.
4. Key each line twice.

Accuracy Improvement

Key two 30-s timings on
each line concentrating on
accuracy as your goal.
Students on individual
progress should key each
line three times with the
accuracy goal in mind.

7 We feel this plant has prepared a satisfactory new contract.

8 She will change the production material for this new lesson.

9 The officer assumed that all traffic could proceed to cross.

10 It appears that all chattels and effects were omitted in it.

• • • • 1 • • • • 2 • • • • 3 • • • • 4 • • • • 5 • • • • 6 • • • • 7 • • • • 8 • • • • 9 • • • •10• • • •11• • • •12

Spread Centering

Spread centering means that *one* space is left between each letter in a word and *three* spaces are left between words. It is a special form of horizontal centering.

Example: I N T E G R A T E D   S O F T W A R E

Prepare Your Machine

1. Set your margin stops at the extreme left and extreme right.
2. Clear all tab stops.
3. Insert your paper.
4. Set a tab stop at the center point.

Steps for Spread Centering

1. Tab to the center point.
2. Backspace once for each character and its following space. Backspace once for each space between words.
   Example: Spread center the word CENTERING.

   C E N T E R I N G *

   Example: Spread center the words PSYCHOLOGY 100.

   P S Y C H O L O G Y   1 0 0 *

   *Do not backspace for the last letter or number in the last word of the line.
3. Key the line leaving one space between every letter or number in each word and three spaces between words.

   C E N T E R I N G

   P S Y C H O L O G Y   1 0 0

Production 1

Spread center your name.

Spread center your address.

Spread center your city and province.

Check your work.

Production 2

Spread center the following titles. Use the Backspace Method.

Principles of Accounting

Pitman Office Handbook

~~Effective~~ Business Letter Writing

Keyboarding

Office Information Systems

Mastering Effective English

Three- or Five-Minute Timing

Assess Your Improvement
Set spacing at 2. Key at least one 3-min *or* 5-min timing. Circle all errors and calculate gross words per minute. Record the timing on your Progress Chart.

	1 CW	3
108	12	4
120	24	8
132	36	12
12	48	16
24	60	20
36	72	24
48	84	28
60	87	29
72	99	33
84	111	37
87	123	41
12	135	45
24	147	49
36	159	53
48	171	57
60	183	61
72	195	65
84	207	69
96	219	73
12	231	77
24	243	81
36	255	85
48	267	89
60	279	93
72	291	97
84	303	101
94	313	104

Electronic typewriters have come a long way since they were first introduced to the business world. Some business consultants in the 1980's were stating that the electronics have an extremely limited lifespan and would quickly be replaced by the microcomputer in every office situation. Now it has become more evident that there is still a need for a machine that can bridge the gaps between a basic typewriter and a computer.

The popular electronic machines used today allow users to store and reprint information, edit by use of screens of various sizes from one to a number of lines in length, bold face or underline text, automatically set margins, center a line automatically, as well as automatically align decimals and tab stops. Word wrap-around has now become as common a feature with electronics as the "on-switch" of the standard electric typewriter of the past. Many models offer repetitive phrase and format storage for labels, memos and letter parts. Most allow the operators to search and replace text in addition to moving, copying, and deleting text blocks.

Machine memory is continuing to climb, allowing numerous pages of a document to be stored for later use. Recent introduction of communications, electronic mail and unit to unit file transfers means that the electronic machines have made it into a new league. And besides, the occasional envelope, which does not fit into list processing jobs on the computer printer, can still be handled on the typewriter at hand without moving to a different work station.

```
• • • • 1 • • • • 2 • • • • 3 • • • • 4 • • • • 5 • • • 6 • • • 7 • • • • 8 • • • 9 • • • •10 • • •11 • • • 12   1 min
           1                    2                    3                    4   3 min
```

SI   1.36
AWL 6.18

17

50-space line
Spacing: 1 and 2
Key two 1-min timings on
each line *or* repeat each line
three times.

**Analyze Your Practice
Needs**
Key two 1-min timings on
each sentence *or* repeat each
sentence three times. Every
alphabetic character is
included in each sentence.

Timing

Set your line space regulator
at 2. Key two 2-min
timings. Circle all errors
and calculate gross words
per minute (GWPM).
Record the better timing on
your Progress Chart.

SI   1.00
AWL 4.19

Block Centering

One-Hand Words

1 tear hilly seed link acre holy fact kink tart loop
2 swat jumpy swab hoop ward polo base hook beat link

Alphabetic Sentences

3 Jack visited the wax museum by the zoo before they
put signs on the lawn that a quarter was required.

4 The young queen waved to the joyous crowd from the
box seats in the private zone kept mainly for her.
· · · · 1 · · · · 2 · · · · 3 · · · · 4 · · · · 5 · · · · 6 · · · · 7 · · · · 8 · · · · 9 · · · · 10

Selected Letter Practice

1. Analyze your errors in the Alphabetic Sentences.
2. Choose the letter or letters giving you difficulty or causing errors.
3. Turn to Lesson 14 and select the appropriate Selected Letter Practice.
4. Key each line twice.

Two-Minute Timing

	1	2
We'll see you and your friend at the fair the	10	5
day after next. Will you be there by two? We see	20	10
that you will try to win in the horse race. There	30	15
will be more of you in the race than last year. I	40	20
hope you have good luck this time. Will Kim start	50	25
the horse in the race for the first time? It will	60	30
be nice to see both of you in the same race if the	70	35
draw works out just right.	75	37

· · · · 1 · · · · 2 · · · · 3 · · · · 4 · · · · 5 · · · · 6 · · · · 7 · · · · 8 · · · · 9 · · · · 10   1 min
1   2   3   4   5   2 min

Block Centering

Block centering means that only the longest line in a group of lines is exactly horizontally
centered. The other lines in the grouping are blocked to begin with the same left margin as
the longest line. Do not consider the title or heading when selecting the longest line. Block
centering is another special form of horizontal centering.

Skill Building

60-space line
Spacing: 1 and 2
Key two 30-s timings on each line *or* repeat each line three times.

Double-Letter Words

1 green steer dollar copper arrears calling shopping essential

2 cross upper cotton rubber college settled arriving officials

One-Minute Timings

1. Turn to the One-Minute Timings, page 421.
2. Select the paragraph that you think you can complete in one minute.
3. Key the One-Minute Timing as a drill.
4. If you had two or more errors, practice Accuracy Improvement.
   If you had fewer than two errors, practice Speed Improvement.

Word-Combination Practice

Skill Building

Key two 30-s timings on each line concentrating on the speed *or* accuracy goal set in your One-Minute Timings.
Students on individual progress should key each line three times with their speed *or* accuracy goal in mind.

3 Reading good books should develop pleasant tastes for books.

4 Roast turkey is served directly from most types of kitchens.

5 Kings should develop policies suitable to their realm's use.

6 Red dresses should sport tiny yellow scarves or white belts.

· · · ·1· · · ·2· · · ·3· · · ·4· · · ·5· · · ·6· · · ·7· · · ·8· · · ·9· · · ·10· · · ·11· · · ·12

Stroking Practice

1. Turn to the Stroking Practice, page 414.
2. Key the lines selected by your instructor or the letter combinations giving you difficulty in the drills just completed.
3. Students on individual progress should select lines.
4. Key each line twice.

Accuracy Improvement

Key two 30-s timings on each line concentrating on accuracy as your goal.
Students on individual progress should key each line three times with the accuracy goal in mind.

7 Season this stew using sage and onion and serve it on bread.

8 Use pink ink to draw carefully on the card to go to Phillip.

9 Your monthly statements will show all purchases made by you.

10 Our office will contact you about purchasing any new shares.

· · · ·1· · · ·2· · · ·3· · · ·4· · · ·5· · · ·6· · · ·7· · · ·8· · · ·9· · · ·10· · · ·11· · · ·12

Prepare Your Machine

1. Set your margin stops at the extreme left and extreme right.
2. Clear all tab stops.
3. Insert your paper.
4. Set a tab stop at the center.

Steps for Block Centering

1. Select the longest word or line which is called the *key line*.
   Example: Block center the following.

   ```
   All these words are not the same length.
   ```

   The key line is *length*.
2. Tab to the center point.
3. Backspace once for every two characters and spaces in the key line.
4. Set a left margin stop at the point you stopped backspacing in step 3.
5. Key all lines beginning at this left margin.

```
All
these
words
are
not
the
same
length.
```

Production Practice

Production 1

Using block centering key the following example. Use the Backspace Method.
Example:

```
O F F I C E    J O B    T I T L E S
                 TS
                    Records Clerk
                    Receptionist
                    Administrative Clerk
                    Administrative Assistant
                    Information Systems Manager *
                    Information Systems Trainee
                    Systems Analyst
```

*Key line: Information Systems Manager

1. Spread center the heading. (*Note:* Titles or headings are not always spread centered.)
2. Triple space.
3. Select the key line. *Information Systems Manager* and *Information Systems Trainee* have 27 strokes.
4. Backspace to center the key line.
5. Set the left margin at this point.
6. Key all names in the column at this left margin.

Three- or Five-Minute Timing

Assess Your Improvement
Set spacing at 2. Key at least one 3-min *or* 5-min timing. Circle all errors and calculate gross words per minute. Record the timing on your Progress Chart.

	1	CW	3

When meeting and operating a new piece of equipment for — 12 | 12 | 4
the first time, it is a sad fact that many people overlook a — 24 | 24 | 8
very important part of the introduction--to carefully peruse — 36 | 36 | 12
the operating instructions. This operating manual is inclu- — 48 | 48 | 16
ded for a very specific purpose. To obtain the best perfor- — 60 | 60 | 20
mance from the machine over a period of time, certain proce- — 72 | 72 | 24
dures have to be followed with regard to operation and main- — 84 | 84 | 28
tenance. — 86 | 86 | 29

Domestic equipment used only occasionally can sometimes — 12 | 98 | 33
be worked effectively for a long period of time based on the — 24 | 110 | 37
trial-and-error method and looking at the exact instructions — 36 | 122 | 41
only when something goes wrong. This is not the case with a — 48 | 134 | 45
piece of office equipment which is required for more contin- — 60 | 146 | 49
uous use. Besides, many office machines have to be operated — 72 | 158 | 53
by different people in the office and the machine must func- — 84 | 170 | 57
tion in the most efficient way. — 90 | 176 | 59

Whenever possible, potential office workers should give — 12 | 188 | 63
serious thought to enrolling in a basic office machine class — 24 | 200 | 67
to learn how to use effectively the common 10-key calculator — 36 | 212 | 71
and copying machines. The typewriter, of course, requires a — 48 | 224 | 75
more systematic and comprehensive training program and these — 60 | 236 | 79
skills can be transferred to many office machines using this — 72 | 248 | 83
basic keyboard as their main operating component. Manufact- — 84 | 260 | 87
urers try their best to produce machines which are very easy — 96 | 272 | 91
to operate but one cannot better invest his or her time than — 108 | 284 | 95
to read carefully the machine manual provided. — 117 | 293 | 98

• • • • 1 • • • • 2 • • • • 3 • • • • 4 • • • • 5 • • • • 6 • • • • 7 • • • • 8 • • • • 9 • • • • 10 • • • 11 • • • 12   1 min
          1   2   3   4   3 min

SI 1.70
AWL 5.06

Production 2

Block center the following material using the principles of the Backspace Method, horizontal centering, spread centering, and block centering where necessary.

B U S I N E S S   E Q U I P M E N T

TS

Photocopier
Personal computer
Laser printer
Computer terminal
Facsimile machine
Plotter
Printing calculator
Postage machine
Paper shredder
Modem
Dictation equipment

SC

Did you find the key line?

Production 3

Block center the following list. Use the Backspace Method.

appliances
bedding
furniture
notions
toys
televisions

DS

P

The symbol ℧ means reverse position.

Skill Building

60-space line
Spacing: 1 and 2
Key two 30-s timings on
each line *or* repeat each line
three times.

Double-Letter Words

1 spoon flood issues really bottles payroll approved installed

2 looks shell seeing billed planned assumed supports submitted

One-Minute Timings

1. Turn to the One-Minute Timings, page 421.
2. Select the paragraph that you think you can complete in one minute.
3. Key the One-Minute Timing as a drill.
4. If you had two or more errors, practice Accuracy Improvement.
   If you had fewer than two errors, practice Speed Improvement.

Skill Building

Key two 30-s timings on
each line concentrating on
the speed *or* accuracy goal
set in your One-Minute
Timings.
Students on individual
progress should key each
line three times with their
speed or accuracy goal in
mind.

Word-Combination Practice

3 Drab brown neckties should darken old drawers, not meetings.

4 This should delay your rotation plans so they can negotiate.

5 Casual labor reports should delay few workers this semester.

6 With your approval I would like to discuss several problems.

Stroking Practice

1. Turn to the Stroking Practice, page 414.
2. Key the lines selected by your instructor or the letter combinations giving you difficulty in the drills just completed.
3. Students on individual progress should select lines.
4. Key each line twice.

Accuracy Improvement

Key two 30-s timings on
each line concentrating on
accuracy as your goal.
Students on individual
progress should key each
line three times with the
accuracy goal in mind.

7 They are making another kind of business equipment delivery.

8 They would like to discuss the need for additional coverage.

9 Feed Jimmy these tart pills with milk before he goes to bed.

10 Weave a loop of pink nylon for the stage cast to swing with.

• • • • 1 • • • • 2 • • • • 3 • • • • 4 • • • • 5 • • • • 6 • • • • 7 • • • • 8 • • • • 9 • • • • 10 • • • • 11 • • • • 12

18

Vertical Centering

50-space line
Spacing: 1 and 2

Key two 1-min timings on each line *or* repeat each line three times.

Skill Building

Key two 1-min timings on each line *or* repeat each line three times. Key these drills as quickly as you can.

Key two 1-min timings on each line *or* repeat each line three times. Try to increase your speed slightly on the second try.

Key one 1-min timing on each line *or* repeat each line twice.

Timing

Set your line space regulator at 2. Key two 2-min timings. Circle all errors and calculate gross words per minute (GWPM). Record the better timing on your Progress Chart.

SI   1.06
AWL 3.47

One-Hand Words

1 beds poll beef mill cage hilly data lump ease milk
2 best hump care pill card yolk dates min seats noon

Alternate-Hand Words

3 body coals dual fuel held lamb male paid rush than
4 born corn duty girl hens land malt pair Ruth theme
5 both dial firm goal idles lane maps pans sick then
6 buck diem fish gowns jams lend melt pant sign they

Common-Word Sentences

7 We hope that this sail is safe to use on our boat.
8 We have a chance to go to the game more often now.
9 Be sure the ice is thick if you plan to skate now.
10 They plan to put a new zoo beside that small lake.

Postal Codes
Set tab stops 12, 24, and 36 spaces from the left margin.

11 P2A 1W3   K8V 5V5   B3A 3J7   G2B 3N9
12 A2N 2Y4   P6B 4P1   V7J 2G6   B1A 2E5
13 J2G 1Z8   A1B 3T0   G4W 3X4   E1V 1P5
         ↑   ↑   ↑
       Tab   Tab   Tab

Two-Minute Timing

     You do not have to own the best clothes in an office to look your best. Your new clothes should be bought with care so that you can use them to be in style yet not part of a fad. If you choose all slacks and tops to mix and match, you will find an extra way to wear them with no extra cost. Try to have a groomed look when you go to work every day.

1	2
10	5
20	10
30	15
40	20
50	25
60	30
70	35

1 min
2 min

Task III – Finalizing Mr. Dasmund's Trip

Today is November 20

Mr. Dasmund has returned from his trip. You give him the tentative itinerary which lists two alternatives. He chooses the arrangements he prefers. (You or your instructor will make the choice for him.) Write letters requesting reservations for the necessary hotel accommodations, car rentals, airline reservations, and the Whistler Ski Package. In the letters for the hotel reservations, request a "hold for late arrival" and have the bills sent to the Toronto office. Include a cheque for the first night at the Four Seasons Hotel in Vancouver and prepay the two nights at Whistler Mountain.

Today is January 15

Fill in and forward the registration form for the AMS convention in Vancouver for Mr. Dasmund. Students without Workbooks should compose a letter for the registration. Send a letter to the conference chairperson. Enclose a copy of Mr. Dasmund's speech.

Today is February 15

Confirmation for hotel reservations has been received from all hotels except from the one in Regina. Write a letter to the Regina hotel inquiring about the reservation.

Today is March 5

Prepare the final itinerary for Mr. Dasmund including the details of the airline reservations, hotel reservations and other arrangements. Inform the western branch manager of Mr. Dasmund's final plans through a memo. Attach a copy of his itinerary.

Vertical Centering

Vertical centering means that the margins at the top and at the bottom of the keyed material are equal.

Attractively formatted material is centered both horizontally and vertically. This allows for a margin of equal proportion on the left and right side of the copy (horizontal centering) and of equal proportion on the top and bottom (vertical centering).

Calculate the Starting Line

1. Count the total number of lines and blank spaces to be used in keying the material.
   - Remember to count one blank line between double spacing and two blank lines between triple spacing.

```
The        1
number     2
of         3
lines      4
needed     5
to         6
key        7
this       8
is         9
ten.       10
```

2. Subtract the total in step 1 from the total number of lines on a page.
$$66 - 10 = 56$$
   - A full sheet of letter-size paper has 66 lines.
   - A half sheet of letter-size paper has 33 lines when the long edge is inserted first and 51 lines when the short edge is inserted first.
3. Divide your answer in step 2 by two, dropping any fraction.
$$\frac{56}{2} = 28$$
4. The answer in step 3 is the number of blank lines you need to leave at the top of the paper.
5. You should start to key on the next line below your top margin. Therefore, add 1 to your answer in step 4 to calculate the starting line.
$$28 + 1 = 29$$

Prepare Your Machine

1. Insert your paper so that the top edge is aligned with the alignment scale on your typewriter or printer.
2. Space down the number of lines you calculated as the starting line.

If you are using a computer, read your software and printer manuals to determine the defaults for top and bottom margins. This could change your calculation.

For vertical centering, read the line number on your status line and move the cursor to the appropriate line position.

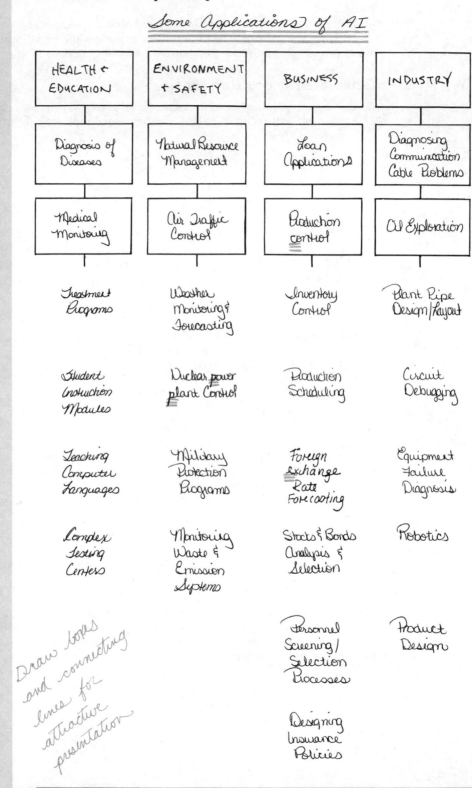

Some Applications of AI

HEALTH + EDUCATION	ENVIRONMENT + SAFETY	BUSINESS	INDUSTRY
Diagnosis of Diseases	Natural Resource Management	Loan Applications	Diagnosing Communication Cable Problems
Medical Monitoring	Air Traffic Control	Production control	Oil Exploration
Treatment Programs	Weather Monitoring & Forecasting	Inventory Control	Plant Pipe Design/Layout
Student Instruction Modules	Nuclear power plant Control	Production Scheduling	Circuit Debugging
Teaching Computer Languages	Military Protection Programs	Foreign exchange Rate Forecasting	Equipment Failure Diagnosis
Complex Testing Centers	Monitoring Waste & Emission Systems	Stocks & Bonds Analysis & Selection	Robotics
		Personnel Screening/ Selection Processes	Product Design
		Designing Insurance Policies	

Draw boxes and connecting lines for attractive presentation

SC

Did you ask your instructor if the word wrap should be *off*?

SC

Did you determine if there is a top/bottom margin default?

Production 1

Center the following paragraph vertically using a half sheet of paper and a 50-space line.

TS↓   WHAT I HAVE LEARNED ABOUT CENTERING

     I have learned a number of things about
centering copy neatly on a page. An attractive
page is very dependent on centering both
vertically and horizontally. Vertical centering
is used in arranging copy so you have even top
and bottom margins. Horizontal centering means
having both the side margins equal. Block
centering and spread centering are variations of
horizontal centering.

Production 2

Center this material both vertically and horizontally on a full sheet of paper. Use the Backspace Method.

INSTRUCTIONS FOR VERTICAL CENTERING

TS↓

Determine the number of lines required

Subtract this number from the
total possible number of lines on the page

Divide the result by two

Align the paper carefully at the top edge and
space down the exact number of lines plus one more

Key the first line of the exercise

Remember to key headings or title in capital letters
and triple space after headings or title

Typewriters and software packages with
automatic centering features simplify these procedures

Task II – Mr. Dasmund's Speech
Overhead Transparency 1

The Quest for Artificial Intelligence

What is intelligence?
What is "Artificial Intelligence"?
Is the concept of AI new?
What are some general applications of AI?

What are some business applications?
What are some shortfalls of AI?
What is the hope for the future of AI?

Overhead Transparency 2

<u>Definitions</u>

<u>Intelligence</u>: "the capacity to acquire and apply knowledge"
(Morris, <u>Heritage Dict</u>., 1973)
"the faculty of making artificial objects,
especially tools to make tools
(Bergson, 1907)

Artificial Intelligence: the ability of a computer to be programmed in such a way as to model the
way a human brain functions in the area
of decision-making and problem-solving
"an approach which rests on the assumption
that thinking can be reduced to a manipulation
(Add others you can find) of symbols representing
facts and relationships
between those facts
(Carpenter, p. 64)
US News & World Report,

Production Review

50-space line
Spacing: 1 and 2
Key two 1-min timings on
each line *or* repeat each line
three times.

Skill Building

Key two 1-min timings on
each line *or* repeat each line
three times.

Analyze Your
Practice Needs
Key two 1-min timings on
each sentence *or* repeat each
sentence three times.

Timing

Set your line space regulator
at 2. Key two 2-min
timings. Circle all errors
and calculate gross words
per minute (GWPM).
Record the better timing on
your Progress Chart.

SI   1.24
AWL 4.07

Alternate-Hand Words

1 if bit dot for lay when dial goal lane eight handy
2 is bow due fox and wish diem gown lend field panel

Common-Word Sentences

3 Ask him if he can bring a silver rock to the camp.
4 He came from afar to see his old friend row again.

· · · · 1 · · · · 2 · · · · 3 · · · · 4 · · · · 5 · · · · 6 · · · · 7 · · · · 8 · · · · 9 · · · 10

Alphabetic Sentences

5 Bring home a litre of fizzy soda water, a litre of
prune juice and a box of black vinyl garbage bags.
6 Vance said that any of the campers who break an ax
handle will quite likely gain just a mark of zero.

· · · · 1 · · · · 2 · · · · 3 · · · · 4 · · · · 5 · · · · 6 · · · · 7 · · · · 8 · · · · 9 · · · 10

Selected Letter Practice

1. Analyze your errors in the Alphabetic Sentences.
2. Choose the letter or letters giving you difficulty or causing errors.
3. Turn to Lesson 14 and select the appropriate Selected Letter Practice.
4. Key each line twice.

Two-Minute Timing

	1	2
They have sent two bills to this office since	10	5
we wrote to them. It seems that they need another	20	10
signed statement before the concern will have very	30	15
much effect. We are surprised at the need to send	40	20
more information since it has been our desire then	50	25
and now that our debts are paid promptly. After a	60	30
further letter, we will have to decide if we would	70	35
do better to deal with a new firm.	77	38

· · · · 1 · · · · 2 · · · · 3 · · · · 4 · · · · 5 · · · · 6 · · · · 7 · · · · 8 · · · · 9 · · · 10   1 min

       1   2   3   4   5   2 min

Farastie, Jean as quoted by Jonathon Green. *Morrow's etc.* (above)

Bergson, Henri as quoted by John Bartlett. *Bartlett's Familiar Quotations*., 14th Ed. Toronto: Little, Brown and Company, 1968

Morris, William, ed. *The Heritage Illustrated Dictionary of the English Language*. New York: American Heritage Publishing Co., Inc., 1985.

Antoninus, Marcus A. as quoted by John Bartlett. *Bartlett's* (copy entry above)

DeLaplace, Pierre Simon as quoted by John Bartlett. . . . (above)

Linden, Eugene. "Putting Knowledge to Work," *Time*, March 28, 1988, pp. 46-50.

Dreyfack, Raymond. "What a Supervisor Should Know About Artificial Intelligence," *Artificial Intelligence*. Chicago: Dartnell Press, 1985.

Simon, Ruth. "The morning after," *Forbes*, October 19, 1987, p. 164+.

Carpenter, Betsy. "Will machines ever think?" *US News & World Report*, October 17, 1988, pp. 64-65.

Shriver, Bruce. "Artificial Neural Systems," *Computer*, March, 1988, pp. 8-9.

Baer, John. "Making Machines That Think," *The Futurist*, January/February, 1988, pp. 8-13.

Shah, K. Tahir. "Electronic Warfare In The World Of Intelligent Machines, "*Electronics & Technology Today*, January, 1988, pp. 20-23

Kandebo, S.W. "Rapid advancements could make Pilot's Associate available for AI," *Aviation Week & Space Technology*, July 4, 1988, pp. 58-59.

Weiss, R. "New technologies emerge in medical AI," *Science News*, August 13, 1988, p. 101.

Hammond, Kristin as quoted in "Chinese food by computer," *USA Today*, June, 1987, pp. 12-13.

Carter, Joe K. "Artificial Intelligence: Current Trends Expanding," *The Office*, January, 1988, p. 82.

Jarvis, Pamela. "Artificial Intelligence: It's Time To Get Ready," *The Office*, August, 1988, pp. 15-16.

Production 1

Horizontally center the following on a half sheet of paper.

MICROCOMPUTER USERS GROUP — *spread center*
MEETS
FIRST MONDAY OF EACH MONTH
AT NOON
IN THE CONFERENCE ROOM
LUNCH IS PROVIDED — *spread center*

} DS

Production 2

Horizontally and vertically center the following on a full sheet of paper.

Time is out running

for our special

Microcomputer purchase price

Avialable Exclusively

to

Employees of

Silver Hill minging Corporation

Production 3

Vertically and horizontally center the following on a half sheet of paper.

You are invited to attend
An Exhibit of Handicrafts
at the Public Library
On Saturday, October 28
During Regular Hours

} DS

Production 4

Block and vertically center the following on a full sheet of paper.

THEATRE PRODUCTION STAFF / Director / Assistant Director / Lighting Director / Assistant Lighting Director / Sound Director / Property Director / Makeup Director / Ticket Manager / Advertising Director / House Manager / Ushers / Technical Crew

P

The symbol ∩ means transpose the position of the letters or words.

P

The symbol / means the end of a line.

Task II – Mr. Dasmund's Speech

nurophysiologists, mathematicians, physicists, psychologists,
computer scientists, and engineers are studying and formulating
theories about how computations actually occurr in nature.
(Shriver, p. 9)

Parallel-processing computers are a further recent development
which we can expect to see somehow coupled in some way with neural
networking. This new type of computer, such as Thinking Machine
Corporation's "Connection Machine" "permits 65,536 independent
processors to operate simultaneously [and these] may solve the
computational paradox that hinders conventional computers"
(Baer, p. 11).

Whether artificial intelligence is a true fact or whether it will
remain an elusive part of man's quest for knowledge remains to be
seen. Bleecker in The Futurist contends the following:

When it has been fully developed, the Bio-Logic Age will give way
to an age of Synthetic Man--where man and machines seem like one,
when prosthetic devices are harvested from cloned cells and when
implanted biochips give infants instant access to thousand of
years of cultural history and scientific fact." (Bleecker,
p. 60)

Another quote from Time also puts the quest for artifical
intelligence into perspective for today:

Like their Greek counterparts, AI scientists can build crude
models and they ahve a rough idea of the principles and
properties involved in achieving their goal. But it may be
centuries, if ever, before all those elements are sufficiently
understood to enable mere mortals to fulfill the dream of AI:
to created electronic replicas of of themselves. (Linden, p. 46)

BIBLIOGRAPHY entries

Beer, Stafford as quoted by Jonathon Green. Morrow's International
        Dictionary of Contemporary Quotations. New York: William
        Morrow and Co., Inc., 1982.

Bleecker, Samuel E. "The Bio-Logic Age...," The Futurist, May/June,
        1988, p. 60.

Magary, James as quoted by Jonathon Green. Morrow's etc (above)

Hoffman, Paul. "Your mindless brain," Discover, September, 1987,
        pp. 84-85.

Coulson, Robert W et al. "Artificial Intelligence and Natural Resource
        Management," Science, July 17, 1987, pp. 262-267

McLuhan, Marshall in Counterblast as quoted by M.R. Rosenburg
        Quotations for the New Age. Secaucus, N.J: The Citadel
        Press, 1978.

Assess Your Progress

Common-Word Sentences

1 I will see that you go along with him to the fair.

2 Is it time for us to go to the tea along with you?

3 Will she try to find her old blue and green books?

4 We wish that the hard rain would stop coming down.

• • • • 1 • • • • 2 • • • • 3 • • • • 4 • • • • 5 • • • • 6 • • • • 7 • • • • 8 • • • • 9 • • • • 10

Two-Minute Timing

Assess Your Speed

Set your line space regulator at 2. Key two 2-min timings. Circle all errors and calculate gross words per minute (GWPM). Record the better timing on your Progress Chart.

SI   1.14
AWL 3.70

Did you achieve the unit objective of 20 words per minute with four errors or less?

	1	2
We would like to advise you that the new mill rate | 10 | 5 |
for your small town will need to be struck at once | 20 | 10 |
to be sure that we have enough funds. Your school | 30 | 15 |
has needs which cannot be met by the present taxes | 40 | 20 |
which are being paid. If you have a question, see | 50 | 25 |
one of our clerks at the office on any week day at | 60 | 30 |
a time that you can arrange. | 65 | 33 |

• • • • 1 • • • • 2 • • • • 3 • • • • 4 • • • • 5 • • • • 6 • • • • 7 • • • • 8 • • • • 9 • • • • 10   1 min

    1   2   3   4   5   2 min

Production 1

Assess Your Production Progress

Can you key Production 1 in 10 min?

Horizontally and vertically center the following on a full sheet of paper. Use the Backspace Method.

TS
I N V I T A T I O N
The Division of Business and Commerce
of
HOLLAND COLLEGE
invites you to attend
their
Graduation Ceremonies
To be held
May 8
16:00
in the
College Gymnasium
R S V P

DS

Task II – Mr. Dasmund's Speech

decision-making process can be reduced to a set of rules that an automaton can follow . . . No machine can yettrecognize a face, distinguish a dog from a cat, or name instantaneously a four-letter flower that rhymes with hose.(Hoffman, p. 84)

James Magary put it another way, "Computers can figure out all kinds of problems, except the things in the world that just don't add up." (Magary as quoted by Green, p. 224)

What is the hope for the future of AI?

Knowlegde in modern society is still increasing at incremental rates. It has been said that man's knowledge has increased more in the last ten years than it has since the beginning records of man. Tremendous inroads into data storage and retrieval have been accomplished since the invention of the modern computer and the improvements and updates in the computer world have been so frequent that one British scientist was led to write, "If it works, it's out of date"(Beer, p. 222).

The real question facing the future of artifical intelligense is: "Can expert systems be beefed up to duplicate human problem-solving abilities, or will they remain simply business tools?" (Carpenter, p. 65) Some researchers maintain that AI will eventually produce machines which can react like the human brain. Others believe that the early predictions for AI were too well rooted in fantasy. However, their critics of the latter group remind their colleagues that today's fact is often based upon yesterday's fantasy. One hope for the future of AI lies in research around neural networking.

Neural networking is a form of software program which aids the program to store the results of problem-solving back into the database, thus aiding the program to benefit from previous "learning" when it solves a similar or related problem. In this way, it is similare to the human brain patterns which result when neuron paths are repeated between synapses. It can be noted that "synaptic transmission in the brain occurs at a snail's pace compared with the speed of electrons in a computer circuit" (Baer, p. 11). Recently, researchers have been concentrating upon using artificial neural networks to perform speech and handwritten character recognition, a task previously only believed possible for the "natural" brain. Bruce Shriver in Computer discusses this new thrust in the world of AI:

Both the literature and the number of professional society meetings focusing on artifical neural systems are growing at an amazing rate. A number of technical disciplines are involved in the wide variety of indipendent industrial, government, and university-based activities and studies. Neurobiologists,

Production 2

Horizontally and vertically center the following double spaced on a full sheet of paper. Use the Backspace Method.

Can you key Production 2 in 10 min?

Reply — *Spread center*

I shall attend the

Graduation Ceremonies

of

The Division of Business and Commerce

Holland College

to be held

May 8

in the

College Gymnasium

Production 3

Horizontally and vertically center the following on a half sheet of paper. Double space. Leave five spaces between columns. Use the Backspace Method.

Can you key Production 3 in 15 min?

British Columbia	B.C.	BC
Alberta	Alta.	AB
Manitoba	Man.	MB
Saskatchewan	Sak → Sask.	SK
Ontario	Ont.	ON
Quebec	P.Q.	PQ
New Brunswick	N.B.	NB
Nova Scotia	N.S.	NS
Prince Edward Island	P.E.I.	PE
Newfoundland	NF ⇄ Nfld.	
Yukon Territory	Yuk.	YT
Northwest Territories	NT ⇄ N.W.T.	
Labrador	Lab.	LB

Task II – Mr. Dasmund's Speech

What are some business applications?

Expert systems have now been developed to the point that some ambiguity and questions of judgment can be dealt with at much higher levels than conventional data processing. "After years of false starts and overblown promises, the new systems, called expert or knowledge-processing systems, have exploded onto the commercial scene." Examples include approval systems for unusual credit requests of clients and Ford Motor Corporation's nationwide computer system to duplicate their expert diagnosis of engine problems (Linden, p. 46).

A few of the other countless applications now available help management to streamline production scheduling, maintain adequate inventory control, seek funding for oil exploration, design and market new products, and process insurance applications. Personnel management programs assist in the desikgn of in-house training for staff. As Linden, in _Time_ points out, "growing numbers of . . . companies are no longer arguing about whether second-wave technology is worth adopting; stead, they are concerned about how best to use it. They are finding all sorts of ingenious applications (Linden, p. 46). Even a restaurant program called CHEF is is giving an entrepreneur the edge in the Chinese food market (Hammond, pp. 12-13).

One developent of AI which has been a boon to the business office has been the development of less expensive software for conventional office computers. Developers of systems can now apply AI principles to office problems using the machines at hand. AI programming languages are still important and will remain so but "many AI-based system development tools are built using conventional programming languages such as C, Pascal, and PL1." (Carter, p. 82) The resulting AI systems will take more of the clerical drudgery out of daily office takss.

What are some of the shortfalls of AI?

As Betsy Carpenter stated in _U.S. News & World Report_, "despite the acceptance of expert sytems as advisers on specialized tasks, no system makes important decisions autonomously or possesses even a modicum of common sense" (Carpenter, p. 65). Many of the expert systems are extremely good at doing what they were developed to do and that could be in choosing the right bonds for you or wherebest to market your product. Terry Winograd, a professor of computer science at Stanford, points out that reducing to rules the logic in a mulitplication question can be quite obvious but "it's too big a jump to say that [rules govern] everything we call intelligence" (Winograd as quoted by Carpenter, p. 65) Paul Hoffman states it well when he wrote:

Thirty years of work in artificial intelligence has demystified certain areas of human expertise by showing that the

Unit II

Objectives

1 The student will develop speed and accuracy on alphabetic and numeric copy.

2 The student will learn the use of symbol keys.

3 The student will learn to format open and ruled tables.

4 The student will work toward developing a minimum speed of 25 words per minute with four or fewer errors on a two-minute timing.

Task II – Mr. Dasmund's Speech

Throughout the 1970's, AI became the coveted area of computer
research. Many usable expirt systems were developed in industry but
the effect on the modern office has only begun to take shape.
However, the predictions of Minsky are still off somewhere in the
elusive future. "Many researchers who expected a machine with the
smarts of a humane to show up by the 1980's or '90s now say such a
computer will take a century or longer to develop. A significant
number believe it will never come about" (Carpenter, p. 64)

What are some general applications of AI?
        Today you can name almost any field of study or a profession and
find some king of application where "smart" computer programs have
been written to assist in the decision-making process. I will mention
only a few examples:
        Natural resource management. The use of AI led to expert systems
with procedures for, among other things, (1) integrated systems
linking natural resource models to management models, (2) intelligent
geographic information systems allowing interpretation of landscape
comparisons, and (3) modeling of animal behavior with various
environmental factors (Coulson et al., p. 262).

        Diagnosing communication cable problems. AT & T Bell
Laboratories produced an expert system which would identify chronic
cable problems at phenomenal speeeds. It helped to take the guesswork
out of the problem-solving process. This program and its updates has
been very cost effective and has been marketed to other communication
companies (Simon, p. 168).

        Diagnosis of diseases. Tremendous inroads have been made in
producing expert systems for the medical field. An example is the
system developed by Control Data Corp. which suggests possible
diagnoses and treatments following a thorough analysis of the database
built up from patient reports, hospital nursing station data, lab
reports, and pharmaceutical histories (Dreyfack, p. 16) If you have a
particular interest in these developments, you may wish to refer to
Weiss' excellent article in Science News (Weiss, p. 101).

        Assisting jet pilots in times of peace and war. Various programs
have been written to assist in the whole area of safety in air traffic
control. A program called PILOT'S ASSOCIATE even simulates the
demands of aircraft warfare and gives clear direction for an advanced
tactical fighter (Kandebo, pp. 58 - 59).   Shah, a Canadian freelance
writer, states that the

        "star wars of tomorrow will be fought by electronics and
        computers;controlling, decoding, jamming, and avoiding those
        little chunks of electromagnetic waves moving back and forth at
        the speed of light. It will be the battle of intelligent
        computers and the electromagnetic spectrum.(Shah, p. 20)

Open Tables

50-space line
Spacing: 1 and 2
Key two 1-min timings on each line *or* repeat each line three times.
Key at your controlled rate for accuracy.

Common-Word Sentences

1 The two girls were late for class nearly all days.
2 Did you get the pail of cold water from the creek?
3 The green and gold chair is put on sale right now.

Skill Building

Key two 1-min timings on each line *or* repeat each line three times. Key these drills as quickly as you can.

One-Hand Words

4 are him car oil egg pin wet hill bags loon dearest
5 car hip bat ion far lip web hump bars look greased
6 cat hop bag ink few oil wee poll cafe yolk acreage
· · · · 1 · · · · 2 · · · · 3 · · · · 4 · · · · 5 · · · · 6 · · · · 7 · · · · 8 · · · · 9 · · · · 10

Key each underlined word three times. Key each line once concentrating on the underlined words.

Concentrate on Correct Spelling

7 They are <u>inquiring</u> about the planned <u>installation</u>.
8 <u>Officially</u>, this <u>occasion</u> warrants a civic social.

Timing

Set spacing at 2. Key two 2-min timings. Circle all errors and calculate gross words per minute. Record the better timing on your Progress Chart.

CW means cumulative word count.

SI   1.24
AWL 3.94

Two-Minute Timing

	1	CW 2
In spite of the trees that have been cut over	10	10	5
the years, this country still has great regions of	20	20	10
forest land. However, we must be certain that new	30	30	15
trees are planted each year.	36	36	18
We rely on our trees for many of the items we	10	46	23
use each day. Homes, boats, beds, and books are a	20	56	28
few of the items that are supplied by our forests.	30	66	33
We can also enjoy their beauty.	36	72	36

· · · · 1 · · · · 2 · · · · 3 · · · · 4 · · · · 5 · · · · 6 · · · · 7 · · · · 8 · · · · 9 · · · · 10   1 min
    1   2   3   4   5   2 min

Presenting Information

Information can be presented in the form of paragraphs or in the form of a table. Read each of the following carefully and decide which presentation of material is the easiest to follow.

Task II – Mr. Dasmund's Speech

computer to amass huge amounts of data with instant and accurate
recall, ~~that~~ has caught the attention of computer specialists and
experts in various disciplines and industries. Samuel Bleecker in
The Futurist explains the evolution from basic data processing in
this way:

> At a time when the Information Age has reached middle age, its
> offspring, the Bio-Logic Age, is crawling out of the cradle. The
> Bio-Logic Age has arrived mostly unannounced. It is the age of
> the merger of man and machine. In pratical terms, the Bio-Logic
> Age combines the revolutions in biotechnology and computers and
> employs the living organism as its model. The Bio-Logic Age uses
> man as its measure. In a sense, the Bio-Logic Age is an age of
> human dimension. The emphasis is on how man operates, both
> physically and mentally. As a result, one of the driving forces
> behind this Bio-Logic Age is artificial intelligence. It holds
> open the promise that computers will be able to work and reason
> as humans do. (Bleecker, p. 60)

Artificial intelligence (AI), then, is the ability of a computer
to be programmed in such a way as to to model the way a human brain
funtions in the area of decision-making and problem-solving. As
Raymond Dreyfack pointed out, in writing for the Dartnell Corporation,
definitions of AI vary considerably but they usually center around the
word "expert". In fact, the term "expert systems" has come to be
synonymous with AI and they are made up of two basic components: (1)
an accurate and complete knowledge or database amassed from input from
many experts in the feild and (2) an inference engine (program) which
examines situations and problems and responds based upon the learning
from former decision-making and problem-solving tasks (Dreyfack,
pp. 5- 6).

Is the concept of AI new?
"Artificial intelligence has been around since 1956, when it was first
recognized as a discipline at a sumner conference at Dartmouth
College" (Jarvis, p. 15). In 1970, Marvin Minsky, a computer
scientist and one of the pioneers of AI was quoted as saying:

> In from three to eight years, we will have a machine with
> the general intelligence of an average human being . . . a
> machine that will be able to read Shakespeare, grease a car,
> play office politics, tell a joke, have a fight. At that point,
> the machine will begin to educate itself with fantastic speed.
> In a few months, it will be at genius level, and, a few months
> after that, its power will will be incalculable. (Minsky as quoted
> by Carpenter, p. 64)

Table Form

MONTHS OF THE YEAR

DS ↓

and Days in Each Month

TS

Month	Days
January	31
February	28*
March	31
April	30
May	31
June	30
July	31
August	31
September	30
October	31
November	30
December	31
TOTAL	365

SS

DS

*Every 4 years (leap year), February
has one additional day making 29 days
and a total that year of 366 days.

Paragraph Form

Line

MONTHS OF THE YEAR

and Days in Each Month

There are 12 months and 365
days in a year. These are divided
in the following way. January, the
first month, has 31 days. February
follows next with 28 days, except
that once every four years it has
an extra day making 29. When this
happens it is called leap year and
there are a total of 366 days in
the year. March is the third month
and has 31 days and it is followed
by April with 30 days, May with 31
days, and June with 30 days.

The second half of the year
begins with July with 31 days, then
August also with 31 days. The
ninth month is September with 30
days, followed by October with 31
days, November with 30 days, and
December has 31 days. The total
of days for 12 months is 365 days.

Tables

A table is material that is condensed and arranged in columns. There are many types of tables including *open tables* and *ruled tables*.

Parts of a Table

Title
- All capitals.
- Double space to subtitle *or* triple space to column headings.

Subtitle
- Principal words capitalized.
- If no subtitle, triple space between the title and column headings.

Column Headings
- Principal words capitalized.
- If the title, subtitle, or the column headings are more than one line, they are single spaced.

Body
- Can be single spaced, double spaced, or grouped.

Footnote
- Separate from the body by an underscore — 18 spaces (elite — 12 pitch) or 15 spaces (pica — 10 pitch).
- Single space before the underscore line and double space after the underscore line.
- Align with the longest line.

Task II – Mr. Dasmund's Speech

(Rough Draft)

THE QUEST FOR ARTIFICIAL INTELLIGENCE

Given for one instant an intelligence which could
comprehend all the forces by which nature is animated and the
respective positions of the beings which compose it, if
moreover this intelligence were vast enough to submit these
data to analysis, it would embarce in the same formula both
the movements of the largest bodies in the universe and those
of the lightest atom; to it nothing would be uncertain, and
the future as the past would be present to its eyes.
(DeLaplace, p. 479)

That statement was made by Pierre Simon DeLaplace in 1820. Man's
fascination with the capabilities of the mind of the homo sapien
has gone on for thousands of years. Famous philosophers such as
Descartes have each given their own interpretation of the Bible's
"mind, body and soul." Marcus Aurelius Antoninus who lived in
A.D. 121 -180 said, "The controlling intelligence understands
its own nature, and what it does, and whereon it works"
(Antoninus, p. 142). Research on the brain and its functions
will continue into the twenty-first century.

What is Intelligence?
The dictionary defines intelligence as "the capacity to acquire and
apply knowledge" (Morris, 1973). In order to apply that knowledge,
there must be good recall of the details that made up that body of
knowledge. Henri Bergson, in 1907, said that "intelligence . . . is
the faculty of making artificial objects, especially tools to make
tools" (Bergson, p. 849). It is one of the fantastic tools invented
by mankind to which we are going to focus our attention today.

That tool, of course, is the computer. It has become commonplace in
both the worlds of work and home life but its capabilities have barely
been tapped. Teh computer is a tool or a machine which has been
invented as a result of man's intelligence but as the French writer,
Jean Fourastie once said, "the machine leads man to specializing in
the human being" (Fourastie quoted by Morrow, p. 222)

What is "artificial intelligence"?

It is the famous Canadian, Marshal McLuhan, who is credited with the
quote that "people never remember but the computer never forgets"
(McLuhan as quoted by Rosenberg, p. 44). It is in the ability of the

Open Tables without Column Headings

Prepare Your Machine

1. Move your margin stops to the extreme left and right.
2. Clear all tab stops.
3. Move your print indicator or cursor to the horizontal center of the paper.

Steps for Keying Open Tables

1. Decide the number of spaces you wish to leave between columns. For the following example, leave six spaces. Note: It is convenient to choose an even number of spaces between columns.
   Example:

   MONTHS

   TS

January	31
February	28
March	31
April	30
May	31
June	30

   Left Margin | 6 spaces | Tab Stop

2. Select the key word in column one: *February.*
3. Select the key word in column two: *28.*
4. The key line is: February   28

   | 6 spaces |

5. Backspace once for every two characters and spaces in the key words in each column:

   Fe br ua ry 28

6. Backspace once for every two spaces between columns: | 12 34 56 |
   - Note the character or cursor position.
   - An extra letter left over in a column is carried over and counted with the next column.
   - An extra letter left over at the end of the key line is ignored.

   For example, if September 30 is the key line it would be necessary to backspace as follows:

   September _____ 30

   | 6 spaces |

   Se pt em be r3 0 * | 12 34 56 |

   *Ignore odd number or letter at the end of key line.
7. Set a left margin at the point you stopped backspacing in step 6.
8. Space forward with the space bar once for each character and space for the key word in column one.
9. Space forward with the space bar once for each space between column one and column two.
   - Note the character or cursor position.
10. Set a tab stop at the point you stopped spacing forward in step 9. Column two will begin at this point.

    February | 123456 |

    Left
    Margin   Tab
                    Stop

11. You are now ready to key the table.

Task II – Mr. Dasmund's Speech

INTEROFFICE MEMORANDUM

TO: *My Assistant*   FROM: *James Dasmund*

DEPT.:   DEPT.:

SUBJECT: *AMS Speech*   DATE: *November 10, 19--*

Attached is a rough draft of my speech. Please do the following during my absence:

Proofread and edit the rough draft notes.

Compose a conclusion, using resources if they are available or using material in the speech as a summary for the conclusion.

Key the speech in report format with two copies. (The AMS editorial committee and the office file)

Put a copy on large index cards (half sheet of paper) to use during the speech.

Attractively key each transparency on a full sheet of paper.

Summarize the speech and transparency materials to prepare a handout for the conference delegates. Determine how this handout will be copied.

Prepare a one-page news release and send it to the *Vancouver Sun* and *The Globe and Mail*. Be sure to include the pertinent items of the speech and give my title with Dasmund.

J. D.

be

SC

Did you key a check list after reading Mr. Dasmund's memo?

If time permits and if resources are available, your instructor may request that you update the speech to reflect the latest information.

Check List For Mr. Dasmund's Speech

Things to be done:	Date Completed:
Proofread and edit rough draft of speech	_____
Prepare conclusion of speech	_____
Key speech in report format with two copies	_____
Key speech on large index cards	_____
Key the transparency material	_____
The Quest for Artificial Intelligence	_____
Definitions	_____
Some Applications of AI	_____
Prepare a Handout for duplication	_____
Prepare a News Release	_____

Keying the Table

1. Calculate the starting line for vertical centering.
   - Nine lines are needed to key the table in the example. Using a half sheet of paper:
     $33 - 9 = 24$

     $$\frac{24}{2} = 12$$
   - The starting line is line 13. If you are having difficulty with vertical centering refer to Lesson 18.
2. Insert your paper and space down to the starting line if you are using a typewriter. OR Space down to the appropriate line allowing for the top margin default if you are using a computer.
3. Horizontally center and key the title in all capitals.
4. Triple space.

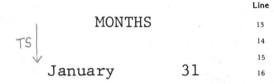

	Line
MONTHS	13
TS	14
	15
January 31	16

5. Set the line spacing for the appropriate spacing of the body of the table.
6. Key the first line in column one.
7. Tab to column two.
8. Key the first line in column two.
9. Return.
10. Repeat until all the lines of the body are keyed.

Production 1

Using the Backspace Method, key the table from the example on page 54. Center the table on a half sheet of paper. Use single spacing.

Production 2

Using the Backspace Method, arrange as an attractive two-column table. Center vertically and horizontally on a half sheet of paper.

Title: DASMUND ENTERPRISES LTD.

Subtitle: Directory of Store Services

Body:

Appliances	Third Floor
Bedding	Lower Floor
Carpets	Fourth floor
Furniture	Second Floor
Housewares	Third Floor
Customer Service	Main Floor
Sporting Goods	Main Floor
Video Recorders	Main Floor
televisions	Second Floor
Computers	Second Floor

SC

Do you know the correct spacing between the parts of the table?

SC

Have you calculated the key line?

SC

Is the table centered both vertically and horizontally?

Task I – Planning Mr. Dasmund's Trip

INTEROFFICE MEMORANDUM

TO: *James Dasmund*   FROM:

DEPT.:   DEPT.:

SUBJECT: *Summary of Hotel Information*   DATE: *19-- 11 12*

<u>*Winnipeg*</u>
1. *Ramada Inn*
   1824 Pembina Highway
   $74-107
2. *Winnipeg Inn*
   2 Lombard Place
   Portage & Main
   $60-80

<u>*Edmonton*</u>
1. *The Westin*
   10135-100 Street
   $130-155
2. *Ramada Renaissance Hotel*
   10155-105 Street
   $62-103

<u>*Regina*</u>
1. *Regina Inn*
   Broad & Victoria
   $87-98
2. *Sheraton Centre*
   1818 Victoria
   $72-89

<u>*Vancouver*</u>
1. *Century Plaza*
   1015 Burrard
   $130-180
2. *Four Seasons Hotel**
   791 W. Georgia at Howe
   $140-195

* Ams conference will be held at The Four Seasons

INTEROFFICE MEMORANDUM

TO: *James Dasmund*   FROM:

DEPT.:   DEPT.:

SUBJECT: *Vancouver Trip*   DATE: *19-- 11 15*

<u>*Whistler Mountain*</u>
1. *Has a 5020 ft. (1530m) vertical rise, 2 Gondolas, 10 double-chairs, 2 T-bars. Lift ticket $33 a day. Lesson $20. Equipment rental is available.*
2. *Accommodations*
   Do you want a condominium or a lodge? Both are available. Approximately $80-190 per day.

<u>*Car Rental*</u>
Medium size is $33.00 per day with unlimited mileage. Cars are available at the airport. Should reserve in advance and specify your arrival so that the car will be ready.

22

Hyphen/Dash/ Open Tables

50-space line
Spacing: 1 and 2

Key two 1-min timings on each line *or* repeat each line three times. Key these drills as quickly as you can.

Skill Building

Use the ; finger. Key each line twice.

Use the ; finger. Key each line twice.

One-Hand Words

1 edge noun face hulk gate pull races mink fast mono
2 eggs only fact pulp gave join rare hill safe jumpy
• • • • 1 • • • • 2 • • • • 3 • • • • 4 • • • • 5 • • • • 6 • • • • 7 • • • • 8 • • • • 9 • • • • 10

Reach to the Hyphen Key

3 ;;; ;p; ;-; ;;; --- ;-; ;-; ;-; ;---; ;---; ;- -;-
4 good-bye eye-opening check-in time-savers trade-in

Reach to the Hyphen or Dash Key

5 Right now - at this very moment - she is swimming.

OR

5 Right then--at the very moment--she went swimming.

Spacing Reminder: Hyphens and Dashes

• No space is left before or after the hyphen in a hyphenated word or number.

   Trade-in   23-28

• There are two ways to key the dash.
  Space hyphen space **or** *No space hyphen hyphen no space*

   now - at   now--at

Common Phrases

6 of the/of it/of them/of their/of his/of its/of our/
7 in the/in it/in them/in their/in her/in its/in our/
8 on it/on them/on our/on his/on their/on the/on its/

Common-Word Sentences

9 Sue went to play nine holes of golf on the course.
10 We had hoped to go to a night ball game with them.
11 The game is played from one end of the open field.
• • • • 1 • • • • 2 • • • • 3 • • • • 4 • • • • 5 • • • • 6 • • • • 7 • • • • 8 • • • • 9 • • • • 10

Key two 1-min timings on each line *or* repeat each line three times. Key these drills as quickly as you can.

Key two 1-min timings on each line *or* repeat each line three times. Key these drills as quickly as you can.

How to use this Timetable
Comment lire cet indicateur

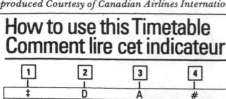

[1]	[2]	[3]	[4]	[5]
‡	D	A	#	†

CALGARY/BANFF, Alta. — [6]
Rsvn (403) 235-1161 Arr/Dep (403) 273-6100
Cargo/Fret (403) 221-2868 — [7]

to/à AMSTERDAM
--3----   14:15   06:45 + 1   CP46 — [10]   0

to/à EDMONTON
12345--   M07:05   07:45   CP*588 — [11]   0

to/à MONTRÉAL
1234567   D11:00   17:01   CP166 — [9]   0   ■ ✗

— [8] — [13] [12]

[1] Frequency/Fréquence.
1 = MO/LU   3 = WE/ME   5 = FR/VE   7 = SU/DI
2 = TU/MA   4 = TH/JE   6 = SA/SA

[2] Departure time (local time)/Heure de départ (heure locale) shown in 24 hour clock/Consultez le cadran de 24 heures.

24 Hr Clock   Cadran 24 heures

(09:00 = 9 a.m.   12:00 = Noon/Midi   22:15 = 10:15 p.m.)

[3] Arrival time (local time)/Heure d'arrivée (heure locale).
Possible time change due to daylight saving or standard time. Check with Canadian Airlines International or your Travel Agent / Il pourrait y avoir des changements avec l'heure normale ou avancée. Vérifiez auprès des Lignes aériennes Canadien International ou votre agent de voyages.

[4] Airline and flight number/Compagnie et no de vol.

[5] Number of stops or enroute connections/Nombre d'escales ou correspondances.

[6] Departure City/Ville de départ.

[7] Arrival City/Ville d'arrivée.

[8] Letter before time indicates airport of departure or arrival for cities served by more than one airport. (Ex. Montreal-Dorval, Mirabel)/Une lettre devant l'heure indique l'aéroport de départ ou d'arrivée pour les villes qui en comptent plus d'un. Ex. Dorval et Mirabel.

[9] Business Class available on all flights shown in red.
La Classe Affaires est offerte sur tous les vols en rouge.

[10] ___Underlined flights operate with B767-300ER aircraft, featuring a 45" seat pitch in Canadian Business Class / Les numéros de vols soulignés sont effectués en B767-300ER, offrant un espacement de 45 po entre les fauteuils en Classe Affaires Canadien.

[11] Specially coded CP flight numbers are operated by our Canadian Partners, Canadi>n Holidays, Wardair or in co-operation with Japan Air Lines or Lufthansa. See Page 3 / Les numéros de vols de CP portant un code spécial sont exploités par les sociétés partenaires de Canadien, Vacances Canadi>n, Wardair, ou en collaboration avec Japan Air Lines ou Lufthansa. Voir page 3.

[12] Meal service / Repas.

[13] ■ Connecting flight departs from a different airport within the same city / Le vol de correspondance quitte un aéroport différent dans la même ville.

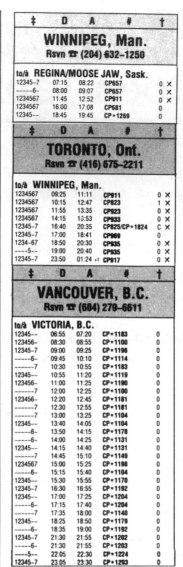

WINNIPEG, Man.
Rsvn ☎ (204) 632-1250

to/à REGINA/MOOSE JAW, Sask.

‡	D	A	#	†
12345-7	07:15	08:22	CP657	0 ✗
-----6-	08:00	09:07	CP657	0 ✗
1234567	11:45	12:52	CP911	0 ✗
1234567	16:10	17:08	CP681	0
12345--	18:45	19:45	CP*1269	0

TORONTO, Ont.
Rsvn ☎ (416) 675-2211

to/à WINNIPEG, Man.

‡	D	A	#	†
1234567	09:25	11:11	CP911	0 ✗
1234567	10:15	12:47	CP823	1 ✗
1234567	11:55	13:35	CP923	0 ✗
1234567	14:15	15:53	CP933	0 ✗
12345-7	16:40	20:35	CP825/CP*1824	C ✗
12345-7	17:00	18:41	CP969	0 -
1234-67	18:50	20:30	CP935	0 ✗
-----5--	19:00	20:40	CP935	0 ✗
12345-7	23:50	01:24 +1	CP917	0 ✗

VANCOUVER, B.C.
Rsvn ☎ (604) 279-6611

to/à VICTORIA, B.C.

‡	D	A	#	†
12345--	06:55	07:20	CP*1183	0
123456-	08:30	08:55	CP*1100	0
12345-7	09:00	09:25	CP*1196	0
-----6-	09:45	10:10	CP*1114	0
-------7	10:30	10:55	CP*1183	0
12345--	10:55	11:20	CP*1119	0
123456-	11:00	11:25	CP*1190	0
-------7	12:00	12:25	CP*1100	0
123456-	12:20	12:45	CP*1181	0
-------7	12:30	12:55	CP*1181	0
12345--	13:40	14:05	CP*1104	0
-----6-	13:50	14:15	CP*1178	0
12345--	14:15	14:40	CP*1131	0
-------7	14:15	14:40	CP*1149	0
1234567	15:00	15:25	CP*1198	0
-----6-	15:15	15:40	CP*1104	0
12345--	15:30	15:55	CP*1170	0
12345-7	16:30	16:55	CP*1192	0
12345--	17:00	17:25	CP*1204	0
-----6-	17:15	17:40	CP*1204	0
-------7	17:35	18:00	CP*1140	0
12345--	18:25	18:50	CP*1179	0
-----6-	18:35	19:00	CP*1192	0
12345-7	21:30	21:55	CP*1202	0
-----6-	21:30	21:55	CP*1203	0
-----5--	22:05	22:30	CP*1224	0
12345-7	23:05	23:30	CP*1203	0

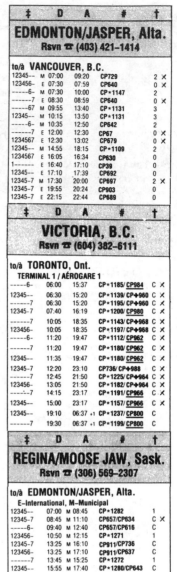

EDMONTON/JASPER, Alta.
Rsvn ☎ (403) 421-1414

to/à VANCOUVER, B.C.

‡	D	A	#	†
12345--	M 07:00	09:20	CP729	2 ✗
123456-	E 07:30	07:59	CP640	0 ✗
-----6-	M 07:30	10:00	CP*1147	0 ✗
-------7	E 08:30	08:59	CP640	0 ✗
-----67	M 09:55	13:40	CP*1131	3
12345--	M 10:15	13:50	CP*1131	3
-----6-	M 10:35	12:50	CP642	2
-------7	E 12:00	12:30	CP67	0 ✗
1234567	E 12:30	13:02	CP679	0 ✗
12345--	M 14:55	18:15	CP*1109	2
1234567	E 16:05	16:34	CP630	0
1------	E 16:40	17:10	CP39	0
12345--	E 17:10	17:39	CP692	0
12345-7	M 17:30	20:00	CP697	2 ✗
12345--	E 19:55	20:24	CP903	0
12345-7	E 22:15	22:44	CP689	0

VICTORIA, B.C.
Rsvn ☎ (604) 382-6111

to/à TORONTO, Ont.
TERMINAL 1 / AÉROGARE 1

‡	D	A	#	†
-----6-	06:00	15:37	CP*1185/CP984	C ✗
12345--	06:30	15:20	CP*1139/CP+960	C ✗
-------7	06:30	15:20	CP*1195/CP+960	C ✗
12345-7	07:40	16:19	CP*1200/CP980	C ✗
-------7	10:05	18:35	CP*1143/CP+968	C ✗
123456-	10:05	18:35	CP*1197/CP+968	C ✗
-----6-	11:20	19:47	CP*1112/CP962	C ✗
-------7	11:20	19:47	CP*1180/CP962	C ✗
12345--	11:35	19:47	CP*1180/CP962	C ✗
12345-7	12:20	23:10	CP736/CP+988	C ✗
-------7	12:45	21:50	CP*1225/CP+964	C ✗
123456-	13:05	21:50	CP*1182/CP+964	C ✗
-------7	14:15	23:17	CP*1191/CP966	C ✗
12345--	15:00	23:17	CP*1157/CP966	C ✗
12345--	19:10	06:37 +1	CP*1237/CP800	C
-------7	19:30	06:37 +1	CP*1199/CP800	C

REGINA/MOOSE JAW, Sask.
Rsvn ☎ (306) 569-2307

to/à EDMONTON/JASPER, Alta.
E-International, M-Municipal

‡	D	A	#	†
12345--	07:00	M 08:45	CP*1282	1
12345-7	08:45	M 11:10	CP657/CP634	C ✗
-----6-	09:40	M 12:40	CP657/CP616	C
123456-	10:50	M 12:15	CP*1271	1
12345--	13:25	M 16:10	CP911/CP736	C
123456-	13:25	M 17:10	CP911/CP637	C
-------7	13:45	M 15:25	CP*1272	1
12345--	15:55	M 17:40	CP*1280/CP643	C
12345--	16:35	M 18:00	CP*1272	1
12345--	17:40	M 20:40	CP681/CP788	C ✗
-----6-	17:40	M 21:20	CP681/CP*1115	C ✗

Set spacing at 2. Key two 2-min timings. Circle all errors and calculate gross words per minute. Record the better timing on your Progress Chart.

SI 1.13
AWL 4.13

Production Practice

P

The symbol ③ means indent runover line three spaces.

Two-Minute Timing

        1   CW   2

The trees at the back of the house were alive 10 | 10 | 5
with the sounds of spring. Some birds had come to 20 | 20 | 10
start the nests that would soon hold large numbers 30 | 30 | 15
of small eggs. 33 | 33 | 17

These same trees were covered with bright new 10 | 43 | 22
leaves that were shiny and green. The flower buds 20 | 53 | 27
were fat, ready to burst forth at any moment. The 30 | 63 | 32
yard would then be full of sweet perfume. 38 | 71 | 36

• • • • 1 • • • • 2 • • • • 3 • • • • 4 • • • • 5 • • • • 6 • • • • 7 • • • • 8 • • • • 9 • • • • 10   1 min
       1   2   3   4   5   2 min

Production 1

Key this table, centered on a half sheet of paper. Runover lines are indented three spaces.

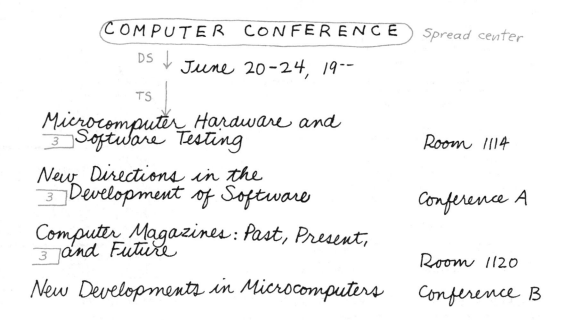

AIR CANADA AS GENERAL SALES AGENT IN CANADA
AIR CANADA AGENT GÉNÉRAL DE VENTE AU CANADA
AIR CANADA ALS ALLGEMEINVERTRETER IN KANADA

HOW TO USE THIS TIMETABLE

Dep	Arr	Flight	Stop	Via/Cl.	Days	Begin	End
MONTRÉAL Ⓐ			Ⓑ			Ⓒ	**EST/HNE**
Reservations/Schedules/Fares 393-3333			Arrivals/Departures				393-3888
Horaires/Tarifs/Réservations			Arrivées/Départs				393-7777
DÜSSELDORF Ⓓ						Ⓔ	**GMT+1/TU+1**
20.00M	10.45 +	AC866	1	FJY	1	567	
20.00M	10.45 +	AC◆866	1	FJY	234		
16.00D	10.45 +	AC419-AC866	3	TOR	5	30.01	30.01
17.30D	10.45 +	AC629-AC856	2	TOR	234		
19.40M	13.35 +	AC870-AF438	1	PAR	1		27.10
Ⓕ Ⓖ	Ⓗ Ⓘ	Ⓙ Ⓚ		Ⓛ Ⓜ	Ⓝ	Ⓞ	Ⓟ

Ⓐ Departure city

Ⓑ Local phone number if only one number applies for all travel information

Ⓒ Time zone of departure city (see below)

Ⓓ Destination city

Ⓔ Time zone of destination city (see below)

Ⓕ Flight departure time from originating city

Ⓖ Departure airport identity if needed (see below)

Ⓗ Arrival time at destination

Ⓘ Destination airport identity if needed (see below)

Ⓙ + indicates arrival on day following departure
++ indicates arrival on second day after departure

Ⓚ Flight number including carrier identification and any special symbols to distinguish this flight's operation
◆ indicates en route change of aircraft. Refer to itineraries for specifics of each flight
★ indicates flight operated by alliance carrier

Ⓛ Total number of stops including transfers

Ⓜ Transfer points
F J Y indicate classes available for AC and AC★ through flights.
F and/or J may not be available on all days although shown. Refer to itineraries, for specifics of each flight.

Ⓝ Days of operation: 1 = Monday, 7 = Sunday

Ⓞ First date if not for full period of timetable (12.10 Day · Month)

Ⓟ Last date if not for full period of timetable (01.09 Day · Month)

TIME ZONES — WINTER

AST — Atlantic Standard Time GMT-4
CST — Central Standard Time GMT-6
EST — Eastern Standard Time GMT-5
GMT — Greenwich Mean Time

MST — Mountain Standard Time GMT-7
NST — Newfoundland Standard Time GMT-3½
PST — Pacific Standard Time GMT-8
YST — Yukon Standard Time GMT-8

RETURN TO DAYLIGHT TIME — UNITED KINGDOM/EUROPE

Most countries in Europe will return to Daylight Time on March 26, 1990. These changes are not reflected in this timetable.

Dep	Arr	Flight	Stop	Via/Cl.	Days	Begin	End
EDMONTON				Reservations/Schedules/Fares	423-1222		
				Horaires/Tarifs/Réservations			
VANCOUVER							**PST/HNP**
07.45E	08.15	AC221	–	Y	1234567		
09.55E	10.25	AC223	–	Y	1234567		
11.45E	12.15	AC225	–	Y	1234567		
13.45E	14.15	AC227	–	Y	1234567		
16.45E	17.15	AC231	–	Y	1234567		
19.30E	20.00	AC233	–	Y	1234567		
REGINA/MOOSE JAW				Reservations/Schedules/Fares	525-4711		
				Horaires/Tarifs/Réservations	359-7575		
EDMONTON							**MST/HNR**
09.05	09.24E	AC223	–	Y	1234567		
08.45	12.20K	AC297-AC★1608	1	CAL	12345		
08.45	12.30K	AC297-AC★1621	1	CAL	6		
17.00	19.20K	AC217-AC★1650	1	CAL	123 5		
17.00	19.50K	AC217-AC★1650	1	CAL	4 7		
TORONTO				Reservations/Schedules/Fares	925-2311		
				Horaires/Tarifs/Réservations	925-2861		
WINNIPEG							**CST/HNC**
09.00	10.41	AC189	–	JY	1234567		09.03
09.00	10.41	AC189	–	JY	1234567	12.03	
12.10	13.47	AC171	–	JY	1234567		
14.05	15.36	AC191	–	JY	1234567		
17.05	18.41	AC195	–	JY	1234567		
19.00	20.42	AC175	–	JY	1234567		
21.05	22.42	AC197	–	JY	12345		
21.45	23.22	AC199	–	JY	7		
VANCOUVER				Reservations/Schedules/Fares	688-5515		
				Horaires/Tarifs/Réservations			
VICTORIA							**PST/HNP**
07.10	07.35	AC★1501	–	Y	123456		
08.10	08.35	AC★1505	–	Y	1234567		
09.00	09.25	AC★1507	–	Y	12345 7		
10.25	10.50	AC★1509	–	Y	1234567		
11.10	11.40	AC223	–	Y	1234567		
11.45	12.10	AC★1511	–	Y	1234567		
13.50	14.15	AC★1515	–	Y	1234567		
15.15	15.40	AC★1519	–	Y	1234567		
16.15	16.40	AC★1521	–	Y	1234567		
17.25	17.50	AC★1523	–	Y	1234567		
18.15	18.40	AC★1525	–	Y	1234567		
19.45	20.10	AC★1527	–	Y	12345 7		
20.45	21.10	AC★1529	–	Y	1234567		
21.35	22.00	AC★1531	–	Y	1234567		
22.45	23.10	AC★1533	–	Y	12345 7		
VICTORIA				☎ 382-9242			
TORONTO							**EST/HNE**
07.05	15.18	AC★1504-AC136	1	VAN	1234567		
07.55	16.18	AC★1506-AC142	1	VAN	1234567		
09.00	17.14	AC★1508-AC116	1	VAN	1234567		
11.05	19.27	AC★1512-AC148	1	VAN	1234567		
14.45	22.58	AC★1516-AC152	1	VAN	12345 7		
19.00	06.11 +	AC★1526-AC156	1	VAN	6		
21.30	06.11 +	AC★1530-AC156	1	VAN	12345 7		
WINNIPEG				Reservations/Schedules/Fares	943-9361		
				Horaires/Tarifs/Réservations			
REGINA/MOOSE JAW							**CST/HNC**
07.30	08.40	AC223	–	Y	1234567		
16.20	17.25	AC191	–	JY	12345 7		

"CANADA'S OFFICIAL LANGUAGES"

The choice is yours . . .
The pleasure to serve you is ours.

Reproduced Courtesy of Air Canada

Production 2

When there are more than two columns, you should remember to do the following:

- Continue to backspace once for every two characters and spaces for the key item in column three (and subsequent columns) and the spaces between all columns.
- Continue to space forward once for each character and space for the key item in column two and the spaces between column two and three to set the tab stop for column three. This should be repeated to set tab stops for all subsequent columns.

Arrange as an attractive three-column table. Center on a half sheet of paper.

CONFERENCE BOOKINGS

TS↓

Monday	Association of Canadian Bankers	Room 1320
Tuesday	Canadian National Railway	Palliser
Wednesday	Occupational Health Nurses	Niagara
Thursday	Information Processing Managers	Wellington
Friday	Hospitality Trainers	Room 209
Saturday	Hospitals Association	Room 704
Sunday	Canadian Tour Operators	Montreal

SC

Check the date of the memos to determine the sequence.

 From the desk of James Dasmund

I have decided this trip will be both business and pleasure. Please find out about a two-day ski package at Whistler Mountain, March 16 & 17. Write: Whistler Area Information Center, Whistler Mtn., B.C. VON 1B0 Ask about accommodation, food, lift tickets, equipment rentals, etc.

J.D.

19-- 11 07

 From the desk of James Dasmund

Will visit the four Western branch stores on this trip. Prepare a flight itinerary. I need a full day at each store including the Vancouver store. I will not be able to visit any store on Sundays. Arrange flights with no early morning or late evening travelling. After Whistler, I would like to go to Victoria to spend two or three days with my brother.
The maximum time I can be away from Toronto is two weeks. Less would be preferable.

J.D.
19-- 11 08

 From the desk of James Dasmund

Check prices on renting a medium-size car. Want to pick it up at the airport and leave it there.
Need accommodation in each city. Ask the branch manager to suggest a couple of good hotels.
Need to know how convenient to airport and store. Prefer to have pool and exercise room.

J.D.
19-- 11 09

 From the desk of James Dasmund

Have a proposed itinerary for me when I return. If possible, I would like two alternatives.
Thanks. Call me at the hotel if you have any questions concerning this trip.

J.D.
19-- 11 10

Underscore/Open Tables

Alternate-Hand Words

1 burn dish flap hair kept lens mend pays soak town
2 busy disk foam half keys lent name pens sock turn

Common Phrases

3 at it/at our/at their/at his/at her/at them/at the/
4 in any/of it/on that/at it/at them/on the/into the/
5 into that/into the/into their/into a/into your own/

Number Practice

6 His address is 43 - 27 St. and mine is 59 Bay Ave.
7 Call me at 782-3624 or try 782-7623 if I'm not in.
8 Kwan can be reached at 782-3561 or 783-4926 today.
• • • • 1 • • • • 2 • • • • 3 • • • • 4 • • • • 5 • • • • 6 • • • • 7 • • • • 8 • • • • 9 • • • • 10

Reach to the Underscore Key

9 ;;; ;P; ;_; ;;; ___ ;_; ;_; ;; __ ;_; ;_; ;__ ;;;;
10 Remember these dates: May 3, June 15, and July 8.
11 Who Has Seen The Wind? was read by W. O. Mitchell.

Two-Minute Timing

	1	CW	2
If you want to travel by car on your holiday,	10	10	5
it is good to plan your jaunt long before you want	20	20	10
to set out. The time spent on plans will help you	30	30	15
to enjoy the trip more.	35	35	18
Get maps of the regions you plan to visit and	10	45	23
chart out your route. Study tour guides to enable	20	55	28
you to select those things that interest you. Get	30	65	33
any items you will need. Have a good trip.	39	74	37

• • • • 1 • • • • 2 • • • • 3 • • • • 4 • • • • 5 • • • • 6 • • • • 7 • • • • 8 • • • • 9 • • • 10   1 min
        1   2   3   4   5   2 min

ADMINISTRATIVE MANAGEMENT SOCIETY

Vancouver Chapter
505 Burrard Street
Vancouver, British Columbia
V7X 1M3

 From the desk of James Dasmund

Inform Mr. Graham I will accept his invitation but need to know the time constraints for the speech. Ask if they have reprographics facilities at the conference or should I bring copies of my handout? Ask for conference program asap. What are the arrangements for my expenses? Will forward copy of speech as soon as it is prepared.
J.D.
19--11 07

19-- 11 02

Mr. James Dasmund
General Manager
Dasmund Enterprises Ltd.
25 York Mills Road
Toronto, Ontario
M2P 1B5

SPEAKING INVITATION

On March 15, 19--, the Vancouver Chapter of the Administrative
Management Society will host the 50th Annual Conference of our
society. We hope you will join us for this conference.

The theme for this conference is Artificial Intelligence. The
latest equipment and systems will be on display.

Since you were the one primarily involved with the office system
changeover at Dasmund, you have already had opportunities to
speak at numerous business workshops. We would like you, as
theme speaker, to set the overall tone of the conference with one
of your convincing speeches on artificial intelligence.

Your acceptance of this invitation will assure us of a terrific
start for the conference. Please let us hear from you soon.

G. R. Graham, CONFERENCE CHAIRPERSON

eb

Skill Building

Key each underlined word three times. Key each line once concentrating on the underlined words.

Concentrate on Correct Spelling

12 We are <u>liable</u> if we <u>intercede</u> in these <u>proceedings</u>.

13 There is little <u>excuse</u> for <u>misspelling</u> a new word.

Open Tables with Column Headings Shorter than Column

Prepare Your Machine

Calculate and set the left margin and tab stops for the columns in the following example.

<u>Month</u>

DS↓

January
February
March

Column heading: Month
Key word: February

Backspace Method

1. To find the center point of the column, space forward from the beginning of the column once for every two letters and spaces in the key word: Fe br ua ry

2. From this center point of the column backspace once for every two characters and spaces in the column heading: Mo nt h

   *Ignore odd letter.
3. Key the column heading at the point you stopped backspacing in step 2.
   • Capitalize the principal words.
   • Underscore the heading.
4. Tab and repeat steps 1 through 3 for each column heading shorter than the column.
5. You are now ready to key the table.

Practice

Using the Backspace Method, center the column heading *Organization* over the key item *Choral Music Group*.

Alternate Method

Arithmetic Method

1. Count the number of characters in the column heading: *Month* has five characters.
2. Count the number of characters in the key word: *February* has eight characters.
3. Subtract the number of characters in the heading from the number of characters in the key word: $8 - 5 = 3$.
4. Divide your answer in step 3 by two, dropping any decimal: $\frac{3}{2} = 1.5$
   • Dropping the decimal, the answer is 1.
5. Space forward from the beginning of the column the number of characters calculated in step 4.
6. Key the column heading.
   • Capitalize the principal words.
   • Underscore the heading.
7. Tab and repeat steps 1 through 6 for each column heading shorter than the column.
8. You are now ready to key the table.

Practice

Using the Arithmetic Method center the column heading *Organization* over the key item *Choral Music Group*.

Dasmund Project

Skill Building

Your instructor will decide when you will key the three Skill Building Lessons in this Unit.

Students on individual progress will decide for themselves when to key the three Skill Building Lessons.

Overview

Welcome to Dasmund Enterprises! You are an assistant to Mr. James Dasmund, General Manager of Dasmund's Head Office in Toronto. Mr. Dasmund has requested that you give priority to three tasks. Before starting these tasks, carefully review the total project (Task I, pages 378 to 382; Task II, pages 383 to 392; and Task III, page 393) so that you will understand the purpose of Mr. Dasmund's request.

The instructions will not always be explicit and you will have to use your judgment. Learn to use your common sense. For each task, determine the order in which the work should be completed, considering the time and the importance of the request.

It is very helpful to key a check list for yourself listing the work to be done. As each item is completed, write the completion date on the check list. This will be useful for future reference.

Plan and organize your time to complete this project in 15 to 19 (or approximately 15 h) class periods. Your Workbook provides you with the necessary forms and letterhead to complete the project.

Good Luck!

Task I - Planning Mr. Dasmund's Trip

Today is November 10
Mr. Dasmund has been invited to be the "theme" speaker at the AMS Annual Conference in Vancouver in march. The invitation has just arrived and Mr. Dasmund has to be out-of-town for the next ten days. He gives you the following notes, pages 378-379 before he leaves.
Check List for Planning Mr. Dasmund's Trip

Things to be done:	Date Completed:
Letter to AMS	_____
Letter to Whistler Mountain	_____
Memos to Branch Managers – request hotel information	_____
Phone car rental agencies	_____
Prepare flight schedules	_____
Prepare tentative itinerary	_____

SC

Did you key a check list after reading the memos?

Preferred Method

The preferred method is the Backspace Method as it increases your production speed.

Keying the Table

1. Calculate the starting line for vertical centering. If you are having difficulty with vertical centering, refer back to Lesson 18.
2. Insert your paper. Space down to the starting line and horizontally center and key the title.
3. Triple space.
4. Calculate and key the column headings.
   - Capitalize the principal words.
   - Underscore each column heading.
5. Double space.
6. Set the line spacing for the appropriate spacing of the body of the table.
7. Key the body of the table.

Production Practice

Production 1

Using the Backspace Method, key the following table, horizontally and vertically centered and double spaced on a full sheet of paper.

SC

Have you calculated the key line?

Officers of the Company

Title	Incumbent
Chairman of the Board	Ralph Bourget
President	Peter Smith
General Manager	Lorraine Chow
Vice President - Sales	Ewald Brennan
Vice President - Finance	Judy Denver
Vice President - Purchasing	Jack O'Neil
Secretary	Harriett Saretsky
Human Resources Manager	Marvin Lynch

Production 2

Using the Backspace Method, arrange as an attractive two-column table. Center and double space the body on a half sheet of paper.

Common Computer Terms

A	B
CPU	Central Processing Unit
RAM	Random Access Memory
DOS	Disk Operating System
I/O	Input/Output

SC

Is the table centered both vertically and horizontally?

Unit VIII

Objectives

1 The student will apply previously learned knowledge and skill related to tabulations, letters, and reports.

2 The student will develop decision-making skills by working through three office-related tasks.

3 The student will learn to assess the importance of each activity in each task.

4 The student will learn to determine the sequence of activities in each task and the specific action to be taken.

5 The student will learn to complete the keyboarding activities in mailable form.

6 The student will learn to organize and present the non-keyboarding activities in a professional way.

7 The student will work toward developing a minimum speed of 55 words per minute with three or fewer errors on a three-minute timing; *or* 50 words per minute with four or fewer errors on a five-minute timing.

24

50-space line
Spacings: 1 and 2
Key two 1-min timings on each line *or* repeat each line three times.

Skill Building

Key two 1-min timings on each line *or* repeat each line three times. Key these drills as quickly as you can.

Sp

neighbor or *neighbour*

Key two 30-s timings on each line *or* repeat each line twice. Key these drills as quickly as you can.

Key two 1-min timings on each line *or* repeat each line three times.

Key each underlined word three times. Key each line once concentrating on the underlined words.

Timing

Set spacing at 2. Key two 2-min timings. Circle all errors and calculate gross words per minute. Record the better timing on your Progress Chart.

SI   1.20
AWL 3.91

Open Tables

One-Hand Words

1 ever pink fade pool gets link rate oily seat holly
2 test hook feeds upon gear hoop read polo vest kink

Alternate-Hand Sentences

3 The six men work with maps but they risk a burial.
4 The lake fish make furor and fight by a city dock.
5 The neighbor is busy with both signs and pen dyes.

Common-Word Sentences

6 Have you read the books about the old ship wrecks?
7 The water in the small pool has not warmed up yet.
8 It should be stated that there are few short cuts.

Number Practice

9 These speed signs on Highway 413 now read 80 km/h.
10 The 17 girls and 22 boys are here at 34 Vue Drive.

• • • • 1 • • • • 2 • • • • 3 • • • • 4 • • • • 5 • • • • 6 • • • • 7 • • • • 8 • • • • 9 • • • • 10

Concentrate on Correct Spelling

11 My secretary requests a raise in salary this year.
12 The principal gave precedence to those with texts.

Two-Minute Timing

		1 CW 2
The use of credit cards is a topic that might	10	10 | 5
be taught in every school. The best place to hear	20	20 | 10
about the pitfalls of credit cards would be in the	30	30 | 15
high school where most young people would hear it.	40	40 | 20
Unless a young person is forced to look right	10	50 | 25
at the problem, he or she may never think of debts	20	60 | 30
that can collect in no time. A budget can be easy	30	70 | 35
to set up but it takes practice to make it work.	40	80 | 40

• • • • 1 • • • • 2 • • • • 3 • • • • 4 • • • • 5 • • • • 6 • • • • 7 • • • • 8 • • • • 9 • • • • 10   **1 min**
      1   2   3   4   5   **2 min**

Mini Project Three

Are you ready to apply this unit in a decision-making project? We challenge you to apply this unit by reading the memo from the desk of James Dasmund and completing the task he has assigned to you.

From the desk of James Dasmund

Please key the report on Electronic Mail (Lesson 123-124) on large index cards (half sheet of paper) that I can use for my speech on this topic.

Please prepare a short news release for The Globe and Mail. Announce I will be delivering this speech at the Electronic Mail Association Conference March 23, in ballroom C at the Skyline Toronto Airport Hotel at noon. The luncheon is open to the public.

Open Tables with Column Headings Longer than Column

When the column heading is longer than the list of items in the body of the table, the column heading is the key item for that column. The column items are blocked centered under the column heading.

<u>Column Heading</u>

    List
    of
    items.

Key item: Column Heading

Prepare Your Machine

1. Move your margin stops to the extreme left and right.
2. Clear all tab stops.
3. Move your print indicator or cursor to the center point of the paper.
4. Backspace once for every two characters and spaces in the key item in each column and the spaces between columns. *Note:* The key item is the column heading.
5. Note the print indicator or cursor position.

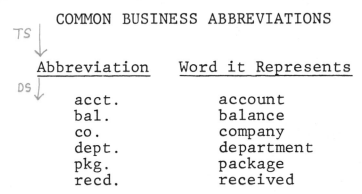

COMMON BUSINESS ABBREVIATIONS

TS

<u>Abbreviation</u>   <u>Word it Represents</u>

DS

        acct.   account
        bal.   balance
        co.   company
        dept.   department
        pkg.   package
        recd.   received

Key line: Abbreviation ⌐spaces⌐ Word it Represents

6. Set the left margin at the point you stopped backspacing in step 4.
7. Space forward with the space bar once for each character and space for the key line in column one and the spaces between columns one and two.
8. Note the print indicator or cursor position.
9. Set a tab stop.

Keying the Table

1. Calculate the starting line for vertical centering. If you have difficulty with vertical centering, refer to Lesson 18.
   - To key the table in the example, 11 lines are needed.
   - Using a full sheet of paper: $66 - 11 = 55$

$$\frac{55}{2} = 27.5$$

   - The starting line is 28.
2. Insert your paper. Space down to the starting line OR to the appropriate line allowing for the top margin default.
3. Key the title.
4. Triple space.

Production 3

Use the Affidavit of Execution form in your Workbook and prepare an Affidavit of Execution for signature today by your instructor. Your instructor watched you sign a legal document.

5. Key column heading one at the left margin.
   - Capitalize the principal words.
   - Underscore the heading.
6. Tab and key column heading two at the tab stop.
7. Double space.

Machine Adjustments for Keying Column Items

Column items are blocked centered under the column heading. This may be done by the Backspace Method or the Arithmetic Method.

Backspace Method

1. To find the center point of the column heading, space forward from the beginning of the column heading once for every two characters and spaces in the column heading:

   Ab br ev ia ti on

2. From this center point of the column heading. Backspace once for every two characters and spaces in the longest item in the column: ac ct .

   *Ignore odd characters.
3. Note the print indicator or cursor position.
4. Reset the left margin at the point you stopped backspacing in step 2.

   <u>Abbreviation</u>

   acct.
   ↑
   New Left Margin

5. To reset the tab stops for each column which has a column heading longer than the column item tab to the column heading. Clear the tab stop. Repeat steps 1 and 2. Note the print indicator or cursor position. Reset the tab stop.

   <u>Word it Represents</u>

   department
   ↑
   New Tab Stop

6. Key the column items line by line in the body.

Alternate Method

Arithmetic Method

1. Count the number of characters and spaces in the column heading: *Abbreviation* has 12 characters.
2. Count the number of characters and spaces in the longest line in the column: *acct.* has five characters.
3. Subtract to calculate the difference between steps 1 and 2: $12 - 5 = 7$
4. Divide your answer in step 3 by two, dropping any decimal. $\frac{7}{2} = 3.5$

   - Dropping the decimal, the answer is 3.
5. From the previously set left margin, space forward the number of characters calculated in step 4. Reset the left margin.
6. Repeat steps 1 through 5 to reset the tab stops for each column which has a column heading longer than the column items.
7. Key the column items line by line.

Preferred Method

The preferred method is the Backspace Method as it increases your production speed.

Production 2

Key the first page of Peter Baker's Will on side-, top-, and bottom-ruled legal paper provided in your Workbook.

THIS IS THE LAST WILL AND TESTAMENT OF me, PETER BAKER, of 8294 Chancellor Boulevard, in the Province of British Columbia.

1. I HEREBY REVOKE all Wills and testamentary dispositions of every nature and kind whatsoever by me heretofore made.

2. IF MY WIFE, EVELYN ISABEL BAKER, survives me for a period of thirty (30) days, I GIVE, DEVISE AND BEQUEATH all my property of every nature and kind and wheresoever situate, including my property over which I may have a general power of appointment, to my said wife for her own use absolutely and I appoint her sole Executrix of this my Will.

3. IN THE EVENT that my wife shall predecease me, or surviving me shall die within a period of thirty (30) days following my decease, I NOMINATE, CONSTITUTE AND APPOINT REGINALD JAMES JOHNSTON, of Vancouver, British Columbia, and KEITH ROBERT ALLAN, of Kamloops, British Columbia, hereinafter referred to as my Trustees, to be the Executors and Trustees of this my Will and I GIVE, DEVISE AND BEQUEATH all my property of every nature and kind and wheresoever situate, including any property over which I may have a general power of appointment, to my said Trustees upon the following trusts, namely:

 (a) To sell, call in and convert into money all my estate not consisting of money at such time or times, in such manner and upon such terms and either for cash or credit or for part cash and part credit as my said Trustees may in their absolute discretion decide upon, with power and discretion to postpone such conversion of such

Production 1

Key this table, centered on a half sheet of paper. Use the Backspace Method.

COMMON BUSINESS ABBREVIATIONS

Abbreviation	Word it Represents
Acct.	account
bal.	balance
co.	company
dept.	Department
pkg.	package
Recd.	received

Production 2

Key the following table on a full sheet of paper. Center attractively and use double spacing. Use the Backspace Method.

Title: Commonly Used Basic Statements

Subtitle: ~~for~~ Action and Control Commands — *Command*

Column Headings Action or Control — Basic Format

Column Items:

Action or Control	Basic Format
Input	Input
Processing	Let
Output	Print
Loop	For/ Next
Decision	If/ Then
Jump	Go To *GOTO*
	Go Sub *GOSUB*
	Return
Halt	Stop
	End

Production 1

Edit and key the second page of the report <u>Desktop Publishing for the Office</u>. The footnote references should be noted within the text, not at the bottom of the page.

needs advanced and varied publishing work. However, other smaller integrated systems are available which allow a secretary to apply publishing capabilities to wp tasks.

↓3
Trends

DS ‖ There has been tremendous movement towards integrated software systems which use the best word processing capabilities together with graphics and color printing. As Megan Jill Paznik points out in

Administrative Management:↓2

SS There is inexorable movement toward bringing column layout, character spacing, and more fonts into word processing. There is also movement to plug the word processor full of aids to improve writing, such as grammar checking, correct word usage (i.e. there or their), and the ability to have your word processor grab information from your database, spreadsheet, and mailing list to write up-to-date letters and reports every week or month without your typing a word.4

Taking Advantage of Opportunities

The smaller businesses have been able to take advantage of the more sophisticated desktop publishing as the cost has come down. Even a small accounting department in a business can use graphics to develop very attractive visual displays for various presentations.5 It is important to survey the vendors in one's areas to assure that there is an excellent match between user need and the product to meet that need.6 A business does not have to take second best with today's list of vendors and products.

Footnote References

4Megan Jill Paznik, "Your Word Processor As Publisher and Secretary," <u>Administrative Management</u>, August, 1987, p. 14.

5Rick Friedman, "Computer Graphics: the Image of Things To Come," <u>The Office</u>, March, 1988, p. 137.

6John Lynn Shanton, "EP Electronic Publishing," <u>Words</u>, May/June, 1988, p. 24.

25

Skill Building

50-space line
Spacing: 1 and 2
Key two 1-min timings on
each line *or* repeat each line
three times.

One-Hand Words

1 no wax him rest noon waste knoll few pin ease lump
2 in wet ink vest kink start plump red lip vast noun
3 my was ply area milk after imply tar pin text pulp

Alternate-Hand Words

4 city dock fork hams laid maid odor risk spans when
5 and dye own them corn hams malt amend flake burial
6 aid eke pan then dial hems maps angle flame burlap

Alternate-Hand Sentences

7 It is a big busy city with docks for 7 fuel firms.
8 Ruth laid a rug down but she did shake half of it.
9 They own 3 bus firms and a quantity of handy keys.

• • • • • 1 • • • • 2 • • • • 3 • • • • 4 • • • • 5 • • • • 6 • • • • 7 • • • • 8 • • • • 9 • • • •10

Skill Building

Key two 30-s timings on
each line *or* key each line
twice.

Key two 30-s timings on
each line *or* key each line
twice.

Number Practice

10 The 17 girls and 22 boys are here at 34 Vue Drive.
11 Melvin's mass is 78 kg and he is 175 cm in height.
12 Pick 6 apples, 25 plums, 7 pears and 20 cucumbers.

Key two 1-min timings on
each line *or* repeat each line
three times.

Common Phrases

13 by the /by a /by that /by their /by them /by our /by any /
14 to it /to the /to that /to them /to her /to his /to this /
15 as the /as it /as they /as that /as their /as any /as to /

• • • • • 1 • • • • 2 • • • • 3 • • • • 4 • • • • 5 • • • • 6 • • • • 7 • • • • 8 • • • • 9 • • • •10

Key two 30-s timings on
each line *or* repeat each line
twice. Key these drills as
quickly as you can.

Alphabetic Sentences

16 The zebra was scared by the starved fox that tried
   to kill by making quick jumps at his scarred neck.

17 The quiet old man brought the heavy blue milk jars
   to Wendy so she could put them on a flat zinc box.

Key two 1-min timings on
each sentence *or* repeat each
sentence three times. Every
alphabetic character is
included in each sentence.

• • • • • 1 • • • • 2 • • • • 3 • • • • 4 • • • • 5 • • • • 6 • • • • 7 • • • • 8 • • • • 9 • • • •10

Assess Your Progress

60-space line
Spacing: 1 and 2
Key two 30-s timings on
each line *or* repeat each line
three times.

**Assess Your
Speed**

Set spacing at 2. Key at
least one 3-min *or* 5-min
timing. Circle all errors and
calculate gross words per
minute. Record the timing
on your Progress Chart.

SI   1.59
AWL 4.71

Did you achieve the unit
objective of 50 words per
minute with 3 errors or less
on a three-minute timing;
or 45 words per minute with
4 errors or less on a five-
minute timing?

One-Hand Words

1 add mum ware noon beat hulk state nylon beaver look retarded
2 crease him estate hill greater hoop attested knoll abstracts

Three- or Five-Minute Timing

1 CW 3

When we accept our first job, it is usually with an as- | 12 | 12 | 4
sumption that we hope to do a good job and to advance up the | 24 | 24 | 8
ladder of success within the firm. Few people have a desire | 36 | 36 | 12
to remain the stock room clerk or the secretary's helper. A | 48 | 48 | 16
desire to advance in status is not merely related to earning | 60 | 60 | 20
more money although this is a definite motivator today. The | 72 | 72 | 24
majority of workers have a deeper need. | 80 | 80 | 27

Most people have a natural and healthy secret desire to | 12 | 92 | 31
achieve that sense of personal accomplishment. It is indeed | 24 | 104 | 35
satisfying to look back upon the roads of success from which | 36 | 116 | 39
you have come, especially when you can share these occasions | 48 | 128 | 43
with fellow workers who have helped along the way. Advance- | 60 | 140 | 47
ment at the expense of other employees will do little to get | 72 | 152 | 51
the job satisfaction that most people desire. | 81 | 161 | 54

An employee who has a good attitude towards the job and | 81 | 173 | 58
fellow workers has discovered the most important ingredients | 24 | 185 | 62
toward receiving recognition and eventual advancement. Most | 36 | 197 | 66
firms have an active and operative promotion system of their | 48 | 209 | 70
own. This means that most workers do not have to seek after | 60 | 221 | 74
recognition. They are constantly rated and recognized for a | 72 | 233 | 78
possible promotion or a raise in pay. | 79 | 240 | 80

• • • • 1 • • • • 2 • • • • 3 • • • • 4 • • • • 5 • • • • 6 • • • 7 • • • 8 • • • • 9 • • • 10 • • • 11 • • • 12 1 min
          1   2   3   4 3 min

Graduated Speed Practice

	15 s	12 s	10 s

Select a sentence that you think you can key in the time indicated by your instructor. If you complete the line within the time limit, try the next line. If not, try again or adjust your goal.

Students on individual progress should key each line twice, as quickly as possible.

Line	Sentence	15 s	12 s	10 s
1	He cut it.	8	10	12
2	Go to fish.	9	11	13
3	It is there.	10	12	14
4	Fix the door.	10	13	16
5	Tie a big rug.	11	14	17
6	I was to visit.	12	15	18
7	The cost is low.	13	16	19
8	Thank him for it.	14	17	20
9	A letter is first.	14	18	22
10	She bid for a dish.	15	19	23
11	They gave us a lamb.	16	20	24
12	He put it in the box.	17	21	25
13	She gave a disk to us.	18	22	26
14	The bus goes very fast.	18	23	28
15	Is that his big old car?	19	24	29
16	We hope to go there soon.	20	25	30
17	They wish to have a theme.	21	26	31
18	Sign and return the cheque.	22	27	32
19	Did you make the mauve gown?	22	28	34
20	That is a very busy old city.	23	29	35
21	The big ship is now at a dock.	24	30	36
22	It is your duty to handle them.	25	31	37
23	He will work for less than that.	26	32	38
24	The invoice due is also enclosed.	26	33	40
25	You should advise me if it is due.	27	34	41
26	He wishes to give us an eighth map.	28	35	42
27	The hens should lay more eggs again.	29	36	43
28	You kept idle while she got us lunch.	30	37	44
29	She hopes to dye her gown bright pink.	30	38	46
30	He can now use both a fork and a knife.	31	39	47
31	The land by the lake was ready for sale.	32	40	48

· · · · 1 · · · · 2 · · · · 3 · · · · 4 · · · · 5 · · · · 6 · · · · 7 · · · · 8

Production 2

Prepare a fully keyed Affidavit of Execution to be sworn today by Jean Moragh McAffer, Barrister and Solicitor, practising in your home town. Ms. McAffer witnessed a Transfer by Lance William Seminiuk, Brian Stenning, and Kathleen Linda Vander Zalm, which was signed at her office today. Use the ruled legal paper provided in your Workbook.

Production 3

Use the Notarial Certificate in your Workbook and prepare a Notarial Certificate for signature by Jean McAffer. Penelope Amy Ng brought Ralph Donald Perrin's Death Certificate No. 31817, dated September 12, 1989, into Ms. McAffer's office this morning to be notarized.

18 We have not <u>interfered</u> because it is <u>indispensable</u>.

19 Use <u>legible</u> printing so the new <u>licence</u> is correct.

Key each underlined word three times. Key each line once concentrating on the underlined words.

Sp

license or licence
Know the preference in your part of Canada and be consistent.

Timing

Set spacing at 2. Key as many 2-min timings as time permits. Circle all errors and calculate gross words per minute. Record the best timing on your Progress Chart.

SI   1.22
AWL 4.05

Two-Minute Timing

		1	CW	2
Credit buying has become a problem in all our		10	10	5
walks of life. This is the scheme whereby someone		20	20	10
can buy now and pay later. If used properly, this		30	30	15
form of buying can be of great help.		37	37	19
Some problems come up when people do not mind		10	47	24
an account to see if the next pay cheque will give		20	57	29
the resources needed to meet the bill. If one has		30	67	34
to use credit beyond that, it is better to wait.		40	77	39

• • • 1 • • • 2 • • • 3 • • • 4 • • • 5 • • • 6 • • • 7 • • • 8 • • • 9 • • • 10 **1 min**
       1   2   3   4   5 **2 min**

Production Review

60-space line
Spacing: 1 and 2
Key two 30-s timings on
each line *or* repeat each line
three times.

Production Practice

Alternate-Hand Words

1 big oak turn burn land down dual duty shake blend shale buck

2 bit own urns busy lane fish flap foam borne shape burns busy

Production 1

Edit and key the first page of the report Desktop Publishing for the Office.
Use the formal footnote style giving the footnote references at the bottom of the page.

DESKTOP PUBLISHING FOR THE OFFICE

SS
5

Desktop publishing is the process of using computer systems to enter, edit, lay out, store, and print
documents containing both text and graphics. All parts 5
of the document preparation process, from text and
graphics entry to the final production of a camera-
ready original, are included. (Dennis et al., p. 26)

The use of the computers in publishing has been firmly estab-
lished for many years. However, the expenses involved in hiring a
typographer, a compositor, and a layout artist were much beyond
the capabilities of many small businesses. In recent years, these
can now be accomplished by one user and a computer terminal.

↓3

Range and Popularity of Products

↓2

The Toronto-based Electronic and Desktop Publishing Association
reported that "94 per cent of its members expect to purchase
equipment in the next 12 months" (Kelly, p. 31) and most of
them were users outside the graphic arts industry. The new
products "feature what-you-see-is-what-you-get (WYSIWYG) screens
with fully made-up pages and the abillity to edit on the screen"
(Wohl, p. 33). Complex systems are available for the office that

¹Alan R. Dennis et al., "Desktop Publishing: What's Right For You?," CMA Magazine, November, 1988, p. 26.

²Tom Kelly, "Everyone's a Publisher," Office Equipment & Methods, July/August, 1988, p. 31.

³Amy Wohl as quoted by Patricia Tracy Callahan, "An Interview with Amy Wohl," Words, May/June, 1988, p. 33.

26

50-space line
Spacing: 1 and 2
Key two 1-min timings on each line *or* repeat each line three times.

Skill Building

Use **;** finger and left shift key. Key each line twice.

Use **F** finger and right shift key. Keep other fingers anchored above home row. Key each line twice.

Key two 1-min timings on each line *or* repeat each line three times.

Timing

Set spacing at 2. Key two 2-min timings. Circle all errors and calculate gross words per minute. Record the better timing on your Progress Chart.

SI   1.15
AWL 3.82

:/$/Open Tables

One-Hand Words

1 in bet hip face join bases onion few non gate oily

2 my cat hop fact hill brass pupil rag lip free holy

Reach to the **:** Key

3 ;;; ;:; ;:; ::: ;:; :;: :;: ;;; ;:; ;:; ::: ;: ;:;

4 The times listed are: 06:42; 23:18; 08:53; 22:30.

Reach to the **$** Key

5 fff f4f f$f f$f fff $$$ f$f f$f f$$f f f$f f$ $f

6 The invoice totals are: $23.15, $9.25 and $49.15.

7 He gave me $5.10 of the $7.50, leaving only $2.40.

Spacing Reminder: Colons and Dollar Signs

- No space before a colon.
- Two spaces after a colon used within a sentence.
- No space before or after a colon used to express time.
- No space after the dollar sign.

Common-Word Sentences

8 We would like to thank you for the valued service.

9 They would have sent the letter to you since that.

10 This will be the first time we have stopped there.

• • • • 1 • • • • 2 • • • • 3 • • • • 4 • • • • 5 • • • • 6 • • • 7 • • • • 8 • • • • 9 • • • • 10

Two-Minute Timing

			1	2
School was over for the day. Donna rushed in	10	5
the house, threw her books on a chair, grabbed her	20	10
helmet and headed for her brand new motorbike. It	30	15
was a thrill to hear a rush of power as she headed	40	20
down the lane. Soon she was out on the open trail	50	25
with thoughts of school and books left far behind.	60	30
This was the life for her.	65	33

• • • • 1 • • • • 2 • • • • 3 • • • • 4 • • • • 5 • • • • 6 • • • 7 • • • • 8 • • • • 9 • • • • 10   1 min

        1   2   3   4   5   2 min

HEREBY APPOINT RICHARD GOWAN, of Portage La Prairie, Manitoba, to be the guardian of my infant children during their respective minorities.

IN WITNESS WHEREOF I have hereunto set my name this   day of June, 19--, to this my Last Will and Testament written on this and the two preceding pages.

SIGNED, PUBLISHED AND DECLARED   )
by the above-named JOAN DEOMING,   )
as and for her Last Will and   )
Testament, in the presence of us,   )
both present at the same time, who   )
at her request, in her presence,   )
and in the presence of each other,   )
have hereunto subscribed our   )
names as witnesses:)
↓4   )
_____   )
Name   )
↓2   )
_____   )
Address   )   line vertically
↓2   )   ↓ centered
_____   )   _____
↓3   )   JOAN DEOMING
)
_____   )
Occupation   )
↓3-4   )
_____   )
Name   )
↓2   )
_____   )
Address   )
↓2   )
_____   )
↓3   )
)
_____   )
Occupation   )

Skill Building

Key two 1-min timings on each line *or* repeat each line three times.

Number Practice

11 Your clerks charged us $324.12 instead of $234.12.
12 Invoice 17469 lists two amounts: $3.42 and $4.98.
13 The postal codes needed are: J2X 4L1 and G5C 1R5.

• • • • 1 • • • • 2 • • • • 3 • • • • 4 • • • • 5 • • • • 6 • • • 7 • • • • 8 • • • • 9 • • • 10

Production Practice

SC

Have you calculated the key line?

Production 1

Center the following on a half sheet of paper. Use the Backspace Method.

TELEVISION LISTINGS

Sports Hi-Lites
March 5-11, 19--

Day	Event	Time	Channel
Saturday	All Star Wrestling	09:00	5
Saturday	Stampede Preview	11:00	4
Saturday	Outdoor Sportsman	12:30	8
Saturday	Canadian College Sport	13:00	6
Sunday	World Junior Curling	14:00	5
Sunday	NBA Basketball	15:45	13

↑ Align the colons.   ↑ Align numbers on the right.

Production 2

Center the following table on a full sheet of paper. Use the Backspace Method. Double space the body. *Note:* The $ symbol is shown only beside the first dollar amount in numerical column listings. Be careful to align the numbers on the right.

Title: DASMUND ENTERPRISES LTD.

Subtitle: Clerical Positions Open

SC

Have you calculated the key line?

Column Headings: Job	Rate	Department
Clerk	$1350	Receiving
Database Management Clerk	1500	Personnel
Desktop Publishing Specialist	1500	Central Services
Records Manager	1650	Central Records
Receptionist	1350	General Office
Secretary	1600	Legal
Administrative Assistant	1800	Land
Information Processing Specialist	1525	General Office
Accounts Payable Clerk	1500	Accounting

Stop here if you cannot get the balance of the Will material on the present page.

Draw a ZED in the unused space of your present page and then continue with the balance of the Will on a new page.

consider necessary shall be used for the maintenance, education and advancement in life of each respective child until he or she attains the age of twenty-one (21) years. The receipt of the guardian, or of such other person satisfactory to my Trustees with whom any child may be living, shall be sufficient discharge to my Trustees for payments made. When each of the said children reaches the age of twenty-one (21) years, his or her share shall be paid to him or her for his or her own use absolutely. PROVIDED that should any of my children predecease me leaving issue him or her surviving, such issue shall take, and if more than one then in equal shares between them, the share of my estate which his, her or their parent would have taken had he or she survived me.

10 →

4.   In the event that my said husband predeceases me, or surviving me, fails to appoint a guardian, I

−3−

27

*/ Open Tables

50-space line
Spacing: 1 and 2
Key two 1-min timings on
each line *or* repeat each line
three times.

Skill Building

Use **K** finger and left shift
key. Key the line once.

Key two 30-s timings on
each line *or* repeat each line
twice. Key these drills as
quickly as you can.

Key two 1-min timings on
each line *or* repeat each line
three times. Concentrate on
accuracy.

Timing

Set spacing at 2. Key two
2-min timings. Circle all
errors and calculate gross
words per minute. Record
the better timing on your
Progress Chart.

SI   1.17
AWL 3.78

One-Hand Words

1 on err mop fare jump bread jolly sag oil fear polo
2 up far you fats link craft imply sex ink rare kink

Reach to the * Key

3 kkk k8k k*k k*k kkk *** k*k k*k k**k *k* k**k k*k*
4 one* two** three*** four**** five ***** six ******
5 We have heard this theory explained to us before.*

Spacing Reminder: Asterisks

- No space before the asterisk at the end of a word or number to indicate a footnote.
- No space after the asterisk at the beginning of a footnote reference.

Common-Word Sentences

6 No other way through the event seems to be better.
7 He might hide his dark brown hat until the men go.
8 The air that day was clear and fresh; a bird sang.

Number Practice

9 The 13 pictures were sold for $45.75 at the store.
10 Just call me at 378-4932 or 483-5265 at this time.

Two-Minute Timing

1	2

Some more work has come to us and needs to be
done by next May. Most of the staff are still unable to handle this kind of work and those who did
last time, are still not back on the job after the
spring break. We need to act quickly and get some
other workers to join our team for the short haul.
Please phone the new firm that lists help for this
kind of work. We need them all by next week.

1 min				
1	2	3	4	5

2 min

6

power of appointment, to my said Trustees upon the following trusts, namely:

10

(a) To sell, call in and convert into money all my estate not consisting of money at such times, in such manner and upon such terms and either for cash or credit or for part cash and part credit as my said Trustees may in their absolute discretion decide upon, with power and discretion to postpone such conversion of such estate or any part or parts thereof for such length of time as they may think best, and I hereby declare that my said Trustees may retain any portion of my estate in the form in which it may be at my death (notwithstanding that it may not be in the form of an investment in which trustees are authorized to invest funds and whether or not there is a liability attached to any such portion of my estate) for such length of time as my said Trustees may in their discretion deem advisable, and I also declare that my Trustees when making any investments for my estate shall not be limited to investments authorized by law for trustees, but may make any investments which in their absolute discretion they consider advisable, and my Trustees shall not be held responsible for any loss that may happen to my estate by reason of their so doing.

10

(b) To pay my just debts, funeral and testamentary expenses.

10

(c) To hold the whole of my estate in trust for my children in equal shares, the income from each share, and so much of the capital thereof as my Trustees may

TS
-2-

TS

Production 1

Center the following table on a half sheet of paper. Single space the body and arrange in the groupings as shown. Use the Backspace Method. *Note:* The asterisk is not included in the count when calculating horizontal placement.

DASMUND ENTERPRISES LTD.
Report of Sales, 19--

Location	Manager	Annual Sales
Vancouver	Fred Baker	$2 201 012*
Edmonton	Mike Dasmund	1 769 000
Regina	Peter Gallin	1 415 211
Winnipeg	Joan Deoming	1 517 100
Toronto	Thomas Rollins	2 720 550**
Montreal	Michelle De Meeres	2 975 617
Halifax	Edward Brinley	1 121 320

#>

↓ SS
↓ DS

*Increase of $250 000 over last year
**Increase of $475 000 over last year

Production 2

Center the following table on a half sheet of paper. Single space the body and arrange in the groupings as shown. Use the Backspace Method. *Note:* Serial numbers are keyed as recorded on the source document and aligned on the right. It is not necessary to separate the serial number by thousands.

Dasmund Enterprises Ltd.
Office Machine Repairs

Brand Name	Serial Number	Type of Repair
IBM PC	2129-2013325	Disk Drive A
Zenith Laptop P.C.	181302-89659	Key Stuck
Dec Mate III	076-L344340	Can't input data
Epson Printer Dot-Matrix	018-EL348651	Piling letters
HP Laser Printer	EL 024-34985	Faded print
IBM Electronic Typewriter	947865240-31	Margin
Canon Electronic Typewriter	457320921	Centering feature

#>

#>

Production

Key Joan Deoming's Will on side-, top-, and bottom-ruled legal paper provided in your Workbook.

12

10 ⟶ THIS IS THE LAST WILL AND TESTAMENT OF me,
JOAN DEOMING, of 16 McNulty Crescent, in the City
of Winnipeg, in the Province of Manitoba.
1.8 TS↓ ⟶ I HEREBY REVOKE all Wills and testamentary
dispositions of every nature or kind whatsoever by
me heretofore made.
2.   TS↓ IF MY HUSBAND, EDWARD DONALD DEOMING,
survives me for a period of thirty (30) days, I GIVE,
DEVISE AND BEQUEATH all my property of every nature
and kind and wheresoever situate, including my property
over which I may have a general power of appointment,
to my said husband for his own use absolutely and I
appoint him sole Executor of this my Will.
3.   TS↓ IN THE EVENT that my husband shall predecease
me, or surviving me shall die within a period of
thirty (30) days following my decease, I NOMINATE,
CONSTITUTE AND APPOINT RICHARD GOWAN, of Portage La
Prairie, Manitoba and my son, MATTHEW CLAYTON DEOMING,
of Calgary, Alberta, hereinafter referred to as my
Trustees, to be the Executors and Trustees of this my
will and I GIVE, DEVISE AND BEQUEATH all my property
of every nature and kind and wheresoever situate,
including any property over which I may have a general

28

Analytical Practice

Key two 1-min timings on each line *or* repeat each line three times.

Analyze Your Practice Needs
Key three 1-min timings on each sentence *or* repeat each sentence five times. Every alphabetic character is included in each sentence.

Circle all errors.

After Selected Letter Practice, key two 1-min timings on each sentence and determine if you have improved your accuracy.

If you have practised the necessary lines before your instructor calls time, begin keying at line **A** and key each line once.

Alternate-Hand Words

1 go air dig fit jam turn coal fuel lamb cycle gland
2 he big dog fix key urns corn girl land digit gowns

Alphabetic Sentences

3 The queen took her prize bags home with her in the
taxi which was driven just half as fast as before.

4 One quiet morning in July, the sick woman sat back
in her sofa, relaxed and admired her prize violet.
• • • • 1 • • • • 2 • • • • 3 • • • • 4 • • • • 5 • • • 6 • • • • 7 • • • • 8 • • • • 9 • • • 10

Selected Letter Practice

1. Analyze your errors in the Alphabetic Sentences.
2. Choose the letter or letters giving you difficulty or causing errors.
3. Select the appropriate Selected Letter Practice.
4. Key each line twice.

A Alice ate an apple as a snack and asked for lunch.
As an ape ran across a paved road a car came near.

B A bad boy better behave or he will be behind bars.
Buy a big bullet before big black bears come back.

C Can a cross child catch an ochre color clay chick?
A city car creeps with care as it comes by cliffs.

D Does a dumb dog decide to dart after a dirty duck?
Does dear daddy make desks and doors for a dollar?

E Ede expects each extra book end to be even enough.
Every event enables each expert to expect empties.

F Fred found four financial files full of few facts.
File the firm's first fine finds for future funds.
• • • • 1 • • • • 2 • • • • 3 • • • • 4 • • • • 5 • • • 6 • • • • 7 • • • • 8 • • • • 9 • • • 10

Wills

60-space line
Spacing: 1 and 2
Key two 30-s timings on
each line *or* repeat each line
three times.

Left-Hand Words

1 fact refer water evaded savers grafted caterers stressed tax

2 fade rests watts exacts screws gravest decrease greatest bag

One-Minute Timings

1. Turn to the One-Minute Timings, page 421.
2. Select the paragraph that you think you can complete in one minute.
3. Key the One-Minute Timing as a drill.
4. If you had two or more errors, practice Accuracy Improvement.
   If you had fewer than two errors, practice Speed Improvement.

Accuracy Improvement

Skill Building

Key two 30-s timings on
line 3 of Accuracy Improvement. Circle any errors. If
you have more than one
error for each timing, continue with the Accuracy
Improvement drill. If you
have one error or less on
each timing, key the Speed
Improvement drill and
concentrate on speed.

3 annum bills better passed arrived express carrying supplying

4 pop up loon moon union jolly mummy Phillip ill oh look imply

5 decree pup excess plop exceeds John decrease nylon aggravate

Speed Improvement

6 The afternoon meeting started at 13:30; it was 2 hours long.

7 That water will be wasted if you start the pump before noon.

8 Keep a summary of express bills to see if we get all crates.

• • • •1• • • •2• • • •3• • • •4• • • •5• • • •6• • • •7• • • •8• • • •9• • •10• • •11• • •12

Punctuation Practice

Key each line once,
concentrating on correct
punctuation.

9 "When do you plan to leave for Vancouver Island?" asked May.

10 After he finished keying, he sat down on the chair to relax.

11 Fred brought the lunch: ham, cheese, pumpernickel and wine.

12 Ms. Jackson, the manager, will return your call later today.

13 Tony wasn't ready; we had to leave for Montreal without him.

14 When could you read The Dog Who Wouldn't Be by Farley Mowat?

G We get great groups who give good guitar programs.
Go get a good gift for Gary; a glad guessing game.

H He has heard that his new hotel is high on a hill.
Harry helped himself by holding the heavier hinge.

I If it is an impossible issue, I am not interested.
Their ideas about investment insurance are issues.

J Jody just jumped with joy over a new judicial job.
A Joke Joint sells jewels, jacks, jugs, and jeans.

K Kiki knows how to keep knees from getting skinned.
The cranky king keeps kicking crooked wicker kegs.

L Long large lots were listed low and sold at sales.
Little notes left local labs at least an hour ago.

M Market men might make much more money most months.
My mortgage manager moved our meetings of members.

N Nina never needs to own nine nice new nylon lines.
Numbers of names never need to be noted in spring.

O Our original office orders are overdue more often.
Our own options offer only one other open opinion.

P Present plan proposals permit product part prices.
Perhaps past people paid previous public policies.

Q He questioned the quantity of quartz in the quota.
Five quality quarters; an equally quick quotation.

· · · · 1 · · · · 2 · · · · 3 · · · · 4 · · · · 5 · · · · 6 · · · · 7 · · · · 8 · · · · 9 · · · 10

Production

Key the following report in non-bound format. If your software has graphics capabilities, use them to design the chart. If not, use your machine, a ruler, and a sharp pencil.

ELECTRONIC MAIL OR COMPUTERIZED MESSAGING SYSTEMS

A dramatic, though quiet, revolution has been taking place in the modern office. This revolution is due to the increasing use of electronic mail or computerized messaging systems. Communication in the office has been revolutionized by this new technology.

The computerized messaging systems have allowed clear and direct instructions to be transmitted in the least amount of time, often providing a better information source for making instant, cost-saving decisions. Management in the past has seldom been so quickly sold on the advantages available to them in the vendor's packages relating to electronic mail.

One type of electronic mail can be described as synchronized communication; messages take place instantaneously between two or more parties. The medium can be voice or hard copy. The telephone falls into this category although telex and facsimile systems can function in this manner as well.

Non-synchronized communication takes place independently of the sender and receiver. The oldest form is the letter, traditionally stored on paper. However, in recent years store-and-forward computers are replacing the need to store messages on paper. An office worker can call up onto his or her video display terminal a copy of the messages or letters stored in the electronic mailboxes. The system available to the receiver will vary but either voice or written text receiver systems are in common usage.

Some of the more common electronic mail systems can be described under one of the headings in the following chart:

SC

Can you draw horizontal and vertical lines on your machine?

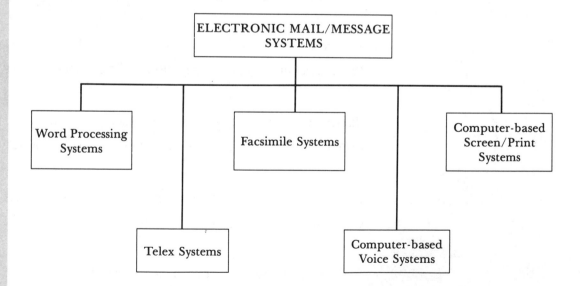

R Ruth read rental reports and recent reply records.
   Re refunds required with regard to room reference.

S Sid sat to see special ships sail in the sea show.
   Several sizes were shown this season at some sale.

T Three of them think that they are the total terms.
   The lot tax is typed today to transfer the titles.

U Usually you are using your unit measure upon that.
   I usually urge you to vacuum up untidy upholstery.

V Violet votes for various village views in Vistavu.
   Very valuable vests vary vastly with each version.

W Shawn will work while Walter walks for well water.
   Which was the way Walt waltzed on Wednesday night?

X Max Sexton fixed six tax boxes for Trixie's taxes.
   Mexican Max fixed Trixie's deluxe saxophone boxes.

Y Yes, your yards of yellow yarn yielded yard goods.
   Molly may say you have years of youth; a yarn yet.

Z Zeke picked twelve bronze zinnias by this new zoo.
   Zorro, the dozy zombie, has a prize razor buzzing.

· · · · 1 · · · · 2 · · · · 3 · · · · 4 · · · · 5 · · · · 6 · · · · 7 · · · · 8 · · · · 9 · · · · 10

Sentence with Numbers

Key three 2-min timings on the sentence *or* repeat the sentence five times. All numbers are included in the sentence.

Circle all number errors.

Class 136 with 241 students will meet in Room 309;
class 178 with 382 students will meet in Room 591;
and class 278 with 65 students will meet in Rooms
4 056 or 4 907.

· · · · 1 · · · · 2 · · · · 3 · · · · 4 · · · · 5 · · · · 6 · · · · 7 · · · · 8 · · · · 9 · · · · 10

Skill Building

60-space line
Spacing: 1 and 2
Key two 30-s timings on
each line *or* repeat each line
three times.

Double-Letter Words

1 gross needs commit arrive assured success bulletin naturally
2 books doors unless recall offered meeting supplies carefully

Graduated Speed Practice

Turn to the Graduated Alphanumerical Speed Practice, page 403. Select a sentence that you think you can key in the time indicated by your instructor.

Alphabetic Sentences

3 This bin of clothing has mixed sizes so look quite carefully

if you plan to have something you will enjoy wearing.

4 The saxophone players squeezed into a very awkward garage so

they could begin their first major practice.

Number Practice

5 The new address is: Box 79, Lakevue Park, Alberta, T3H 5S0.
6 To see my 2- and 3-bedroom suites call 355-6648 or 365-6319.

Stroking Practice

1. Turn to the Stroking Practice, page 414.
2. Key the lines selected by your instructor or the letter combinations giving you difficulty in the drills just completed.
3. Students on individual progress should select lines.
4. Key each line twice.

Accuracy Building

Key two 30-s timings on each line concentrating on accuracy as your goal. Students on individual progress should key each line three times with the accuracy goal in mind.

Accuracy Improvement

7 desert Jim feared pull graders poll excavate jolly detracted
8 fats saved waxes exerts seeded rafters excavate affected ear

Speed Improvement

9 We will enclose the material requested by your office staff.
10 Lou had ink to stamp the pupil who was seated by the crates.

• • • • 1 • • • • 2 • • • • 3 • • • • 4 • • • • 5 • • • 6 • • • 7 • • • • 8 • • • • 9 • • • • 10 • • • • 11 • • • • 12

Skill Building

Key two 30-s timings on line 7 of Accuracy Improvement. Circle any errors. If you have more than one error for each timing, continue with the Accuracy Improvement drill. If you have one error or less on each timing, key the Speed Improvement drill and concentrate on speed.

Three- or Five-Minute Timing

Turn to the timing in Unit VII of your Working Papers. Students without Working Papers should key the timing in Lessons 134-35, page 358.

Selected Number Practice

1. Analyze your errors in the Sentence with Numbers.
2. Choose the number or numbers giving you difficulty or causing errors.
3. Select the appropriate Selected Number Practice.
4. Key the line twice.

After Selected Number Practice, key two 2-min timings on the sentence and determine if you have improved your number accuracy.

1 1 or an 11 or 111 and 12 for a 31 by 1 among 1 121
2 by 12 since 212 by 2 and a 2 or 21 and 2 122 or 12
3 3 and 33 by 313 yet 3 131 or 3 323 by 3 but 3 or 3
4 4 but 14 and 4 141 by 44 among 41 for 4 424 and 14
5 55 or 515 by 51 but 25 at least 5 251 for 51 and 5
6 6 since 616 then 61 but 16 626 for 16 or 66 but 62
7 7 or a 71 or 7 171 and 7 for a 72 by 7 among 7 737
8 8 and 88 by 818 yet 8 181 or 8 828 by 8 but 8 or 8
9 9 but 19 and 9 191 by 9 among 949 for 9 929 and 19
0 0 or 400 by 30 but 20 at least 1 040 for 200 and 0

• • • • 1 • • • • 2 • • • • 3 • • • • 4 • • • • 5 • • • • 6 • • • • 7 • • • • 8 • • • • 9 • • • • 10

Production

Production Timing

Adjust your machine to set your margins and tabs. Calculate the vertical placement. Insert your paper. Space down to begin. Backspace to horizontally center the title. **Stop.** Your instructor will tell you when to begin the actual timing. Students on individual progress should time themselves when they begin keying the table.

Can you complete the table in 10 min?

Key the following table as a production timing. It should be centered, double spaced, and attractively set up on a full sheet of paper. Use the Backspace Method.

BIRTHSTONES AND FLOWERS

Month	Birthstone	Flower
January	Garnet	Carnation
February	Amethyst	Violet
March	Bloodstone	Jonquil
April	Diamond	Sweet Pea
May	Emerald	Lily of the Valley
June	Pearl	Rose
July	Ruby	Larkspur
August	Sardonyx	Gladiolus
September	Sapphire	Aster
October	Opal	Calendula
November	Topaz	Chrysanthemum
December	Turquoise	Narcissus

Production 2
(See instructions on page 359.)

Affidavit Of Execution

CANADA ①

PROVINCE OF ALBERTA

TO WIT:

I,   SAUL ISAAC WARBURG ②   , of the City of   Calgary ③ , in the Province of Alberta ,   MAKE OATH AND SAY:

1.   THAT I was personally present and did see MARTIN KARL KOWALCHUK and ALICIA TANIA KOWALCHUK ④

named in the within instrument, who are personally known to me to be the persons named therein, duly sign and execute the same for the purpose named therein.

2.   THAT the same was executed at the   City of   Calgary ⑤ , in the Province of Alberta and that I am the subscribing witness thereto.

3.   THAT I know the said MARTIN KARL KOWALCHUK and TANIA KOWALCHUK and they are ④ , in my belief, of the full age of eighteen years.

SWORN before me at Calgary,
in the Province of Alberta,
this 18th day of April, ⑥
19 94

     ———————————————
     SAUL ISAAC WARBURG

———————————————————————————
A Commissioner for Oaths in and for the Province of Alberta

Production 3

Use the Affidavit of Execution form in your Workbook and prepare an Affidavit of Execution for signature today by Mary Teresa Joe, a barrister and solicitor in your home town. The name of the client is Dominic Alex Porteous-Fyfe.

29

Ruled Tables

50-space line
Spacing: 1 and 2
Key two 1-min timings on each line *or* repeat each line three times.

Skill Building

Key two 1-min timings on each line *or* repeat each line three times. Key these drills as quickly as you can.

Key two 30-s timings on each line *or* repeat each line twice. Key these drills as quickly as you can.

Key each underlined word three times. Key each line once concentrating on the underlined words.

Key one 1-min timing on each line *or* repeat each line twice. Circle any errors to determine if there is need for extra drill on the number reaches.

Timing

Set spacing at 2. Key two 2-min timings. Circle all errors and calculate gross words per minute. Record the better timing on your Progress Chart.

SI   1.09
AWL 3.59

Common-Word Sentences

1 Ask him if he can bring a silver rock to the camp.
2 I will see that you go along with him to the fair.

One-Hand Words

3 on tax ill wave yolk agree nylon saw you feet only
4 up set mum wear pull award union get joy raft look
5 no beg him ever upon swear plunk fed hum gave hoop

Alternate-Hand Sentences

6 Did the girls cut and fit keys or is it a key jam?
7 She paid us for eight pens and six pairs of socks.
8 Girls fit hems for the height of their duty socks.

· · · · 1 · · · · 2 · · · · 3 · · · · 4 · · · · 5 · · · · 6 · · · · 7 · · · · 8 · · · · 9 · · · · 10

Concentrate on Correct Spelling

9 Aid was <u>offered</u> before the <u>occurrence</u> demanded it.
10 Is it <u>feasible</u> to have it completed by <u>February</u> 3?

Number Practice

11 701 and 35 and 471 and 94 and 318 and 2 and 27 020
12 512 and 80 and 670 and 50 and 492 and 30 and 2 942

· · · · 1 · · · · 2 · · · · 3 · · · · 4 · · · · 5 · · · · 6 · · · · 7 · · · · 8 · · · · 9 · · · · 10

Two-Minute Timing

	1	2
The boys had not stopped to see if Kwan might	10	5
need some help with his old car. He seemed not to	20	10
notice them as they went past him. He spent a lot	30	15
of time under the hood with a set of wrenches. On	40	20
Friday he hoped to have his old car ready to start	50	25
the big race. He would have to work on it without	60	30
stopping.	62	31

· · · · 1 · · · · 2 · · · · 3 · · · · 4 · · · · 5 · · · · 6 · · · · 7 · · · · 8 · · · · 9 · · · · 10   **1 min**

1　　　　2　　　　3　　　　4　　　　5   **2 min**

Production 1

(See instructions on page 359.)

↓ 7

AFFIDAVIT OF EXECUTION

↓ TS

CANADA   )
PROVINCE OF BRITISH COLUMBIA   )
TO WIT:)

↓ TS

→ 10 →   I, THOMAS ROALD DUSEVIC, Barrister and Solicitor,

of the Municipality of Burnaby, in the Province of British

Columbia, MAKE OATH AND SAY:

↓ TS

1.   THAT I was personally present and did see LORNA

PATRICIA ECKARDT, named in the within instrument, who is

personally known to me to be the person named therein, duly

sign and execute the same for the purpose named therein.

2.   THAT the same was executed at the Municipality of

Burnaby, in the Province of British Columbia, and that I am

the subscribing witness thereto.

3.   THAT I know the said LORNA PATRICIA ECKARDT and

she is, in my belief, of the full age of eighteen years.

SWORN BEFORE ME at the   )
Municipality of Burnaby, in   )
the Province of British   )
Columbia, this 10th day of   )
December, 1992.   )
)   _____
)   THOMAS ROALD DUSEVIC
↓ 3-4   )
_____   )
A Commissioner for taking   )
Affidavits for British   )
Columbia   )

Ruled Tables

Ruled tables are similar to open tables when it comes to horizontal centering. However, ruled tables are different from open tables in three ways:
- Vertical centering is different.
- In the ruled table, there is a solid line of underscoring above and below the column headings and at the bottom of the table.
- In the ruled table, the column heading is not underscored.

The underscore key is usually used for horizontal lines. Some word processing software also uses the underline option for horizontal lines. Know your software.

An Open Table

GRANDE PRAIRIE REGIONAL COLLEGE

DS

Course Enrollments
1990-91

TS

Program	Full Time	Part Time
DS		
Arts	701	35
Business	471	94
Health	318	22
Nursing	270	20
Physical Education	512	80
Science	670	50
TOTAL	2 942	301

Lines 1–16 marked in right margin.

A Ruled Table

GRANDE PRAIRIE REGIONAL COLLEGE

DS

Course Enrollments
1990-91

SS

DS

Program	Full Time	Part Time
SS		

DS

Arts	701	35
Business	471	94
Health	318	22
Nursing	270	20
Physical Education	512	80
Science	670	50

SS

DS

TOTAL	2 942	301

SS

Lines 1–19 marked in right margin.

Skill Building

Key two 30-s timings on line 3 of Accuracy Improvement. Circle any errors. If you have more than one error for each timing, continue with the Accuracy Improvement drill. If you have one error or less on each timing, key the Speed Improvement drill and concentrate on speed.

Accuracy Improvement

₃ up at least 31 to the 830 save all 41 in all 17 up to the 16

₄ to bow lane blame widow ritual entitle authentic town eighth

₅ decade pop exceed plum evaders kink caterers imply afterward

Speed Improvement

₆ The emblem of the island is a visitor on a map of the world.

₇ Phillip will pin the badge on Joy when he awards pupil work.

₈ Your program has been receiving assistance for eleven years.

• • • • 1 • • • • 2 • • • • 3 • • • • 4 • • • • 5 • • • • 6 • • • • 7 • • • • 8 • • • • 9 • • • •10 • • • •11 • • • •12

Stroking Practice

1. Turn to the Stroking Practice, page 414.
2. Key the lines selected by your instructor or the letter combinations giving you difficulty in the drills just completed.
3. Students on individual progress should select lines from 46 to 60.
4. Key each line twice.

Affidavit of Execution

Required Information

1. Province in which Affidavit of Execution will be used.
2. Name (and occupation) of witness.
3. City or Municipality in which the witness resides.
4. Name of person who signed the accompanying document.
5. City or Municipality where the accompanying document was executed (signed).
6. Place and date on which the witness appeared before a Commissioner and signed the Affidavit of Execution.

Production Practice

Production 1

Prepare the fully keyed Affidavit of Execution to be sworn by Thomas Roald Dusevic (see page 360).

Production 2

Use the Affidavit of Execution form in your Workbook to prepare the Affidavit of Execution to be sworn by Saul Isaac Warburg (see page 361).

Spacing Reminder: Underscores

- The underscore is keyed at the bottom of the line and should not be counted in addition to the space.

$$SS \downarrow \underline{\text{This is the last line.}}$$

- Single space above a line of underscoring and double space below.

Keying Ruled Tables

Keying the Table

1. Clear all tabs.
2. Calculate and set the left margin and tab stops for the column headings.
3. Set the right margin even with the longest item in the last column.
4. Calculate the starting line for vertical centering.
   - Refer to the preceding example of a ruled table.
   - For a full sheet of paper: $66 - 19 = 47$

$$\frac{47}{2} = 23.5$$

The starting line is 24. If you are having difficulty with vertical centering refer to Lesson 18.

Remember:
- There is a single space between the subtitle and the line of underscoring.
- There is a single space above each line of underscoring and a double space below.

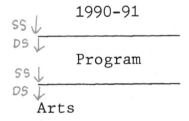

5. Insert your paper.

Prepare Your Machine

1. Space down to the starting line.
2. Horizontally center and key the title and subtitle.
3. Single space.
4. Underscore from the left margin to the right margin. The underscoring should end even with the longest item in the last column.
5. Double space.
6. Key the column headings.
7. Single space.
8. Underscore from the left margin to the right margin.
9. Double space.
10. Key the body of the table.

Bottom Rule

11. The totals are ruled within a solid line of underscoring. Single space after the last line of the list in the body.

SC

Do you know how to set the appropriate right margin?

Affidavit of Execution

60-space line
Spacing: 1 and 2
Key two 30-s timings on
each line *or* repeat each line
three times.

Alternate-Hand Words

1 air men they body keys dial diem dish audit risks augur born

2 bid map town buck lamb disk dock firm rocks rotor blame both

**Assess Your
Improvement**
Set spacing at 2. Key at
least one 3-min *or* 5-min
timing. Circle all errors and
calculate gross words per
minute. Record the timing
on your Progress Chart.

Three- or Five-Minute Timing

	1	CW	3
Most people are interested in looking and feeling their	12	12	4
best. Perhaps the best, and least expensive way to help the	24	24	8
way we look and feel, is through regular exercise. The hope	36	36	12
of achieving an acceptable level of fitness will probably be	48	48	16
the motivating factor in the beginning stage of any exercise	60	60	20
program. The choice of exercise is strictly a personal one.	72	72	24
Jogging, swimming and cycling are excellent. The goal is to	84	84	28
increase the heart rate for 30 min three times a week.	95	95	32
Any exercise program requires self-discipline and using	12	107	36
a regular period of time. Before embarking on any strenuous	24	119	40
program a medical checkup is a good idea. Exercising with a	36	131	44
friend can make the program more interesting and challenging	48	143	48
for the people concerned. Novices should work up gradually,	60	155	52
not trying a 30 min run the first day out. However, it is a	72	167	56
fact that any program will fail if it is not a regular habit	84	179	60
at least three times a week.	90	185	62
What benefit can we expect from an exercise program? A	12	197	66
number of very delightful things might happen. Some of them	24	209	70
might be: (1) a desire to eat less, since regular exercises	36	221	74
help to control appetite, (2) energy levels will increase in	48	233	78
other areas of our lives, (3) our systems will become vastly	60	245	82
more efficient as the pulse rate slows, (4) perhaps the real	72	257	86
big plus is the fact that we will feel better and will be so	84	269	90
much more alert. This makes the program a success.	96	279	93

• • • • 1 • • • • 2 • • • • 3 • • • • 4 • • • • 5 • • • • 6 • • • • 7 • • • • 8 • • • • 9 • • • • 10 • • • • 11 • • • • 12 **1 min**

1   2   3   4 **3 min**

SI   1.53
AWL 4.48

12. Underscore from the left margin to the right margin.
13. Double space.
14. Key totals.
15. Single space.
16. Underscore from the left margin to the right margin.
   Remember:
   • A ruled table always ends with a final line of underscoring single spaced below the body.
   • A footnote is keyed below the final line of underscoring.

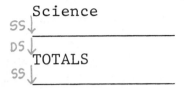

Ruling Totals on a Typewriter

• A ruling should be as wide as the longest number in the column.
• A single line in a column of numbers indicates addition or subtraction.
• A double line in a column of numbers indicates a final total.
To key a double line of rulings:
1. Underscore the column.
2. Open the ratchet release.
3. Turn the cylinder up slightly.
4. Key the second line of underscoring.
5. Close the ratchet release.
6. Turn the cylinder back to the writing line.

Ruling Totals on a Computer

• Ask your instructor or read the software manual to determine how to double rule.

Practice

Drill on Ruling Totals

670	291	50	37 592
2 942	6 938	301	104 687

19	57	306	2.157 3
823	104	4 967	52.346 7

Production Practice

Production 1

Turn to page 78. Center and key the open table, Grande Prairie Regional College, on a half sheet of paper.

Production 2

Turn to page 78. Center and key the ruled table, Grande Prairie Regional College, on a half sheet of paper.

Production 2

Use the Notarial Certificate form in your Workbook and prepare a Notarial Certificate for signature by DONALD JAMES BELL, a Notary Public in your city or municipality. DONNA MARIE ARCHAMBAULT brought her Birth Certificate No. 498247 dated January 18, 1968, into the office today to be notarized.

Production 3

Use the Notarial Certificate form in your Workbook and prepare a Notarial Certificate for signature by Constance Amelia Saracino, a Notary Public in your city or municipality.

The document to be notarized is the Last Will and Testament of Elizabeth Jane Tanaka signed by (insert appropriate name) and dated November 17, 1984. This document was shown to Ms. Saracino by Sean Patrick O'Shea today.

30

Ruled Tables

50-space line
Spacing: 1 and 2
Key two 1-min timings on
each line *or* repeat each line
three times.

Analyze Your Practice Needs
Key three 1-min timings on
each sentence *or* repeat each
sentence five times. Every
alphabetic character is
included in each sentence.

Circle all errors.

One-Hand Words

1 ax no be joy cab lip raw hill bear mink fees knoll
2 we in at him bat oil egg plum draw noun gave plump

Alphabetic Sentences

3 Vaughn could buy a size fifteen jacket for himself
  or maybe with a bit of help he could fix this one.

4 The taxes on the lake property in this zone aren't
  quite as bad as some just west of this vivid crag.

· · · · 1 · · · · 2 · · · · 3 · · · · 4 · · · · 5 · · · · 6 · · · · 7 · · · · 8 · · · · 9 · · · · 10

Selected Letter Practice

1. Analyze your errors in the Alphabetic Sentences.
2. Choose the letter or letters giving you difficulty or causing errors.
3. Turn to Lesson 28 and select the appropriate Selected Letter Practice.
4. Key each line twice.

Key each underlined word
three times. Key each line
once concentrating on the
underlined words.

Concentrate on Correct Spelling

5 Is it conceivable that the councilor is too tired?
6 His deceit followed her desperate attempt to hide.

Timing

Key two 2-min timings on
the paragraphs *or* repeat the
paragraphs twice. Circle all
errors. Compare any errors
made with those in the
timings of lines 3 and 4.

Two-Minute Timing

		1	CW	2

     A trip through the mountains in the spring is   10 | 10 | 5
worth the time it takes.   At this time the cars on 20 | 20 | 10
the roads are few and the banks of white snow fill   30 | 30 | 15
each crevice.   33 | 33 | 17
     It is a thrill to see the wild goats and some   10 | 43 | 22
bighorn sheep feeding at the side of the road.   On 20 | 53 | 27
a ledge one might be able to spot a white mountain   30 | 63 | 32
goat looking down from the safety of the cliff.   40 | 73 | 37

· · · · 1 · · · · 2 · · · · 3 · · · · 4 · · · · 5 · · · · 6 · · · · 7 · · · · 8 · · · · 9 · · · · 10   **1 min**
            1   2   3   4   5   **2 min**

SI   1.11
AWL 3.84

Notarial Certificate

Required Information

1. Province in which Notarial Certificate will be used.
2. Name of Notary Public.
3. City or Municipality in which Notary Public resides.
4. Name of the person who shows Notary Public the original and copy of the document.
5. Description of original document. For example, Birth Certificate No. 10195 in the name of (Name) dated (Date).
6. Day, month, and year when Notary Public signs the Notarial Certificate.

Production 1

Key the Notarial Certificate on the printed form in your Workbook.

Notarial Certificate

CANADA

PROVINCE OF ALBERTA ①

TO WIT:

} TO ALL TO WHOM THESE PRESENTS MAY COME BE SEEN OR KNOWN

I, JATINDER BANSAL ②

of the City of Calgary ③, in the Province of Alberta ①, a Notary Public by royal authority duly appointed, **DO CERTIFY** that the paper writing hereto annexed is a true copy of a document produced and shown to me from the custody of

KATHERINE YAU ④

and **purporting to be** an Agreement between KATHERINE YAU and LILY ALICE LUI, ⑤ dated the 5th day of May, 19--,

the said copy having been compared by me with the original document an act whereof being requested. I have granted under my notarial form and seal of office to serve as occasion shall or may require.

IN TESTIMONY WHEREOF I have hereunto subscribed my name and affixed my seal of office at the City of Calgary, ③ in the Province of Alberta, ① this 19th day of August, 19-- ⑥

(SEAL)

_____

A Notary Public in and for the Province of Alberta ①

Production 1

Center attractively on a half sheet of paper. Use single spacing.
- Set your right margin to help you in ending the solid line of underscores.
- A one-line column heading aligns horizontally with the second line of a two-line column heading.
- Two line column headings may be centered or block centered.

Title: DASMUND ENTERPRISES LTD.
Subtitle: Price List of Paper Stock and Reprographics Costs

SC
Did you set a right margin?

Type	Size	Cost	Reprographic Cost
20 lb Bond	8½ x 11	6.93/M	.02 per page
20 lb Carnaby Bond	8½ x 11	17.06/M	.025 " "
Linen Stocks	8½ x 11	28.00/M	.045 " "
Mayfair Covers	8½ x 11	10.00/M	.045 " "

Production 2

Center attractively on a half sheet of paper. Use the line groupings as shown.

Dasmund Enterprises Ltd.
Styles of Print Wheels Available, 19--

Catalogue No.	Pitch	Typestyle
763-02101	Pica	Bookface Academic
763-01201	Pica	Courier—English
763-01501	Pica	Courier—Bilingual
763-01701	Pica	Orator
763-01801	Pica	Prestige
763-00701	Elite	Courier
763-01901	Elite	Dual Gothic
763-02001	Elite	Courier Italic
763-20301	Elite	Prestige
763-00201	15	Gothic

SC
Did you use the underscore key or the underline option for the rulings?

Legal Documents

Paper Size

Standard size paper is used in legal offices. In the past, longer sheets of paper or legal size (21.5 cm × 35.5 cm) were popular. Legal size paper is still used for many printed legal forms which may be purchased in a stationery store.

Rulings

Legal paper can be ruled. Vertical side rulings are popular, but many legal offices use paper with an additional top and bottom rule, especially for Wills.

Reference Guide for Legal Documents

Left and Right Margins

On ruled paper, the left and right margins should be one or two spaces inside the side vertical rule. This usually gives a 60-65 space line (pica) or a 70-75 space line (elite).
On unruled paper, the left margin should be 15 (pica) or 18 (elite) spaces from the left edge if the document is to be sidebound; the right margin should be 8-10 spaces from the right edge.

Spacing

Double space the paragraphs. Triple space between paragraphs. (Some legal firms single space paragraphs with a double space between paragraphs.)

Top Margin

Page one — Start keying on line 7 (line 13 for a Will) or double space after the top rule.
Page two — Center and key the page number on line 4.
Allow for the top margin default if you are using a computer.
Triple space and continue the text.

Bottom Margin

Stop keying 6-9 lines from the bottom edge of the paper or 2-3 lines above the bottom rule. Allow for the bottom margin default if you are using a computer.

Page Numbering

Page one — No page number.
Page two — Center and key the page number of line 4. Key a hyphen before and after the page number.
Triple space and key the text.
Note: On a Will, the page number is keyed 6 lines from the bottom edge of the paper or 2-3 lines above the bottom rule.

Title

Center the title.

Indentations

Indent 10 spaces.

Enumerations

Key at the margin or indent 10 spaces.

Note: Introductory words are frequently capitalized. Reference to numbers in the text are keyed in words and figures and in legal instruments but not in correspondence or on court documents. On some documents, corrections are not permitted to names, money, figures, or dates.

SC

Many legal documents have standard wording so you should use the macro capabilities of your software whenever possible. Macro capabilities allow you to record such standard wordings under one name and play them back exactly as they were recorded.

31

Ruled Tables

50-space line
Spacing: 1 and 2
Key two 1-min timings on each line *or* repeat each line three times.

Alternate-Hand Words

1 dot map tug clay hair make sock firms rotor theory
2 due oak urn coal half male span flair shake visual

Skill Building

Key two 1-min timings on each line *or* repeat each line three times. Key these drills as quickly as you can.

Common-Word Sentences

3 Yes, these have been good years for winter sports.
4 I hope to get the same kind of treatment from him.
5 You will find that the case is too small for them.

Alphabetic Sentences

Key three 1-min timings on each sentence *or* repeat each sentence five times. Every alphabetic character is included in each sentence. Circle all errors. Make note of any letter drills you should practise from Lesson 28.

6 Liza questioned whether the crew on this voyage is able to solve the problem of just keeping relaxed.

7 Maxine could view the quality of the job done by a zealous group that managed to rake the area clean.

Key two 1-min timings on each line *or* repeat each line three times. Key at your controlled rate.

Number Practice

8 Mosen walked 20.03 km, but Charan walked 31.42 km.
9 Telephone them at 782-4563 at 18:30 on 1990 06 25.
10 Her address is 6721 - 24 Street, Calgary, Alberta.

· · · · · 1 · · · · 2 · · · · 3 · · · · 4 · · · · 5 · · · · 6 · · · · 7 · · · · 8 · · · · 9 · · · 10

Timing

Set spacing at 2. Key two 2-min timings. Circle all errors and calculate gross words per minute. Record the better timing on your Progress Chart.

Two-Minute Timing

	1	CW	2
Good taste in dress is a matter of choice not	10	10	5
chance. It isn't a matter of money but of knowing	20	20	10
what suits you and your life style. It isn't just	30	30	15
a case of latching on to the latest fad.	38	38	19
When you go to buy clothes try to see them as	10	48	24
you would a piece of art work. The way you wear a	20	58	29
piece of clothing has to do with style. Your idea	30	68	34
of yourself shows in the way you dress.	38	76	38

· · · · · 1 · · · · 2 · · · · 3 · · · · 4 · · · · 5 · · · · 6 · · · · 7 · · · · 8 · · · · 9 · · · 10   1 min
      1   2   3   4   5   2 min

SI   1.15
AWL 3.54

Notarial Certificate

60-space line
Spacing: 1 and 2
Key two 30-s timings on
each line *or* repeat each line
three times.

Double-Letter Words

1 issue error attach street discuss letters shipping committee

2 small allow cannot settle address carried actually according

One-Minute Timings

1. Turn to the One-Minute Timings, page 421.
2. Select the paragraph that you think you can complete in one minute.
3. Key the One-Minute Timing as a drill.
4. If you had two or more errors, practice Accuracy Improvement.
   If you had fewer than two errors, practice Speed Improvement.

Skill Building

Key two 30-s timings on
line 3 of Accuracy Improvement. Circle any errors. If
you have more than one
error for each timing, continue with the Accuracy
Improvement drill. If you
have one error or less on
each timing, key the Speed
Improvement drill and
concentrate on speed.

Accuracy Improvement

3 so box lend blend works signal emblems amendment they cosign

4 face reefs waste evades sagged grafter carefree stresses bar

5 mop on yolk look nylon onion pupil opinion my you ill in kin

Speed Improvement

6 The increase in stock values has been returned to customers.

7 Buy 3 kg of ground beef for Al's barbecue at 16:30 tomorrow.

8 Both of us held a sign to signal the visit of the civic men.

• • • • 1 • • • • 2 • • • • 3 • • • • 4 • • • • 5 • • • • 6 • • • • 7 • • • • 8 • • • • 9 • • • • 10 • • • • 11 • • • • 12

The Colon

1. Use a colon between two independent clauses when there is **no** coordinating conjunction (and, but, or, nor) or transitional expression joining the two clauses.
2. Use a colon between a clause and a series (words, phrases, or clauses) when the clause contains an anticipatory expression such as "the following".
3. Use a colon before an enumerated list or series.
4. Use a colon in expression of time, proportion, after salutations, and in reference to books or publications.

Key each line once,
concentrating on correct
punctuation.

9 You suggest the following: 17 lamps, 8 stands and 3 shades.

10 We will need notebooks for: English, Physics and Chemistry.

11 The workshop starts at 08:45 and might continue until 16:30.

12 We left the store in a hurry: I was fearful of the message.

Production 1

Key the following material as a ruled table. Center on a full sheet of paper. Double space the body of the table.

KEYBOARDING SPEED CHARTS

Five-minute Tests*

Student's Name / Semester 1 / Semester 2 / Improvement

Ann Corrio - 25, 38, 13
Reg Northman - 29, 37, 8
Evelyn Hannignan - 32, 45, 13
Dwayne Matejko - 20, 30, 10
Eva Ovingbridge - 42, 52, 10
Garry Stanford - 35, 46, 11
Bev Wertz - 39, 48, 9

*Scores are given as gross words per minute.

Production 2

Key the following material as a ruled table. Center on a full sheet. Single space the body with line groupings as shown.

Television Shows

Week of March 14, 19--

day / show / time / channel

Monday / Noon News / 13:00 /3
Monday / Family Feud / 13:00/6

#>

Tuesday / Oprah Winfrey /11:00/3
Tuesday / Super Password / 14:00/10
Tuesday / Body Works/ 15:00 / 5

#>

Wednesday / Canada AM /07:00 /3
Wednesday /Wheel of Fortune / 15:30 / 13

#>

Thursday / Donahue /10:00/8
Thursday / Jeopardy /12:00/8
Thursday / People's Court /13:30/2
Thursday / Classic Theatre /15:00/7

b. Conference.

Motion: Mike Dasmund/Joan Deoming, "that the Annual General Conference be held at Toronto, October 16, 19-- (current year). Carried.

7.   OTHER BUSINESS

Thomas Rollins gave a short report on AMS and the upcoming conference to be held at New York, July 24-29, 19-- (current year).

8. ADJOURNMENT

Mike Dasmund adjourned the meeting at 15:50.

_____

President - Thomas Rollins

_____

Secretary - Michelle De Meeres

Production 3

Key the following news release. The body may be single or double spaced.

Center →

Line 13 →

NEWS RELEASE   From: Michelle De Meeres
                             Secretary-Treasurer
                             Board of Directors
                             Dasmund Enterprises Ltd.
                      DS ↓ (416) 363-5133
                             Release: Immediately
                      DS↓
                             Date: October 15, 19--

Use a 60-space line

TS ↓

NATIONAL FIRM DISCUSSES HEAD OFFICE RELOCATION

TS ↓

A recommendation to move the head office from Toronto to Edmonton will be presented and discussed at the 19-- Annual General Meeting of Dasmund Enterprises Ltd. Shareholders of the company will have an opportunity to study the proposal at their annual meeting on October 16, 19--. Company president, Thomas Rollins will release details on the proposed relocation after the October meeting.

32

Skill Building

50-space line
Spacing: 1 and 2
Key two 1-min timings on
each line *or* repeat each line
three times.

Skill Building

Key two 30-s timings on
each line *or* repeat each line
twice. Key these drills as
quickly as you can.

Key two 30-s timings on
each line *or* repeat each line
twice. Key these drills as
quickly as you can.

Key two 1-min timings on
each sentence *or* repeat each
sentence three times. Every
alphabetic character is
included in each sentence.

One-Hand Words

1 ear mop bar nil gas ink wax plum cast ploy address
2 eat pop sad nip wax ion was plop dart hook adverse

Alternate-Hand Words

3 air end pay they diem hand melt audit flaps ritual
4 bib eye pep town dish held mend augur foams cosign

Alternate-Hand Sentences

5 She got a big dog dish for a pair of problem dogs.
6 Ruth pays for a title for an island by the eighth.

Alphabetic Sentences

7 The child went to a zoo to see the quick fox, four
 yak, a big jaguar, a monkey and a violet porpoise.
8 Hazel was quite proud of the way the six cylinders
 in her truck brought them over the mountain jaunt.

Graduated Speed Practice

1. Turn to Lesson 25 on page 67.
2. Drill on the appropriate Graduated Speed Practice.

Timing

Set spacing at 2. Key as
many 2-min timings as time
permits. Circle all errors
and calculate gross words
per minute. Record the best
timing on your Progress
Chart.

SI   1.10
AWL 3.50

Two-Minute Timing

		1	2
I watch as a small bird flits by my elm tree.		10	5
She slows, then returns to find a resting place on		20	10
one of the top branches. Soon her small head goes		30	15
back and a sweet song comes forth from her throat.		40	20
I hear the happy tune and my own work is made easy		50	25
by the anthem that comes from this small herald of		60	30
spring. But soon the song is done and the bird is		70	35
off to search for a place for her new nest.		79	39

• • • • 1 • • • • 2 • • • • 3 • • • • 4 • • • • 5 • • • • 6 • • • • 7 • • • • 8 • • • • 9 • • • • 10   **1 min**
          1   2   3   4   5   **2 min**

Production 2

Key the following minutes for the Annual General Meeting of Dasmund.

DASMUND ENTERPRISES LTD.

MINUTES

ANNUAL GENERAL MEETING, HALIFAX OCTOBER 12, 19-- *(last year)*

The meeting was called to order at 13:00 by President Thomas Rollins. There were 150 share-holders present. An Agenda was distributed.

1. AGENDA ADOPTION

Motion: Mike Dasmund/Joan Deoming, "that the Agenda be adopted as distributed." Carried.

2. MINUTES APPROVAL

Secretary, Michelle De Meeres, read the Minutes of the Annual General Meeting, held at Vancouver, October 8, 19-- *(two years ago)*

Motion: Fred Baker/Peter Gallin, "that the Minutes be adopted as read." Carried.

3. BUSINESS ARISING FROM THE MINUTES

Brochure – Edward Grinley reported that no progress has been made on this.

4. REPORTS

Reports from the President, Chairperson of the Board, and seven Regionals were distributed. Verbal reports were made by the Vice-President, Treasurer, Secretary and Peter Gallin of the Saskatchewan Regional.

Motion: Peter Gallin/Fred Baker, "that the reports as distributed and given be accepted." Carried.

5. ELECTION OF NEW REGIONAL CHAIRPERSONS

Maritimes	Edward Grinley
Quebec	Michelle De Meeres
Ontario	Walter Holowatiuk
Manitoba	Joan Deoming
Saskatchewan	Peter Gallin
Alberta	Jacques Gosselin
B. C.	Fred Baker

Spell out

Motion: Edward Grinley/Joan Deoming, "that the above slate of chairpersons be accepted." Carried.

6. NEW BUSINESS

a. Constitution (revised). Fred Baker--Item 4e "AMS representative to be appointed at the first Executive Meeting to be held after the General Meeting."

Motion: Joan Deoming/Peter Gallin, "that the revised Constitution be accepted as circulated and corrected." Carried.

33

#/Business Forms

50-space line
Spacing: 1 and 2
Key two 1-min timings on
each line *or* repeat each line
three times.

Skill Building

Key two 30-s timings on
each line *or* repeat each line
twice. Key these drills as
quickly as you can.

Key two 1-min timings on
each line *or* repeat each line
three times.

Use the **D** finger and the
right shift key. Try to keep
both **A** and **F** fingers
above home row. Key each
line twice.

Key each underlined word
three times. Key each line
once concentrating on the
underlined words.

Timing

Set spacing at 2. Key two
2-min timings. Circle all
errors and calculate gross
words per minute. Record
the better timing on your
Progress Chart.

SI   1.18
AWL 3.42

Alternate-Hand Words

1 cub hen sit born fork lame risk cycle proxy height
2 cut ham six both form lane rock digit rifle island

Common-Word Sentences

3 She hopes to go through the whole program by noon.
4 There is a great need to trust in every man there.

Number Practice

5 We have a new mortgage. He still needs $3 758.90.
6 Tom ran the race in 2.5 min while Ty took 2.8 min.
7 Some Ontario codes: K9H 4G7, M5H 1W1 and P9A 3M2.

• • • • 1 • • • • 2 • • • • 3 • • • • 4 • • • • 5 • • • • 6 • • • • 7 • • • • 8 • • • • 9 • • • 10

Reach to the # Key

8 ddd d3d d#d d#d ddd ### d#d d#d #d# .#d#d d#d d# #d
9 #1 #2 #3 #4 #5 #6 #7 #8 #9 #10 #11 #12 #13 #14 #15
10 We have paid these invoices: #75, #578 and #1423.

Concentrate on Correct Spelling

11 That man gave his <u>niece</u> a bright shiny new <u>nickel</u>.
12 The <u>ninetieth</u> <u>piece</u> has just now been reassembled.

Two-Minute Timing

		1 CW 2

    A dog can be a good pet if one is prepared to | 10 | 10 | 5
spend the time needed to train and care for it. A | 20 | 20 | 10
small dog is often the best choice for people that | 30 | 30 | 15
live in a town or city. | 35 | 35 | 17

    Often people will buy a cute pup as a pet for | 10 | 45 | 22
a small child. This pup grows and the child isn't | 20 | 55 | 27
able to give the care a dog needs. The dog is now | 30 | 65 | 32
looking for a new home. | 35 | 70 | 35

• • • • 1 • • • • 2 • • • • 3 • • • • 4 • • • • 5 • • • • 6 • • • • 7 • • • • 8 • • • • 9 • • • 10   1 min

    1   2   3   4   5   2 min

Production 1

Review keying an outline in Lessons 66-67 pages 180-181. Key the agenda on a feel sheet of letter-size paper. Your word processing software may have an outline option.

DASMUND ENTERPRISES LTD.

SHAREHOLDERS ANNUAL GENERAL MEETING

Head Office

Toronto, *ontario* October 16, 19--

center

13:00

AGENDA

1. Minutes of the Annual General Meeting, October 12, 19-- (last year)

2. Approval of the Minutes

3. Business arising from Minutes

4. Reports
   a. Chairperson of the Board of Directors
   b. President
   c. Vice-President
   d. Treasurer
   e. Secretary
   f. Regional Directors
      3 { Maritimes
      Quebec
      Ontario
      Manitoba
      Saskatchewan
      Alberta
      British Columbia

5. Elections of Officers for 19--/-- (Use next year's date)

6. New Business
   a. Dividend distribution
   b. Capital spending requirements
      3 { this year
      five-year projections
   c. Recommendations from reports

7. Other Business

SC

Did you ask your instructor or read the software manual to determine if there is an outline option?

Keying on Lines

Move your cylinder forwards or backwards by depressing the left cylinder knob or the variable line spacer. Key slightly above the line. Use your alignment scale as a guide.

This is too high.

This is too low.

This is just right.

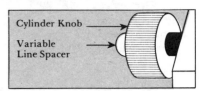

Cylinder Knob

Variable
Line Spacer

Key the following with appropriate underscores. Then remove the paper from the machine and reinsert to key on the lines.

Name: _____

Address: _____

_____

Postal Code: _____

Telephone No: _____

Name of School or College: _____

Marina got first prize in the fair.

The invoices amounted to $216.20 and $136.15 .

A cheque for $35.35 was sent to Joe.

Three boys' names are: _____

Three tree fruits are _____

My favorite vegetables are _____ and _____

Make sure Johan gets three hundred dollars ($300).

Two of my friends are: _____ and _____

Business Forms

Many business documents are of a similar nature. Rather than key an individual table for each document, a standardized form is often designed.

Keying Business Forms

1. Determine if your left margin should align with the form heading or the body of the form.
   - If the left margin aligns with the form heading, set the margin stop two spaces after the colon of the longest word.
   - If the left margin aligns with the form body, set the margin stop for the first column.
2. In the form heading, set tab stops two spaces after the colon of the longest word in any column.
3. In the body, set tab stops according to the following rules:
   - Number columns line up at the right with at least 1 or 2 blank spaces between the vertical line on the form and the number.
   - Word columns line up at the left with at least 1 or 2 blank spaces between the vertical line on the form and the word.
   - Set a common left margin and common tab stops, if possible for the heading and the body of the form.
   - Columns may be centered visually under the column headings in the body.

Practice

SC

Did you ask your instructor if you should do this exercise if you are using a computer?

Sp

favorite or *favourite*
Know the preference in your part of Canada and be consistent.

SC

If you are using a computer, you may be asked to design and create master forms to use with the following exercises. Once created, the master form would be retrieved for the production exercise.

Assess Your Improvement
Set spacing at 2. Key at least one 3-min *or* 5-min timing. Circle all errors and calculate gross words per minute. Record the timing on your Progress Chart.

	CW	3

All people find themselves having to do portions of as-
signments or jobs which they do not find stimulating. Those
kinds of activities can become more pleasant by applying raw
doses of self-discipline. This does not mean merely regula-
ting outward behavior. Gritting teeth usually helps little.
What we are referring to is applying a healthy dosage of in-
ner discipline to the basic attitude.

A first step to make this change must come from the basic realization that we are no longer children. When in our
teens, our reaction to parental authority was often one that
asserted our need for independence. We now have to reassess
our motives for reacting in a similar way and accept the re-
sponsibilities that go along with the package of adult life.
One of these is the realization that not all activity can be
of free choice and without regulation and restriction.

As Saint Paul once wrote: "When I was a child, I spake
as a child, understood as a child, I thought as a child; but
when I became a man, I put away childish things." All of us
now have to accept the challenge to attack the task in front
of us even though a basic childish urge would cause us to go
play. Time is allotted for leisure, much more than ever before in the history of labor. Therefore, we need to reshape
our attitudes toward the task at hand and learn to enjoy it.

12	12	4
24	24	8
36	36	12
48	48	16
60	60	20
72	72	24
79	79	26
12	91	30
24	103	34
36	115	38
48	127	42
60	139	46
72	141	50
84	153	54
95	164	57
12	176	61
24	188	65
36	200	69
48	212	73
60	224	77
72	236	81
84	248	85
96	260	89

• • • • 1 • • • • 2 • • • • 3 • • • • 4 • • • • 5 • • • 6 • • • 7 • • • • 8 • • • • 9 • • • 10 • • • 11 • • • 12   1 min

1   2   3   4   3 min

SI   1.48
AWL 4.43

4. Double space between the horizontal line and the form body. It is acceptable to single space if the body is long.
5. Single space the form body. Double space the form body if the body is short.

Refer to Production 1 for the correct method of keying one type of business form called an *invoice*.

Invoices

An invoice is a bill sent to a customer for money owing from a sales transaction. The invoice shows the quantity, unit price (price per item), total amount owed for each item purchased, and the total owed by the customer for all items purchased.

Production 1

Key the following invoice on the form provided in the Working Papers.

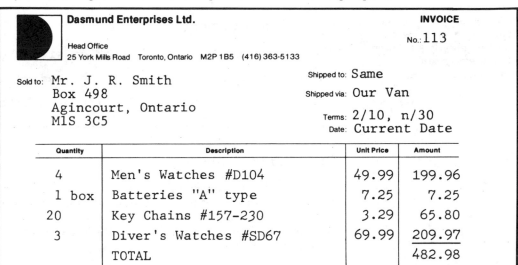

	Dasmund Enterprises Ltd.				INVOICE

Head Office
25 York Mills Road   Toronto, Ontario   M2P 1B5   (416) 363-5133

No.: 113

Sold to: Mr. J. R. Smith
Box 498
Agincourt, Ontario
M1S 3C5

Shipped to: Same
Shipped via: Our Van
Terms: 2/10, n/30
Date: Current Date

Quantity	Description	Unit Price	Amount
4	Men's Watches #D104	49.99	199.96
1 box	Batteries "A" type	7.25	7.25
20	Key Chains #157-230	3.29	65.80
3	Diver's Watches #SD67	69.99	209.97
	TOTAL		482.98

Production 2

Key the following information on the invoice form that is provided in the Working Papers. Use the current date.

Sold to: Red Deer College
Box 5005
Red Deer, Alberta
T4N 5H5

Ship to: Red Deer College   #114
Red Deer, Alberta
T4N 5H5

Terms: 2/10, n/30

Ship via: Byers Transport

14	Electronic Typewriters	$1050	$14700
4	Dataphone Transcribers	420	1680
8	Calculators	175	1400
2	Desk-top Copiers	1200	2400

Production Practice

SC

If you are using a computer you may be asked to create a master invoice which would be saved and retrieved for each production exercise.

SC

What is your employer's preference for keying dates? Alphabetic dating: *month day year* as November 5, 19 - -
Numeric dating: *year month day* as 19 - - 11 05
Dasmund uses numeric dating.

The dollar sign ($) is not keyed on business forms.

SC

Did you remember that dollar signs are not keyed on business forms?

SC

Did you calculate the total?

Agenda/Minutes

60-space line
Spacing: 1 and 2
Key two 30-s timings on
each line *or* repeat each line
three times.

Skill Building

Key two 30-s timings on
line 3 of Accuracy Improvement. Circle any errors. If
you have more than one
error for each timing, continue with the Accuracy
Improvement drill. If you
have one error or less on
each timing, key the Speed
Improvement drill and
concentrate on speed.

Right-Hand Words

1 on up no in my him joy you lip oily minimum opinion monopoly

2 oh non mink milk pulpy kinky pully million up plum loon pump

Accuracy Improvement

3 added calls agreed differ getting proceed planning currently

4 debate mop exacts poll estates polo carefree plunk addresses

5 by the 90 so then 34 to 56 for all 103 give them 5 to the 74

Speed Improvement

6 The operation mentioned a problem with the original records.

7 Cotton, coffee and copper are shipped on approval as needed.

8 Jill wore a rare mink stole with a pink scarf to the formal.

• • • • 1 • • • • 2 • • • • 3 • • • • 4 • • • • 5 • • • • 6 • • • • 7 • • • • 8 • • • • 9 • • • •10 • • • •11 • • •12

Stroking Practice

1. Turn to the Stroking Practice, page 414.
2. Key the lines selected by your instructor or the letter combinations giving you difficulty in the drills just completed.
3. Students on individual progress should select lines from 31 to 45.
4. Key each line twice.

Semicolon

Use a semicolon:

1. when two independent clauses are **not** joined by a coordinating conjunction (and, but, or, nor).
2. when two independent clauses are joined by a transitional expression. Use a semicolon before the transitional expression and a comma after it. (however, therefore, although)
3. to separate items in a series that has internal punctuation.

Key each line once,
concentrating on correct
punctuation.

9 My work isn't done; I must stay home and try to complete it.

10 Sue-Ann hopes to pass her exam; however, she is not worried.

11 I visited Olds, Alberta; Gimli, Manitoba; and Peel, Ontario.

12 He read "Western Lights"; I read "North to Great Bear Lake."

34

Business Forms

50-space line
Spacing: 1 and 2
Key two 1-min timings on each line *or* repeat each line three times.

Alternate-Hand Words

1 did key the buck fuel lend rush eight right panels
2 die lay tie burn girl lens soak field rigid ritual

Skill Building

Key two 1-min timings on each line *or* repeat each line three times.

Number Practice

3 The discount of $40 is more than 0.5 of the total.
4 The times for the swim were: 2.3 min and 3.7 min.
5 All Atlantic codes: E1B 5B1, A1E 3X1 and B1A 2E5.

Common-Word Sentences

Key two 30-s timings on each line *or* repeat each line twice. Key these drills as quickly as you can.

6 We are required to pay our tax by the end of June.
7 All of the order should be here by the next month.
8 We will never know how much has been paid for aid.

• • • • 1 • • • • 2 • • • • 3 • • • • 4 • • • • 5 • • • • 6 • • • • 7 • • • • 8 • • • • 9 • • • • 10

Concentrate on Correct Spelling

Key each underlined word three times. Key each line once concentrating on the underlined words.

9 It was <u>embarrassing</u> that we had not <u>enclosed</u> them.
10 We need <u>personnel</u> who can <u>perform</u> well on the job.

Graduated Speed Practice

1. Turn to Lesson 25, page 67.
2. Drill on the appropriate Graduated Speed Practice.

Two-Minute Timing

Timing

Set spacing at 2. Key two 2-min timings. Circle all errors and calculate gross words per minute. Record the better timing on your Progress Chart.

SI   1.14
AWL 4.05

	1	2
The air was strangely still as we rushed from	10	5
the boat to our waiting truck. Thick black clouds	20	10
hung over the lake where we had been sailing. One	30	15
large ragged flash streaked above our heads. Then	30	20
a crashing sound of thunder came. As Pai tried to	50	25
fit the key in the lock on the truck door, the big	60	30
clouds opened and we got soaked.	66	33

• • • • 1 • • • • 2 • • • • 3 • • • • 4 • • • • 5 • • • • 6 • • • • 7 • • • • 8 • • • • 9 • • • • 10   1 min
       1   2   3   4   5   2 min

Kelly, Tom. "Got a letter? Get a bargain," <u>Canadian Secretary</u>, March 1988, pp. 18-20.

Kelly, Tom. "Data links for the lay user," <u>Office Equipment & Methods</u>, January/February, 1988, pp. 49-51.

*Insert→ Mortensen, Erik. "Adapting Electronic Mail To Management's Needs," <u>Administrative Management</u>, August, 1987, pp. 26-31.

Pratt, Ron. "Ride the next wave," <u>Office Equipment & Methods</u>, March, 1988, p. 36.

Reiman, Tyrus. "Send your fax in 3 secs flat," <u>Office Equipment & Methods</u>, June, 1988, pp. 36-39.

Rowh, Mark C. "Today's Copiers: They Cost Less and Do More," <u>The Office</u>, March, 1988, pp. 71-72.

Totty, Patrick. "Facsimile: the Hottest Office Machine to Date," <u>The Office</u>, February, 1988, pp. 15-16, 24.

*Place, Irene and Yetha, Alice M. <u>Management of the Electronic Office</u>, Fourth Ed. Englewood Cliffs, N.J.: Prentice-Hall, 1986.

Production 3

The report, <u>Electronic Mail</u>, was written by Michelle De Meeres of Dasmund, Montreal Office. This paper will be presented to the AMS meeting, St. Stephen's Club on September 13, 19--. Copies of the paper will be duplicated for distribution at the meeting. Key a title page.

Credit Memorandum

A credit memorandum is issued when goods are returned that were originally recorded on an invoice. A credit memo is issued to reduce the original charges made to the customer.
1. Review the instructions for Keying Business Forms in Lesson 33.
2. Study the example of a credit memorandum in Production 1.

Production Practice

SC

If you are using a computer you may be asked to create a master credit memorandum which would be saved and retrieved for each production exercise.

Production 1

Key the following credit memorandum on the form provided in the Working Papers.

 Dasmund Enterprises Ltd.   No.: 73

Head Office
25 York Mills Road   Toronto, Ontario   M2P 1B5   (416) 363-5133

CREDIT MEMORANDUM

To: Red Deer College   Date: Current Date
     Box 5005
     Red Deer, Alberta
     T4N 5H5

Your Account has been credited as follows:

Quantity	Description	Unit Price	Amount
2	Electronic Typewriters	900.00	1800.00
1	Printing Calculator	175.00	175.00
	TOTAL		1975.00

Production 2

Key the following information on the credit memorandum that is provided in the Working Papers. Use the current date.

To: Mr. J.R. Smith   # 72
    Box 498
    Agincourt, Ontario M1S 3C5

1 Diver's Watch #SD67 $69.99

SC

What is your employer's preference for keying dates?

SC

Did you omit the dollar sign when you keyed the credit memo?

Production 1

Review the keying of a table of contents in Lessons 74-75 page 200. Use the information in Lessons 123-124 and key a table of contents for the report, <u>Electronic Mail</u>. Fill in the page numbers for the first topics to agree with the first part of the report you keyed in Lessons 125-26.

Table of Contents   *Page*

A replacement for postal services? . . . .

Growth in the market . . . .

Use of facsimile equipment . . . .

#> Centralized networks . . . .
Determining communication patterns *4*

System interconnects *4*

Interface with facsimile *5*

Range of features *7*

Need for training *8*

Future trends *10*

<u>Bibliography</u> *12*

Production 2

Review the keying of a bibliography in Lessons 74-75 pages 199-200. Key the following bibliography.

```
                         BIBLIOGRAPHY
```
 TS

```
Bakst, Shelley.  "FACSIMILE:  The Buying Boom Accelerates," The
        Office, May, 1988, pp. 15 - 20.

Gross, Daniel.  "The Emerging Trends in Facsmile Technology," The
        Office, February, 1988, pp. 58 - 59.

Kalow, Samuel J. "Copiers:  A New Era Will Be Ushered In," The
        Office, January, 1988, p. 84.
```

Production Practice

SC

Did you ask your instructor or read the software manual to determine if there is a special feature for doing a Table of Contents.

SC

Did you ask your instructor or read the software manual to determine if there is a special feature for doing a Bibliography?

35 Business Forms

50-space line
Spacing: 1 and 2
Key two 1-min timings on
each line *or* repeat each line
three times.

Skill Building

Key two 30-s timings on
each line *or* key each line
twice.

Key two 30-s timings on
each line *or* key each line
twice.

Key two 30-s timings on
each line *or* key each line
twice.

Key two 1-min timings on
each line *or* repeat each line
three times.

Key each underlined word
three times. Key each line
once concentrating on the
underlined words.

Timing

Set spacing at 2. Key two
2-min timings. Circle all
errors and calculate gross
words per minute. Record
the better timing on your
Progress Chart.

SI   1.10
AWL 3.74

Alternate-Hand Words

1 dig man toe busy goal lent sick fight risks signal
2 dog men tow city gown maid sign forms rocks social

One-Hand Words

3 as my ad you tax ink few null test pool race imply
4 aw up we pin eat non rad loon feed kink crew onion

Alternate-Hand Word Sentences

5 A rigid tow rod is an aid for their tight signals.
6 A fish odor by the lake did rid them of a big bug.

Common-Word Sentences

7 They want to be the first to give such a new gift.
8 The whole church board will meet to discuss music.

Number Practice

9 Order now. The price is $25.90 instead of $45.69.
10 Some Western codes: V3J 6W6, T8N 2S4 and R9A 0B3.

• • • • 1 • • • • 2 • • • • 3 • • • • 4 • • • • 5 • • • • 6 • • • • 7 • • • • 8 • • • • 9 • • • • 10

Concentrate on Correct Spelling

11 The <u>financial</u> statement is done <u>except</u> for keying.
12 Her <u>fiery</u> temper is always <u>grievous</u> to the people.

Two-Minute Timing

	1	2

The night was still and warm as Gena made her
way along the lane that led through the tall trees
to the door of her quaint log cabin. How good she
felt knowing that this long hike at last was done.
Now Gena could take off her heavy pack and stretch
the muscles along her back. At last she could sit
and enjoy a hot cup of tea.

1	2
10	5
20	10
30	15
40	20
50	25
60	30
65	33

• • • • 1 • • • • 2 • • • • 3 • • • • 4 • • • • 5 • • • • 6 • • • • 7 • • • • 8 • • • • 9 • • • • 10   1 min

1 • • • • • • 2 • • • • • • 3 • • • • • • 4 • • • • • • 5   2 min

Table of Contents/ Bibliography

Alternate-Hand Words

1 me but maid burnt right turkey bicycle authentic body burlap

2 of bus lent burns rifle theory bifocal endowment born handle

One-Minute Timings

1. Turn to the One-Minute Timings, page 421.
2. Select the paragraph that you think you can complete in one minute.
3. Key the One-Minute Timing as a drill.
4. If you had two or more errors, practice Accuracy Improvement.
   If you had fewer than two errors, practice Speed Improvement.

Skill Building

Key two 30-s timings on line 3 of Accuracy Improvement. Circle any errors. If you have more than one error for each timing, continue with the Accuracy Improvement drill. If you have one error or less on each timing, key the Speed Improvement drill and concentrate on speed.

Accuracy Improvement

3 creeds hop evaded hump erratic holy averages plump addressee

4 hop my hook ploy plump plunk imply minimum up lion lily oily

5 glass speed accept excess install dollars accident corrected

Speed Improvement

6 The staff barber barged past the jolly imp and hit the lily.

7 Normally the meeting is called to assess the current losses.

8 For this dress you need 3.40 m of the 90 cm width of fabric.

• • • • 1 • • • • 2 • • • • 3 • • • • 4 • • • • 5 • • • • 6 • • • • 7 • • • • 8 • • • • 9 • • • • 10 • • • • 11 • • • • 12

The Apostrophe

An apostrophe is used:

1. in a contraction. The apostrophe is keyed at the point where a letter has been omitted when two words are joined.
2. to show possession (singular and plural).

Key each line once, concentrating on correct punctuation.

9 Jerry isn't here and Yvonne won't be able to stay very long.

10 The ladies' teams try to beat the men's teams in ice hockey.

Statement of Account

A statement of account is a summary of the transactions for a customer during a specific period of time. It shows the invoices charged, the credit memo issued, any money paid on the account, and the balance owing at the date of the statement.
1. Review the instructions for Keying Business Forms in Lesson 33.
2. Study the example of a statement of account in Production 1.

Production Practice

SC

If you are using a computer you may be asked to create a master statement of account which would be saved and retrieved for each production exercise.

SC

What is your employer's preference for keying dates?

Production 1

Key the following statement of account on the form provided in the Working Papers.

Dasmund Enterprises Ltd.

STATEMENT OF ACCOUNT

Head Office
25 York Mills Road   Toronto, Ontario   M2P 1B5   (416) 363-5133

In Account with: Mr. J. R. Smith
Box 498
Agincourt, Ontario
M1S 3C5

Date: Last day of current month

Please return this stub with your cheque: Amount Enclosed $

Date	Reference	Credits	Charges	Balance
19-- 10 01	Balance Forward			1 217.00
19-- 10 23	Invoice #113		482.98	1 699.98
19-- 10 25	Credit Memo #72	69.99		1 629.99
19-- 10 31	Balance Due			1 629.99

Production 2

Key the following information on the statement of account that is provided in the Working Papers.

To: Red Deer College
Box 5005
Red Deer, Alberta
T4N 5H5

Date: June 30, 19--

June 1	Balance Forward		$17 520
June 14	Invoice #114	$20180	
June 26	Credit Memo #73	1975	

SC

Did you total the statement?

Production

Key the following report in non-bound format. If your software has graphing capabilities, use them to prepare the graph at the end. If not, use your machine, a ruler, and a sharp pencil.

THE COST OF A BUSINESS LETTER

The office worker in training, or even, sometimes one in the work force, has the mistaken notion that the cost of a business letter is made up of the simple total of the cost of the paper and the cost of the stamp. These costs are merely the least expensive of some more indirect costs.

To find the true cost of producing a business letter, consider these additional costs. The largest portion of the costs relates to the salaries of the individuals involved in the letter production. For example, the originator of the letter, if an executive of a company, has a large dollar figure associated with each minute of his or her time. The cost of a secretary, or other employee, although usually paid in a lower salary bracket, still adds the next highest cost factor in letter production. An employee who does not have the best of clerical skills can add a considerable cost to the total every time there is time taken out for corrections. A letter which needs re-keying can double this portion of the total expense.

Added to the costs already mentioned, there are many other components which add to the real cost of a business letter. These costs include equipment and the equipment maintenance, the office space required and the associated costs of rent, insurance, etc.

The cost of a business letter has risen drastically over the past few years. The following graph, based on research of The Dartnell Corporation, illustrates more fully the real cost of producing a business letter. Employees can be a valuable asset to their firm if they can initiate ways of streamlining the communication process and take steps to produce better office efficiency.

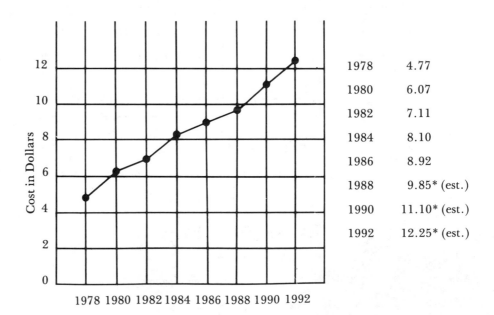

Year	Cost
1978	4.77
1980	6.07
1982	7.11
1984	8.10
1986	8.92
1988	9.85* (est.)
1990	11.10* (est.)
1992	12.25* (est.)

*Estimate not from Dartnell

Skill Building / Interoffice Memorandum

One-Hand Words

1 far joy tar non war nil tea pill east link arrears
2 fat you rat nun ads non tar hulk deaf loop asserts
3 fed hum dab ohm add nun sex pull fast lump attract

Alternate-Hand Words

4 big fit rid urns dock idle odor blame forks emblem
5 bit fix rig when down jams owns blend forms embody
6 bow for rod wish dual kept paid borne furor enamel

Alternate-Hand Sentences

7 We go to the lake to fish and to visit the island.
8 The city pays the eight chairmen to make bus maps.
9 The girls fit, make or mend formal gowns for them.

Number Practice

10 We plan for 25 children, 16 adults and 9 pet dogs.
11 We meet at 06 10 11:30, which is morning, June 10.
12 Deliver this letter to 76 - 12 St. by 13:00 today.

Common-Word Sentences

13 The house that is up for sale is built with stone.
14 The hot beach was lined with scores of tanned men.
15 Meat tastes good when it is cooked on open flames.

Alphabetic Sentences

16 How high could Zeke jump when he first got back to
   the quaint little village on the sixth of January?

17 We have just found six ways to freeze the spinach,
   kale or red cabbage more quickly than ever before.

• • • • 1 • • • • 2 • • • • 3 • • • • 4 • • • • 5 • • • • 6 • • • • 7 • • • • 8 • • • • 9 • • • • 10

Skill Building

60-space line
Spacing: 1 and 2
Key two 30-s timings on
each line *or* repeat each line
three times.

One-Hand Words

1 deface joy exerts mill exerted hill deserves onion attracted

2 defect you extras pill fastest Jill deserved pupil decreased

Graduated Speed Practice

Turn to the Graduated Alphanumerical Speed Practice, page 403. Select a sentence that you think you can key in the time indicated by your instructor.

Alphabetic Sentences

3 The lazy fox jumped quickly over the big stone wall when the

lone coyote came into sight.

4 The exhaust fumes from the ancient bulldozer pollute the air

and are blocking my view of the jittery squirrels.

Number Practice

5 Jack Wong is over 175 cm tall and has a mass of about 81 kg.

6 About 15 of the 90 new campers are registered for camp 2436.

Selected Letter Practice

1. Analyze your errors in the Alphabetic Sentences and Number Practice.
2. Choose the letters or numbers giving you difficulty or causing errors.
3. Turn to page 405 and select the appropriate Selected Letter and Number Practice.
4. Key each line twice.

Accuracy Building

Key two 30-s timings on each line concentrating on accuracy as your goal. Students on individual progress should key each line three times with the accuracy goal in mind.

Accuracy Improvement

7 rooms mills assure assets billing install assembly referring

8 go aid kept world title flange signals entitlement worn them

Speed Improvement

9 The cow, the lamb and the hens kept us awake half the night.

10 She planned to collect a dollar for all noon dinner tickets.

• • • • 1 • • • • 2 • • • • 3 • • • • 4 • • • • 5 • • • 6 • • • 7 • • • • 8 • • • 9 • • • • 10 • • • 11 • • • 12

Skill Building

Key two 30-s timings on line 7 of Accuracy Improvement. Circle any errors. If you have more than one error for each timing, continue with the Accuracy Improvement drill. If you have one error or less on each timing, key the Speed Improvement drill and concentrate on speed.

Three- or Five-Minute Timing

Turn to the timing in Unit VII of your Working Papers. Students without Working Papers should key the timing in Lessons 123-24, page 337.

Key each underlined word three times. Key each line once concentrating on the underlined words.

18 Can you <u>achieve</u> the <u>allotted</u> goals for each title?

19 No <u>committee</u> member can <u>conceive</u> that to be right.

Graduated Speed Practice

1. Turn to Lesson 25, page 67.
2. Drill on the appropriate Graduated Speed Practice.

Two-Minute Timing

Timing

Set spacing at 2. Key at least one 2-min timing. Circle all errors and calculate gross words per minute. Record the timing on your Progress Chart.

	1	CW	2

        There is nothing like a real painting to give   10 10   5
your room the look you wanted to achieve. Adopt a   20 20 10
theme that you can live with the year around and a   30 30 15
painting which portrays that theme for you.   39 39 19

        Once you have purchased the picture and frame   10 49 24
for your room, then it is time to add other extras   20 59 29
to the decor. The best choice of color will focus   30 69 34
on those in your picture and complement them.   39 78 39

• • • • 1 • • • • 2 • • • • 3 • • • • 4 • • • • 5 • • • 6 • • • 7 • • • 8 • • • 9 • • • 10 **1 min**
          1   2   3   4   5 **2 min**

SI   1.24
AWL 4.22

Sp

color or *colour*
Know the preference in your part of Canada and be consistent.

Interoffice Memorandum

An interoffice memorandum is a written communication used for correspondence between departments and individuals within a company. It is faster and cheaper than keying a letter because the memorandum is keyed on a printed form using letter quality paper.

Keying the Interoffice Memorandum

1. Determine if the left margin should align with the beginning of the printed lines in the heading or the colon following the printed line in the form heading.
   • Use your judgment as both ways are acceptable.
   • Set the right margin the same width as the left margin to center the information on the memorandum.
2. Triple space between the heading and the body.
3. Single space the body. Double space between paragraphs. It is acceptable to double space the body if the message is short. If double spacing is used, indent the paragraphs.
4. Key the sender's initials at the close of the memo. A formal signature is not usually used.
5. Key the operator's initials at the left margin.

11 Deme, Mark, Bob, and Alice will drive to Halifax and Queens.

12 It is a long, hard bicycle ride from Jasper to Maligne Lake.

13 While the manager explained the project, the employee slept.

14 Ms. Wilms, the personnel manager, will see you very shortly.

Comparison of the Two Methods of Referencing

Method 1 (See *Reference Guide for Footnotes*, Lesson 123-24, page 338.)

In the modern office, the office worker "may not need to become a data processing expert, but . . . should be aware of what a computer can do and how it does it."[1] This . . .

[1]Pat Smith et al, <u>Pitman Office Handbook</u> (Toronto: Copp Clark Pitman Ltd., 1988), p. 79.

Method 2 (See *Reference Guide for In-text References*, Lesson 71-73, page 193.)

In the modern office, the office worker "may not need to become a data processing expert, but . . . should be aware of what a computer can do and how it does it" (Smith, 1988, p. 79). This . . .

Production Practice

Production 1

Turn to Lessons 123-24, pages 338-341 and re-key the report using in-text references (APA Style). This method is faster for the operator. The former method is more convenient for the reader to make a quick and easy reference of the quoted material.

Production 2

Key a Bibliography for the report completed in Production 1. The Reference Guide for a Bibliography is in Lessons 74-75.

If you are using a computer you may be asked to create a master interoffice memorandum which would be saved and retrieved for each production exercise.

Production 1

Key the following interoffice memorandum on the form provided in the Working Papers.

 Dasmund Enterprises Ltd.　　　　　　**INTEROFFICE MEMORANDUM**

To: Store Managers　　　　　　From: Thomas Rollins
Dept.:　　　　　　　　　　　　Dept.:

Subject: Expense Accounts　　　　Date: Current Date

TS ↓

It has been brought to my attention that expense accounts are being submitted without the appropriate receipts and authorized signature.

Would you please explain to your sales staff that we cannot pay expense claims without the appropriate receipts attached. Also please be sure you have authorized these expense claims before they are forwarded to us for payment.

These simple checks will help us process the claims more quickly and we will be able to reimburse the salesperson involved almost immediately. Thanks for your cooperation.

DS ↓ T.R.

oi ↓ DS

Production 2

Key the following interoffice memorandum on the form provided in the Working Papers.

Thomas Rollins　　　　　　　　　　M. S. Dasmund

Expense Accounts

Thom, here are the expense accounts for my sales staff for last week. I have checked them and initialled them accordingly.

You will note that there are some receipts missing. This is because the staff were not made aware they needed them in time. They have assured me this will not happen again.

I was wondering if you had ever considered giving an advance to the sales staff at the beginning of each month. They could use this for their expenses and at the end of the month send a statement with either a cheque attached for the portion they did not spend or a request for money still owing to them. I know this would be greatly appreciated by my sales staff here.

M. D.

Reports with Footnotes

60-space line
Spacing: 1 and 2
Key two 30-s timings on each line *or* repeat each line three times.

One-Hand Words

1 wax nun sage lump swat plum sewer Jimmy barber null redrafts

2 wad ohm stab milk swab plop staff plump barges loom referred

One-Minute Timings

1. Turn to the One-Minute Timings, page 421.
2. Select the paragraph that you think you can complete in one minute.
3. Key the One-Minute Timing as a drill.
4. If you had two or more errors, practice Accuracy Improvement.
   If you had fewer than two errors, practice Speed Improvement.

Skill Building

Key two 30-s timings on line 3 of Accuracy Improvement. Circle any errors. If you have more than one error for each timing, continue with the Accuracy Improvement drill. If you have one error or less on each timing, key the Speed Improvement drill and concentrate on speed.

Accuracy Improvement

3 or bug lens borne world social element entitlement them then

4 set all 50 with the 35 but not 90 of 98 all the 52 of the 62

5 ever reeds wares estate sacred graders averages starters eat

Speed Improvement

6 We understand that we can lease or purchase this new office.

7 Joy and Lily feared that the extra staff would create worry.

8 The height of the shelf kept them from seeing the new gowns.

• • • • 1 • • • • 2 • • • • 3 • • • • 4 • • • • 5 • • • • 6 • • • 7 • • • • 8 • • • • 9 • • • •10 • • •11 • • •12

The Comma

A comma helps clarify a sentence, and there are many rules for using the comma. Here are a few of the basic rules.

Use a comma:
1. before a coordinate conjunction such as *and, but, or,* or *nor* which joins two independent clauses in a compound sentence.
2. to separate three or more items in a series (words, phrases, or clauses).
3. to separate two or more consecutive adjectives that modify the same noun. Never place a comma between the last adjective and the noun it modifies.
4. after an introductory phrase or an introductory subordinate clause in a sentence.
5. to set off a parenthetical or transitional expression (word, phrase, or clause) from the rest of the sentence.
6. to indicate divisions in dates, geographical references, and addresses.

Key each line once, concentrating on correct punctuation.

9 I want black coffee, but Mary would really prefer clear tea.

10 This letter was sent from Barrie, Ontario on March 22, 1990.

Production Practice

50-space line
Spacing: 1 and 2

Key two 1-min timings on each sentence *or* repeat each sentence three times. Every alphabetic character is included in each sentence.

Alphabetic Sentences

1 Bring a dozen sharp porcupine quills to fix to our jacket trim; always try for our very neatest work.

2 This quiz isn't very hard if all answered problems are clear; jot them on the top of six blank pages.

• • • • 1 • • • • 2 • • • • 3 • • • • 4 • • • • 5 • • • • 6 • • • • 7 • • • • 8 • • • • 9 • • • • 10

Timing

Set spacing at 2. Key two 2-min timings. Circle all errors and calculate gross words per minute. Record the better timing on your Progress Chart.

SI   1.04
AWL 3.59

Two-Minute Timing

	1	2
We need to buy five new cars and three trucks	10	5
for our new firm. Do you have some for sale which	20	10
we could see next week? We hope to have all these	30	15
bought by the time our firm is ready to open doors	40	20
for the fall sales. We have great joy to think of	50	25
the speed with which the men have worked to meet a	60	30
date in early fall. The cars and trucks will give	70	35
us a chance to have the stock ready for the sales.	80	40

• • • • 1 • • • • 2 • • • • 3 • • • • 4 • • • • 5 • • • • 6 • • • • 7 • • • • 8 • • • • 9 • • • • 10   1 min
　　　　　1　　　　　2　　　　　3　　　　　4　　　　　5   2 min

Production Practice

Production 1

Key the following as an open table. Center on a half sheet of paper.

BANK OF MONTREAL
Term Savings Deposits
May 24, 19--

Account Number	Amount of Deposit	Due Date
376851	$10 000	November 30, 1991
748539	75 000	June 15, 1995
674385	8 000	December 1, 1998
823451	55 000	May 15, 1996
231451	15 000	May 1, 1992
475869	4 000	January 1, 1993

office machines are being replaced with newer streamlined desktop models which can fit easily into a well-planned office work station. However, even in the area of facsimile document transfer, we are left with this bit of warning:

As fax software improves, it will integrate with other applications such as word processing and database management. Eventually, it will be possible to send "mail-merged" facsimiles to lists of recipients, ushering in the era of "fax junk mail." (Gross, p. 58)

Electronic messaging systems are typically divided further into two distinct types of centralized networks. The first is a software package used privately within the firm, usually centralized from a mainframe or minicomputer. Examples of this type are IBM's "DISOSS" and "Professional Office System" (PROFS) and Digital's "All-In-One" and "VaxMail". The second system is typified by a growing number of public service systems which are accessible by subscription. Examples already available include "AT&T Mail," "Telemail," "EasyLink," and "Comet" (Mortensen, p. 29).

Electronic mail is still in its infancy and as more integrated software is made available to the ordinary user of a personal computer, there is no prediction what the end use will be. Philip Walker of the Electronic Mail Association, sums it up this way: "As innovations in communications software for personal computers make messaging even more convenient, more e-mail users are being brought on-line" (Walker, p. 120).

Production 2

Edit and key the following as an open table on a full sheet of paper. Center and arrange the items in the body in alphabetical order.

Title: GREENVIEW EMPLOYMENT AGENCY - spread center

Subtitle: Vacancies in office positions

May 17, 19--

Column Headings:	Position Open	Hours per Week	Experience Required	Weekly Salary
Body Items:	Bookkeeper	37.5	2 years	$440
	Clerk Administrative	37.5	1 year	470
	Clerk	35.0	none	350
	credit clerk	37.5	2 Years	410
	Records Manager	37.5	1 Year	500
	Receptionist	35.0	0-1 year	360
	Secretary	35.0	1 year	425
	Database Management Clerk	37.5	2 years	440
	Administrative Assistant	37.5	3 years	570
	Legal Secretary	35.0	5 years	580

Production 3

Key the following as a ruled table. Center on a full sheet of paper.

Directory of Microcomputer Software

Report	Report Number	No. of Pages	Publication Date
File Management	MS20-400-101	25	10/89
Authoring Systems	MS22-150-101	12	11/88
Energy Management	MS26-350-101	17	4/89
Law Enforcement	MS32-200-101	11	5/89
Property Management	MS34-300-101	7	3/89
Electronic Spreadsheets	MS38-400-101	12	6/89
Purchasing Management	MS40-450-101	14	12/88

ment distribution (including hard copy delivery) and voice-storage-and-forward technologies. (Mortensen, p. 26)

There has been a tremendous growth in the market for electronic messaging systems. According to The Electronic Mail Association, there were over five million users of computer-based messaging in North America in the late 1980's. For 1990, there were over 20 billion pieces of electronic mail predicted and 86 billion messages by the year 2000 (Mortensen, p. 26). As the computer technology becomes cheaper to purchase, electronic mail will continue to flourish at compounding rates.

One enhancement of the electronic messaging systems is the ability to send and receive files containing formatted documents such as spreadsheets and graphics. Draft reports can now contain excellent, readable tables and graphs which make editing reports easier and clarity of communications more sure. Not only do the "words" of the text get sent -- the exact machine tabulations, paragraphing, spacing between text, boldfacing, underlining, and centered titles are received in exactly the same format.

A further enhancement is the use of facsimile equipment which sends an exact copy of illustrations, typewritten documents, charts, or photographs. This long distance copying is accomplished by an electronic scanner which breaks images down into miniscule electronic components which can be transferred over telephone wires. A transceiver and modem are required at each station and these can be operated automatically to take advantage of lower off-hour transmission charges. The real beauty of this technology is in its smaller size. Older large

Production Practice

60-space line
Spacing: 1 and 2
Key two 1-min timings on
each sentence *or* repeat each
sentence three times. Every
alphabetic character is
included in each sentence.

Alphabetic Sentences

1 Jacques Vogel read a funny news story about a lazy silver fox which might try unusual naughty pranks.

2 A pastel mink jacket is a needless luxury; however you should quietly buy one in my size as our gift.

• • • • 1 • • • • 2 • • • • 3 • • • • 4 • • • • 5 • • • • 6 • • • • 7 • • • • 8 • • • • 9 • • • •10

Timing

Set spacing at 2. Key two
2-min timings. Circle all
errors and calculate gross
words per minute. Record
the better timing on your
Progress Chart.

Two-Minute Timing

	1	CW	2

Take a close look at your files. Can you see | 10 | 10 | 5
your way clear to keep them up to date or does the | 20 | 20 | 10
time seem to slip away each day? Do you leave the | 30 | 30 | 15
filing to the last, spending all your time on some | 40 | 40 | 20
other tasks and finding that the files get no real | 50 | 50 | 25
work? Have you tried to find a file and thought a | 10 | 60 | 30
quick look in the main file would do, only to find | 20 | 70 | 35
that the one you need is still on your desk? Take | 30 | 80 | 40
a few minutes and look at our ad which will show a | 40 | 90 | 45
real aid to your filing blues. | 46 | 96 | 48

• • • • 1 • • • • 2 • • • • 3 • • • • 4 • • • • 5 • • • • 6 • • • • 7 • • • • 8 • • • • 9 • • • •10   1 min
        1   2   3   4   5   2 min

SI   1.06
AWL 3.59

Production Practice

Production 1

Prepare an invoice for the following sale. Use the form provided in the Working Papers. If you are using a computer retrieve your master invoice OR display in appropriate table format. Be sure to total all necessary columns. Ship via CP Express.

On December 17, Dasmund Enterprises sold 2 IBM Electronic Typewriters, Serial Numbers 93116201 and 93116304 at $1395 each to Gestetner Corporation, 3000 Yonge Street, Toronto, Ontario M4N 2K5. They also sold them 3 four-drawer filing cabinets, #1707L at $520 each and one computer desk, #S3360 at $627. Invoice number 1527.

(Terms: 2/10, n/30)

Now key the following information as a side-bound report.

Electronic Mail

A Challenge in Office Communications

With the growing need for becoming more competitive in the world of business, there has arisen the need for immediate and accurate communications upon which to make those important decisions. Now that modern computer terminals and personal computers are an integral part of the modern office, managers must face the challenges of communicating in a more complex world. Electronic mail, although it has been around for some period of years, is being analyzed more thoroughly as a necessary communications tool for the future.

Originally, electronic mail was thought of in terms of a replacement for our postal services. Promoters of electronic mail "argued that companies would grab the chance to avoid the rising cost and erratic delivery of traditional mail" (Gordon, p. 35). Messages over the telephone wires, between computers, could be received instantaneously.

The sending of simple messages from place to place has increased considerably but this has not been the main usage of the systems. Not until the majority of clients are on compatible communications systems will we see this particular usage in wholesale quantity. Instead, it is in its related capabilities that we see electronic mail flourishing.

Electronic mail can be implemented with such diverse technologies as: facsimile, telex, micro-computers, communicating word processors, a variety of computer-based message systems, electronic docu-

Production 2

Use the forms provided in the Working Papers to record the following transactions. If you are using a computer retrieve your master interoffice memorandum OR display in appropriate table format.

 Dasmund Enterprises Ltd. INTEROFFICE MEMORANDUM

To: Accounts

From: Sales.

Subject: Exchange of Goods

Date: December 20, 19--

On December 20, Gestetner returned one cabinet for credit and purchased a smaller cabinet #1604L at $355. Prepare the appropriate credit memorandum (No. 715) and invoice (No. 1528) for this transaction.

Production 3

Use the form provided in the Working Papers to prepare the statement of account. If you are using a computer retrieve your master statement of account OR display in appropriate table format.

 Dasmund Enterprises Ltd. INTEROFFICE MEMORANDUM

To: L. Beauchamp

From: G. Porozny

Dept.: Accounts

Dept.: Accounting

Subject: December Statement

Date: January 3, 19--

Prepare a December statement of Account for Gestetner. The balance forwarded from November 30 is $1217. Cheques were received on December 10 for $717 and on December 19 for $500. Acknowledge the credit memorandum (No. 715) and the invoices (Nos. 1527 and 1528) appropriately.

Steps for Planning Footnotes

1. Use a backing sheet (extended to right of keying page) with the numbers keyed in reverse order at the bottom of the page.
2. Start keying the body of the report.
3. After keying the first footnote reference, calculate four blank lines (ruling line plus first footnote).
4. Add this number to six (bottom margin).

   6 + 4 = 10

   If there is only one footnote, stop keying the body of the report ten lines from the bottom of the page. Use the backing sheet as a guide.
5. If there is more than one footnote on a page, add three lines for each additional footnote.

   Example: three footnotes   6 + 4 + 3 + 3 = 16
               Stop keying 16 lines from the bottom of the page.
   Note: Calculate the allowance for the bottom margin you are keying.

Reference Guide for Footnotes

> **Footnotes**   Single space each footnote. Double space between footnotes and indent the first line 5-10 spaces.
> - If the footnotes are keyed on the same page as the body, they are separated from the body by a horizontal line with a single space above and below the line.
> - There should be a 6-10 line bottom margin after the footnotes are keyed.

Production Practice

Production

The report entitled ELECTRONIC MAIL is a business report which has been written in the APA style (see Lessons 74–75) where the references are keyed as in-text references. Change the format to the formal footnoting style where the references are recorded at the bottom of the page where they occur. If you need help, refer to Lessons 121–122.

Footnote/Bibliography Information for ELECTRONIC MAIL

Manuel Gordon, "The Mail Imperative," *Office Management & Automation*, January, 1988, pp. 25-27.

Irene Place and Alice M. Yetka, *Management of the Electronic Office*, 4th ed. (Englewood Cliffs, N.J: Prentice-Hall, 1986.

Philip Walker, "Electronic Mail Offers Growing Range of Uses," *The Office*, January, 1988, p. 120.

Gross, Daniel (1988, February). The Emerging Trends in Facsimile Technology. *The Office*, pp. 58-59.

Erik Mortensen, "Adapting Electronic Mail to Management Needs," *Administrative Management*, August, 1987, pp. 26-31.

Latocha, Walter (1988, August) Electronic Mail: Slow Start but Moving Now. *The Office*, p. 56.

Skill Building

One-Hand Words

1 fee pin eat ply ace him saw null fade milk average
2 few nip ear ill awe hop set loom stew mink awarded
3 gas lip raw mum age hum add moon raze noon baggage

Alternate-Hand Words

4 box fox row with duty keys pair burns girls enrich
5 bug fur rug work firm laid pans burnt gland entity
6 bus got rye worn fish lake pant chair gowns handle

Alternate-Hand Sentences

7 To rush a bushel box of corn to the men, augur it.
8 She also pays for a pair of socks and six turkeys.
9 Both firms wish to work with them to make signals.

· · · · 1 · · · · 2 · · · · 3 · · · · 4 · · · · 5 · · · · 6 · · · · 7 · · · · 8 · · · · 9 · · · 10

Number Practice

10 The new show starts at 19:30 and is over at 21:45.
11 Suphat drove 820.03 km, but Nizar drove 931.42 km.
12 N4B 7B7 and V9W 4T7 and L9C 6J4 were postal codes.

Common-Word Sentences

13 The stones are used to mark the edge of the lanes.
14 The old man had his red case with him at the door.
15 The vine has grown up the pole to the bird houses.

Alphabetic Sentences

16 Kaye wore her best quilted pyjamas as she realized
   there were just five or six nights to get to camp.

17 A keyboarding contest for zone five has seen quite
   a jump in male entrants with a total of sixty-six.

· · · · 1 · · · · 2 · · · · 3 · · · · 4 · · · · 5 · · · · 6 · · · · 7 · · · · 8 · · · · 9 · · · 10

Assess Your Improvement
Set spacing at 2. Key at least one 3-min *or* 5-min timing. Circle all errors and calculate gross words per minute. Record the timing on your Progress Chart.

1   CW   3

The world of business or the marketplace is neither the	12	12	4
gentle nor the forgiving learning place that you find in the	24	24	8
college. Are you surprised by this? The business world out	36	36	12
there is under no obligation to give you any set time length	48	48	16
or chance to prove yourself. In college you are assessed on	60	60	20
the grades you obtain for the most part. Much time and help	72	72	24
is generously heaped upon you to help you to do your best.	84	84	28

In the business world an evaluation will not wait for a	12	96	32
set of tests or assignments to come in. The main reason for	24	108	36
this is that businesses give out money instead of grades. A	36	120	40
big difference in attitude is found here because business is	48	132	44
not happy about giving away money that isn't earned from its	60	144	48
point of view. Unlike college, a business hires you because	72	156	52
of the immediate impression you make.	79	163	54

After you have been hired, you will be evaluated by the	12	175	58
immediate impressions you continue to make as much as by the	24	187	62
demonstration of skills and your attitude to your work. You	36	199	66
should try to cultivate a healthy set of skills in the areas	48	211	70
of personal communications and good manners. Taking part in	60	223	74
activities involving oral communications will help you raise	72	235	78
your self-confidence and allow you to gain good mileage from	84	247	82
the first impressions you make.	90	253	85

• • • • 1 • • • • 2 • • • • 3 • • • • 4 • • • • 5 • • • 6 • • • • 7 • • • • 8 • • • • 9 • • • • 10 • • • 11 • • • • 12   **1 min**
1　　　　　2　　　　　3　　　　4   **3 min**

SI   1.46
AWL 4.54

Footnotes

If necessary, review keying formal footnotes in Lessons 121-122, pp. 331-335. Determine when to stop keying the body of the report and insert the footnotes at the bottom of the page so that the page has a bottom margin of 6-10 lines. If you have a word processing software package that will help you to allow for the footnotes at the bottom of the page, ask your instructor if it is allowable to use it in this instance. It is important to know the method outlined below in case you have to prepare a report with formal footnoting on a typewriter or a microcomputer without a special word processing software package.

Concentrate on Correct Spelling

18 They are <u>dissatisfied</u> with the way ink <u>disappears</u>.

19 It is <u>convenient</u> to use a <u>dictionary</u> for spelling.

Graduated Speed Practice

1. Turn to Lesson 25, page 67.
2. Drill on the appropriate Graduated Speed Practice.

Timing

Set spacing at 2. Key as many 2-min timings as time permits. Circle all errors and calculate gross words per minute. Record the best timing on your Progress Chart.

SI 1.09
AWL 3.58

Two-Minute Timing

	1	2
We went for a week of camping in the big park	10	5
at the edge of the mountains. We found a spot off	20	10
to the north of Birch Mountain. It was well treed	30	15
and we had no close neighbors. We set up our tent	40	20
and prepared to relax and enjoy the peace. As our	50	25
last tent peg went in the ground, we heard a noise	60	30
at the back of our van. A black bear and two cubs	70	35
were eating our lunch.	74	37

. . . 1 . . . 2 . . . 3 . . . 4 . . . 5 . . . 6 . . . 7 . . . 8 . . . 9 . . . 10 **1 min**

1　　　　　2　　　　　3　　　　　4　　　　　5 **2 min**

Reports with Footnotes

60-space line
Spacing: 1 and 2
Key two 30-s timings on each line *or* repeat each line three times.

Alternate-Hand Words

1 and lay them also kept clay coal corn rifle right ambit amen

2 am aid man then born chair risks mend amend angle rigid also

Skill Building

Key two 30-s timings on line 3 of Accuracy Improvement. Circle any errors. If you have more than one error for each timing, continue with the Accuracy Improvement drill. If you have one error or less on each timing, key the Speed Improvement drill and concentrate on speed.

Accuracy Improvement

3 bow pan when city lend fork fuel girl shelf burnt eight city

4 hip in link hull mommy knoll Jimmy uphill no ohm mink pinion

5 errs reads wards erects safest garages attracts staggers add

Speed Improvement

6 We have 7 new 3-bedroom bungalows left, total price $98 679

7 Len and Ruth were busy with their problem of antique enamel.

8 Pull this car up the hill to that garage for grease and oil.

• • • • 1 • • • • 2 • • • • 3 • • • • 4 • • • • 5 • • • • 6 • • • • 7 • • • • 8 • • • • 9 • • • •10• • • •11• • • •12

Stroking Practice
1. Turn to the Stroking Practice, page 414.
2. Key the lines selected by your instructor or the letter combinations giving you difficulty in the drills just completed.
3. Students on individual progress should select lines from 16 to 30.
4. Key each line twice.

Quotation Marks
Quotation marks enclose:
1. a direct quotation or the exact words of a writer or speech.
2. titles of published material in magazines, books, or other media.
3. words for special emphasis.

Rules for the final punctuation at the end of quoted material are:
1. The comma and period are keyed inside the quotation marks.
2. The question mark can be keyed either inside or outside the quotation marks.
3. The semicolon and colon are keyed outside the quotation marks.

Key each line once, concentrating on correct punctuation.

9 Alice said, "Why are you taking those files to the meeting?"

10 The News Review featured an article called "Property Taxes."

11 "The car," said Samuel, "is not worth the price you stated."

12 My letter was stamped "Moved--Address Unknown" and returned.

40

Assess Your Progress

Common-Word Sentences

1 The craft store hired one of the girls from class.

2 It was hard to see them go at the end of the year.

Alphabetic Sentences

3 Most zebras do not enjoy wearing quilted or violet pyjamas; they often favor sexy striped nightgowns.

4 Clara will try to find one dark jade vase for Zane or she might pay quite a lot to get a crack fixed.

· · · · 1 · · · · 2 · · · · 3 · · · · 4 · · · · 5 · · · · 6 · · · · 7 · · · · 8 · · · · 9 · · · · 10

Two-Minute Timing

Assess Your Speed

Set spacing at 2. Key two 2-min timings. Circle all errors and calculate gross words per minute. Record the better timing on your Progress Chart.

SI   1.19
AWL 3.71

Did you achieve the unit objective of 25 words per minute with four errors or less?

		1 CW 2
In our country we have a great chance to be a		10 | 10 | 5
part of the great outdoors. We still have quite a		20 | 20 | 10
few places that do not have a lot of people living		30 | 30 | 15
there all year round.		34 | 34 | 17
One has only to choose what he wants to do in		10 | 44 | 22
the outdoors. There are many good places to camp,		20 | 54 | 27
canoe, fish, hike, or backpack. Any of these will		30 | 64 | 32
let you see a part of Canada that is off the usual		40 | 74 | 37
paths.		41 | 75 | 38

· · · · 1 · · · · 2 · · · · 3 · · · · 4 · · · · 5 · · · · 6 · · · · 7 · · · · 8 · · · · 9 · · · · 10   1 min
         1   2   3   4   5   2 min

Production 1

Key the following as an open table. Center on a half sheet of paper.

Important Wedding Anniversaries

years	Theme
5th	Silverware
10th	Diamond Jewel
15th	Watches
20th	Platinum
25th	Sterling Silver Jubilee
50th	Golden Jubilee
60th	Diamond Jubilee

#>

When a footnote refers to a work fully identified in an earlier footnote but not the one immediately preceding it, it may be shortened as follows: Author's surname, page number.[6]

Ellipsis. An ellipsis is another way of shortening quoted material by leaving out parts of the quote which you do not really want to use. An ellipsis is three spaced periods . . . and if the material left out comes at the end of a sentence, four spaced periods . . . .

There are many things to remember when writing and keying a report. A wise operator will keep a style guide close at hand.

---

[6]Campbell, p. 5.

Production 2

Key the following as a ruled table. Center on a full sheet of paper.

Can you complete
Production 2 in 15 min?

METRIC MEASUREMENT

Unit	Symbol	Relationship
kilometre	km	1 000 m
metre	m	10 dm
decimetre	dm	10 cm
centimetre	cm	10 mm
millimetre	mm	--
tonne	t	1 000 kg
kilogram	kg	1 000 g
gram	g	--
litre	L	1 000 mL
millilitre	mL	--

Production 3

Can you complete
Production 3 in 10 min?

Key the following invoice on the form provided in the Working Papers. If you are using a computer use the master invoice you created OR display using appropriate table format.

Sold To: J. C. Dallas and Company, 15703 – 116 Street, Edmonton, Alberta T5X 2M8
Invoice: #1971
Date: Today
Ship Via: Freight
Ship to: Same

12 only   Calculator watches   at   39.99 each = 479.88

6 only   Proctor-Silex Toasters #85 at 47.98 each = 287.88

24 only   Table lamps #674-553 at 49.99 each = 1199.76

Total Invoice   1967.52

Keying the Footnoted Material

Short Quotations. A short reference quoted in a report is keyed within the report by showing the quotation with quotation marks around the actual quote. An example of this style is given by Campbell when he explains, "Direct quotations shorter than four keyed lines, or less than a complete sentence, should be run into the text and enclosed in double quotation marks."[3]

Longer Quotations. A reference of more than three lines in length is considered a long reference and is displayed separately by leaving a double space, then indenting five spaces on each side and keying the quote with single spacing. Here is an example of how to show a long footnote quotation:

A bibliography at the end of a manuscript or a report typically lists all the works consulted in the preparation of the material as well as all the works that were previously cited in the footnotes. The format of a bibliography is also used for any list of titles, such as a list of recommended readings or a list of new publications.[4]

When preparing a formal report the author often uses the same reference sources more than once.

Ibid. When a footnote refers to a work that was fully identified in the footnote immediately preceding it, it may be shortened by use of the abbreviation Ibid. This replaces all parts that would otherwise be carried over. Ibid. is not usually underscored.[5]

---

[3]William Giles Campbell, et al., Form a Style: Theses, Reports, Term Papers, 6th Edition (Boston: Houghton Mifflin Company, 1982), p. 55.
[4]Sabin, p. 286.
[5]Ibid., p. 285.

Unit III

Objectives

1 The student will learn to format business letters in full block style with mixed punctuation.

2 The student will learn to format personal business letters in full block style.

3 The student will learn to format envelopes.

4 The student will learn to prepare copies of business letters.

5 The student will learn to correct errors.

6 The student will improve keyboard control.

7 The student will work toward developing a minimum speed of 30 words per minute with six errors or less on a three-minute timing.

This form of footnoting is very easy for the reader to follow; however, it is difficult for the operator not using a special word processing package. Be careful to have 6-10 lines left at the bottom margin after the footnote references have been completed. The footnote source must appear on the same page as the footnote material.

One helpful hint for the operator using this form of footnoting is to use a backing sheet. A backing sheet is made by inserting a blank sheet of paper and keying the number 1 in the extreme top right-hand corner. Then the number is followed by 2 on the next line. Twenty lines from the bottom of the page reverse the order until number 1 ends on the bottom line. By inserting this page behind the paper being keyed and with the numbers showing on the right-hand margin, you can check to see how many lines are left on the page. This will help you to decide where to stop keying the text of the report, and still have room to include the necessary footnotes on the page with an acceptable bottom margin.

Another form of footnoting is to put in parentheses the author's last name and the page number of the reference source immediately after the material is quoted in the report.[2] When using this method, footnotes are not numbered and a separate footnote page is not necessary. The alphabetized bibliography is the only reference list required in this format.

A third form of footnoting is simply showing a number in parentheses (1) following the quoted material. The source is then given on a separate footnote page at the end of the report. Footnotes are numbered consecutively within the report and then documented consecutively on the footnote page.

---

[2]Pat Smith, et al., Pitman Office Handbook (Toronto: Copp Clark, Pitman, 1982) p. 41.

41

''/!/Business Letters

60-space line
Spacing: 1 and 2
Key two 1-min timings on each line *or* repeat each line three times.

Alternate-Hand Words

1 by bib hen and both buck lamb pant audit risks cosign ritual

2 go bid jam aid turn flap make dial augur rocks eighth signal

Use the ; finger and left shift key. Keep other fingers anchored above home row. Key the line once.

Reach to the '' Key

3 ;;; ;"; ;"; ;;; ;"; ;"; ;;; ";" ";" ;;; ;"; ;"; ";" ";" ;";"

4 "Won't you come," asked Leann's friend, "to the conference?"

5 I said, "Yes." Her answer came, "Are you sure that's true?"

The exclamation mark is either the shift of the top row numeral **1** key or this combination of keys: apostrophe - backspace - period. Use the **!** key if there is one on your machine. Key line 6 once and lines 7 and 8 twice each.

Reach to the ! Key

6 aaa aqa a!a qqq a! q! a!a aaa a!q a!a qqq !a! a!a !a! !q! a!

OR

6 ;;; ;!; ;!; ;;; ;! !; ;!; ;;; !;! !;! ;;; ;!; ;!; !;! !;! ;!

7 Yes! No! Alas! Never! Always! Certainly not! Problems!

8 Stop! Look! Good boy! Come back here! You know him well!

Speed Building

Key at least two 30-s timings on each line *or* repeat each line twice. Try to increase your speed on each successive try.

Sentences with Double-Letter Words

9 The yellow wall in the accounting office looked green to me.

10 The staff will offer to attend all three weeks if necessary.

11 Gemma was happy to be called to carry the sheets for a book.

• • • • 1 • • • • 2 • • • • 3 • • • • 4 • • • • 5 • • • • 6 • • • • 7 • • • • 8 • • • • 9 • • • 10 • • • 11 • • • 12

Common-Word Sentences

12 The above price was too high for the meeting to accept then.

13 We would like to thank you for the kind remarks given to us.

14 The cost has been kept well under the maximum suggested now.

• • • • 1 • • • • 2 • • • • 3 • • • • 4 • • • • 5 • • • • 6 • • • • 7 • • • • 8 • • • • 9 • • • 10 • • • 11 • • • 12

Production

Read the report carefully before beginning to key it. Then prepare the material as a side-bound report. Be careful in making allowance for your footnotes and bottom margin. If you need additional assistance, see the review of the steps for planning footnotes on page 338. If you have a word processing software package which will assist you in preparing a report with formal footnoting, you may check with your instructor regarding using it to do the following production.

FORMAL REPORTS

Including Footnotes

Footnote references are a common part of every report. Whenever the author of a report uses a reference source, it must be acknowledged properly. There are different acceptable ways of showing footnotes. The style used will depend upon company policy or the wishes of the person for whom the report has been written.

Formal Footnoting Style.

The most formal, but still a popular form of footnoting, is to show the source of the material at the bottom of the same page. If a footnote refers to a book, it is necessary to show the author's name, book title (underscored), publishing company, place and year of publication, and the page number where the reference may be located.[1] Footnotes are always separated from the body of the report by a line of underscores approximately 15 spaces long. A single space is left before the line of underscores and a double space follows the line. Footnotes are single spaced with a double space between them, and numbered consecutively. The first line is indented five spaces.

Footnote reference numbers are keyed, first following the material quoted, in a superior position (one-half line above the writing line) and then they are again keyed before the source information given at the bottom of the page.

[1]William A. Sabin, Reference Manual for Secretaries and Typists SI METRIC, 2nd Canadian Edition (Toronto: McGraw-Hill Ryerson Limited, 1978), p. 278.

Key at least two 30-s timings on each line *or* repeat each line twice. Try to increase your speed on each successive try.

Number Practice

15 Buy 5 m of fabric, 3 spools of blue thread, and 4 m of felt.

16 The largest of the 5 meeting rooms will be about 8 m by 9 m.

• • • • 1 • • • • 2 • • • • 3 • • • • 4 • • • • 5 • • • • 6 • • • • 7 • • • • 8 • • • • 9 • • • •10• • • •11• • • •12

Skill Building

Word Division – Rule 1

Divide words between speech syllables.
bea-con ban-quet bank-ing band-age beau-ti-ful bor-der

Key each line once, inserting a hyphen between each speech syllable. Correct lines should end evenly on a 60-space line. Check your work carefully.

Word Division Practice

17 buildings burglar charter clusters compass compensate

18 candidate captures climate conditions custom discuss

19 gentlemen glandular governor graciousness furnished

20 governmental outrage others outlived output outright

Key each underlined word three times. Key each line once concentrating on the underlined words.

Concentrate on Correct Spelling

21 She is in a dilemma because he tried to deceive us.

22 Did he emphasize the familiar nature of the problem?

Timing

Three-Minute Timing

All timings are expressed in words per minute. Therefore a 3-min timing would require that the total words keyed be divided by three. For ease in scoring, a 3-min timing scale has been added for your convenience. This scale is already shown in words per minute so it is not necessary to divide by three.

Set spacing at 2. Key at least one 3-min timing. Circle all errors and calculate gross words per minute. Record the timing on your Progress Chart.

	1	3
We hope to go to the big air show which is to be held a	12	4
month from now. You may try to get tickets to go with us if	24	8
you can obtain the day off from work. We could pick them up	36	12
in town if you would like us to do it. It looks like a real	48	16
top show this year since a group will be here with many acts	60	20
from the east as well as the west. The fact that the better	72	24
pilots will be here will bring out a great crowd. Since the	84	28
show will be in late June instead of in May, more people may	96	32
turn out than we at first thought.	103	34

• • • • 1 • • • • 2 • • • • 3 • • • • 4 • • • • 5 • • • • 6 • • • • 7 • • • • 8 • • • • 9 • • • •10• • • •11• • • •12   1 min

       1   2   3   4   3 min

SI   1.06
AWL 3.41

| 3. Sideheadings | At left margin Capitalize first letter of key words and underscore *or* all capital letters |
| 4. Paragraph Headings | Indent at the beginning of the paragraph. Underscore |

Formal Footnoting Style

Short Quotations. A...

Footnotes

Whenever the author of a report quotes a reference source, the reference must be properly acknowledged by an in-text reference, an endnote, or a *footnote*.

Reference Guide for Footnotes

This is the last line of the text on the page.

SS ← 15 spaces →

DS 5 [1] Author, Book Title (City of Publication: Publisher, Date of Publication), SS
page number.

Example:

This is the last line of the text on the page.

_____

[1]Marg Melanson, Time It! (Toronto: Copp Clark Pitman Ltd., 1983), p. 5.

Alternate Method

SS This is the last line of the text on the page.

← 15 spaces →

DS

Author, Book Title, Publisher, City of Publication, Date of Publication, page number.

↓ Six lines to bottom of page.

Example:

This is the last line of the text on the page.

_____

[2]Sandra D. Ubelacker et al., Mastering Keyboarding Skills, Copp Clark Pitman Ltd., Toronto, 1989, p. 42.

SC
Use et al. when there are three or more authors.

Letters

There are many different styles of business letters being used in offices. This unit will deal with only one type of business letter which is called *full block style*.

1. Study the illustration of the full block letter style on page 108.
2. Read the letter carefully. It explains the full block letter style and mixed punctuation.
3. Set a 60-space line (elite — 12 pitch) or 50-space line (pica — 10 pitch) because the letter is considered to be an average length. An experienced office worker uses a standard line length for letters and adjusts the spacing between letter parts to create a balanced effect. However, a very short letter or a very long letter may require the line length to be changed. Use the line-length default if you are using a computer.
4. Key the *current date* on line 15 (or 2-3 lines below the letterhead). This is only a guide to help you while learning to format letters. Allow for the top margin default if you are using a computer.
5. Space down six* times to key the *inside address*.
6. Double space after the inside address and key the *salutation*.
7. Double space after the salutation and key the *body of the letter*. Remember to double space after each paragraph.
8. Key the *complimentary closing*.
9. Double space. Key the *company name* in capital letters. The use of the company name on business letters is optional. Determine the policy of your employer.
10. Space down four* times and key the *signature lines*.
11. Key the *operator's reference initials* (oi) a double space* after the writer's official title.
12. Key *copy* or *enclosure notations* a single space below the operator's initials.

*This is where the experienced operator adjusts spacing to balance the letter.

Reference Guide for Full Block Letters

Line length   Set a 60-space line (elite — 12 pitch) or a 50-space line (pica — 10 pitch) OR use the line-length default.

Date line   Key on line 15 or 2-3 lines below the letterhead.

Use your judgment.

Inside address   Space down 6 lines or use your judgment. Space down further for a short letter.

Salutation   Double space above and below the salutation. For women, Ms. is preferred unless Miss or Mrs. is indicated in previous correspondence with the particular woman.

Body   Single space but double space between paragraphs. *Note:* There is no paragraph indentation.

Complimentary closing   Double space before the complimentary closing.

Determine company policy.

Company name (optional)   Double space before the company name. Key the company name in capital letters.

Use your judgment.

Signature space   Space down 4 lines or use your judgment according to the length of the letter.

Signature lines   Key sender's name and sender's official title.

Use your judgment.

Operator's initials   Key a double space below the last line of the signature lines. Adjust space according to the length of the letter. Initials may be on the same line as the last line of the signature line.

Notations   Key a space below the operator's initials (*Enclosure*, *c*, etc.).

Assess Your Improvement

Set spacing at 2. Key at least one 3-min *or* 5-min timing. Circle all errors and calculate gross words per minute. Record the timing on your Progress Chart.

Three - or Five-Minute Timing

1   CW   3

In studying consumer trends, it has been noted that the relationship between one's beliefs and one's needs is an important factor in sales. Belief and need are closely linked together. A person tends to believe what he or she needs to believe. Also, the extent of one's desires is partly determined by beliefs. The need for the esteem of others may aid a man to believe that the purchase of a large car will raise him in the eyes of his neighbor.

People are slow to change many of their beliefs because to do so would create an imbalance in their total systems of beliefs. Their system is important to them because it gives the desired order to their lives. The only beliefs that are easy to give up are those that involve very little change to their system of beliefs. In preparing advertisements, it is this latter kind of belief that is under attack.

When a product is purchased for the first time a change of an inconsequential belief is often involved. The persuader needs to establish a need for the product and try to get consumers to change their beliefs in the area of the product without upsetting deeply held beliefs. Appeals that tend to conflict with deeply held beliefs tend to become barriers to making the purchase.

SI   1.45
AWL 4.54

```
•  •  •  • 1 •  •  •  • 2 •  •  •  • 3 •  •  •  • 4 •  •  •  • 5 •  •  •  • 6 •  •  •  • 7 •  •  •  • 8 •  •  •  • 9 •  •  •  • 10 •  •  •  • 11 •  •  •  • 12   1 min
           1                        2                        3                        4   3 min
```

Reports

Review the format for keying a report in Lessons 61 and 62-63, pages 168 and 172-173 as well as the Reference Guide for Reports on page 176, Lessons 65-65. There are many styles of format for keying headings in a report. The hierarchy of headings used in this text is:

1. Title   Centered
        All capital letters   FORMAL REPORTS

2. Subheadings   Centered and underscored
        Capitalize the first letter of key   Including Footnotes
        words

Full Block Letter Style

Date

Inside Address

Salutation

Body

Complimentary Closing

Company Name (Optional)

Signature Lines

Operator's Initials Notations

Dasmund Enterprises Ltd.

Head Office
25 York Mills Road   Toronto, Ontario   M2P 1B5   (416) 363-5133

↓ Line 15 or 2-3 spaces from letterhead

Numeric Date

↓ 6

Key the
Inside Address
Here

↓ DS
Salutation:

↓ DS
This letter is an example of the full block letter style
with mixed punctuation.

In the full block letter style, the letter parts are blocked
at the left margin. This includes the date, inside address,
salutation, and the closing lines. Paragraphs are not
indented in the body of the letter.

Mixed punctuation means that the punctuation at the end of
the letter parts is limited to a colon after the salutation
and a comma after the complimentary closing. Of course, if
you are using abbreviations, it is necessary to include a
period after these. The body of the letter is punctuated
according to accepted English usage.

The full block letter style is the most popular letter style
used in business today. We hope that you will like it!
↓ DS
Yours truly,
↓ DS
DASMUND ENTERPRISES LTD.

↓ 4-6

Name
Official Title
↓ DS
oi
SS ↓ Notations

Mixed punctuation is also known as *two-point punctuation*.

Reports with Footnotes

60-space line
Spacing: 1 and 2
Key two 30-s timings on
each line *or* repeat each line
three times.

Skill Building

Key two 30-s timings on
line 3 of Accuracy Improvement. Circle any errors. If
you have more than one
error for each timing, continue with the Accuracy
Improvement drill. If you
have one error or less on
each timing, key the Speed
Improvement drill and
concentrate on speed.

Double-Letter Words

1 offer apply manner assist arrange selling approval discussed

2 weeks sorry supply called current support supplied effective

Accuracy Improvement

3 in all 94 through the 82 but the 17 in all 64 but then 4 379

4 agree seems issued lessee shipped allowed progress different

5 create hip evades Jill erected oily attracts Jimmy addressed

Speed Improvement

6 The payroll account has been allowed to get too low in June.

7 We were able to open three new customer services this month.

8 Give that enamel handle to us and we will fix it for Helena.

• • • • 1 • • • • 2 • • • • 3 • • • • 4 • • • • 5 • • • • 6 • • • • 7 • • • • 8 • • • • 9 • • • •10• • • •11• • • •12

Stroking Practice

1. Turn to the Stroking Practice, page 414.
2. Key the lines selected by your instructor or the letter combinations giving you difficulty in the drills just completed.
3. Students on individual progress should select lines from 1 to 15.
4. Key each line twice.

The Underscore

In keyed copy, underscore words which would be italic in print. This includes:
1. titles of published materials for books, magazines, and newspapers.
2. technical and foreign words not commonly used.
3. words for emphasis.
4. proper names given to objects such as ships.

Key each line once,
concentrating on correct
punctuation.

9 According to Time Review, the opera Tosca will be presented.

10 Those eight professors gathered to discuss lexicostatistics.

11 Do not confuse salon and saloon in writing up a news report.

12 The Ocean Queen and Silver Sail are two beautiful sailboats.

SC
Did you determine company
policy on the use of the
company name on business
letters?

Production 1

Key a copy of the full block letter on page 108. Use the current date.

Production 2

Key the following letter on the Dasmund Enterprises Toronto letterhead provided in the Working Papers. Use the current date. *Note:* Dasmund Enterprises always uses *numeric dating*. This means that the year is keyed first, followed by the month, and then the day. A space separates each section. For example:

October 21, 1989 is keyed 1989 10 21

May 1, 1990 is keyed 1990 05 01

SC
If you are using a computer,
• Did you use word wrap
for the body of the letter?
• Did you check the
manual to determine if
there are software or
printer defaults for top/
bottom margins?
• Did you use your line-
length default?

Dasmund Enterprises Ltd.

Head Office:
25 York Mills Road   Toronto, Ontario   M2P 1B5

Current Date

Use your judgment for spacing.

J. C. Dallas and Co.
1221 Weber Street East
Kitchener, Ontario
N2A 1C2

Gentlemen:

Thank you for your letter of (use date of last Monday) and your cheque for $1 000.

After crediting your account, there is a balance outstanding of $394.44. As you have not indicated any reason for your partial payment, we are somewhat confused. Please forward the balance or provide an explanation as to why you did not pay your account in full.

We hope you are pleased with the merchandise and look forward to a pleasant and profitable business with your company.

Sincerely yours,

Use your judgment for spacing.

Thomas Rollins
Manager

oi

Unit VII

Objectives

1 The student will review and format reports and other related material learned in Unit IV.

2 The student will learn to format reports with the formal footnote references at the bottom of the page.

3 The student will learn to format agendas and minutes of meetings.

4 The student will learn to format selected legal documents.

5 The student will learn to format the "fill-in" portion of printed legal documents.

6 The student will work toward improving keyboard control.

7 The student will work toward developing a minimum speed of 50 words per minute with three or fewer errors on a three-minute timing; *or* 45 words per minute with four or fewer errors on a five-minute timing.

> Note: Students are encouraged to use automatic options (e.g. headers and footers) if they are available on their typewriters or computers.

42

Business Letters/ Correcting Errors

60-space line
Spacing: 1 and 2

Key two 1-min timings on each line *or* repeat each line three times.

Speed Building

Key at least two 30-s timings on each line *or* repeat each line twice. Try to increase your speed on each successive try.

If you do not have a degree symbol on your keyboard, open the ratchet release, turn the roll back, and key the small letter **o**.

Skill Building

Key each line once, inserting a hyphen between each speech syllable. Correct lines should end evenly on a 60-space line. Check your work carefully.

Timing

Set spacing at 2. Key at least one 3-min timing. Circle all errors and calculate gross words per minute. Record the timing on your Progress Chart.

SI   1.21
AWL 3.69

Alternate-Hand Words

he big key air urns foam male diem bible rotor emblem social
if bit lay bib when fork malt dish blame shake embody theory

Common-Word Sentences

3 Which of you want to go with us to see an equipment display?
4 We have written a letter to your company regarding the cost.
5 That case was used as a basis for making up the firm policy.

Number Practice

6 The temperature today was 24°C but tomorrow it will be 30°C.
7 Eri's temperature was 40.5°C; it should only have been 37°C.

• • • • 1 • • • • 2 • • • • 3 • • • • 4 • • • • 5 • • • • 6 • • • 7 • • • • 8 • • • • 9 • • • • 10 • • • • 11 • • • • 12

Word Division – Rule 2

Never divide words of one syllable.
should   acts   aged   aides   dressed   brushed   cashed   caused   changed

Word Division Practice

8 climbed combed dropped height doubt draped edged eighth fast
9 iced inched inked junction meaning masked milled misguide
10 mishap misplaced missed needle neighbor perspired paved
11 tiled phoned postcard portion spoiled poultry programmed

Three-Minute Timing

	1	3
The road to success is never an easy one. You can make	12	4
a mark upon the world only after a lot of hard work and many	24	8
charts and plans along the course. Events happen at each of	36	12
the stages of life to cause you to check your course and the	48	16
changes to be made to adjust to the voice of experience. To	60	20
do this, you must take heed of that advice of your peers and	72	24
use it for your very own best interest. Know the importance	84	28
of others in the world for success is a hard-earned right.	96	32

• • • • 1 • • • • 2 • • • • 3 • • • • 4 • • • • 5 • • • • 6 • • • 7 • • • • 8 • • • 9 • • • • 10 • • • • 11 • • • • 12   1 min
          1   2   3   4   3 min

pick you up at the store.

15:00   Leave Vancouver, Air Canada
Flight 226 to Winnipeg

20:39   Arrive Winnipeg. Stay at
Winnipeg Inn — 2 Lombard Place
(Portage & Main)

Thursday, August 4
09:00 — 11:30 — Meetings with Winnipeg Staff

12:10 Leave Winnipeg for Montreal, Air
Canada, Flight 176
16:40 Arrive Montreal
Stay at Le Shangrila — 3407 rue Peel,
Montreal. Phone 288-4141
Michelle De Meeres has tickets for
you for baseball game

Friday, August 5
08:30 — 12:00 — Meetings with Montreal staff
13:45   Leave Montreal for Halifax on
Air Canada, Flight 612
16:05   Arrive Halifax
17:00 — 18:00 Meetings with Halifax Staff
Accommodations at <u>Nova Scotian</u> Hotel.
19:00   Staff BBQ & Social at E. Grinleys home.

Saturday, August 6
08:35   Leave Halifax, Air Canada Flight 605
to Toronto
09:47   Arrive Toronto. Wife will pick you up.

Skill Building

Key each underlined word three times. Key each line once concentrating on the underlined words.

Concentrate on Correct Spelling

12 Did they <u>overestimate</u> the <u>permanent</u> visual damage?

13 If their plans were not so <u>changeable</u>, we would go.

Correcting Errors Using a Typewriter

Error correction may be made with an eraser, correction fluid, correction paper, or correction tape. Many machines have a correction key and correction tape built into the machine.

Try to correct each error as soon as you make it. It is much easier to correct your error while the paper is still in the machine than to have to reinsert and realign your work. Your paper bail can be used very effectively to help you proofread the material line by line while your paper is in the machine.

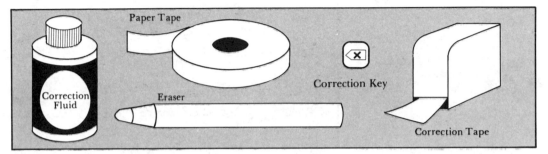

Correcting Errors Using an Eraser

A hard eraser is best for correcting an original copy. A softer eraser works best for corrections on carbon copies.

1. Lift the paper bail. Turn the paper so that the error will be at the top of the cylinder even with the erasing table or roller.
2. Use an eraser shield, if possible. This protects the rest of your material from smudging.
3. Erase gently using a light circular motion following the outline of the letter being erased.
4. Blow or brush the eraser particles away from the machine.
5. Return to the writing position and key the correction.

Error Correction Drill

Key the following sentences as shown. Then erase or use the insert/delete feature and make the necessary corrections. Can you correct the error so well that you cannot see an error has been made?

1 Take it awau.   2 Turm right here.   3 Join tge group.

Correcting Errors Using a Correction Key

Your machine may be equipped with one of the following correction keys.

Electric Correction Key

1. Space or backspace to the letter or space directly to the right of the letter to be corrected.
2. Depress the correction key to position the machine to the letter to be changed (activating the correction tape mechanism).
3. Re-key the error to lift off the original error.
4. Key the correct letter or space.
5. Repeat as necessary.

Itinerary
James Diamund

Toronto – Regina – Edmonton – Vancouver –
Winnipeg – Montreal – Halifax – Toronto

Monday, August 1
09:40   Leave Toronto, Air Canada Flight 107
        to Regina
10:47   Arrive Regina
11:30 – 17:00   Meetings with Regina staff

        Evening free to spend with your
        son. He will pick you up at
        store.

Tuesday, August 2
08:45   Leave Regina, Air Canada Flight 269 to
        Edmonton
10:00   Arrive Edmonton
11:00 – 16:00   Meetings with Edmonton staff
17:00   Leave Edmonton, Air Canada Flight 231
        for Vancouver
17:30   Arrive Vancouver
        Accommodation – Coast Plaza at Stanley Park
        1733 Comox Street   Phone 688-7711

Wednesday, August 3

08:30 – 12:00 – Meetings with Vancouver staff
12:00   Lunch Ms. Switzu, Architect, Hewill

Electronic Memory Correction Key

1. Space or backspace to the letter or space directly to the right of the letter(s) to be corrected.
2. Depress the correction key to remove the letter to the left.
3. Repeat as necessary.
4. Key the correct letter(s).

Correcting Errors on Your Computer Monitor

To correct an error when inputting material:

Know the function of the backspace key, the insert key, and the delete key. This will allow you to insert and delete characters, words, lines, paragraphs, and larger blocks of text. The insert and delete modes are the two most commonly used text-editing features of any word processing program. Know your software.

The backspace key moves the cursor one space to the left, removing the character it passes.

The delete key removes the character at the cursor.

The insert key adds characters to the left of the cursor.

Read the software manual or ask your instructor how to set the insert/delete mode. Some word processing programs have a spell-check feature. This can help you find some of your errors.

To correct an error after the material has been input:

1. Read the monitor using the scrolling option.
2. Move the cursor to the error.
3. Correct the error using the backspace key, or the insert/delete option.
4. Know your software and use the most efficient method.

Error Correction Key Drill

Key the first sentence. Then, use the error correction key or the insert/delete feature to change it to the second sentence.

Change: `Make these corrrection.`   *To:* `Make this correction.`

Change: `Use thj appropriate key.`   *To:* `Use the designated book.`

Squeezing or Spreading Letters in a Word Using a Typewriter

To squeeze or add an extra letter in a word:

1. Determine if your machine has a half-space key or bar.
2. The print position may be moved half a space forward or backwards by using the carriage release and watching the print indicator on the alignment scale.
3. With some typewriters you may press gently with your hand against the ribbon pack mechanism and watch the print indicator on the alignment scale.

Squeezing an Extra Letter into a Word

1. Erase the word.
2. Move each letter one-half space to the left.
3. The corrected word will have one-half space between it and the next word.

`com with`

`come with`

One-half space

Mini Project Two

Are you ready to apply this unit in a decision-making project? We challenge you to apply this unit by reading the memo from the desk of James Dasmund and completing the task he has assigned to you.

From the desk of James Dasmund

Please key the attached itinerary and forward it to the branch managers with a covering memo advising I would like them to meet me at the airport when I arrive. If they can't please have them arrange for someone else and let me know who will be there. I also want them to set up the staff meetings in their stores and advise me what has been arranged when they meet me.

From the desk of James Dasmund

Please prepare a cheque request form for a $500 advance to cover my expenses on this trip.

SC

Did you use the scroll option?

SC

Did you read your software manual for the insert/delete option?

Practice

Erase and squeeze.

SC

Does your software have a spell-check feature?

Squeezing and Spreading Letters in a Word Using a Computer

On a computer, words are usually corrected using the insert/delete option. Therefore, it is not necessary to squeeze or spread letters in a word. The lines will adjust to the line length which has been set.

If the right margin has been set for right justification, extra spaces may be automatically inserted between some of the words in each line so the right margin will align. Know your software. Is justification a system default? Is justification *on* or *off*?

Sentence Practice for Squeezing Letters

Key: Can you com with us tomorow?

Erase and squeeze
letters to correct: Can you come with us tomorrow?

Key: The lase printer is locate on the fifth floor.

Erase and squeeze
letters to correct: The laser printer is located on the fifth floor.

Key: The anual meeting wil be held a Friday.

Erase and squeeze
letters to correct: The annual meeting will be held on Friday.

Key: The brown table and chair are on sale.

Erase and squeeze
letters to correct: The yellow table and chairs are on sale.

Spreading or Removing an Extra Letter from a Word

1. Erase the word.
2. Move each letter one-half space to the right.
3. The corrected word will have one and one-half spaces between it and the next word.

coome with

come↑with

One and one-half spaces

Sentence Practice for Spreading Letters

Key: The newer printers have done a good job.

Erase and spread
letters to correct: The new printer has done a good job.

Key: The 2400-baud modems are on sale today.

Erase and spread
letters to correct: The 2400-baud modem is on sale today.

Key: The large warehouses were built last summer.

Erase and spread
letters to correct: The tiny warehouse was built last summer.

Key: The latest color copiers were on display.

Erase and spread
letters to correct: The large color copier was on display.

Practice

Erase and spread.

SC

Does your software have a spell-check feature?

Production 3

Key the following ruled table on a full sheet of paper with the long edge inserted first. This gives you a sideways table. Double space the body.   Center it vertically and horizontally.

Shoppers' Specials
December 16, 19--

Department	Floor	Description	Regular Price	Sale Price
Women's Wear	Second	Cowl Neck Tops	$ 65.00	$49.00
Loungewear	Second	Caftans and Dresses	80.00	55.99
Juniors	Second	Corduroy Pants	44.00	25.49
Men's Wear	Main	Leather Jackets	295.00	170.00
Men's Shoes	Main	Hush Puppies	59.95	37.50
Leather Goods	Main	Leather Purses	70.00	39.99
Sporting Goods	Lower	Exercise Bikes	499.99	219.99
Toys	Lower	Kites	12.49	4.19

Production

Key the following letter on the Dasmund Enterprises Edmonton letterhead provided in the Working Papers. Use the current numeric date.

 Dasmund Enterprises Ltd.

6817 - 119 Avenue Edmonton, Alberta   T5B 4L8
(403) 464-8551

Current Date

Mr. S. J. Bahbahami
12185 - 116 Avenue
Surrey, British Columbia
V3V 3S1

Dear Mr. Bahbahami:

Welcome to our growing list of new customers!

We are sending, under separate cover, our most recent catalogue together with our current sales catalogue which features many exciting sales items. Please note that the sales catalogue expires at the end of next month.

If you would like to open a convenient charge account with us, complete the enclosed "Application for Credit" form. Upon receipt of this application, we will send you a personalized charge card.

Enclosed, for your convenience, is an order form with a stamped addressed envelope to be returned to our Edmonton store. Telephone orders to either our Edmonton or our Vancouver stores are also accepted.

Thank you for your interest in Dasmund Enterprises. We look forward to your first order and the opportunity to serve you.

Sincerely yours,

M. S. Dasmund
General Manager

oi
Enclosures 2

SC

Did you use your judgment for the signature space?

SC

Did you key the enclosures notation?

Production 1

Key the following Profit and Loss Statement for the Scarborough Management Company Limited for the year ending December 31, 19--. Center both horizontally and vertically according to the format illustrated. Use a full sheet of paper.

GROSS RENT RECEIVED		$55 575.00
EXPENSES:		
Brokerage Fee to obtain mortgage	$1 635.00	
Insurance:		
Central Mortgage and Housing	$ 590.69	
Fire Insurance	183.00	773.69
Interest:		
Adjustment	$ 124.79	
Interim Financing	753.76	
Mortgage	8 063.55	8 942.10
Legal		1 668.95
Repairs and Maintenance		1 318.48
Surveyor's Certificate		490.00
Taxes		1 475.46
Utilities		223.28
Total Expenses		16 526.96
NET PROFIT		$39 048.04

Production 2

Key the following table in boxed style on a full sheet of paper. Double space the body. Center it vertically and horizontally.

(Information About Cash-Flow Loans) all caps

Amount of Loan	Terms		Cost	
	Months	Payments	Interest	Total
1 000	12	89.08	68.96	1 068.96
1 500	18	91.82	162.76	1 662.76
2 000	24	94.61	270.64	2 270.64
2 500	30	97.46	423.80	2 923.80
3 000	36	100.36	612.96	3 612.96
4 000	42	118.07	958.94	4 958.94
5 000	48	132.90	1 379.20	6 379.20
7 000	60	147.49	2 449.40	9 449.40
9 000	60	202.48	3 148.80	12 148.80

@ / ¢ / Business Letters

One-Hand Words

cat mop bet Jim bars poll feed upon dear milk verge plump ad

bat pop car pin bare plum fade join debt min verse plunk awe

Reach to the @ Key

3 sss s2s s@s s@s sss @@@ s@s s@s @s@ @s@s s@s s@ @s

4 240 @ $1.40 ea.; 300 @ $4.10 ea.; 220 @ $21.05 ea.

5 Try to buy 5 @ $0.10, 250 @ $3.15, and 35 @ $4.55.

Reach to the ¢ Key

6 jjj j6j j¢j j¢j jjj ¢¢¢ j¢j j¢j ¢j¢ ¢j¢j j¢j j¢ ¢j

7 These are the prices: 9¢, 35¢, 45¢, 69¢, and 99¢.

8 350 boxes @ 99¢; 100 boxes @ 75¢; 350 boxes @ 89¢.

Double-Letter Words

9 all lass will meet three carry letter appear account correct

10 add loon been keep shall fully office accord suggest appears

Sentences with Double-Letter Words

11 Ross will collect the full proceeds, and credit the account.

12 Smood and Gibbons feel we need a new sheet feeder very soon.

• • • • 1 • • • • 2 • • • • 3 • • • • 4 • • • • 5 • • • • 6 • • • • 7 • • • • 8 • • • • 9 • • • 10 • • • • 11 • • • • 12

Word Division – Rule 3

Do not divide off syllables with one letter.
able aboard about omit open ready ably acute ago

Word Division Practice

13 edition abundant equipped chairman learned sandwich site

14 called anatomy filed knives locked luncheon picked simple

15 stapled stitched styled abandon abundant along amend apex

Assess Your Progress

Assess Your Speed

Set spacing at 2. Key at
least one 3-min *or* 5-min
timing. Circle all errors and
calculate gross words per
minute. Record the timing
on your Progress Chart.

Double-Letter Words

1 occur asset across latter booklet collect commence assistant
2 walls fleet bottom summer usually arrival officers connected

Three - or Five-Minute Timing

1 CW 3

The long cold winters are hard on our cars and they are | 12 | 12 | 4
usually in need of an engine tuneup when spring finally gets | 24 | 24 | 8
here.   The annual tuneup should tell you about the condition | 36 | 36 | 12
of your car's engine.   A bonus is that a well-tuned car will | 48 | 48 | 16
usually give you better gas mileage.   This is good news if a | 60 | 60 | 20
person is concerned about conserving fuel and cutting down a | 72 | 72 | 24
lot of high fuel bills. | 77 | 77 | 26

Since there are a lot of places doing tuneups, it is so | 12 | 89 | 30
important to shop around so you are sure of getting the work | 24 | 101 | 34
done on your car at a reasonable price.   Find out what parts | 36 | 113 | 38
of the car will be checked as part of the tuneup price.   The | 48 | 125 | 42
garage that will merely check the fan belts and change spark | 60 | 137 | 46
plugs is probably not the place to take your car.   Ask for a | 72 | 149 | 50
manual that defines each repair task. | 79 | 154 | 52

When you finally choose a garage to do a tuneup on your | 12 | 166 | 56
car, give the mechanic all the information you can to enable | 24 | 178 | 60
the mechanic to do fast, complete work.   If your auto is not | 36 | 190 | 64
easy to start be sure to mention this.   If the steering does | 48 | 202 | 68
not respond as it should tell your mechanic about it.   After | 60 | 214 | 72
you get your car back, if you are unhappy with either prices | 72 | 226 | 76
charged or work done, check with the Better Business Bureau. | 84 | 238 | 80

• • • • 1 • • • • 2 • • • • 3 • • • • 4 • • • • 5 • • • • 6 • • • • 7 • • • • 8 • • • • 9 • • • •10 • • • •11 • • • •12   1 min

1　　　　　　2　　　　　　3　　　　　　4   3 min

SI   1.34
AWL 4.07

Did you achieve the unit
objective of 45 words per
minute with 3 errors or less
on a three-minute timing;
or 40 words per minute with
4 errors or less on a five-
minute timing?

Basic English Skill

affect: v. to influence   *effect:* n. result   v. to bring about

16 The change in the weather does not (affect, effect) our plans for holidays.

17 What is the main (affect, effect) of the new trend in fashion?

18 We hope to (affect, effect) a change in our present procedures and this should bring the desired (affect, effect).

Two-Minute Timing

	1	2
Hannah Bradsell, a 17-year-old Moose Jaw golfer, shot a	12	6
5 over par 78 Friday for an 8-stroke victory in the northern	24	12
junior women's golf championship. She beat out Joanne Kwok,	36	18
also 17, of Calgary. Miss Kwok held single-shot leads after	48	24
18 and 36 holes. Bradsell was at 248.	56	28

• • • • 1 • • • • 2 • • • • 3 • • • • 4 • • • • 5 • • • • 6 • • • • 7 • • • • 8 • • • • 9 • • • • 10 • • • • 11 • • • • 12   1 min

1   2   3   4   5   6   2 min

Production 1

Key the following letter on the Chang's Appliance Store letterhead provided in the Working Papers. *Note:* Chang's Appliance Store does not use numeric dating, but rather the traditional alphabetic dating.

November 1, 19--

Dasmund Enterprises Ltd.
560 Main Street
Winnipeg, Manitoba
R3B 1C6

Use your judgment for spacing.

Gentlemen:

I have just received your new winter catalogue and would like to place an order with you.

Please ship two Macintosh II hard disk computers at $3800 each and one Laserwriter printer, model number SC MO 188 at $690 I would ask you to ship the order by Canadian National Express, COD

I am interested in establishing credit with your organization. Please forward the necessary forms for credit privileges.

Sincerely yours,
J. R. Chang

Sidebar

Key each sentence once, inserting the correct choice from the words in parentheses. Your right margin will not be even.

Timing

Set spacing at 2. Key two 2-min timings. Circle all errors and calculate gross words per minute. Record the better timing on your Progress Chart.

SI   1.63
AWL 4.17

Production Practice

P
The symbol ✗ means delete.

SC
Did you listen for the margin signal to indicate the end of the line? OR Did you use word wrap?

Production Review

Production 1

Use the information in the computer printout below and set up an open-style table. The table heading is: Historic Statement of Account / Account 12348 / as of March 3, 1990. / The column headings are: Date / Transaction Amount / Principal Allocation / Interest Calculated / and Mortgage Balance. You should not use the Transaction Code and the Tax Balance columns. In the date column use metric numeric dating and in the transaction amount column use metric format.

DATE	TRAN CODE	TRANSACTION AMOUNT	PRINCIPAL ALLOCATION	INTEREST CALCULATED	MORTGAGE BALANCE	TAX BALANCE
00/00/00					.00	.00
29/09/89	02	644.42	644.42−	.00	644.42−	.00
29/09/89	15	34 730.86	34 730.86	.00	34 086.44	.00
19/12/89	15	30 976.25	31 775.93	799.68	65 862.37	600.00
18/01/90	02	1 784.53	1 215.25−	569.22	64 647.12	603.00
18/01/90	15	25 344.07	25 344.07	.00	89 991.19	603.00
21/02/90	02	644.41−	1 511.26	866.85	91 582.45	603.00
21/02/90	15	16 051.18	16 051.18	.00	107 553.63	603.00
21/02/90	15	16.68	16.68	.00	107 570.31	603.00
01/03/90	01	1 144.01	796.85−	247.16	106 773.46	703.00

Production 2

Key the following Table of Contents for Dasmund's Employees' Manual. Use a 50-space line and open-leader style.

Production 3

Turn to Lesson 104, Production 1, page 280. Key the table as a boxed table, changing the title to "Sporting Goods Sales" and bracing the word "comparison" over the columns "this year" and "last year".

Production 2

Key the following letter on the Dasmund Enterprises Winnipeg letterhead provided in the Working Papers. Use the current numeric date.

 Dasmund Enterprises Ltd.

560 Main Street Winnipeg, Manitoba   R3B 1C6
(204) 651-1332

Current Date

Mr. J.R. Chang
Chang's Appliance Store
1212 Main Street South
Dauphin, Manitoba
R7N 1M8

Dear Mr. Chang

Thank you for your letter of November 1 and your order for two Macintosh II hard disk computers and one Laserwriter printer, model SCM0188. These were shipped to you yesterday via CNX, COD, express prepaid.

Enclosed is the Application for credit privileges. As soon as we receive the completed form, we will process it and advise you as to the amount of your credit limit.

We hope you will be pleased with your shipment and look forward to doing business with you in the near future.

Sincerely yours,

Joan Deoming
Manager

oi

Enclosure

P

The symbol / through a letter means use a lower case or small letter.

Production 1

Use the form provided in the Working Papers to complete the purchase requisition.

SC

Did you use the forms in
your workbook?

SC

If you are using a computer,
you may be asked to create
a master interoffice
memorandum which would
be retrieved for each
production exercise.

 Dasmund Enterprises Ltd. INTEROFFICE MEMORANDUM

To: *Purchasing*
Dept.:
Subject: *Office Supplies*

From: *Office Services*
Dept.:
Date: *Current date*

*Prepare a purchase requisition for the Montreal Office
Service Manager, H. Gaudette.*

*The supplier is United Office Products Ltd., 1612 Eglinton
Avenue West, Toronto, Ontario, M6E 2G8. The Account Code is
7413 and the Expenditure Code is 1229.*

*The items requested are: 1 Steel Filing Cabinet Grey (No. 1810) at
$499.50; 10 boxes of legal-size file folders (No. 9486) at $11.50/box;
6 sets of manila indexes (No. 1105) at $3.50/set; and 16 rolls
of folder tabs (No. 17) at $2.19/roll.*

Be sure to extend the amounts and total the requisition.

Production 2 and 3

Use the forms provided in the Working Papers and complete the purchase order and the
voucher cheque.

 Dasmund Enterprises Ltd. INTEROFFICE MEMORANDUM

To: *R. Bohnet*
Dept.: *Purchasing*
Subject: *P.O. - United Office Prod.*

From: *T. Grisel*
Dept.: *Purchasing*
Date: *Current date*

*Prepare the purchase order to send to United Office Products
for the purchase requisition you have just completed. Ship via
Reliant Trucking. Terms: 2/10, n/30.
Be sure to transfer the necessary information and note on
the purchase requisition the P.O. Issuing Date. Michelle
De Meeres will authorize the purchase order.*

 Dasmund Enterprises Ltd. INTEROFFICE MEMORANDUM

To: *Accounting*
Dept.:
Subject: *Cheque - United Office Prod.*

From: *R. Bohnet*
Dept.: *Purchasing*
Date: *Current date*

*Prepare a voucher cheque to send with the purchase order
to United Office Products Ltd.*

Envelopes

60-space line
Spacing: 1 and 2
Key two 1-min timings on
each line *or* repeat each line
three times.

Right-Hand Words

1 no up him hip hop hill Jill hump poll plum knoll Jimmy plump

2 in mop pop nip no. plop mill pill hulk pull loom plunk imply

Accuracy Building

Key at least two 1-min
timings on each line *or*
repeat each line three times.
Count all errors. If you had
more than two errors in
each attempt, concentrate
on individual letters. Your
aim should be to maintain
keyboard control.

Left-Hand Words

3 ax are cab cat bade cede draw sags bears dated bearer crease

4 at bat bag bar bags adds drew save waste debts freeze create

One-Hand Words

5 bag pup cat nip bear plop adds hill deed mink vests imply as

6 bar joy ear lip cage mill acre jump draw mono wages nylon ax

Sentences with One-Hand Words

7 We ate a few raw red beets and bread as we sat at a freezer.

8 No, I saw no moon, only hill faded upon hill; few were pink.

• • • • 1 • • • • 2 • • • • 3 • • • • 4 • • • • 5 • • • • 6 • • • • 7 • • • • 8 • • • • 9 • • • •10 • • • •11 • • • •12

Skill Building

Word Division – Rule 4

Avoid dividing off two-letter syllables if possible.
copy   absent   acted   alley   already   also   camera   detect   usual   ago

Word Division Practice

In all exercises, it is assumed that no two-letter syllables are divided.

9 angle badges engage females indexed accede moulded appointed

10 affairs attitudes latitude onions rumor rifle started also

11 doctors matched movement enforce pharmacy scarcely radios

12 dictate digit incomplete marked agenda against amount area

Key each line once, inserting a hyphen between each
speech syllable. Correct
lines should end evenly on a
60-space line. Check your
work carefully.

Basic English Skill

all together: in one group   *altogether:* completely

13 We hope to dine (all together, altogether) at The Chateau Laurier

but we may be (all together, altogether) too tired by that time.

all ready: completely ready   *already:* at a previous time

14 Darin was (already, all ready) at the seminar when the telephone

call came to see if he was (all ready, already) to leave.

Key each sentence once,
inserting the correct choice
from the words in
parentheses. Your right
margin will not be even.

Business Forms

60-space line
Spacing: 1 and 2
Key two 30-s timings on
each line *or* repeat each line
three times.

Right-Hand Words

1 in pup joy you hum loop lump milk loin mink mono union pupil

2 my pin nip lip oil look yolk ploy hook hull link nylon imply

One-Minute Timings

1. Turn to the One-Minute Timings, page 421.
2. Select the paragraph that you think you can complete in one minute.
3. Key the One-Minute Timing as a drill.
4. If you had two or more errors, practice Accuracy Improvement.
   If you had fewer than two errors, practice Speed Improvement.

Skill Building

Key two 30-s timings on
line 3 of Accuracy Improvement. Circle any errors. If
you have more than one
error for each timing, continue with the Accuracy
Improvement drill. If you
have one error or less on
each timing, key the Speed
Improvement drill and
concentrate on speed.

Accuracy Improvement

3 if cut malt coals rocks burial audible quantity flake rotary

4 ax ear tax far rare dear raze fees cedar grass ceases freeze

Speed Improvement

5 It was our plan to put the proposal forward at this meeting.

6 Mom was ill when we darted to the edge of the knoll to look.

• • • • 1 • • • • 2 • • • • 3 • • • • 4 • • • • 5 • • • • 6 • • • • 7 • • • • 8 • • • • 9 • • • •10 • • • •11 • • • •12

Summary of Rules for Keying Numbers

1. Numbers that begin a sentence are always spelled out.
2. Numbers ten and under are spelled out unless used with larger or related numbers or when used for special emphasis.
3. Numbers above ten are usually written in figures.
4. Numbers with the word "percent" or with decimals should be keyed in figures.
5. When two unrelated numbers follow one another, spell out the smaller number. This allows for better reading comprehension.
6. A space should separate numbers in groups of three to the left and right of the decimal marker.
7. Approximate numbers should be spelled out.
8. Use figures to express time except when used with the word "o'clock".
9. Use figures when a number follows a noun.
10. Use figures for numbers when used in a compound adjective and write out numbers when used as an ordinary adjective.
11. Amounts of money are written in figures. Leave out zeroes and decimal marker if it is an even dollar amount.
12. When a date is preceded by the month, do not use th, d, rd, nd or st. Dates which come before the month may be written in words or as figures with endings.
13. Key numbers as figures when they are used with a symbol.
14. Key numbers according to those in the source document, i.e., invoice, memo, page, etc.
15. Key numbers as figures when referring to measures, mass, dimensions, and distances.

Two-Minute Timing

In the 1840's many persons immigrated to those colonies which would later join together to become Canada. They came in large numbers, averaging 25 000 each year at the start of the decade. In 1847, 90 000 arrived at Quebec to look for a new home. Population in Upper Canada leaped from 455 000 in 1841 to 942 000 in 1851.

	1 min	2 min
	12	6
	24	12
	36	18
	48	24
	60	30
	65	32

Number 10 Envelopes (105 mm x 242 mm)

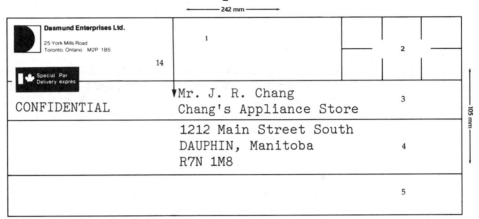

Sections of an Envelope

1. This space is for the printed or keyed return address and the postal code. Postal stickers such as *Special Delivery* or *Air Mail* are placed below the return address within sections 1 and 3.
2. This space is for postage stamps or meter impression.
3. The address can be written or keyed in any part of sections 3 and 4. Special instructions like *Attention* or *Personal and Confidential* must be placed in section 3 only.
4. The postal code must appear as the last item of the address. It can be on the same line as the city and province as long as it is separated from the name of the province by at least two spaces as in the sample return address. *Note:* The postal code is preferred as the last line of the address.
5. Leave this space (approximately five lines) entirely blank.
6. Because of high speed processing it is very important that all envelopes are fully sealed to prevent air from *ballooning* them. Windows on an envelope must also be covered with see-through material for the same reason. *Note:* The address must be clearly visible through the window on the envelope.

Postal Code Reminders

1. Always key or print the code in block letters.
2. Do not use periods or other punctuation marks anywhere in the code.
3. Never underline the code.
4. Leave a clear space between the two parts of the code. Do not join the code in any way.
5. No part of the address should appear below the code. The word *CANADA* should be above the code or the item before the code.
6. The postal code is a permanent part of the address.

Wednesday. He will pick up his rental car at the hotel and drive to Tulsa where he has an appointment at 11:00 with M. J. Young and at 13:30 with Don Arnold. He will drive back to Oklahoma City and take American Airlines Flight 456 for Dallas at 17:25 arriving in Dallas at 18:50. He has a reservation at the American Inn of the Six Flags. This has been confirmed as it is a late arrival. He should leave the rental car at the airport.

Thursday. He has an appointment and luncheon meeting with J. A. Master of the Dallas Chamber of Commerce at 11:00. He will leave the Dallas/Fort Worth Airport at 15:15 on Delta Airlines Flight 753 arriving in Edmonton at 21:50.

Production 2

Below is a summary of Mike Dasmund's expenses for his trip.
(a) Complete the Dasmund Travel Request Form in the Working Papers.
(b) Complete the Dasmund Travel Expense Form in the Working Papers.
Students without Working Papers should set up the material as attractive tables.

The term per diem means for each day.

<u>Expense</u>
1. Airfare: Edmonton-Oklahoma City-Dallas-Edmonton $749.
2. Car Rental - $36.95.
3. Hotels - Oklahoma City 2 nights @ $95.
        - Dallas 1 night @ $115.
4. Per diem allowance 4 days @ $70.
5. Special Meals
        - Business dinner - Monday - $60.
        - Luncheon - Tuesday - $35.
        - Luncheon - Thursday - $25.
6. Taxi fares $70.
<u>Note</u>: Receipts are attached.

Production 3

Use the cheque in the Working Papers to cover the expenses for Mike Dasmund's trip.

Reference Guide for Envelopes (No. 10)

The address is blocked five characters to the left of the vertical center and two lines below the horizontal center.

Return Address   Key 3 spaces in from the left edge and 3 lines down from the top edge.
Special Instructions   Key 3 spaces in from the left edge and 10 lines down from the top edge.
Address (No. 10 Envelope)   Begin keying 50 spaces (elite — 12 pitch) or 42 spaces (pica — 10 pitch) in from the left edge and 14 lines down from the top edge.
- The city is preferably keyed in capital letters.
- The province or territory is preferably spelled out in full.
- The postal code is preferred as the last line of the address.
- For foreign addresses, the country of destination should be capitalized on the last line.

Use your judgment.

Canadian Provinces and Territories

Preferred	Optional	Preferred	Optional
Alberta	AB	Nova Scotia	NS
British Columbia	BC	Ontario	ON
Labrador	LB	Prince Edward Island	PE
Manitoba	MB	Quebec	PQ
Newfoundland	NF	Saskatchewan	SK
New Brunswick	NB	Yukon Territory	YT
Northwest Territories	NT		

- Two-letter symbols for provinces and territories may be used by large volume mailers.

Production Practice

SC

If you are using a computer, can you print envelopes? OR Is it easier to print envelope labels?

Production 1

Key the following five envelopes on the forms provided in the Working Papers.

MasterCard
P.O. Box 3000
Place d'Armes
Montreal, Quebec
H2Y 3M1

Eaton's
P.O. Box 2900
Winnipeg, Manitoba
R3G 3G1

Confidential

Columbia House
1414 Warden Avenue
Scarborough, Ontario
M1R 5A7

Imperial Oil Limited
Box 7100
Don Mills, Ontario
M3C 2Z5

Confidential

Registrar's Office
University of Calgary
2920 - 24 Avenue N. W.
Calgary, Alberta
T2N 1N4

Three- or Five-Minute Timing

1 CW 3

The diet of the average North American consumer will be | 12 | 12 | 4
made up of many products that have sugar added to them. The | 24 | 24 | 8
amount of sugar in some foods will come as a surprise to any | 36 | 36 | 12
person who has not carefully analyzed the food being brought | 48 | 48 | 16
home. For instance, ketchup might be found to have a higher | 60 | 60 | 20
percentage of sugar than does ice cream or canned apples. A | 72 | 72 | 24
can of corn will probably have sugar added. | 81 | 81 | 27

It is sometimes hard to realize how much sugar there is | 12 | 93 | 31
in a product because different types of sugar might be added | 24 | 105 | 35
and listed individually. Sugar, corn syrup and honey can be | 36 | 117 | 39
listed separately on the label of a certain food product but | 48 | 129 | 43
they are all forms of sugar and could mean that sugar is the | 60 | 141 | 47
main ingredient in that food. For this reason the consumers | 72 | 152 | 51
must study labels very carefully. | 79 | 160 | 53

Are there any problems with the consumption of all this | 12 | 172 | 57
sugar? It would seem that there are problems. There is now | 24 | 184 | 61
no doubt that tooth decay can be linked to sugar. Sugar can | 36 | 196 | 65
also contribute to obesity and all the health problems which | 48 | 208 | 69
go along with being overweight. Children might fill up with | 60 | 220 | 73
sweetened foods and miss out on the vital nutrients in other | 72 | 232 | 77
foods such as fruits, vegetables and cereal products. | 83 | 243 | 80

•••1•••2•••3•••4•••5•••6•••7•••8•••9•••10•••11•••12 1 min

1   2   3   4 3 min

SI   1.49
AWL 4.49

Production Practice

Production 1

Mike Dasmund is planning a trip to Oklahoma City, Tulsa, and Dallas from Monday, June 7 to Thursday, June 10.
(a) Key attractively on a full sheet of paper the itinerary for this trip.
(b) Complete the Itinerary Form in the Working Papers. This form summarizes the flight information and notes the hotel reservations for each city.

Monday. 06:55 leaves Edmonton International Airport, Delta
Airlines Flight 476 to Oklahoma City (via Salt Lake City). The
flight arrives at 12:26. Reservations are confirmed at the Holiday
Inn. He has an appointment at 15:00 with Mr. Jackson and a
dinner meeting at 19:00 with Mr. Ralph Reimer.

Tuesday. He has an appointment at 09:45 with Mr. Ray Berger;
lunch at 12:00 with R. Berger and J. Caswell; and a conference
with the Oklahoma Chamber of Commerce at 15:00.

Production 2

Key the following five envelopes on the forms provided in the Working Papers.

Mrs. P. E. Rowe
Southview Cottage
Southview Drive
HOLLAND-ON-SEA
Essex CO15 5TP
ENGLAND

Higher College of Technology
Box 17155
AL AIN, ABU DHABI
UNITED ARAB EMIRATES

International Education Services
Shin Taiso Building
10-7, Dogenzaka 2-chome
SHIBUYA-KU, TOKYO 150
JAPAN

Signora J. Siggia
Via Vettor Pisani 4
30126 VENEZIA LIDO
ITALY

Miss U. Riechers
126 Ryesgade
DK-2100 COPENHAGEN 0
DENMARK

Production 3

Key the following letter on the Dasmund Enterprises Halifax letterhead provided in the Working Papers. Key an appropriate envelope or envelope label.

Current Date / Mrs. Annabelle Kiyooka / 519 Saint Anne Street / Bathurst, New Brunswick / E2A 2N5 / Dear Mrs. Kiyooka: / Mr. Hank Russell has applied for the position of bookkeeper and has given your name as a reference. / ¶ Mr. Russell has an excellent background on paper, showing very high grades in his academic studies and relevant work experience. However, when we interviewed Mr. Russell, we were concerned about his ability to relate to people. We think that this may have been because of a difficult interview situation. Once employed, he may be more relaxed and possibly relate better. / ¶We would appreciate your honest and direct comments about this particular problem, as well as any other information. All information provided will be held in strictest confidence. Sincerely yours, / Edward Grinley / Manager

Travel Forms

One-Hand Words

1 raw lip dear moon adds hoop safer plump agreed Jill deserves

2 egg oil deaf loon acre oily saves plunk arrest hump deserved

Accuracy Improvement

3 ad wax sad was feed deed rest gave craft trace stages severe

4 in all 15 up at least 80 but up to 73 to the 716 save all 30

5 three carry letter appear account correct possible necessary

Speed Improvement

6 John put the junk on the baggage cart beside the staff pool.

7 The schools and colleges are wholly committed to the issues.

8 The quotation included instructions regarding water systems.

• • • • 1 • • • • 2 • • • • 3 • • • • 4 • • • • 5 • • • • 6 • • • • 7 • • • • 8 • • • • 9 • • • •10• • • •11• • • •12

Stroking Practice

1. Turn to the Stroking Practice, page 414.
2. Key the lines selected by your instructor or the letter combinations giving you difficulty in the drills just completed.
3. Students on individual progress should select lines from 46 to 60.
4. Key each line twice.

Number Keying

Rule 15: Key numbers as figures when referring to measures, mass, dimensions, and distances.
Example:

The box had a mass of 75 kg but he carried it 50 m.

Practice

9 We live about 60 km from the nearest city and fifteen km to town.

10 The totals for the experiment were: 8.3 g, 2.7 g and 0.8 g.

11 We took eleven L of milk on July 2nd and 10 L are left on the 4th.

12 The result showed 4,734.7213, 20 more than that in May.

½/¼/Skill Building

60-space line
Spacing: 1 and 2
Key two 1-min timings on
each line *or* repeat each line
three times.

Skill Building

Use the ; finger. Key each
line once.

Key two 1-min timings on
each line *or* repeat each line
three times. Circle all errors.
If most of your attempts
have two errors or less,
proceed to line 11. If not,
repeat this drill.

Key two 1-min timings on
each line *or* repeat each line
three times as quickly as you
can. Assess your speed
progress.

Timing

Set spacing at 2. Key two
3-min timings. Circle all
errors and calculate gross
words per minute. Record
the better timing on your
Progress Chart.

SI   1.23
AWL 3.92

One-Hand Words

1 ads mum see pop ware mono card moon gate kink stage nylon ax

2 add him set joy wart noon care loon gave hill saves onion at

Reach to the ½ and ¼ Keys

3 ;;; ;½; ;½; ;;; ½½½ ;½; ;½; ;½½; ;½½; ;½ ½; ;½ ½½;

4 ;;; ;¼; ;¼; ;;; ¼¼¼ ;¼; ;¼; ;¼¼; ;¼¼; ;¼ ¼; ;¼ ¼¼;

5 Here are 2 examples of simple fractions: ½ and ¼.

6 Examples of mixed fractions are: 3½, 5¼, and 17¼.

Accuracy Improvement

7 as beg web bet dear swab fare tees after erred agreed drawer

8 on ink nil non ohm noon only pink pool pulp pump molly nylon

9 gee well food door press proof vessel assume keeping summary

10 wee loot roof pass rooms mills assure assets billing install

Speed Improvement

11 The fire bell for this building will ring for eight minutes.

12 All odd jeeps are billed according to their full book price.

13 My pump on the east edge of the place acts as if it is worn.

14 Jon asked Jim to get on the pink car as we pulled the lever.

• • • • 1 • • • • 2 • • • • 3 • • • • 4 • • • • 5 • • • • 6 • • • • 7 • • • • 8 • • • • 9 • • • • 10 • • • • 11 • • • 12

Three-Minute Timing

	1	3
Plants can be used well to help bring a warm feeling to	12	4
the office scene. The large office can be broken into small	24	8
areas around a desk or a group of desks by placing a few big	36	12
plants between them. Besides adding color to the scene, the	48	16
plants seem to absorb some of the sound of the office. When	60	20
clients visit us, they tend to relax more if they are put at	71	23
ease right from the start. Live plants give an extra sense	82	27
of caring that no amount of green plastic plants can ever	93	31
achieve.	94	31

• • • • 1 • • • • 2 • • • • 3 • • • • 4 • • • • 5 • • • • 6 • • • • 7 • • • • 8 • • • • 9 • • • • 10 • • • • 11 • • • 12   **1 min**

          1   2   3   4   **3 min**

Production

Key the following itinerary for Thomas Rollins on a full sheet of paper.
Center it horizontally and vertically.

I T I N E R A R Y

THOMAS ROLLINS
MONTREAL – HALIFAX – VANCOUVER

MONDAY, May 3

07:00   Leave Lester B. Pearson *International* Airport, Air Canada
             Flight 400 to Montreal.

08:10   Arrive in Montreal. Michelle De Meeres will meet
             you.

14:30   Meet with Montreal branch manager, office manager,
             and union representatives.

17:25   Leave Montreal, Air Canada Flight 160 to Halifax.

19:45   Arrive in Halifax. Stay at the Holiday Inn.
             Reservation is guaranteed for late arrival.

TUESDAY, May 4

09:30   Picked up at Hotel by Edward Grinley.

12:00   Guest Speaker at Chamber of Commerce luncheon.
             Speech is in your briefcase. *Ed will accompany you.*

             Afternoon is free to spend as you wish. There is
             an excellent Golf course next to your Hotel.
                          l.c.   *l.c.*

WEDNESDAY, May 5

08:15   Leave Halifax, Air Canada Flight 105 to Vancouver.

12:00   Arrive Vancouver. Fred Baker will meet you.
             Reservation at Hotel Vancouver.

14:00   Meet with Vancouver branch manager, office
             manager, and union representatives.

17:30   Staff ~~are~~ is having a BBQ at Stanley Park.

THURSDAY, May 6

09:15   Leave Vancouver, Air Canada Flight 136 to
             Toronto.

16:25   Arrive at Lester B. Pearson International.

Graduated Speed Practice

Select a sentence that you think you can key in the time indicated by your instructor. If you complete the line within the time limit, try the next line. If not, try again or adjust your goal.

Students on individual progress should key each line twice, as quickly as possible.

		20 s	15 s	12 s
1	We wish to go there.	12	16	20
2	The man cuts the hay.	13	17	21
3	Please come to see us.	13	18	22
4	He owns a herd of cows.	14	18	23
5	Use spray to kill slugs.	14	19	24
6	They sit under fir trees.	15	20	25
7	The price of fuel is high.	16	21	26
8	She tried to burn the coal.	16	22	27
9	The soil needs to be worked.	17	22	28
10	He has tried to pan for gold.	17	23	29
11	They just bought a dog collar.	18	24	30
12	The land firm was given notice.	19	25	31
13	Ruth saw the sight from the bus.	19	26	32
14	An odor from the lake was strong.	20	26	33
15	Rush the sick child to the doctor.	20	27	34
16	The band will form a line up ahead.	21	28	35
17	We have paid all our bills for fuel.	22	29	36
18	Len hopes to bid on the chairs today.	22	30	37
19	The large span of the bridge is ready.	23	30	38
20	The two boys will compete on the panel.	23	31	39
21	The girls' title has been given to them.	24	32	40
22	She lent her keys to the girls from town.	25	33	41
23	He hopes to work for the same oil company.	25	34	42
24	We can paint signs for the annual air show.	26	34	43
25	The little dog tried to dig under the fence.	26	35	44
26	He built a handy shelf for their living room.	27	36	45
27	Give us the title of the book you wish to get.	28	37	46
28	Their own fishing rods are just like this make.	28	38	47
29	They will either fix the plans or make new ones.	29	38	48
30	She cannot hope to please customers all the time.	29	39	49
31	We hope to go to the island again for our holiday.	30	40	50

• • • • 1 • • • • 2 • • • • 3 • • • • 4 • • • • 5 • • • • 6 • • • • 7 • • • • 8 • • • • 9 • • • • 10

Itinerary

60-space line
Spacing: 1 and 2
Key two 30-s timings on
each line *or* repeat each line
three times.

Alternate-Hand Words

1 an due owns fight shelf embody suspend auditory digit ritual

2 am dot odor field shape emblem turkeys chairman eight signal

One-Minute Timings

1. Turn to the One-Minute Timings, page 421.
2. Select the paragraph that you think you can complete in one minute.
3. Key the One-Minute Timing as a drill.
4. If you had two or more errors, practice Accuracy Improvement.
   If you had fewer than two errors, practice Speed Improvement.

Skill Building

Key two 30-s timings on
line 3 of Accuracy Improvement. Circle any errors. If
you have more than one
error for each timing, continue with the Accuracy
Improvement drill. If you
have one error or less on
each timing, key the Speed
Improvement drill and
concentrate on speed.

Accuracy Improvement

3 far Lou fear look aged holy saved imply assert poll detracts

4 shall fully office accord suggest appears addition attention

5 eats rafts vests egress rested exceeds assessed rewarded vex

Speed Improvement

6 We shall assess the value of the mill when we obtain access.

7 My joy in this case was nil because I saw my tax fee stated.

8 The morning meeting will begin at 09:30; please be punctual.

• • • • 1 • • • • 2 • • • • 3 • • • • 4 • • • • 5 • • • • 6 • • • • 7 • • • • 8 • • • • 9 • • • •10• • • •11• • • •12

Number Keying

Rule 14: Key numbers according to those in the source document, i.e., invoice, memo
page, etc.
Example:

Invoice 1378 should match Requisition 147-B.

Practice

Key each line once, cor-
recting the numbers when-
ever necessary. Correct lines
should end evenly on a
60-space line. The last two
lines review rules taken to
date. Check your work
carefully.

9 My social insurance number is 620 506 7947; shall I copy it?

10 Cheque 14734 was sent to cancel the debt on invoice 146B-32.

11 She signed a 9-year lease on the property at $550.00 per month.

12 At least 3.5% of the $14,734.70 is due here March 17.

&/Letters

60-space line
Spacing: 1 and 2
Key two 1-min timings on
each line *or* repeat each line
three times.

Alternate-Hand Words

1 is bow man bid wish form maps disk blend shale enamel turkey

2 it box men big with fuel melt dock borne shape enrich visual

Use **J** finger and left shift
key. Keep other fingers
above home row keys. Key
each line twice.

Reach to the & Key

3 jjj j7j j&j j&j jjj &&& j&j j&j &j& &j&j j&j j& &j

4 1 & 2; 3 & 4; 5 & 6; 7 & 8; 9 & 10; 11 & 12; 7 & 6

5 We sent the cheque to Rainesly, Wagner & Swainson.

Speed Building

Key at least two 30-s
timings on each line *or*
repeat each line twice.
Try to increase your speed
on each successive try.

Sentences With Double-Letter Words

6 The fellows will meet to arrive at some agreement on issues.

7 We are sorry that the bills differ; it was indeed our error.

8 The current bulletin will arrive for an association meeting.

Common-Word Sentences

9 They sent another cheque to cover the total amount of taxes.

10 Our new credit department has been opened to serve you well.

11 Further copies will need to be given to them to use them up.

• • • • 1 • • • • 2 • • • • 3 • • • • 4 • • • • 5 • • • 6 • • • • 7 • • • • 8 • • • • 9 • • • • 10 • • • • 11 • • • • 12

Skill Building

Word Division – Rule 5

Divide words between double letters of speech syllables.
beg-gar baf-fle bal-loon book-keeper cat-tle lit-tle

Word Division Practice

Key each line once, inserting a hyphen between each
speech syllable. Correct
lines should end evenly on a
60-space line. Check your
work carefully.

12 collapsed college commerce commute connects committee

13 settle omitted offset referral shallow stringent affix

14 barrister cellophane occurred shelter stripped scarlet

15 screened dispatched slotted smoothed supply village ally

Number Practice

Key one 1-min timing on
each line *or* repeat each line
twice.

16 Please put 25 L of gasoline in this tank and add 1 L of oil.

17 Some box sizes are 4 L, 6 L and 8 L; the basket size is 2 L.

• • • • 1 • • • • 2 • • • • 3 • • • • 4 • • • • 5 • • • 6 • • • • 7 • • • • 8 • • • • 9 • • • • 10 • • • • 11 • • • • 12

Production 1 (continued)

SC

Did you count the number of lines needed for the right side of the balance sheet?

I S E S   L I M I T E D

December 31, 19--

L I A B I L I T I E S

CURRENT LIABILITIES:

Accounts Payable	$ 1 667 481.20	
Air Travel Contract Deposits	96 350.00	
Chattel Mortgage notes payable	131 111.21	
Equipment purchase obligations	428 211.20	
Interest accrued	44 011.00	
Salaries and Wages accrued	871 881.75	
Other accrued liabilities	25 127.08	$ 3 264 173.44

LONG TERM DEBT:

Bank Loan	$ 2 273 870.80	
Chattel Mortgages	3 097 091.20	
Equipment purchase obligations	761 633.59	6 132 595.59

CAPITAL

Share Capital		
Common Shares of $100 par value Authorized 10 000 shares	$ 1 000 000.00	
Retained Earnings	19 159 424.00	20 159 424.00

move up ↑

TOTAL LIABILITIES AND CAPITAL $29 556 193.03

18 We are <u>changing</u> the date due to dual <u>cancellation</u>.

19 Try <u>convincing</u> the clerk that fees are <u>chargeable</u>.

Timing

Set spacing at 2. Key at least one 3-min timing. Circle all errors and calculate gross words per minute. Record the timing on your Progress Chart.

Three-Minute Timing

	1	3
It is not always easy to shop for an unusual gift for a	12	4
friend. One wants to find that gift which is just right yet	24	8
fits into a meagre budget. Each store seems to have an item	36	12
to offer but it is the wrong color or the wrong size. Firms	48	16
may offer to get the right one for you but you have left the	60	20
shopping too late for an order to arrive on time. Is this a	72	24
state in which you often find yourself? If it is, our store	84	28
can help you solve your problem of shopping. We have a good	96	32
selection of gifts that are truly different for that special	108	36
person on your gift list.	113	38

SI   1.22
AWL 3.83

• • • • 1 • • • • 2 • • • • 3 • • • • 4 • • • • 5 • • • • 6 • • • • 7 • • • • 8 • • • • 9 • • • 10 • • • 11 • • • 12 1 min

　　　　　1　　　　　　　　　2　　　　　　　　　3　　　　　　　　4 3 min

Personal Business Letters

A personal business letter varies from a regular business letter in two ways. First, letterhead paper is not used. Therefore, a return address must be keyed on the letter. Second, the operator's initials are omitted as the same person who writes the letter usual keys it.

1. The return address is keyed above the date line.

↓ 12

Street Address
City, Province
Postal Code
Date

Block the return address at the left margin.

2. Key the complimentary closing followed by the name of the person writing the letter. A title is not usually shown on a personal business letter.

Sincerely yours

Name

3. Operator's initials are omitted. Enclosure notations follow the keyed signature, properly spaced to create the necessary pleasant balanced appearance of the letter.

Production Practice

SC

Did you count the number of lines needed for the left side of the balance sheet?

Did you decide what adjustments should be made so that the two sides of the balance sheet will end on the same line?

Production

The following Balance Sheet should be keyed on two pages which can be put together as the complete financial statement. Center it horizontally and vertically. Do this Balance Sheet as a two-page table even if your software and printer has a feature allowing it to be done as a one-page table.

<pre>
              D A S M U N D   E N T E R P R

                    Balance Sheet as of

                       A S S E T S

CURRENT ASSETS:

    Cash in Bank $ 1 268 308.33
    Accounts Receivable:
       Accounts and notes
          receivable $ 1 440 599.71
       Customer Accounts
          receivable   1 620 304.46
       Government of Canada   6 067.96   3 066 972.13

FIXED ASSETS:

    Buildings $18 501 608.92
       Less Reserve for
          Depreciation   1 850 160.89   16 651 448.03
    Furniture and Fixtures $ 3 220 404.46
       Less Reserve for
          Depreciation   322 040.44   2 898 364.02
    Property   5 323 076.32

DEFERRED CHARGES:

    Maintenance Work in Progress   129 773.03
    Prepaid Taxes   146 001.17
    Prepaid Utilities   72 250.00

                                                   move up ↑

TOTAL ASSETS $29 556 193.03
</pre>

Production 1

Key the following personal business letter on plain paper. Be sure to include the return address in the appropriate place.

12185 - 116 Avenue
Surrey, BC
V3V 3S1
November 15, 19--

Dasmund Enterprises Ltd.
7025 Granville Street
Vancouver, BC
V6P 4X6

Gentlemen:

Enclosed is my "Application for Credit" with your company. I trust everything is in order and that you will soon forward my personalized charge card.

I would like to order one Redwood picnic table, Model No. D173 @ $70. My cheque in payment is enclosed. Please deliver as soon as possible.

Sincerely yours,

S. J. Bahbahami

Enclosures

Production 2

Key the following personal business letter on plain paper. Be sure to include the return address in the appropriate place. Use the current numeric date.

105 Rochford St.
Charlottetown, P.E.I.
C1A 7N8

Current Date

Business Technology
P.O. Box 2810
Boulder, CO 80322-1279
U.S.A.

Gentlemen;

I am interested in subscribing to your magazine, *Business Technology*.

Please send me an application form and information concerning a one-year subscription. Should the subscription be paid in Canadian or U.S. funds?

Sincerely,
Bruce Arbuckle

The American postal code or *Zip Code* is keyed on the same line as the city and state, two spaces after the state.

SC
Did you use your judgment to create a balanced appearance in this letter?

Two-Page Tables

Two-page tables must be planned so that when the two pages are taped together the information will line up in tabular form.

Steps

1. Decide where the data divides horizontally into two equal or logical halves.
2. Count the number of lines and spaces needed to key the left half.
3. Count the number of lines and spaces needed to key the right half.
4. If your answers in steps 2 and 3 are not the same, decide where extra spaces can be added or deleted so that the same number of lines and spaces are needed for each half of the table.
5. **Left Page**

   The table may be keyed to the right edge of the left page or a right margin may be set. If the table is keyed to the right edge:
   a) From the right edge of the paper **pivot** or backspace the key line of the left half of the table. Note the print or cursor position.
   b) Set the left margin at the point at which you stopped backspacing.

   If the table has a right margin:
   a) Set the right margin 12 spaces (elite — 12 pitch) or 10 spaces (pica — 10 pitch) from the edge of the paper.
   b) From the right margin **pivot** or backspace the key line of the left half of the table. Note the print or cursor position.
   c) Set the left margin at the point at which you stopped backspacing.
6. **Right Page**

   The table may be keyed from the left edge of the right page or a left margin may be set.

   If a left margin is set:
   a) Set the left margin 12 spaces (elite — 12 pitch) or 10 spaces (pica — 10 pitch) from the edge of the paper.
   b) The line length of the right page should be the same length as the key line of the left page. Therefore, the material will be horizontally centered.

Keying the Table

1. Key the table starting each half of the table title on the same line.
2. The table for each half should end on the same line.
3. Tape the two pages together on the back.
4. If margins were set, fold the right margin of the left page and the left margin of the right page before taping the pages together.

   Note: If you are using a computer
   • Set a right and left margin for both the left page and the right page.
   • View the two pages side by side before printing if your software has this special feature.

Letters

60-space line
Spacing: 1 and 2
Key two 1-min timings on
each line *or* repeat each line
three times.

Alternate-Hand Words

1 me bug map bit work girl mend down burns shelf entity handle
2 do bus oak bow worn goal name dual burnt sight lapels height

Common-Word Sentences

3 Five hundred shares will be put up for sale during the year.
4 They hoped to learn English quickly since jobs awaited them.
5 Please advise which office equipment they should now handle.

Number Practice

6 In the cupboard we have 500 g of cheese and 250 g of butter.
7 Bring home 500 g of rice, 425 g of cereal and 250 g of bran.

· · · · 1 · · · · 2 · · · · 3 · · · · 4 · · · · 5 · · · · 6 · · · · 7 · · · · 8 · · · · 9 · · · ·10· · · ·11· · · ·12

Speed Building

Key at least two 30-s
timings on each line *or*
repeat each line twice.
Try to increase your speed
on each successive try.

Three-Minute Timing

	1	CW	3

You must realize that every job has some unfavorable or | 12 | 12 | 4 |
negative things about it. You cannot expect a class at col- | 24 | 24 | 8 |
lege or a job at work to be filled with a bed of roses. One | 36 | 36 | 12 |
job may have more favorable things than another and you will | 48 | 48 | 16 |
do well to balance your books on that side, but you must re- | 60 | 60 | 20 |
member that there is no perfect job or position. | 70 | 70 | 23 |

The important thing to keep in mind is that you must be | 12 | 82 | 27 |
looking continually on the favorable aspects of your job and | 24 | 94 | 31 |
playing down the unfavorable. As you strive to do this, you | 36 | 106 | 35 |
will gradually make a habit of looking for the factors which | 48 | 118 | 39 |
are favorable. You will slowly develop yourself into a more | 60 | 130 | 43 |
positive person. | 63 | 133 | 44 |

Timing

Set spacing at 2. Key two
3-min timings. Circle all
errors and calculate gross
words per minute. Record
the better timing on your
Progress Chart.

· · · 1 · · · · 2 · · · · 3 · · · · 4 · · · · 5 · · · · 6 · · · · 7 · · · · 8 · · · · 9 · · · ·10· · · ·11· · · ·12 1 min

1   2   3   4 3 min

SI   1.48
AWL 4.34

Skill Building

Word Division – Rule 6

Divide only between complete words of a compound word.
low-grade   mid-day   mid-eastern   long-range

Two-Page Tables

60-space line
Spacing: 1 and 2
Key two 30-s timings on
each line *or* repeat each line
three times.

Right-Hand Words

1 no upon oily holy loom nip non ply ill yolk hook knoll imply

2 in pin lip oil ion link lump milk mink noun only Jimmy pupil

One-Minute Timings

1. Turn to the One-Minute Timings, page 421.
2. Select the paragraph that you think you can complete in one minute.
3. Key the One-Minute Timing as a drill.
4. If you had two or more errors, practice Accuracy Improvement.
   If you had fewer than two errors, practice Speed Improvement.

Skill Building

Key two 30-s timings on
line 3 of Accuracy Improvement. Circle any errors. If
you have more than one
error for each timing, continue with the Accuracy
Improvement drill. If you
have one error or less on
each timing, key the Speed
Improvement drill and
concentrate on speed.

Accuracy Improvement

3 ease radar verse effect regret evaders asserted reverses awe

4 few ion fast yolk ages polo sawed nylon assess plum excavate

5 he did maps cubic rotor burlap antique problems flair visual

Speed Improvement

6 Kenneth assures us that he will need aid to cross the creek.

7 What we plan to do next week is a topic to be discussed now.

8 Canada's population was at 25 354 064 by statistics of 1986.

. . . . 1 . . . . 2 . . . . 3 . . . . 4 . . . . 5 . . . 6 . . . . 7 . . . . 8 . . . . 9 . . . 10 . . . 11 . . . 12

Number Keying

Rule 13: Key numbers as figures when they are used with a symbol.
Example:

Taxi #472 arrived at the hotel.

Practice

Key each line once, cor-
recting the numbers when-
ever necessary. Correct lines
should end evenly on a
60-space line. The last two
lines review rules taken to
date. Check your work
carefully.

9 Bus #nine hundred ten was supposed to arrive but Bus #eighty-six
thirty-one arrived first.

10 At least ten % of the total $3000 was raised by Wednesday.

11 Aziz received .5 of the total $9 000 before the 4 of May.

12 A 3-way switch cost $3.88 on June 3rd but went on sale for
$3.00.

8 good-will long-term make-believe mock-up run-down short-term

9 postage-paid armchair amber self-contained apron axle awful

10 asked sixty-one vaguely bacteria safe-keeping saleswomen

11 shut-downs shopworn sincerely plywood victims up-to-date

Concentrate on Correct Spelling

12 We are introducing a new brand of leisure luggage.

13 The management will be moving into staff quarters.

Production 1

Key the following personal business letter on plain paper. Use the current alphabetic date. This letter is from Mrs. L.A. Howard, secretary of the Sherbrooke Optimist Club. Her return address is 407, rue Prince Rupert, Sherbrooke, Quebec J1G 1Z9. *Note:* Ms. is normally used to indicate a woman unless she has specified Miss or Mrs. in previous correspondence. Many women do not indicate their marital status when they sign a letter. Therefore, Ms. is used in addressing the reply.

Oasmund Enterprises Ltd.
300, rue Lepailleur
Montréal, Quebec
H1L 6J1

Gentlemen:

I am writing on behalf of the Sherbrooke Optimist Club. They would like to order 30 good quality sleeping bags, six 3 m x 4 m tents, 10 Coleman coolers, and 10 three-burner Coleman stoves. Could you submit a quotation for these items?

Our Club is a non-profit community organization. We would appreciate any discount you may offer.

Sincerely yours,

Mrs. L. A. Howard
Secretary

Production 2

Plan and key a copy of the following chart on a full sheet of paper

INFORMATION SERVICES ORGANIZATION CHART

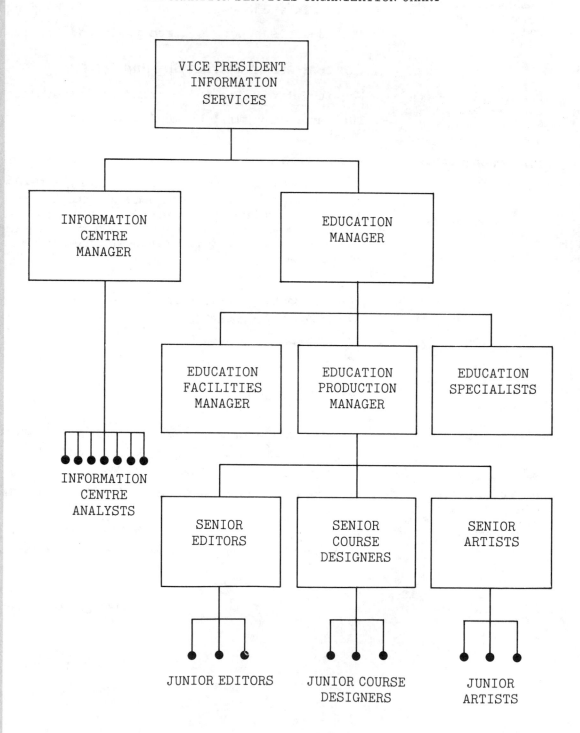

Production 2

Key the following personal business letter on plain paper. Use the current numeric date.
Note: When it is necessary to divide a long line into two to keep a balanced effect in the inside address, the run-over line is indented three spaces.

206 Rockwood Avenue
Fredericton, N B
E3B 2M3

Current Date

Cabot Institute of Applied
[3] Arts & Technology
Box 1693
St. John's, Newfoundland
A1C 5P7

Gentlemen:

I am planning to attend college next year and would like to receive information concerning the programs offered at Cabot.

Please forward, as soon as possible, a general calendar of programs. Do you have student residences? If you do, please include this information.

Sincerely yours,

Jean Anne Chiaverini

Production 1

Plan and key a copy of the following chart on a full sheet of paper. Ask your instructor or read the software manual to determine if it is possible to draw vertical and horizontal lines on your typewriter or computer.

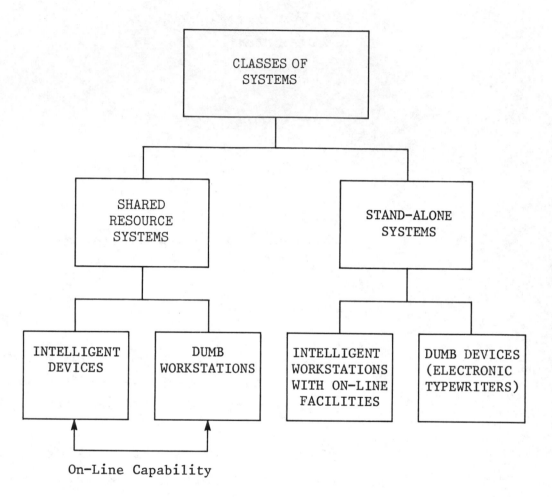

48 Letters/Subject Lines

60-space line
Spacing: 1 and 2
Key two 1-min timings on each line *or* repeat each line three times.

Speed Building

Key at least two 30-s timings on each line *or* repeat each line twice. Try to increase your speed on each successive try.

Key at least two 30-s timings on each line *or* repeat each line twice. Try to increase your speed on each successive try.

Key at least two 30-s timings on each line *or* repeat each line twice. Try to increase your speed on each successive try.

Timing

Set spacing at 2. Key two 3-min timings. Circle all errors and calculate gross words per minute. Record the better timing on your Progress Chart.

SI   1.24
AWL 4.13

Alternate-Hand Words

1 of but own box also gown odor duty chair signs formal island
2 or cow pan bug body hair owns firm civic slant handle panels

Common-Word Sentences

3 It is now time again to look at our needs for car insurance.
4 It is our plan to have more than one payment made by summer.
5 This has been our best opportunity to return the good favor.

Sentences with Double-Letter Words

6 The planning committee was successful in their news release.
7 We fully agree with you on that matter; I will attend to it.
8 Do feel free to offer advice if you see that an error looms.

Number Practice

9 Sharin ran the race in 3 min 42 s but Gerald took 4 min 19 s.
10 The speed limit is 50 km/h in town and 100 km/h on highways.

 • • • • 1 • • • • 2 • • • • 3 • • • • 4 • • • • 5 • • • • 6 • • • • 7 • • • • 8 • • • • 9 • • • •10• • • •11• • • •12

Three-Minute Timing

		1	3
Jobs may be hard to get this year so we need to start a		12	4
bit early this year to try to place our students. One thing		24	8
is on the side of students with business training: more job		36	12
openings have occurred in this field than in any other. The		48	16
demand for clerical and secretarial skills has topped career		60	20
charts for the last three years. The long-term trend claims		72	24
that there will soon be a shortage of office workers even if		84	28
some other fields may be in trouble. Have the students fill		96	32
out this form so we can best match them to jobs of their own		100	36
choice. However, to get their start in an office this year,		120	40
they may have to accept their second or third choices.		131	44

 • • • • 1 • • • • 2 • • • • 3 • • • • 4 • • • • 5 • • • • 6 • • • • 7 • • • • 8 • • • • 9 • • • •10• • • •11• • • •12   1 min

          1   2   3   4   3 min

Skill Building / Charts

60-space line
Spacing: 1 and 2
Key two 30-s timings on
each line *or* repeat each line
three times.

Left-Hand Words

1 fare safer waves exceed seated greases deserves averaged tar

2 fast saves waver excess secret greased deserved abstract far

Graduated Speed practice

Turn to the Graduated Alphanumerical Speed Practice, page 403. Select a sentence that you
think you can key in the time indicated.

Alphabetic Sentences

3 That same book is an excellent source of quotations for just

about every good poet who took a prize.

4 She hopes to qualify for the job in the zoo office but seven

other women would like to get exactly the same job.

Number Practice

5 Class 246 and 135 will meet in Room 1079 at 09:30 on Monday.

6 The school zone speed of 30 km/h would begin at 08:30 today.

Accuracy Building

Key two 30-s timings on
each line concentrating on
accuracy as your goal.
Students on individual
progress should key each
line three times with the
accuracy goal in mind.

Stroking Practice

1. Turn to the Stroking Practice, page 414.
2. Key the lines selected by your instructor or the letter combinations giving you difficulty in
the drills just completed.
3. Key each line twice.

Accuracy Improvement

7 degree hum faster hulk garages hump detracts union decreases

8 no nun kink polo phony lymph holly pinion knoll lymph in you

Skill Building

Key two 30-s timings on
line 7 of Accuracy Improvement. Circle any errors. If
you have more than one
error for each timing, continue with the Accuracy
Improvement drill. If you
have one error or less on
each timing, key the Speed
Improvement drill and
concentrate on speed.

Speed Improvement

9 His book went to press before the error was fully corrected.

10 The haughty girl laid the box by the bicycle and gave a cry.

• • • • 1 • • • • 2 • • • • 3 • • • • 4 • • • • 5 • • • • 6 • • • • 7 • • • • 8 • • • • 9 • • • • 10 • • • • 11 • • • • 12

Three- or Five-Minute Timing

Turn to the timing in Unit VI of your Working Papers. Students without Working Papers
should key the timing in Lesson 112, page 303.

Subject Lines

When a writer wishes to draw special attention to the purpose of a letter, the subject line notation may be used. It always follows the salutation by a double space. The subject line is similar to a title for the body of the letter because it refers to the information in the body.

Some accepted forms of subject lines follow. Notice that the word *Re* is interchangeable with the word *Subject*. Subject lines may be indented or centered. Because this step takes longer, the preferred business practice is to block the subject lines with the left margin.

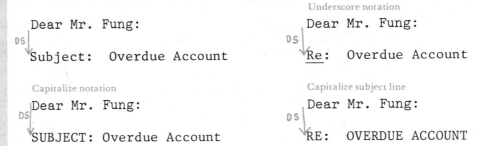

```
Dear Mr. Fung:                          Underscore notation
                                        Dear Mr. Fung:
Subject:  Overdue Account
                                        Re:  Overdue Account

Capitalize notation                     Capitalize subject line
Dear Mr. Fung:                          Dear Mr. Fung:

SUBJECT: Overdue Account                RE:  OVERDUE ACCOUNT
```

Production Practice

Production

Key the following personal business letter on plain paper. Use the current alphabetic date.

```
26 Allan Street
Red Deer, AB
T4R 1A8
Current Date

Liberty House
400-1975 Scarth Street
Regina, Sask.
S4P 2H1

Gentlemen:

Re:  Membership Number 55115875925 01795

I have received your statement showing a balance due of
$31.98.  This amount does not agree with my records.

My last statement showed a balance owing of $23.15 and
I paid this in full. Recently, I purchased one compact
disc for $19.95 and this should be the amount owed.

Enclosed is my cheque for $20.80 which includes the handling
charge of $0.85.

Please credit my account.

Sincerely yours,

Don J. Dusik

Enclosure
```

SC

Did you use your judgment to create a balanced appearance in this letter?

Production 1

Key the following Statement of Mortgage Proceeds on a half sheet of paper. Use open leaders and a 60-stroke line. Center it horizontally and vertically.

Dupuis Rental Properties Ltd.
Statement of Mortgage Proceeds
as at March 1, 19--

Loan		$112 632.00
Tax Account	$ 600.00	
Interest to December 1	644.42	
Legal Account	392.40	
Mortgage Discount	4 000.00	
Mortgage Insurance	1 632.00	
Interest to February 1	1 140.12	
Advance Number 1	29 662.04	
Advance Number 2	30 976.25	
Advance Number 3	23 559.54	
Advance Number 4	16 712.29	109 319.06
Seasonal Deficiencies		$ 3 312.94

Production 2

Key the following Income Statement for Dasmund Social Club (Toronto) for the year 19-- to 19-- on a full sheet of paper. Center vertically and horizontally. Do not use leaders. Capitalize centered headings and underscore side headings.

Receipts and Disbursement of Funds

Receipts:		
January Banquet	$1 345.00	
Advertising Contest	575.00	$1 920.00
Payments:		
Catering	$840.00	
Hall Rental for Jan. Banquet	142.56	
Postage and Printing	63.72	
Bank Service Charge	0.41	1 046.69
PROFIT		$ 873.31

Financial Condition

Opening Balance	$171.86	
Receipts	1 920.00	
Total		$2 091.86
Payments		1 046.69
ADJUSTED BALANCE		$1 045.17

49

%/Letters

60-space line
Spacing: 1 and 2
Key two 1-min timings on
each line *or* repeat each line
three times.

Use **F** finger and right shift
key. Keep other fingers
above home row. Key
each line twice.

Accuracy Building

Key at least two 1-min
timings on each line *or*
repeat each line three times.
Count all errors. If you had
more than two errors in
each attempt, concentrate
on individual letters. Your
aim should be to maintain
keyboard control.

Skill Building

Key each line once, inserting a hyphen between each
speech syllable. Correct
lines should end evenly on a
60-space line. Check your
work carefully.

Key each underlined word
three times. Key each line
once concentrating on the
underlined words.

One-Hand Words

1 tax you eat oil cast pill aged link drew noon wages onion re

2 tar hum ear Lou dart hulk ages hoop ease noun wards pupil be

Reach to the % Key

3 fff f5f f%f f%f fff %%% f%f f%f %f%f %f%f f%f f% %

4 10%; 20%; 30%; 40%; 50%; 60%; 70%; 80%; 90%; 100%.

5 The two groups range from 3% to 9% and 20% to 50%.

Right-Hand Words

6 my ohm ill joy you null moon loon look yolk ploy imply nylon

7 on ply ill mum pop hook hull link loop lump milk onion pupil

Double-Letter Words

8 see soot feel need staff happy follow assure between process

9 fee deep well bill still steel matter sheets follows looking

Sentences with Double-Letter Words

10 Their green cook book will now sell for three small loonies.

11 Agree to sell the yellow wool dresses but issue the tariffs.

12 It took a good week to sell the staff football pool to them.

• • • • 1 • • • • 2 • • • • 3 • • • • 4 • • • • 5 • • • • 6 • • • • 7 • • • • 8 • • • • 9 • • • • 10 • • • • 11 • • • • 12

Word Division – Rule 7

A single syllable in the middle of a word should be left on the first line of **keying**. If there are two single syllables, divide between them.
docu-ment gradu-ation grati-tude regu-late sani-tary via-ble

Word Division Practice

13 reputations salutations stimulus simulated valuations

14 civilization communication jubilation tedious ideas

Concentrate on Correct Spelling

15 Did you <u>exceed</u> the limit or become <u>exhausted</u> first?

16 That was dated before the <u>factory</u> was in <u>existence</u>.

113 Financial Statements

60-space line
Spacing: 1 and 2
Key two 30-s timings on
each line *or* repeat each line
three times.

One-Hand Words

1 rat hum dare hulk seed join reeds union access polo averages

2 dab Jim daze pull feed hill reefs jolly aerate kink carefree

One-Minute Timings

1. Turn to the One-Minute Timings, page 421.
2. Select the paragraph that you think you can complete in one minute.
3. Key the One-Minute Timing as a drill.
4. If you had two or more errors, practice Accuracy Improvement.
   If you had fewer than two errors, practice Speed Improvement.

Accuracy Improvement

3 still steel matter sheets follows looking accounts immediate

4 for all 83 by the 82 so then 37 to 43 to the 26 give them 13

5 at rag cat raw seed debt reef case draft grate crafts starts

Speed Improvement

6 Such information could cause a problem if the date is wrong.

7 The pupil darted up the hilly knoll to see an excavated car.

8 The hood of the jeep and its steel wheel need small repairs.

· · · · 1 · · · · 2 · · · · 3 · · · · 4 · · · · 5 · · · · 6 · · · · 7 · · · · 8 · · · · 9 · · · · 10 · · · · 11 · · · · 12

Skill Building

Key two 30-s timings on
line 3 of Accuracy Improvement. Circle any errors. If
you have more than one
error for each timing, continue with the Accuracy
Improvement drill. If you
have one error or less on
each timing, key the Speed
Improvement drill and
concentrate on speed.

Number Keying

Rule 12: When a date is preceded by the month, do not use th, d, rd, nd, or st. Dates which come before the month may be written in words or as figures with endings.
Example:

We will leave on July 20. We will arrive around the

3rd of August.

Practice

Key each line once, cor-
recting the numbers when-
ever necessary. Correct lines
should end evenly on a
60-space line. The last two
lines review rules taken to
date. Check your work
carefully.

9 The rodeo is scheduled for May 28 but it may be changed now.

10 We will arrive at your place by the 23 or 24 of October.

11 33 scouts arrived on July 3rd to use 15 canoes.

12 On the 7th of March we spent $15000.00 for 4 new computers.

Two-Minute Timing

Timing
Set spacing at 2. Key two
2-min timings. Circle all
errors and calculate gross
words per minute. Record
the better timing on your
Progress Chart.

SI   1.69
AWL 4.36

A new concept in apartment dwelling will open very soon	12	6
at 92 Birch Road. There are 75 new suites and it features a	24	12
covered car park. Two-bedroom suites rent for $850 a month.	36	18
A limited number of 3-bedroom suites, each with vast storage	48	24
and living space, are now renting for $995 a month. For in-	60	30
formation on these suites, please phone 836-4972.	70	35

• • • • 1 • • • • 2 • • • • 3 • • • • 4 • • • • 5 • • • • 6 • • • • 7 • • • • 8 • • • • 9 • • • • 10 • • • 11 • • • 12   1 min
1   2   3   4   5   6   2 min

Production 1

Production Practice

Key the following letter on the Dasmund Enterprises Toronto letterhead provided in the
Working Papers. Key an appropriate envelope or an envelope label for the letter.

Current Date

Mr. W. S. Kahn
14 Willingdon Avenue
London, ON
N6A 3Y6

Dear Mr. Kahn:

Subject: Account #17-342-74 in the Amount of $175

Your account is with our attorney for collection. This
action is regretted.   You are advised that your credit
privileges with our firm are cancelled.

Your account #17-342-74 in the amount of $175 is now three
months overdue.

When you applied for credit, you signed an application
form agreeing to make regular monthly payments on the
balance owing at the end of each billing period.   However,
this does not appear to be happening.

On November 1, 19--, you were notified that your account
was two months overdue.   You were advised again on November 15
and reminded by registered mail on November 30.   It appears
that you have chosen to ignore these letters.   We have no
alternative but to turn your account over to our legal
department.

Yours truly,

Thomas Rollins
Manager

oi

SC

Did you use your judgment
to create a balanced
appearance in this letter?

Production 1

Key the following Profit and Loss Statement on a full sheet of paper. Center it vertically and horizontally.

Dupuis Rental Properties Ltd.

PROFIT AND LOSS STATEMENT

For the year ended December 31, 19--

Rent Income		$116 075.00
Expenses		
Appraisal for 2nd Mortgage	$ 75.00	
Development Costs	3 000.00	
Discount on Mortgage	4 000.00	
Insurance :		
Fire	$ 802.00	
Mortgage	2632.00	3 434.00
Interest :		
Bank of Montreal	$ 2841.44	
Canada Trust	816.57	
Mortgage	1 799.68	5 457.69
Legal		1 627.90
Maintenance & Repairs		555.57
Mortgage Appraisal Fee		400.00
Supplies		833.24
Taxes – Prepayment		1 600.00
Total Expenses		20 983.40
NET PROFIT		$95 091.60

SC

Did you indent three spaces for the items under expenses?

SC

Do you have an automatic decimal alignment option?

Production 2

Key the Profit and Loss Statement in Production 1. Use a 70-stroke line with open leaders. Remember that the leaders should stop to align with the end of the first money column.

Production 2

Key the following personal business letter on plain paper. Use the current alphabetic date. *Note:* Titles and qualifications may be keyed with or without periods when they are abbreviated. For example, *B.A.* or *BA* is the abbreviation for Bachelor of Arts.

21 Carlington Avenue
London, Ontario
N5B 2J3

Current Date:

Dasmund Enterprises Ltd.
25 York Mills Road
Toronto, Ontario
M2P 1B5

Gentlemen:

Re: H.S. Kahn, Account # 17-342-74

Today I contacted Mr. Kahn concerning his outstanding account. At first, he was very uncooperative. Mr. Kahn decided instead of a wage garnishee he would pay the account in full.

Enclosed is a cheque for $140 which represents the $175 owed to you by Mr. Kahn less my usual collection fee of 20 percent of the balance collected.

Sincerely yours,

M.R. Duhamel, B.A., LL.B.

Enclosure

Example:

PAYMENTS:

3[Supplies	$150
[Insurance:	
3[Fire	300
[Mortgage	800
Hall rental for	
3] January banquet	50 $1 300

Three- or Five-Minute Timing

1 CW 3

Since the economy of our nation is in a continual state

of flux, the job market is hard to predict. Many a graduate

of university programs has found it difficult to get the job

for which he or she was training. Perhaps it worked for the

student's parents in the 1950's or someone in the 1970's but

the 1980-90's are giving more problems. One cannot outguess

easily the state of the job market in 4 or 5 years.

The number of graduates on the market will continue the

upward trend until at least 1993. No one predicts a compar-

able expansion in jobs. Enrollments in most universities in

the nation continue to rise. In 1961, only 13% of those el-

igible went beyond high school; in 1977, 25%; and by 1995 it

could be as high as 40%. The traditional correlation stated

between education and employment is being weakened.

More women are entering the job market to compete for a

growing scarcity of jobs. The female work force has had an-

nual growth rates of 5% compared to a male work force growth

of only 2% a year. The same trend is apparent in university

and college. The ratio of men to women in Ontario universi-

ties in 1982 was 1:15:1 and should be 1.06:1 by 1995. After

and during secondary school, students must seek out good vo-

cational counselling in order to find a probable job after a

lengthy training program.

12	12	4
24	24	8
36	36	12
48	48	16
60	60	20
72	72	24
82	82	27
12	94	31
24	106	35
36	118	39
48	130	43
60	142	47
72	154	51
82	164	54
12	176	58
24	188	62
36	200	66
48	212	70
60	224	74
72	236	78
84	248	82
96	260	86
101	265	88

• • • • 1 • • • • 2 • • • • 3 • • • • 4 • • • • 5 • • • • 6 • • • • 7 • • • • 8 • • • • 9 • • • • 10 • • • 11 • • • 12 1 min

1   2   3   4 3 min

SI 1.78
AWL 4.43

Sidebar:

Assess Your Improvement

Set spacing at 2. Key at least one 3-min *or* 5-min timing. Circle all errors and calculate gross words per minute. Record the timing on your Progress Chart.

50

Letters/Attention Lines

60-space line
Spacing: 1 and 2
Key two 1-min timings on each line *or* repeat each line three times.

Accuracy Building

Key at least two 1-min timings on each line *or* repeat each line three times. Count all errors. If you had more than two errors in each attempt, concentrate on individual letters. Your aim should be to maintain keyboard control.

Left-Hand Words

1 ad tax tar rat bars acre ease saws grass deeds facade creeds

2 aw dab eat ear bare aged deed scar razed defer fester debate

Alternate-Hand Words

3 an aid ham via then born laid pair amend right burlap island

4 am air hay dug they town lake pans angle rigid bushel panels

One-Hand Words

5 rat Jim ear ion dare pull acts oily eats O.K. wares union we

6 dab pin far ink daze null fact holy edge only waste jolly at

Sentences with One-Hand Words

7 As you start to pump extra gas, my car will race down hills.

8 Hop up on the aged lumpy raft after you pull on my wet gear.

• • • • 1 • • • • 2 • • • • 3 • • • • 4 • • • • 5 • • • 6 • • • • 7 • • • • 8 • • • • 9 • • • •10 • • • •11 • • •12

Skill Building

Key each sentence once, inserting the correct choice from the words in parentheses. Your right margin will not be even.

Basic English Skill

can: power or capabilities   *may:* permission

9 We (can, may) all key at least 30 words per minute.

10 Kuldip (can, may) swim twenty lengths of the pool in 10 min.

any one: usually followed by "of"; accent one   *anyone:* accent any

11 Has (any one, anyone) left a message for me while I was out?

12 (Any one, Anyone) of my clients could have tried to contact me.

Timing

Set spacing at 2. Key two 2-min timings. Circle all errors and calculate gross words per minute. Record the better timing on your Progress Chart.

SI   1.86
AWL 5.11

Two-Minute Timing

	1	2
The village of Glennview requires a part-time secretary	12	6
to begin work November 15. Duties consist of responsibility	24	12
for this office 24 hours each week and taking the minutes at	36	18
2 meetings each month. Applicants should apply prior to the	48	24
meeting on October 5, giving details of previous experience,	60	30
qualifications, salary expected, and references. Apply to:	71	35
Box 679, Glennview.	74	37

• • • • 1 • • • • 2 • • • • 3 • • • • 4 • • • • 5 • • • 6 • • • • 7 • • • • 8 • • • • 9 • • • •10 • • • •11 • • •12   1 min

1   2   3   4   5   6   2 min

Financial Statements

60-space line
Spacing: 1 and 2
Key two 30-s timings on
each line *or* repeat each line
three times.

Skill Building

Key two 30-s timings on
line 3 of Accuracy Improvement. Circle any errors. If
you have more than one
error for each timing, continue with the Accuracy
Improvement drill. If you
have one error or less on
each timing, key the Speed
Improvement drill and
concentrate on speed.

Alternate-Hand Words

1 or eye pant flame snake flange paucity ornament civic handle

2 so end pans flake slant entity problem problems coals height

Accuracy Improvement

3 then the 57 signed up 14 to the 38 when all 89 still have 31

4 staff happy follow assure between process business agreement

5 sax non raze loop tart poll seeds knoll badges pull recessed

Speed Improvement

6 Lou had to pump up water to use in the pool on your acreage.

7 The poor cook spilled the three eggs all over the inn floor.

8 At first, it was our wish to see this through to completion.

· · · · 1 · · · · 2 · · · · 3 · · · · 4 · · · · 5 · · · · 6 · · · · 7 · · · · 8 · · · · 9 · · · 10 · · · 11 · · · 12

Stroking Practice

1. Turn to the Stroking Practice, page 414.
2. Key the lines selected by your instructor or the letter combinations giving you difficulty in the drills just completed.
3. Students on individual progress should select lines from 31 to 45.
4. Key each line twice.

Number Keying

Rule 11: Amounts of money are written in figures: leave out zeroes and decimal marker if it is an even dollar amount.
Example:

We hoped to collect $47.50 but $30 was the most we could get.

Practice

Key each line once, cor-
recting the numbers when-
ever necessary. Correct lines
should end evenly on a
60-space line. The last two
lines review rules taken to
date. Check your work
carefully.

9 The invoices were recorded as follows: $8.18, $9.90 and $7.00.

10 The cost of the furniture was listed at $1860.99, down $99.00.

11 She handed me $15.00 to pay for the 3 rolls of camera film.

12 She took a 3-week vacation to Cape Breton for 7 autumns.

Indentations

Indent three spaces for each subdivision under a heading. If a description takes more than one line, indent the second line three spaces. If possible, use the indent option of your word processing program.

Attention Lines

When writing to a specific individual in a company, an attention line may be used. Key the attention line a double space below the inside address at the left margin. Leave a double space before the salutation. The attention line, like the subject line, can be keyed in many ways. Some acceptable forms are:

Attention: Mr. J. R. Parmar

DS↓

Gentlemen:

Underscore notation

Attention: Mr. J. R. Parmar

DS↓

Gentlemen:

Capitalize notation

ATTENTION: Mr. J. R. Parmar

DS↓

Gentlemen:

Capitalize attention line

ATTENTION: MR. J. R. PARMAR

DS↓

Gentlemen:

When keying an envelope, the attention line is included in the special instructions section between the return address and the main address.

Production Practice

Production

Key the following personal business letter on plain paper. Use the current alphabetic date.

```
4100 - 4th Avenue
Whitehorse, Yukon
Y1A 1H5

Current Date


Confederation College of
    Applied Arts & Technology
Box 398, Postal Station F
Thunder Bay, ON
P7C 4W1

Attention: Registrar

Gentlemen:

I am registered to attend Confederation College next term
and have received my acceptance letter.

The general calendar showing important dates and deadlines
has been misplaced.  Please forward a new calendar or
duplicate these pages.

Information concerning student housing would be appreciated.

Sincerely yours,

Denise Ehlert
```

SC
Did you remember to adjust spacing for a well balanced appearance?

Production 1

Key the following Balance Sheet on a full sheet of paper. Center it horizontally and vertically.

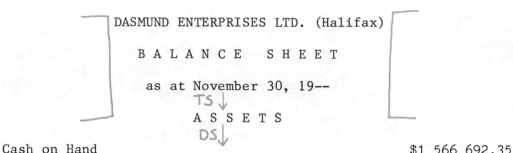

DASMUND ENTERPRISES LTD. (Halifax)

B A L A N C E   S H E E T

as at November 30, 19--

TS↓

A S S E T S

DS↓

Cash on Hand		$1 566 692.35
Accounts Receivable	$ 443 117.07	
3]Less Bad Debts Reserves	44 225.00	398 892.07
Furniture and Fixtures	$1 444 850.00	
3]Less Depreciation Reserves	44 850.00	1 400 000.00
Merchandise Inventory		1 897 450.00
Prepaid Insurance		43 776.40
Total Assets		$5 306 810.82

TS↓

L I A B I L I T I E S

DS↓

Accounts Payable	$ 422 720.00
Accrued Interest Payable	142 285.00
Notes Payable	366 000.00
Total Liabilities	$ 931 005.00

TS↓

C A P I T A L

DS↓

Capital, November 1, 19--	$3 352 718.00	
Accumulated Profit	1 023 087.82	
Capital, November 30, 19--		4 375 805.82
Total Liabilities and Capital		$5 306 810.82

SC

Did you clear all tabs?

SC

Do you have a decimal alignment option?

SC

Did you find the key line?

Production 2

Key the Balance Sheet in Production 1, but use a 60-stroke line with open leaders. Remember to leave at least one space between the word and the first leader. In this exercise the leaders should stop to align with the end of the first column of numbers in the section Assets.

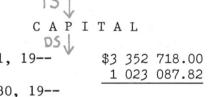

Cash on Hand		$1 566 692.35
Accounts Receivable	$ 443 117.07	
Accounts Payable		$ 422 720.00

Letters

60-space line
Spacing: 1 and 2
Key two 1-min timings on
each line *or* repeat each line
three times.

Accuracy Building

Key at least two 1-min
timings on each line *or*
repeat each line three times.
Count all errors. If you had
more than two errors in
each attempt, concentrate
on individual letters. Your
aim should be to maintain
keyboard control.

Timing

Set spacing at 2. Key two
2-min timings. Circle all
errors and calculate gross
words per minute. Record
the better timing on your
Progress Chart.

SI   1.28
AWL 3.38

Skill Building

Key each sentence once,
inserting the correct choice
from the words in
parentheses. Your right
margin will not be even.

One-Hand Words

1 eat nip fat nil east loom raft polo eggs pink water knoll ad

2 ear lip fed nip dear moon arts kink errs pool watts Jimmy aw

Left-Hand Words

3 as raw egg fat bear ages eats seas staff deter grease decade

4 re few gag gas cafe acts edge seat stage draft rarest decree

Double-Letter Words

5 bee beep good sell offer apply manner assist arrange selling

6 ill leek meet cell weeks sorry supply called current support

Sentences with Double-Letter Words

7 The book proof sheets need to be proofread for added errors.

8 We see that too many errors appear in office asset accounts.

• • • • 1 • • • • 2 • • • • 3 • • • • 4 • • • • 5 • • • • 6 • • • • 7 • • • • 8 • • • • 9 • • • • 10 • • • • 11 • • • • 12

Two-Minute Timing

	1	CW	2
We have a very special offer for you if you write to us	12	12	6
in the next week. We would like you to try our exciting new	24	24	12
product at no cost to you. Our company is so sure that most	36	36	18
people will be just as thrilled with this new product as all	48	48	24
of us are and will want to buy more after a free trial.	59	59	29
Our product is a brand new concept in skin care using a	12	71	35
costly blend of natural ingredients found only in the yellow	24	83	41
blooms of the dandelion. We guarantee that there is nothing	36	95	47
else on the market that is like Dandle Mist Cream. Write to	48	107	53
us today to get a large jar of this cream for yourself.	59	118	59

• • • • 1 • • • • 2 • • • • 3 • • • • 4 • • • • 5 • • • • 6 • • • • 7 • • • • 8 • • • • 9 • • • • 10 • • • • 11 • • • • 12   1 min

  1   2   3   4   5   6   2 min

Basic English Skill

complement: to complete   *compliment:* words of praise

9 This letter is the (compliment, complement) of our correspondence with that particular firm.

Leaders

Some businesses use a fixed line length (e.g., 60-stroke line) when keying financial statements. Therefore, there may be more than eight spaces between the descriptive column and the first money column. Leaders or a line of periods are added to make it easier to read from the descriptive column to the money column.

A leader is a period. A line of leaders is always preceded and followed by a space. Leaders may be keyed in open sequence (one space between periods) or in closed sequence (no spaces between periods).

Keying a Line of Open Leaders

1. Key the first line in the descriptive column.
2. Space **once**. Note if the print or cursor position is at an odd or even number.
3. Key *period space* repeatedly; stopping two or three blank spaces before the beginning of the first money column.
4. Key the money column(s) for the first item.
5. Key the second line in the descriptive column.
6. Space **once**. Note if the print or cursor position is at an odd or even number. If the number is similar (odd or even) to your answer in step 2, key a line of leaders. If the number is **not** similar (odd or even) to your answer in step 2, space once more and key a line of leaders.
7. The leaders should end at the same point and should align vertically under each other.
8. If there is more than one money column, the line of leaders usually stops before the first money column.

Example:

```
Supplies . . . . . . . . . . $   150
Insurance  . . . . . . . . .   1 100
Rental . . . . . . . . . . .      50
                                 ____

Total Payments . . . . . . .   $1 300
```

Note: There is one blank space after *supplies* and two blank spaces after *insurance*. This is so the leaders will align vertically. **Never** begin the leaders without spacing at least once.

Keying a Line of Closed Leaders

1. Key the first line of the descriptive column.
2. Space once.
3. Key the period repeatedly, stopping one or two blank spaces before the second column.
4. Key the second line of the descriptive column.
5. Repeat steps 2 and 3.

Example:

```
Supplies ................. $   150
Insurance ................ 1 100
Rental ...................    50
                            ____
Total Payments ...........  $1 300
```

Preparing to Key a Leader Table

1. Set the margins for the desired line length.
2. Center and key the title and subtitle.
3. Clear all tabs.
4. To set the tabs for the columns, pivot or backspace from the right margin.
5. Leave two or three spaces between money columns if there is more than one money column.

10 This letter is to (compliment, complement) you on the fine service we received from your company.

continual: actions which have repeated breaks at close intervals
continuous: actions which are repeated without interruption

11 The automatic timer on this oven has given (continual, continuous) service, when needed, for over 20 years.

12 The drip from that faucet has been (continuous, continual) for the past hour.

Production Practice

Production 1

Key the following letter on the Dasmund Enterprises Montreal letterhead provided in the Working Papers. Use the current date. Key the appropriate envelope or envelope label.

Master Card
Box 3000
Place d'Armes
Montréal, Québec H2Y 3M1

Attention: Credit Manager

Gentlemen:

Re: Account Number 223 0033 5566 131
Dasmund Enterprises Ltd.

¶ Your recent statement showing money owed to us has an error with one of our customers, Jules Sinclair.

¶ It appears that there has been a double billing of Mr. Sinclair's account. Our records show that he had one charge at our store on June 6. Your records indicate two charges on that day, both of equal amounts.

¶ Please make the necessary correction. We would appreciate it if you would advise Mr. Sinclair of this adjustment.

Sincerely,

Michelle De Meeres
Manager

111

60-space line
Spacing: 1 and 2
Key two 30-s timings on
each line *or* repeat each line
three times.

Leaders

Left-Hand Words

1 be web bag wet tare date rear face cater grade caveat feared

2 we far wax set rear dead reed base casts graft ceased feeder

One-Minute Timings

1. Turn to the One-Minute Timings, page 421.
2. Select the paragraph that you think you can complete in one minute.
3. Key the One-Minute Timing as a drill.
4. If you had two or more errors, practice Accuracy Improvement.
   If you had fewer than two errors, practice Speed Improvement.

Skill Building

Key two 30-s timings on
line 3 of Accuracy Improvement. Circle any errors. If
you have more than one
error for each timing, continue with the Accuracy
Improvement drill. If you
have one error or less on
each timing, key the Speed
Improvement drill and
concentrate on speed.

Accuracy Improvement

3 gag ink fade ploy acts kink scars onion assets plop exceeded

4 is cub male civic risks rotary auditor sorority flame burial

5 up non noon mono jumpy lumpy milky Phillip in joy kin I lump

Speed Improvement

6 In 1976 Saskatchewan had a total population of just 921 323.

7 She was happy to see small shells on the reef by the vessel.

8 We feared a monopoly was started so we had to act very fast.

• • • • 1 • • • • 2 • • • • 3 • • • • 4 • • • • 5 • • • • 6 • • • 7 • • • • 8 • • • • 9 • • • • 10 • • • 11 • • • 12

Number Keying

Rule 10: Use figures for numbers when used in a compound adjective; and write out numbers if used as an ordinary adjective.
Example:

This is the fifth time we have taken an 8-day hike.

Practice

Key each line once, cor-
recting the numbers when-
ever necessary. Correct lines
should end evenly on a
60-space line. The last two
lines review rules taken to
date. Check your work
carefully.

9 After spending 2 years in the 5th grade, I was promoted.

10 This was the 7th annual graduation of the 12 grade.

11 14 of us remained behind while the other forty-two skied out.

12 The 3rd recipe called for 9 red peppers and 2 onions.

Production 2

Key the following personal business letter from Ashton K. Kjellbotn, 5 Wright's Cove Road, Dartmouth, NS B3B 1M8. Use plain paper and the current alphabetic date.

Nova Scotia Institute of Technology / Box 2210 / 5685 Leeds Street / Halifax, NS B3K 2T5 / Attention: Mr. C.R. Maclean, Principal / Gentlemen: / I would like to inquire about a position at your Institute. / ¶ On April 25, I am moving to Halifax and will be available for employment. I would be interested in working in the area of accounting as I just completed the requirements for CMA certification. Enclosed is my résumé which contains information on my qualifications and experience. / ¶ An opportunity to discuss my application would be appreciated. I can be contacted by telephone at 902-762-4120. / Sincerely yours,

Production 2

Key the following Bank Reconciliation Statement for the Business Club for the month of March, 19--. Center it horizontally and vertically.

Bank Balance, March 1 $7 123

Outstanding Deposits:
March 17	$ 719	
March 20	2 014	
March 24	2 916	
March 28	7 111	
March 30	1 123	13 883
		21 006

Outstanding Cheques:
Cheque 4101	$ 125	
Cheque 4103	318	
Cheque 4217	1 001	
Cheque 4218	916	
Cheque 4222	4 003	
Cheque 4225	2 018	8 381

Correct Bank Balance, March 31 $12 625

*Note: The amounts have been rounded off to the nearest dollar.

52

Analytical Practice

60-space line
Spacing: 1
Key two 1-min timings on
each line *or* repeat each line
three times.

**Analyze Your
Practice Needs**
Key three 1-min timings on
each sentence *or* repeat each
sentence five times. Every
alphabetic character is
included in each sentence.

Circle all errors.

After Selected Letter
Practice, key two 1-min
timings on each sentence
and determine if you have
improved your accuracy.

If you have practised the
necessary lines before your
instructor calls time, begin
keying at line **A** and key
each line once.

Alternate-Hand Words

1 do and lay them also kept ambit rifle burial ambient antique

2 do and end lay them also kept paid ambit rifle burial height

Alphabetic Sentences

3 One might say of an avid gardener that he just quietly rests

by his bed of zinnias while he watches his phlox take a nap.

4 Zoe was busy learning to play the saxophone every night, but

she just had to quit all of her activities to make the band.

• • • • 1 • • • • 2 • • • • 3 • • • • 4 • • • • 5 • • • • 6 • • • • 7 • • • • 8 • • • • 9 • • • • 10 • • • 11 • • • 12

Selected Letter Practice

1. Analyze your errors in the Alphabetic Sentences.
2. Choose the letter or letters giving you difficulty or causing errors.
3. Select the appropriate Selected Letter Practice.
4. Key each line twice.
5. Assess your improvement.

A as was any year sales area take day name car accept air game

Mary asked Alison to add any extra articles to this account.

B be been but above being both basis before business back bond

Brian will bring the big bags of bait to his brother's boat.

C can could each account received cost cheque cover back place

Can Candice carry each crate of canned peaches to the truck?

D and made due good dock dual odor end kind does found address

Does a dog named Duke draw a sled or just drag an old board?

E be ear reef bears eager effect grace evade edge beds greases

Ethel does not even eat eggs but she likes to eat red plums.

F fee of cafe fat fish fight staff safer affect fast fix rafts

The fare on this ferry is fifty-five dollars for the family.

G dig girl grass agree grace badges digit sag garage gate cage

The girls will give Glen a gift if he gets a good game goal.

• • • • 1 • • • • 2 • • • • 3 • • • • 4 • • • • 5 • • • • 6 • • • • 7 • • • • 8 • • • • 9 • • • • 10 • • • 11 • • • 12

Financial Statements

Each business has its own style of format for keying financial statements. Some of the more popular styles are used in this unit.
- Financial statements are usually keyed in tabular form.
- If the financial statement is horizontally centered:
1. Leave six to eight spaces between the descriptive column and the first money column.
2. Leave two or three spaces between money columns.
3. Align the dollar signs and the decimal markers in the money columns.
   Some word processing software and electronic typewriters have an automatic decimal alignment option.

Note: Before keying a financial statement which is horizontally centered, find the key line.

Production Practice

Production 1

Key the following Bank Reconciliation Statement on a full sheet of paper. Center it horizontally and vertically according to the format illustrated.

SC

Did you capitalize the name of the statement?

SC

Did you clear all preset tabs?

SC

Do you have an automatic decimal alignment option?

SC

Did you find the key line?

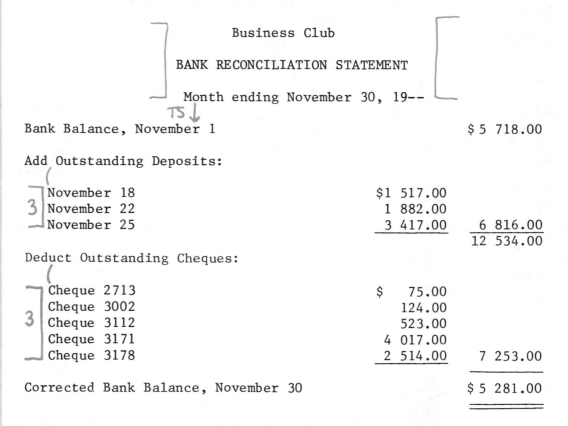

Business Club

BANK RECONCILIATION STATEMENT

Month ending November 30, 19--

Bank Balance, November 1	$ 5 718.00
Add Outstanding Deposits:	
November 18 $1 517.00	
November 22 1 882.00	
November 25 3 417.00	6 816.00
	12 534.00
Deduct Outstanding Cheques:	
Cheque 2713 $ 75.00	
Cheque 3002 124.00	
Cheque 3112 523.00	
Cheque 3171 4 017.00	
Cheque 3178 2 514.00	7 253.00
Corrected Bank Balance, November 30	$ 5 281.00

Key line: Corrected Bank Balance November 30 |6 spaces| $1 517.00 |3 spaces| $ 5 718.00

H he fish ham both chair right whale this the what hope handle
Help Hannah with her math while I have a hand at helping Al.

I if big rid iced with sit rigid island him item pin is social
If Iris eats the white icing on the pies she might get sick.

J join jam joke jelly jeep jaw just jungle janitor join jargon
Joan's jacket and jeans are just about adjusted for her use.

K keen kitten make knows kip keys lark knife joke knoll turkey
I asked if Kent would keep the key rack in the back kitchen.

L lab laid rail lamb call salt laurel leader local lost luxury
A busy little lady took a ladle to the lake to play in sand.

M major man women marble meal came metric miner mobile mystery
Many men might make the same kind of mistake as Marvin made.

N upon loan name an needs noise noted noun town number nursery
Nancy needs new knitting needles to finish her next garment.

O oak obey omit lone opaque often odd outfit outside over polo
She will only open this door if someone else is not at home.

P hip upon plump pant pin shape problem proper protein opinion
Papa paid the planned price to purchase a pair of big pants.

Q equal quarter sequel question qualify quite quantities quota
The quiet queen quickly quartered a quantity of quince jell.

R rack range burlap reason recovery rice roof oar rush rip rig
Ralph raked the rolls of rotted rubber from roofs of trains.

S safe sales second grass size snow forks soar space his sight
Sarah said she will salt the fresh salad greens in a second.

T to but kept trends trust tyrant twine right attest cat great
I might take the walnut table to the front of the tiny room.

U use until us unable under visual unusual union utilize augur
Seven of us used your unusual umbrella under the summer sun.

• • • • 1 • • • • 2 • • • • 3 • • • • 4 • • • • 5 • • • • 6 • • • • 7 • • • • 8 • • • • 9 • • • •10• • • •11• • • •12

Financial Statements

60-space line
Spacing: 1 and 2
Key two 30-s timings on
each line *or* repeat each line
three times.

One-Hand Words

1 tax joy cast mill rear pump rated onion accede oily attested

2 tar you dart pill rare upon reads pupil arrest holy attracts

One-Minute Timings

1. Turn to the One-Minute Timings, page 421.
2. Select the paragraph that you think you can complete in one minute.
3. Key the One-Minute Timing as a drill.
4. If you had two or more errors, practice Accuracy Improvement.
   If you had fewer than two errors, practice Speed Improvement.

Skill Building

Key two 30-s timings on
line 3 of Accuracy Improvement. Circle any errors. If
you have more than one
error for each timing, continue with the Accuracy
Improvement drill. If you
have one error or less on
each timing, key the Speed
Improvement drill and
concentrate on speed.

Sp

neighbor or *neighbour*

Accuracy Improvement

3 do dig mend digit shale cosign visitor neighbor fight theory

4 tee seem moor boom grass deeds stress bottle omitted vessels

5 on nip O.K. noun jolly mummy hilly pylon oh you him nil moon

Speed Improvement

6 Attach the holly to the upper part of the wall in an office.

7 What amount do you hope to obtain from the sale of old hats?

8 By 1941 Canada's population had jumped to 14 009 429 people.

• • • • 1 • • • • 2 • • • • 3 • • • • 4 • • • • 5 • • • • 6 • • • • 7 • • • • 8 • • • • 9 • • • • 10 • • • • 11 • • • • 12

Number Keying

Rule 9: Use figures when a number follows a noun.
Example:

Cabin 26 is not in use.

Practice

Key each line once, cor-
recting the numbers when-
ever necessary. Correct lines
should end evenly on a
60-space line. The last two
lines review rules taken to
date. Check your work
carefully.

9 Rooms 3124 and 4632 are scheduled for grade two in the winter.

10 We travelled via Route Six Sixteen and Route Seven Hundred on
the return trip.

11 When counted, Kwan got nineteen votes, May got seven, and
Sean got 21.

12 During 1990, 23 new college programs were started.

v visit voyage live every vitamin vein vacant vacuum vats vast
  Valery values the violet velvet vest given to her by Vaughn.

w wore woe drew hollow wish world whale wade wart waste screws
  Wally went with Wilma while we waited and watched a western.

x x-ray box ax six pixie relax flex tax sex extra waxes x-rays
  Trixie Knox fixed a box to mix her extra six salads for Max.

y yard you year yours yellow young eye play by fly typed forty
  Yesterday I used a yard of your yellow yarn for my own ball.

z zero zone zany daze zodiac zipper doze zealous zippy zooming
  This bronze zinnia is in the same zone as the azure lobelia.
  • • • • 1 • • • • 2 • • • • 3 • • • • 4 • • • • 5 • • • 6 • • • • 7 • • • • 8 • • • • 9 • • • 10 • • • 11 • • • 12

Sentence with Numbers

Please phone these people: Mary Ann 347-6015, Uwe 885-2089,
Anita 476-5312, Terry 348-7021, Kim 359-6037, Jose 343-7218,
Lindsay 476-3456, and Marge 472-8101.
  • • • • 1 • • • • 2 • • • • 3 • • • • 4 • • • • 5 • • • 6 • • • • 7 • • • • 8 • • • • 9 • • • 10 • • • 11 • • • 12

Selected Number Practice

1. Analyze your errors in the Sentence with Numbers.
2. Choose the number or numbers giving you difficulty or causing errors.
3. Select the appropriate Selected Number Practice.
4. Key each line twice.

1 a 1 and a 1 or an 11 or 111 and 12 for a 31 by 1 among 1 121
2 a 2 or 22 by 12 since 212 by 2 and a 21 or 21 and 2 122 or 2
3 the 3 or 13 and 33 by 31 yet 3 131 or 3 323 by 31 but 3 or 3
4 or 4 and 41 but 14 and 4 141 by 44 among 414 for 4 424 and 4
5 a 5 and a 55 or 515 by 51 but 5 at least 5 251 for 515 and 5
6 the 6 or 16 since 616 then 61 but 16 626 for 16 or 66 but 26
7 a 7 and a 7 or a 71 or 7 171 and 7 for a 72 by 7 among 7 737
8 the 8 or 18 and 88 by 81 yet 8 181 or 8 828 by 83 but 8 or 8
9 or 9 and 92 but 19 and 9 191 by 99 among 949 for 9 929 and 9
0 a 0 and a 3 or 040 by 39 but 20 at least 1 040 for 200 and 0
  • • • • 1 • • • • 2 • • • • 3 • • • • 4 • • • • 5 • • • 6 • • • • 7 • • • • 8 • • • • 9 • • • 10 • • • 11 • • • 12

Key three 2-min timings on the sentence *or* repeat the sentence five times. All numbers are included in the sentence.

Circle all number errors.

After Selected Number Practice, key two 2-min timings on the sentence and determine if you have improved your number accuracy.

Production 1

Key the following table on a full sheet of paper with the long side inserted first. Center it horizontally and vertically.

Dasmund Enterprises Ltd.
Number of Employees by Branch, 19--

Age	Halifax M	Halifax F	Montreal M	Montreal F	Toronto M	Toronto F	Winnipeg M	Winnipeg F	Regina M	Regina F	Edmonton M	Edmonton F	Vancouver M	Vancouver F	Total*
Under 18	4	2	5	2	5	3	2	1	2	2	3	2	3	2	38
18–25	10	8	12	14	17	23	20	15	13	12	15	13	22	22	216
26–30	22	10	29	17	35	35	24	23	30	17	28	24	30	28	352
31–40	20	21	29	27	28	17	25	17	25	26	29	26	28	25	343
41–50	20	11	27	15	34	31	29	20	18	12	21	21	23	23	305
51–55	10	8	15	14	12	9	11	7	8	5	9	6	7	4	125
56–60	8	5	12	7	10	7	7	4	7	6	8	4	5	5	95
61–65	5	1	9	3	7	3	5	1	6	2	2	1	3	1	49
Over 65	2	–	2	1	2	–	1	1	2	–	–	–	1	–	12
Totals	101	66	140	100	150	128	124	89	111	82	115	97	122	110	1535

* Head Office employees not included

Set margins for an appropriate line length. Insert your paper and space down to the date line. Wait until your instructor tells you to begin keying. Students on individual progress should start to time themselves when they begin keying.

Can you complete the letter in 10 min?

Production

Key the following letter on the Dalhousie University letterhead provided in the Working Papers. Use the current alphabetic date.

Mr. Lin Sung
Xinghua University
Haidian District
Beijing, People's Republic of China

Dear Mr. Lin:

¶ I am very pleased to learn of your interest in Oceanography and that you have written to Dalhousie for specific information. I hope that my office can be of assistance to you when you enter the University.

¶ I believe Dalhousie can offer you the advantages of an outstanding education and superior preparation for your chosen career. We like to involve our students in department activities as they progress through their studies, and we have available student assistantships for those qualified after they enter the University.

¶ Please feel free to contact me at any time if you have questions or desire further information. My office hours are 08:00 through 16:30, Monday to Friday.

¶ If you attend one of our Summer Orientation Programs for entering freshmen, I hope you will come by my office and introduce yourself. I look forward to meeting you and working with you every way possible after you enter Dalhousie University.

Sincerely,

S. K. Broecker, Dean
Faculty of Science

SC
Did you include your reference initials?

Assess Your Improvement

Set spacing at 2. Key at least one 3-min *or* 5-min timing. Circle all errors and calculate gross words per minute. Record the timing on your Progress Chart.

SI 1.48
AWL 4.43

We are bombarded with the spoken word every day through
many mediums. The radio, the television, the telephone, the
teacher, the boss, our friends. The list goes on and on. A
person learns to block out and ignore many of these messages
that hit our ears. Often, however, we are blocking out some
voices that we should be hearing. Many of us are quite poor
listeners and we miss important information.

Good listening skills are important for all of us. Our
ability to listen will help us in school, in our jobs and in
our relations with our friends on a social basis. Mastering
good listening skills will require effort, but the effort is
sure to pay off in many ways. It can result in a better job
done and in better relationships with friends and with other
members of our families.

To start off, be interested in what the speaker is saying and do not interrupt. When taking notes record only key
words and phrases. Concentrate even if the subject is something you find heavy. Try to understand the speaker's point
of view even if you do not agree with it. Train yourself to
block out distractions. Read widely so you can be genuinely
interested in a variety of topics.

	12	12	4
	24	24	8
	36	36	12
	48	48	16
	60	60	20
	72	72	24
	81	81	27
	12	93	31
	24	105	35
	36	117	39
	48	129	43
	60	141	47
	72	153	51
	77	158	52
	12	170	56
	24	182	60
	36	194	64
	48	206	68
	60	218	72
	72	230	76
	79	237	78

• • • • 1 • • • • 2 • • • • 3 • • • • 4 • • • • 5 • • • • 6 • • • • 7 • • • • 8 • • • • 9 • • • •10• • • •11• • • •12 1 min
　　　　　1　　　　　　　2　　　　　　　3　　　　4 3 min

53 Letters with Tables

60-space line
Spacing: 1 and 2
Key two 1-min timings on each line *or* repeat each line three times.

Speed Building

Key at least two 30-s timings on each line *or* repeat each line twice. Try to increase your speed on each successive try.

Timing

Set spacing at 2. Key two 3-min timings. Circle all errors and calculate gross words per minute. Record the better timing on your Progress Chart.

SI   1.29
AWL 4.09

Alternate-Hand Words

1 us did pro cow buck hems pans foam cycle their bushel social

2 do die rid cub burn hand pant fork digit theme cosign theory

Sentences with One-Hand Words

3 The hulls are carted east to my pulp mill and then sawed up.

4 We can join him in a debate on the free use of the ski hill.

5 Look at a few pages of my free verse on sea reefs and water.

Common-Word Sentences

6 Both of our departments will try to give you speedy service.

7 Two men were taken to the local hospital in the same period.

8 Your account has been overdue for a month without a payment.

Number Practice

9 At 6 years of age Sean is 117 cm tall and his mass is 20 kg.

10 Dinner is at 18:30 and their meeting will start about 20:30.

• • • • 1 • • • • 2 • • • • 3 • • • • 4 • • • • 5 • • • • 6 • • • • 7 • • • • 8 • • • • 9 • • •10• • •11• • •12

Three-Minute Timing

		1	3
Winter in Alberta can be a long, cold stretch of months		12	4
if you happen to be a sun lover. But it is not necessary to		24	8
sit and mope and count the days until spring. The people of		36	12
the province will tell you that winter can be as much fun as		48	16
summer if you are prepared to bundle up. Cross country ski-		60	20
ing is enjoyed by many people. On Sunday afternoon you will		72	24
see whole families out gliding across the fresh fallen snow.		84	28
For those who enjoy a slower pace, a pair of snowshoes might		96	32
be just right. Anyone who savors the thrill of heights with		108	36
brisk winds and dizzy speed will love down hill skiing. And		120	40
for those who hate snow there is a warm fireplace and a good		132	44
book.		133	44

• • • • 1 • • • • 2 • • • • 3 • • • • 4 • • • • 5 • • • • 6 • • • • 7 • • • • 8 • • • • 9 • • •10• • •11• • • 12   1 min

       1   2   3   4   3 min

Sideways Tables

60-space line
Spacing: 1 and 2
Key two 30-s timings on
each line *or* repeat each line
three times.

Skill Building

Key two 30-s timings on
line 3 of Accuracy Improvement. Circle any errors. If
you have more than one
error for each timing, continue with the Accuracy
Improvement drill. If you
have one error or less on
each timing, key the Speed
Improvement drill and
concentrate on speed.

Right-Hand Words

1 up non ply ill hum loom look hook link lump milk ion minimum

2 no joy ill ink Jim kink polo oily hoop join upon jolly knoll

Accuracy Improvement

3 through the 72 but the 91 in all 73 and all 17 but for 3 759

4 sad non draw link arts bump seats jolly awards hulk recesses

5 nee tell hood mood breed dress middle occurs annuity barrels

Speed Improvement

6 We will attach the interest receipt to a prepared statement.

7 We called to see if he might assist us unless he cannot dig.

8 Look to see if Jill will link the oily hoop to the wet hook.

· · · · 1 · · · · 2 · · · · 3 · · · · 4 · · · · 5 · · · · 6 · · · · 7 · · · · 8 · · · · 9 · · · · 10 · · · · 11 · · · · 12

Stroking Practice

1. Turn to the Stroking Practice, page 414 .
2. Key the lines selected by your instructor or the letter combinations giving you difficulty in the drills just completed.
3. Students on individual progress should select lines from 16 to 30.
4. Key each line twice.

Number Keying

Rule 8: Use figures to express time except when used with the word "o'clock".
Examples:

The seminar will finish at 14:50 today and 09:30 tomorrow.

We should arrive by five o'clock.

Practice

Key each line once, cor-
recting the numbers when-
ever necessary. Correct lines
should end evenly on a
60-space line. The last two
lines review rules taken to
date. Check your work
carefully.

9 It was seven o'clock before the meeting was called to order.

10 The same class is available at 900, 1100, 1330 or 1400.

11 Nine had arrived by 9:30 but the other eighteen arrived at 955.

12 The Toronto Stock Exchange sold 473 573 462 stocks by 1300.

Skill Building

Key each underlined word
three times. Key each line
once concentrating on the
underlined words.

Concentrate on Correct Spelling

11 We hope the report is <u>acceptable</u> to the six of you.

12 Are they <u>acknowledging</u> efforts <u>across</u> the country?

Letters with Tables

When statistical material needs to be included with a business letter, a separate table may be keyed and attached to the letter or the table may be keyed within the body of the letter.

A table keyed within the body of a letter should have a double space above and below it. Such a table may be set up in two ways:

1. The table is aligned with the left and right margins of the letter by adjusting the number of spaces between columns.
2. The table is indented from the left and right margins of the letter. This may be done by either backspacing the key line of the table from the center point (the table should not go beyond the normal line length of the body) or indenting equal number of spaces from the right and left margins and adjusting the number of spaces between columns.

Either method of keying tables is acceptable business practice.

Production Practice

Production 1

Using the Government of British Columbia letterhead provided in the Working Papers, key the following letter. Key an appropriate envelope or an envelope label.

```
Mr. Felix Helle
Fraser Valley College
3616 Tretheway
Abbotsford, British Columbia
V2T 4C1


Dear Mr. Helle:


Thank you for your recent letter and the inquiry for information
on metrication.


The SI (Système international d'unités) uses the following metric
prefixes:
        DS
```

Number of Units	Prefix	Symbol
1 000 000	mega	M
1 000	kilo	k
100	hecto	h
10	deca	da

```
        DS
I hope that this information will be of assistance to you.


Sincerely yours,


R. E. Wiseman, Ph.D.
Coordinator, Metric Commission

oi
```

Production

Key the following table on a full sheet of paper with the long side inserted first.
Center it horizontally and vertically. Your printer may require specialized software to print sideways if you are using a computer.

(Number of Dasmund Employees by Age and Sex, 19——) all caps

Age	Male		Female		Total	
	Number	Percent[1]	Number	Percent[2]	Number	Percent[3]
Under 18	24	2.40	15	1.92	39	2.12
18–25	129	12.88	137	17.49	266	14.92
26–30	233	23.28	186	23.75	419	23.50
31–40	212	21.18	180	22.98	392	21.98
41–50	197	19.68	145	18.52	342	19.18
51–55	85	8.48	58	7.41	143	8.03
56–60	67	6.70	46	5.88	113	6.34
61–65	42	4.20	14	1.79	56	3.14
Over 65	12	1.20	2	0.26	14	0.79
Total	1001	100.00	783	100.00	1784	100.00

[1] Indicates percentage of total males
[2] Indicates percentage of total females
[3] Indicates percentage of employees, male and female

SC

Does your printer have the capability of printing sideways if you are using a computer?

Production 2

Key the following letter on the Dasmund Enterprises Vancouver letterhead provided in the Working Papers. Key an appropriate envelope or an envelope label.

Mr. Guy Almberg
6029 Tisdale Street
Vancouver, British Columbia
V5Z 3N1

Dear Mr. Almberg:

The information you requested in your letter of October 13 concerning current salaries paid to our clerical staff is as follows:

Job Title	Annual Salary Range
Clerk	15 156 - 18 756
Administrative Clerk	20 472 - 24 348
Receptionist	16 956 - 21 468
Secretary	20 472 - 24 348
Information Processing Specialist	18 756 - 22 248

In addition, we provide a full range of fringe benefits to our employees. These benefits include group-life insurance, paid sick-leave, medical and dental insurance, and a company pension plan.

I trust this information will be helpful. We would be interested in receiving a copy of your completed report.

Sincerely,

Fred Baker
Manager

108

60-space line
Spacing: 1 and 2
Key two 30-s timings on
each line *or* repeat each line
three times.

Skill Building

Key two 30-s timings on
line 3 of Accuracy Improvement. Circle any errors. If
you have more than one
error for each timing, continue with the Accuracy
Improvement drill. If you
have one error or less on
each timing, key the Speed
Improvement drill and
concentrate on speed.

Key each line once, cor-
recting the numbers when-
ever necessary. Correct lines
should end evenly on a
60-space line. Check your
work carefully.

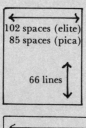

```
┌─────────────────────┐
│102 spaces (elite)   │
│85 spaces (pica)     │
│                     │
│                     │
│  66 lines  ↕        │
│                     │
└─────────────────────┘

┌───────────────────────┐
│                 ↑     │
│132 spaces (elite)     │
│110 spaces (pica)      │
│                       │
│  51 lines  ↓          │
└───────────────────────┘
```
Full sheet of paper sideways

Sideways Tables

Left-Hand Words

1 ad vat age vex wade cast rare west bread gases better excess
2 aw wad bad war wage crew wets area breed gates brazed exerts

One-Minute Timings

1. Turn to the One-Minute Timings, page 421.
2. Select the paragraph that you think you can complete in one minute.
3. Key the One-Minute Timing as a drill.
4. If you had two or more errors, practice Accuracy Improvement.
   If you had fewer than two errors, practice Speed Improvement.

Accuracy Improvement

3 in ion pull poll plunk imply nylon minimum in hip pupil kink
4 up at least 67 but up to 85 in all 32 save all 17 to the 853
5 it cow make chair rigid visual augment amendment also ritual

Speed Improvement

6 In my opinion, that lumpy pink cushion deserves to be saved.
7 Attend college in the summer if the class should be offered.
8 We appreciate your account and hope we can continue service.

· · · · 1 · · · · 2 · · · · 3 · · · · 4 · · · · 5 · · · · 6 · · · · 7 · · · · 8 · · · · 9 · · · ·10· · · ·11· · · ·12

Number Keying

Rule 7: Approximate numbers should be spelled out.
Example: We hope nearly thirty people will go.

Practice

9 At least 2 000 people attended the spring conference.
10 Between 40 and 50 students came out for that practice.

Standard Sized Paper Inserted Sideways

A table with many columns may be too wide for a full sheet of paper. The table may fit if the paper is inserted in the machine sideways or with the long edge first.

For a full sheet of paper inserted sideways, horizontally there are 132 spaces (elite — 12 pitch) or 110 spaces (pica — 10 pitch).

If the left edge of paper is at zero on the margin scale, the center point is 66 (elite — 12 pitch) or 55 (pica — 10 pitch).

54 Letters

60-space line
Spacing: 1 and 2
Key two 1-min timings on each line *or* repeat each line three times.

Speed Building

Key at least two 30-s timings on each line *or* repeat each line twice. Try to increase your speed on each successive try.

Skill Building

Key each underlined word three times. Key each line once concentrating on the underlined words.

Timing

Set spacing at 2. Key at least one 3-min timing. Circle all errors and calculate gross words per minute. Record the timing on your Progress Chart.

SI 1.33
AWL 4.30

Alternate-Hand Words

1 so cub pay bus born half paid fish coals snake burial ritual
2 to cut pep but both hams pair flap cubic socks burlap signal

Common-Word Sentences

3 They will be able to put their complete trust in the theory.
4 We appreciate the fact that the goods will not be available.
5 Any future request should be given to the firm in good time.

Number Practice

6 The average door was about 200 cm (2 m) high and 100 m wide.
7 At 3 years of age Peter is 96 cm tall and his mass is 16 kg.

• • • • 1 • • • • 2 • • • • 3 • • • • 4 • • • • 5 • • • • 6 • • • • 7 • • • • 8 • • • • 9 • • • • 10 • • • • 11 • • • • 12

Concentrate on Correct Spelling

8 The <u>policies</u> were not <u>labeled</u> according to <u>effect</u>.
9 Larry was able to <u>accumulate</u> <u>accurate</u> information.

Three-Minute Timing

	1	CW	3
The mail pours into the office each day and needs to be	12	12	4
sorted before it is put on the desks. If this firm is quite	24	24	8
large, a clerk will be assigned to sort the huge pile of in-	36	36	12
coming mail before it is taken to the various offices within	48	48	16
the firm. At the next stage, the secretary must check every	60	60	20
piece of mail that arrives on the desk and make decisions as	72	72	24
to what level of priority each should receive.	81	81	28
The less important mail should be set to one side until	12	93	31
the rest of the mail has been dispatched. This type of mail	24	105	35
would include newspapers, magazines and brochures. The more	36	117	39
important mail would be the first-class mail which has keyed	48	129	43
or handwritten addresses on them. Of course, you should pay	60	141	47
close attention to any special mail for which the sender has	72	153	51
spent extra cash.	75	156	52

• • • • 1 • • • • 2 • • • • 3 • • • • 4 • • • • 5 • • • • 6 • • • • 7 • • • • 8 • • • • 9 • • • • 10 • • • • 11 • • • • 12   1 min

1   2   3   4   3 min

Profit Sharing Plan...continued ↓TS

Name	Branch	Date of Employment
Falenbrenza, Mike	Toronto	85 02 20
Gagnon, Andre	Toronto	90 02 17
Grant, Elizabeth	Vancouver	88 07 15
Gudlaugson, Omar	Montreal	89 09 15
Hamilton, Gordon	Halifax	87 08 01
Hendrickson, Glenda	Toronto	86 10 07
Irvine, Norma	Vancouver	89 08 03
Jamison, Randy	Regina	90 05 12
Jean, Lucien	Montreal	88 06 15
Knight, Ronald	Halifax	90 01 01
Kufeld, Max	Edmonton	85 12 15
Lamoureaux, Bernard	Regina	89 11 15
Longmore, Robert	Winnipeg	87 09 23
MacKintosh, Ian	Halifax	89 07 08
McIntyre, Michael	Winnipeg	88 09 10
Nicholson, Jim	Edmonton	87 12 15
Nolette, Andres	Montreal	89 07 15
Olsenberg, Allan	Regina	88 09 01
Pfeifer, Martin	Montreal	89 03 10
Quinn, Russell	Vancouver	90 01 02
Robertson, William	Vancouver	87 04 15
Runge, Victor	Halifax	89 05 07
Schoepp, Clifford	Edmonton	89 06 17
Scott, Wilma	Regina	86 07 14
Steinke, Donna	Halifax	88 11 09
Tardif, Marcel	Edmonton	90 03 07
Tarrant, Lucille	Halifax	88 04 05
Tremblay, Noel	Montreal	90 03 10
Unruh, Neil	Toronto	90 04 15
Volden, Philip	Winnipeg	86 07 01
Watling, James	Vancouver	90 01 15
Weismiller, James	Regina	88 06 01
Young, Charles	Toronto	89 02 15

page 2 of 2 ↑6

SC
Did you key the heading for page two?

Production 1

Key the following letter on the Northern Alberta Institute of Technology letterhead provided in the Working Papers. Use the current numeric date. Key an appropriate envelope or an envelope label. *Note:* The initials of the person who has written the letter are shown before the operator's initials when the writer's name is not included in the signature lines.

Mr. Mel Henderson
Box 5005
Red Deer College
Red Deer, Alberta
T4N 5H5

Dear Mr. Henderson:

Subject: Text Transfer

Further to our recent conversation, enclosed is a copy of a recent summary prepared at NAIT on the problems involved with text transfer.

The summary of the report is divided as follows:

Guide notes	Pages 1-4
Table of transfer types	Page 5
Hardware required	Page 6
Specific Applications	Page 7
Exercises	Pages 8-12

The enclosed material was prepared by a faculty member at NAIT. I hope you will find it useful. Please contact my office if we may be of further assistance.

Sincerely yours,

Staff Training Director

Enclosure

Continuation Tables

If a table is long and requires more than one page, key it as follows:

Page One
1. Start 6-12 blank lines from the top of the page.
2. Stop 9 blank lines from the bottom of the page. Allow for any top or bottom margin default.
3. Triple space.
4. Key page 1 of --.

Page Two
1. Start keying on line seven of page two. Allow for any top margin default.
2. Do not repeat the table title but use a short description to identify the table. Horizontally center and key the description followed by three periods and the word 'continued' underscored.

   Example: Profit Sharing Plan...<u>continued</u>

3. Triple space.
4. Key the column headings.
5. Complete the table.

Production Practice

Production

This table will take two pages. Key it as a ruled table.

DASMUND EMPLOYEES

SS (Participating in Profit Sharing Plan

as at March 31, 19--) SS

<u>Name</u>	<u>Branch</u>	<u>Date of Employment</u>
Albinati, Andre	Toronto	87 03 01
Audit, Emile	Montreal	90 01 18
Bawden, Charles	Regina	89 06 01
Bruneau, Paul	Halifax	82 12 28
Campbell, Albert	Halifax	88 07 17
Campbell, Deanna	Vancouver	89 09 21
Couturier, Roland	Winnipeg	90 01 15
Dixson, Glenn	Winnipeg	89 10 03
Dobson, Patricia	Edmonton	90 05 15
Dunbar, Peter	Regina	88 02 02
Elliott, Ken	Toronto	77 10 12
Erickson, Roy	Vancouver	79 12 15

page 1 of 2 ↑6

SC

Did you decide where to end page one?

Production 2

Using the Dasmund Enterprises Montreal letterhead provided in the Working Papers, key the following letter. Key an appropriate envelope or an envelope label.

Current Date / Cross, Hanover & Blackmore / 1700, rue University / Montreal, Quebec / H3B 3X4 / Gentlemen: / Re: Bid Submission / We have received your letter of (use date of two weeks ago) and the request for a bid quotation on some items. The following table lists our prices. / Thermal Blankets 180 x 225 cm @ 59.99 / Thermal Blankets 200 x 250 cm @ 69.99 / Reversible Comforter 180 x 225 cm @ 88.99 / Reversible Comforter 200 x 250 cm @ 99.99 / Tablecloths 130 x 177 cm @ 22.99 / Tablecloths 152 x 259 cm @ 34.99 / Bath Towels 61 x 117 cm @ 11.99 / Hand Towels 38 x 64 cm @ 6.99 / Face Cloths 33 x 33 cm @ 3.99 / ¶ Within one week of receipt of your order, these materials will be shipped. Our credit terms are 25 percent payable with your order, the balance within 30 days. / Sincerely yours, / Michelle De Meeres / Manager

Continuation Tables

60-space line
Spacing: 1 and 2
Key two 30-s timings on
each line *or* repeat each line
three times.

Alternate-Hand Words

1 to eke pair flair signs enrich signals quantity cubic island

2 us dye paid firms sight enamel socials sorority cycle panels

One-Minute Timings

1. Turn to the One-Minute Timings, page 421.
2. Select the paragraph that you think you can complete in one minute.
3. Key the One-Minute Timing as a drill.
4. If you had two or more errors, practice Accuracy Improvement.
   If you had fewer than two errors, practice Speed Improvement.

Skill Building

Key two 30-s timings on
line 3 of Accuracy Improvement. Circle any errors. If
you have more than one
error for each timing, continue with the Accuracy
Improvement drill. If you
have one error or less on
each timing, key the Speed
Improvement drill and
concentrate on speed.

Accuracy Improvement

3 ill meet loon moon cools hoods looked offset classes outlook

4 aw age act red fade deed safe care cress grave tracts secret

5 when all 64 then the 31 signed up 85 to the 99 still have 68

Speed Improvement

6 The losses mean we cannot afford to exceed a smaller tariff.

7 Only holly was planted on the east hill of the hilly estate.

8 Normal body temperature is 37°C but 39°C means a high fever.

• • • • 1 • • • • 2 • • • • 3 • • • • 4 • • • • 5 • • • • 6 • • • • 7 • • • • 8 • • • • 9 • • • • 10 • • • • 11 • • • • 12

Number Keying

Rule 6: A space should separate numbers in groups of three to the left and right of the
decimal marker.
Example:

The result was 3 476.732 49.

Practice

Key each line once, cor-
recting the numbers when-
ever necessary. Correct lines
should end evenly on a
60-space line. The last two
lines review rules taken to
date. Check your work
carefully.

9 The results showed 3467.42 and 57 493.46 224 before Monday.

10 The 3 totals were: 17 463.72, 4782.463 and 368.54 573.

11 Of the class, 3 students had 4 216.24 367 for an answer.

12 Although there was a total of two hundred thirty, 70 plants
were sold.

55

Letters

60-space line
Spacing: 1 and 2
Key two 1-min timings on each line *or* repeat each line three times.

Speed Building

Key at least two 30-s timings on each line *or* repeat each line twice. Try to increase your speed on each successive try.

Skill Building

Key each underlined word three times. Key each line once concentrating on the underlined words.

Timing

Set spacing at 2. Key at least one 3-min timing. Circle all errors and calculate gross words per minute. Record the timing on your Progress Chart.

SI   1.43
AWL 4.42

Alternate-Hand Words

1 an dig rig cut busy held pays form eight tight eighth turkey

2 am dog rod did city hens pens fuel field title emblem visual

Common-Word Sentences

3 Interest will be charged on your account after the contract.

4 Regular benefits will be paid to each firm with this policy.

5 Give us your personal comments about the way we have served.

Number Practice

6 Classes are given 3 times a week and go from 10:45 to 12:15.

7 The 4 boys will be back from their 9 km hike at about 08:45.

• • • • 1 • • • • 2 • • • • 3 • • • • 4 • • • • 5 • • • • 6 • • • • 7 • • • • 8 • • • • 9 • • • •10 • • • •11 • • • •12

Concentrate on Correct Spelling

8 We preferred to seek other possibilities for them.

9 Have you suffered by being referred to the courts?

Three-Minute Timing

	1	CW	3
Our firm has new models of the latest in mini dictation	12	12	4
equipment. No longer does your office desk have to be clut-	24	24	8
tered with large equipment which reduces your working space.	36	36	12
Our new machines are built with the newer electronic modules	48	48	16
which can be repaired, when necessary, by simply snapping in	60	60	20
a new module. The machine can be repaired in seconds.	71	71	24
The machines come with an attachment that allows you to	12	83	28
fix the receiver unit on any side of your desk or perhaps in	24	95	32
a drawer. Its dainty case will hardly be noticed nor can it	36	107	36
cause any tears in clothing because it has smooth round cor-	48	119	40
ners. They are available in many colors as well if you wish	60	131	44
to add to your office decor. If you would like the conveni-	72	143	48
ence of one of our units, call us for a two-week free trial.	84	155	52

• • • • 1 • • • • 2 • • • • 3 • • • • 4 • • • • 5 • • • • 6 • • • • 7 • • • • 8 • • • • 9 • • • •10 • • • •11 • • • •12   1 min

            1   2   3   4   3 min

Production 2

Plan and key a line graph from the following rough draft information on a full sheet of paper.

SC

Did you determine if and how to do a line graph if you are using a computer?

EMPLOYER FEEDBACK*

Areas of Improvement Needed for Entry-Level Office Workers

%

		%
100	1. Willingness to start at bottom	74%
90	2. Preparedness for interview	73%
80	3. Work habits	72%
70	4. Ability to work under pressure	69%
etc.	5. Ability to read instructions	67%
	6. Concern for productivity	66%
	7. Willingness to retrain	65%
	8. Ambition/motivation	64%
	9. Quality of work	64%
	10. Responsibility	63%

1   2   3   . . . . etc. . . . . 10 →

Responsibility

*Top ten concerns in order of priority from an office survey.

Production 1

Use the Dasmund Enterprises Toronto letterhead provided in the Working Papers.
This letter should be sent to Mr. Saul Warburg, 207 Beverley Street, Toronto, Ontario
M5T 1Z4. Key an appropriate envelope or an envelope label.

Dear Mr. Warburg

Re: Special Advance Showing of New Merchandise to Preferred Customers

Dasmund Enterprises Ltd. are pleased to invite you as one of our preferred customers to a special advance showing of our new fall line of merchandise.

Monday and Tuesday, ~~May 30~~ June 29 and ~~31~~ 30, our main warehouse at 25 York Mills Road in Toronto will remain open from ~~17:35~~ 16:00 to 21:00 to enable you and other preferred customers to browse and purchase your selections from our new fall line. The merchandise will be available on Wednesday to the general public for their shopping pleasure.

Enclosed is a list of the merchandise which will be available — many are limited quantity and we recommend that you shop early. Please be advised that this is personal shopping only.

This special shopping privilege is our way of saying "Thank You" for being a Dasmund credit account customer.

Sincerely yours,

Thomas Rollins
Manager
oi

Production 2

Using the Dasmund Enterprises Regina letterhead provided in the Working Papers, key
the following letter. Key an appropriate envelope or an envelope label.

Current Date / **Mrs. Dorothy O'Shea** / 1803 – 15 Street S.W. / Prince Albert, Saskatchewan /
S6V 3T8 / Dear Mrs. O'Shea: / Re: Credit for Merchandise Returned / Thank you
for your letter of *(use date of Monday last week)* . We are sorry and very surprised
to hear that you are unhappy with your recent order. ¶ Thousands of sleeping
bags of the same model you received have been sold and we have had no
complaints. To receive full credit for these sleeping bags, return them by Midland
Superior Express, express collect. / ¶ Upon receipt of these sleeping bags, you will
be issued a credit to your account. We hope that this will be satisfactory and that
we may have the pleasure of serving you in the near future. / Yours sincerely, /
Peter Gallin / Manager

Production 1

Plan and key a line graph with the information given below on a full sheet of paper. Ask your instructor or read the software manual to determine if and how graphics can be done.

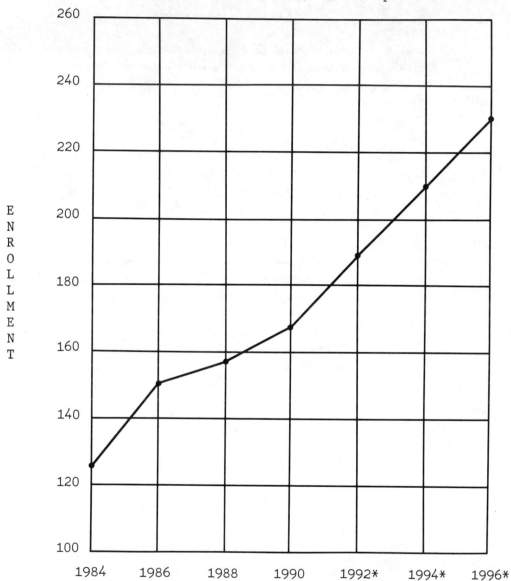

SUMMARY OF PART-TIME ENROLLMENTS

Wascana Office Administration Department

*Estimated.

Information for plotting graph points:

1984 – 125; 1986 – 150; 1988 – 157; 1990 – 168; 1992 – 190;

1994 – 210; 1996 – 230

Skill Building

Skill Building

Key two 1-min timings on
each line *or* repeat each line
three times. Circle all
errors. If most of your
attempts have two errors or
less, proceed to line 7. If
not, take additional timings
on lines 3-6.

Key two 1-min timings on
each line *or* repeat each line
three times as quickly as you
can. Assess your speed
progress.

Key each underlined word
three times. Key each line
once concentrating on the
underlined words.

Key each sentence once,
inserting the correct choice
from the words in
parentheses. Your right
margin will not be even.

One-Hand Words

1 ace hip sex you wade noun cart look gear hump start pupil ad

2 awe hop tar ion wage O.K. case yolk gets poll state union aw

Accuracy Improvement

3 re car wet cat fear base fats test draft evade arrest dredge

4 all free took deed wheel carry arrive degree offices matters

5 eel call poor roll occur asset across latter booklet collect

6 up lump milk kink jump hill join upon imply minimum monopoly

•••1•••2•••3•••4•••5•••6•••7•••8•••9•••10•••11•••12

Speed Improvement

7 The cabbage and lettuce will freeze if the breeze stops now.

8 Eri will pull the loops of pink nylon thread on Jill's loom.

9 We cannot understand why you have not charged us for credit.

10 They hope to produce another kind when they open production.

•••1•••2•••3•••4•••5•••6•••7•••8•••9•••10•••11•••12

Concentrate on Correct Spelling

11 We hope to be transferring a quantity of accounts.

12 This signature line is quite similar to that model.

Basic English Skill

farther: distance   *further:* extent or degree

13 The service station is six kilometres (farther, further)
down the road.

14 We hope to get (farther, further) advice on this matter from
the company lawyer.

between: discussing two   *among:* discussing three or more

15 The managers chose (between, among) Cheryl and Armando.

16 The five members of the new executive will decide (between,
among) themselves when the first meeting should take place.

Skill Building / Graphs

60-space line
Spacing: 1 and 2
Key two 30-s timings on each line *or* repeat each line three times.

Alternate-Hand Words

1 us bit lame bible whale panels haughty endowment turn emblem

2 an big land augur visit island memento entitlement urns when

Graduated Speed Practice

Turn to the Graduated Alphanumerical Speed Practice, page 403 . Select a sentence that you think you can key in the time indicated.

Alphabetic Sentences

3 The vocabulary portion of this quiz is exactly twice as hard

as the same kind of question on the exam just graded.

4 The back axle on my jeep is very weak and is quite likely to

wiggle if the tire is the wrong size.

Accuracy Building

Key two 30-s timings on each line concentrating on accuracy as your goal. Students on individual progress should key each line three times with the accuracy goal in mind.

Number Practice

5 For a down payment of $11 495 you can move into this estate.

6 This 117.8 m^2 bungalow has 3 bedrooms and sells for $98 695.

Stroking Practice

1. Turn to the Stroking Practice, page 414.
2. Key the lines selected by your instructor or the letter combinations giving you difficulty in the drills just completed.
3. Key each line twice.

Accuracy Improvement

7 feed scars wears faster sewers receded grafters asserted rad

8 in ohm holy oily mommy knoll Jimmy minimum joy oil ink union

Skill Building

Key two 30-s timings on line 7 of Accuracy Improvement. Circle any errors. If you have more than one error for each timing, continue with the Accuracy Improvement drill. If you have one error or less on each timing, key the Speed Improvement drill and concentrate on speed.

Speed Improvement

9 Focus both eyes on the field and try to distinguish the dot.

10 The batter for the bread is lumpy so the bread will be poor.

• • • • 1 • • • • 2 • • • • 3 • • • • 4 • • • • 5 • • • • 6 • • • 7 • • • • 8 • • • • 9 • • • • 10 • • • • 11 • • • 12

Three- or Five-Minute Timing

Turn to the timing in Unit VI of your Working Papers. Students without Working Papers should key the timing in Lesson 103, page 276.

1. Turn to Lesson 45.
2. Drill on the appropriate Graduated Speed Practice.

Timing

Set spacing at 2. Key two 3-min timings. Circle all errors and calculate gross words per minute. Record the better timing on your Progress Chart.

SI   1.48
AWL 5.66

Three-Minute Timing

	1	CW	3
Have you ever thought about the need to protect what is | 12 | 12 | 4 |
stored in the memory of your computer? Keeping this data in | 24 | 24 | 8 |
a safe place has caused computer programmers to do thousands | 36 | 36 | 12 |
of lines of code to help insure that the unwanted user can't | 48 | 48 | 16 |
have access to the files. In fact, the computer industry is | 60 | 60 | 20 |
now producing cabinets which are being called data safes and | 72 | 72 | 24 |
these safes are said to be fraud free. | 79 | 79 | 26 |
One of the basic safeguards for protecting the computer | 12 | 91 | 30 |
files is to make sure that all file copies are put away into | 24 | 103 | 34 |
a protected area. Data safes are available that provide the | 36 | 115 | 38 |
protection needed from fires, from wet conditions, and gives | 48 | 127 | 42 |
the dust-free environment to add the desired life to all the | 60 | 139 | 46 |
electronic files. This is so crucial to providing for needs | 72 | 151 | 50 |
to safeguard data in modern office data management systems. | 83 | 162 | 54 |

```
· · · · 1 · · · · 2 · · · 3 · · · · 4 · · · 5 · · · 6 · · · 7 · · · · 8 · · · 9 · · · ·10 · · · ·11 · · · 12    1 min
            1                    2                    3                    4    3 min
```

Production 2

Key the following table on a half sheet of paper. Single space the body. Center it horizontally and vertically.

Table of Monthly Payments *) all caps

) double line optional

Amount Financed	Number of Payments		
	24	18	12
100	5.21	6.60	9.38
200	10.42	13.19	18.75
300	15.63	19.79	28.13
400	20.83	26.39	37.50
500	26.05	32.99	46.88
600	31.26	39.58	56.25
700	36.47	46.18	65.63
800	41.68	52.78	75.00
900	46.89	59.38	84.38
1 000	52.10	65.97	93.75
1 500	78.13	98.96	140.63
2 000	104.17	131.94	187.50

*Interest rate is 12.5% calculated on the monthly balance.

57

Letters/Copies

60-space line
Spacing: 1 and 2
Key two 1-min timings on each line *or* repeat each line three times.

Accuracy Building
Key at least two 1-min timings on each line *or* repeat each line three times. Count all errors. If you had more than two errors in each attempt, concentrate on individual letters. Your aim should be to maintain keyboard control.

Skill Building

One-Hand Words

1 raw oil fee no. deaf loon tart hill ever pull waves plump as
2 far Lou few non fear look swat Jill face pulp waver plunk re

Right-Hand Words

3 up nip ion ink nil mill mink mono noon noun O.K. union jolly
4 no Lou oil lip pup only pink pool pull oily holy plump imply
5 in joy hum Jim nun pulp pump upon join hill jump plunk nylon

• • • • 1 • • • • 2 • • • • 3 • • • • 4 • • • • 5 • • • • 6 • • • • 7 • • • • 8 • • • • 9 • • • • 10 • • • 11 • • • 12

Word Division – Summary of Rules

1. Divide words between speech syllables.
2. Never divide words of one syllable.
3. Do not divide syllables with one letter.
4. Avoid dividing two-letter syllables if possible.
5. Divide words between double letters of speech syllables.
6. Divide only between complete words of a compound word.
7. A single syllable in the middle of a word should be left on the first line of keying. If there are two single syllables, divide between them.

Key each line once, inserting a hyphen between each speech syllable. Correct lines should end evenly on a 60-space line. Check your work carefully.

6 non-maintenance omit omitted opened odor offset pamphlets
7 salutations scanning trainees touched trade-marked title
8 triumphant translation twenty undesirable useless ago
9 unions value vegetable video weddings warfare whichever
10 wrapped youngsters yesterday zealously year-round tapped
11 wonderland witness vaccine via visa vacation unsalable
12 unusually validated unprofessional unskilled undersize
13 tuition two-party traditional transferred through touchy
14 taxi terminated radius diligence deter radiator matter
15 corridor terribly telegrams sunshine summaries upper
16 suicide run-off rushed scattered straight seven busy hurry
17 manager maximum painting pencilled renovation purpose

Key each sentence once, inserting the correct choice from the words in parentheses. Your right margin will not be even.

Basic English Skill

correspond to: matches, is similar   *correspond with:* to exchange communication

18 The fabric in this swatch corresponds (to, with) the new coat.

Production 1

Key the following boxed table with braced column headings on a full sheet of paper. Center it horizontally and vertically.

DASMUND ENTERPRISES LTD.

center ⌐

Number of Employees by Age and Sex, 19-- ⌐

Age (or ↑)	Male		Female	
	Number	Percent[1]	Number	Percent[2]
Under 18	24	2.40%	15	1.92%
18–25	129	12.88%	137	17.49%
26–30	233	23.28%	186	23.75%
31–40	212	21.18%	180	22.98%
41–50	197	19.68%	145	18.52%
51–55	85	8.48%	58	7.41%
56–60	67	6.70%	46	5.88%
61–65	42	4.20%	14	1.79%
Over 65	12	1.20%	2	0.26%
Total	1001	100.00%	783	100.00%

DS↓

[1]Indicates percentage of total males

[2]Indicates percentage of total females

19 Kari has corresponded (to, with) Mrs. Freid for a number of years.

Two-Minute Timing

	1	2
We have 2 offices available immediately at 4903 Stanton | 12 | 6 |
Street. They are well located in the new business area. To | 24 | 12 |
fully appreciate the possibilities for 2 fine offices please | 36 | 18 |
call Lisa at 343-1740. To see, drop by on August 3 or 4 be- | 48 | 24 |
tween the hours of 09:30 and 18:45. You'll be glad you took | 60 | 30 |
the time. | 62 | 31 |

• • • • 1 • • • • 2 • • • • 3 • • • • 4 • • • • 5 • • • • 6 • • • • 7 • • • • 8 • • • • 9 • • • 10 • • • 11 • • • 12 1 min

1　　　　2　　　　3　　　　4　　　　5　　　　6 2 min

Timing

Set spacing at 2. Key two 2-min timings. Circle all errors and calculate gross words per minute. Record the better timing on your Progress Chart. Proofread numbers carefully to determine if extra practice is necessary.

SI   1.82
AWL 4.33

Copies

In business, it is often necessary to send a copy of an original letter to another person. The original copy of the letter is sent to the person to whom the letter is addressed. A copy notation is made on the bottom of this original letter and the copy is sent to the person who is acknowledged as receiving the copy. *Note:* The copy notation is *cc* if you use carbon paper and *c* if you use any other copying method. It is also common business practice to make a copy of most communications keyed in the office; however, this is not acknowledged on the original as it is considered to be routine business practice.

Copies are made by using copying machines or carbon paper. Read the following so that you will know how to use carbon paper. Use carbon paper for one of your production practices.

How to Use Carbon Paper

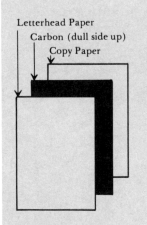

Letterhead Paper
Carbon (dull side up)
Copy Paper

You will need one sheet of carbon paper and one sheet of copy paper for each copy you wish to make. Note that the carbon paper has a shiny side and a dull side. The shiny side has the carbon on it and you must be careful not to smudge or smear this on your work, hands, and clothing.

To assemble the carbon pack, place the copy paper on your desk. Now place the carbon paper (shiny side down) on the copy paper, then the original letterhead paper goes on top of the carbon paper. Be sure the carbon paper is the right way around or the copy will be keyed on the back of the original, only in a reverse or mirror image.

When the carbon pack is assembled, pick up the pack so that the copy paper (and the shiny carbon side of the carbon paper) is toward you. Insert the pack into the typewriter and use the paper release to straighten the pages if necessary. Before starting to key check again to make certain that the dull side of the carbon paper is now toward you and the glossy side is away from you.

Correcting Errors on Carbon Copies

When errors are made on the original copy they are, of course, also made on the carbon copies. If an error is made, it is necessary to correct the original and each individual carbon copy. Begin with the last carbon copy first, and using a soft eraser, make the correction. Brush away the eraser particles from the paper. Then insert a piece of scrap paper, or an eraser shield between the copy and the carbon paper to prevent smudging when correcting the next sheet.

Braced Column Headings

A heading centered over two or more column headings is called a braced heading.

1. Key the title and subtitle of the table.
2. Space down to the line of braced heading(s) but do NOT key it.
3. Space down and key the line of column headings.

   Number   Percent

4. Turn the cylinder back or move the cursor to the line for the braced heading.
5. To center the braced heading over the two column headings, find the midpoint of the two column headings.
   Refer to Lesson 23, page 60, Column Headings Shorter than Columns.
   - Locate the midpoint of the column headings by forward spacing from the beginning of the first column heading, one for every two characters and spaces of the two columns to be braced and the spaces between columns.
   - From the midpoint, backspace once for every two characters and spaces in the heading to be braced.

6. Key the braced heading.
7. Repeat steps 5 through 6 for each braced heading. The backspace method is preferred as it is faster and reduces the chance of arithmetic error.

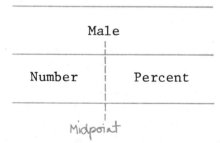

Erase the next sheet. Insert a protective paper between this sheet and the carbon also and continue erasing until you have completed the original copy. Be sure to remove all protection sheets before keying the correction. *Note*: Do not get carbon on your fingers because you may leave fingerprints on the original.

Production Practice

Production

Using the Dasmund Enterprises Edmonton letterhead provided in the Working Papers, assemble a carbon pack. Key the following letter with a carbon copy for Grimshaw Trucking. Key envelopes or envelope labels for Mrs. A. P. Bartoshewski and Grimshaw Trucking, 7707 - 161 Street, Edmonton, Alberta T5R 2K4.

```
Current Date


Mrs. A. P. Bartoshewski
807 Parkwood Drive S.E.
Calgary, Alberta
T2J 3W6

Dear Mrs. Bartoshewski:

Subject:  Damaged Merchandise

We are sorry to hear that the last shipment sent to you
was received in damaged condition.  Our carrier, Grimshaw
Trucking, has been contacted and advised of your concern.

Grimshaw Trucking will deliver a duplicate shipment of
your order, pick up the damaged merchandise, and return it
to us.  The damage claim will be settled by us.

You will receive your duplicate order within the next few
days.  We hope this will be satisfactory.  If there is
anything further we may do to assist you, please let me know.

Sincerely yours,


M. S. Dasmund
General Manager

oi
cc Grimshaw Trucking
```

SC

Did you remember to change cc to c, if you used a copying method other than carbon paper?

SC

Did you remember to make a copy?

Tables with Braced Headings

Right-Hand Words

1 `my you lip loon non ply noun only pool pulp pump lip minimum`

2 `on pin joy pup mop hump plum mill hulk link noun pin opinion`

One-Minute Timings

1. Turn to the One-Minute Timings, page 421.
2. Select the paragraph that you think you can complete in one minute.
3. Key the One-Minute Timing as a drill.
4. If you had two or more errors, practice Accuracy Improvement.
   If you had fewer than two errors, practice Speed Improvement.

Skill Building

Key two 30-s timings on line 3 of Accuracy Improvement. Circle any errors. If you have more than one error for each timing, continue with the Accuracy Improvement drill. If you have one error or less on each timing, key the Speed Improvement drill and concentrate on speed.

Accuracy Improvement

3 `draw great greed Easter refers erected abstract retreads are`

4 `err look loom jeep rooms looks cattle losses approve chattel`

5 `rad nip stew hull raft Jill screw union averts pill reassess`

Speed Improvement

6 `In 1867 Canada's full population was about 3 463 000 people.`

7 `More than ever, we would like to use your latest tax report.`

8 `I agree to meet with all staff and discuss the latter issue.`

• • • • 1 • • • • 2 • • • • 3 • • • • 4 • • • • 5 • • • • 6 • • • • 7 • • • • 8 • • • • 9 • • • • 10 • • • • 11 • • • • 12

Number Keying

Rule 5: When two unrelated numbers follow one another, spell out the smaller number. This allows for better reading comprehension.
Example:

`When reaching 300, twenty-five will have to make another choice.`

Practice

Key each line once, correcting the numbers whenever necessary. Correct lines should end evenly on a 60-space line. The last two lines review rules taken to date. Check your work carefully.

9 `When the total reached 1 375, twelve of the men were phoned.`

10 `Since the score was already thirty-six, 13 players left ahead.`

11 `Our goal is 5 000, 200 of which was in by 6 weeks.`

12 `19 of us were cramped into 3 tents and 2 cabins.`

58

Letters/Copies

Accuracy Building

Key at least two 1-min timings on each line *or* repeat each line three times. Count all errors. If you had more than two errors in each attempt, concentrate on individual letters. Your aim should be to maintain keyboard control.

One-Hand Words

1 few ion gas nun fast yolk swab hump fact pump waxes imply be

2 gag ink get ohm fade ploy ward poll face upon waxed nylon we

Left-Hand Words

3 be rad raw sad cast fact eggs sees start draws accede deface

4 we sax wax wad dart raft errs seed waded dread arrest defect

Right-Hand Words

5 my ply ohm non pop link hoop oily polo kink holy pupil onion

6 on pin hum you joy lump loop ploy yolk plop hump union jolly

Common-Word Sentences

7 Separate cheques have been sent to cover all the fuel bills.

8 It is their decision not to perform during the construction.

9 We were not aware of their recent proposal to the companies.

10 The lake property has recently been put up for sale in town.

• • • • 1 • • • • 2 • • • • 3 • • • • 4 • • • • 5 • • • • 6 • • • • 7 • • • • 8 • • • • 9 • • • •10• • • •11• • • •12

Timing

Set spacing at 2. Key two 2-min timings. Circle all errors and calculate gross words per minute. Record the better timing on your Progress Chart.

SI   1.1
AWL 3.64

Two-Minute Timing

	1	2
Now that you have finished a large part of your year at	12	6
school, you should be able to choose the best set of courses	24	12
to get you where you want to go. You have one more year yet	36	18
to complete so now the time is right to make the next choice	48	24
so you can be sure to get the desired classes. Make time in	60	30
the next week to see me in my office. We need to talk about	72	36
your progress so far and whether or not there needs to be an	84	42
adjustment in your short or long-term goals. Plan to fit an	96	48
hour into your schedule but we will try to take less.	107	53

• • • • 1 • • • • 2 • • • • 3 • • • • 4 • • • • 5 • • • • 6 • • • • 7 • • • • 8 • • • • 9 • • • •10• • • •11• • • •12   1 min
　　　　　1　　　　　2　　　　　3　　　　　4　　　　　5　　　　　6   2 min

To make vertical lines by keying on a typewriter:

1. Key the table as a ruled table.
2. Remove the paper.
3. Re-insert the paper sideways.
4. Be sure the paper is aligned evenly.
5. Locate the midpoint between the first and second column.
6. Key a line of underscores from the column heading to the bottom of the column.
7. Repeat steps 5 and 6 for each vertical ruling.

Double Underscore

Some businesses prefer a double underscore for the first ruled line in ruled tables.

Example 1

Department	Amount

Example 2

Department	Amount

Review keying double lines in Lesson 29, page 80. If you are using a computer, ask your instructor or read the software manual to determine how to double underscore rule.

Review keying double lines in Lesson 29, page 80.

Production Practice

Production 1

Key the following as a boxed table. Center it horizontally and vertically on a half sheet of paper. Use automatic options, if available.

COMPARISON OF SPORTING GOODS SALES ✳

l.c.   FOR SPRING AND SUMMER, 19-- and 19--

Store	This Year	Last Year	Increase Or Decrease
Edmonton	1 417 411	1 397 023	20 388
Halifax	917 006	898 505	18 501
Montreal	2 375 500	2 420 550	(45 050)
Regina	1 120 000	1 105 315	14 685
Toronto	2 495 950	1 985 850	510 100
Vancouver	2 420 397	2 390 300	30 097
Winnipeg	1 295 575	1 250 500	45 075
Total	12 401 839 ~~12 401 540~~	11 448 044³	593 796

#7

✳ *amounts expressed to the nearest dollar.*

Production 2

Key the table, Keying Symbols, on page 279 as a boxed table on a full sheet of paper. Center the headings and center the table horizontally and vertically. Use automatic options, if available.

Key the table, Keying Symbols, on page 279 as a boxed table on a full sheet of paper.

Basic English Skill

different from: correct usage   *different than*: incorrect usage

11 My computer is different (from, than) yours.

except: to leave out   *accept*: take what is offered, assent

12 All of the executive members (except, accept) Mr. Brown will (except, accept) the contract that has been proposed.

Production

Key the following letter on the Dasmund Enterprises Edmonton letterhead provided in the Working Papers. Prepare a copy for Mrs. A. P. Bartoshewski. Key the envelopes or envelope labels for Appliance Repair Company and for Mrs. A. P. Bartoshewski.

Appliance Repair Company
1867 Second Street N.W.
Calgary, Alberta
T2M 2W5

Gentlemen:
Re: Estimate to Repair Damaged Appliances

We recently shipped an order of kitchen appliances to a customer in Calgary and have been advised that they appliances were received in a damaged condition.

We are very concerned about repairing any damage to these appliances but would like to do so quickly so that our customer may use the goods. In talking to our customer, we believe there are no major repairs required. Would you inspect the appliances and advise us before making any repairs? If damage is extensive, it would be better to replace the appliances rather than repair the damage.

The customer is Mrs. A. P. Bartoshewski at 807 Parkwood Drive S.E., Calgary. Please telephone Mrs. Bartoshewski at 245-6716 and make an appointment.

We wait for your authorization of the repairs or your advice that these appliances be replaced.

Sincerely yours,

M. S. Dasmund
General Manager

oi

c   Mrs. A. P. Bartoshewski
    807 Parkwood Drive S.E.
    Calgary, Alberta
    T2J 3W6

Keying Symbols

Symbol	How to Key	Example
1. Insertion	Key diagonal in space. Key insertion above.	missing Insert/words.
2. Exclamation Mark	Key apostrophe. Backspace. Key period.	Wow!
3. Ditto	Key quotation mark.	"
4. Pound (money)	Key "l" upper case. Backspace. Key hyphen.	£213
5. Degree	Open ratchet. Turn up cylinder. Key "o" lower case. Close ratchet. Turn cylinder back to original keyed line.	25°
6. Minute	Key apostrophe.	45'
7. Second	Key quotation mark.	24"
8. Add	Key hyphen. Backspace. Key diagonal.	12 $\neq$ 10
9. Subtract	Key hyphen.	12 - 10
10. Equals	Open ratchet. Turn cylinder up slightly. Key hyphen. Backspace. Turn cylinder down slightly. Key hyphen. Close ratchet. Turn cylinder and find the original keyed line.	12 $\neq$ 10 = 22 12 - 10 = 2
11. Multiply	Key "x" lower case.	12 x 12 = 144
12. Divide	Key colon. Backspace. Key hyphen.	12 $\div$ 12 = 1

Boxed Tables

Vertical lines can be added to separate the columns in a ruled table to make the table easier to read. This table is called a boxed table. The boxed-table format can be used for statistical tables or tables giving a great deal of information.

To make the vertical lines by drawing on a typewriter:

1. Key the table as a ruled table.
2. Take a black pen or pencil.
3. Place the pen in the "notch" of the cardholder.
4. Move the print position and the cylinder so that the pen is resting a) at the midpoint of the distance between the two columns and b) on the horizontal line at the bottom of the table.
5. Open the ratchet release.
6. Hold the pen firmly. Turn the cylinder up until the pen stops at the horizontal line at the bottom of the table.
7. Close the ratchet release.
8. Repeat steps 1 through 7 for each vertical ruling.

Note: If you are using a computer, ask your instructor or read the software manual to determine if and how vertical lines can be inserted.

Production Review

60-space line
Spacing: 1 and 2
Key two 1-min timings on
each line *or* repeat each line
three times.

One-Hand Words

1 no oil lip hum you hulk null loon look hull noun plunk union

2 see look seed pool watts freed darted pompom crafted refract

• • • • 1 • • • • 2 • • • • 3 • • • • 4 • • • • 5 • • • • 6 • • • • 7 • • • • 8 • • • • 9 • • • • 10 • • • • 11 • • • • 12

Production Practice

Production 1

Key the following letter using the Dasmund Enterprises Vancouver letterhead provided in
the Working Papers. Key an appropriate envelope or an envelope label.

Mrs. Isabel Hamatake
500 Jefferson Avenue
New Westminster, BC
V3J 3T6

Dear Mrs. Hamatake:

Thank you for your order of (one week ago). We have shipped
the goods and they are scheduled to be delivered to you
tomorrow.

Enclosed is our invoice. You will notice that our terms of
sale have changed to 4 percent discount if paid within 10
days, 2 percent discount if paid within 20 days, or net 30
days.

Thank you for the opportunity to serve you. We look forward
to hearing from you soon.

Sincerely yours,

Fred Baker
Manager

oi
Enclosure

Prepare the following invoice for Mrs. Hamatake on the form provided in the Working
Papers. Use the current date and invoice #3421. Calculate the extensions and total the
invoice. Ship via ABC Trucking.

2 Calculators, Canon SR793 at 154.99
3 boxes Personal File Folders at 5.75
12 Photo Albums at 9.99
4 Polaroid Sun System Cameras at 56.88

Boxed Tables

60-space line
Spacing: 1 and 2

Key two 30-s timings on each line *or* repeat each line three times.

Left-Hand Words

1 as was bet wax wars crew rate raft cares gears breast extras

2 re wee sad wed tear data read dear cases grace career faster

One-Minute Timings

1. Turn to the One-Minute Timings, page 421.
2. Select the paragraph that you think you can complete in one minute.
3. Key the One-Minute Timing as a drill.
4. If you had two or more errors, practice Accuracy Improvement.
   If you had fewer than two errors, practice Speed Improvement.

Accuracy Improvement

Skill Building

Key two 30-s timings on line 3 of Accuracy Improvement. Circle any errors. If you have more than one error for each timing, continue with the Accuracy Improvement drill. If you have one error or less on each timing, key the Speed Improvement drill and concentrate on speed.

3 all the 34 of the 80 set all 41 with the 56 but not 23 of 50

4 go die melt cycle shake bushel ambient ornament firms turkey

5 no oil pump pulp knoll Jimmy plump uphill I no him hill upon

Speed Improvement

6 Credit purchases from all departments are up over last week.

7 Phil looked at the data and linked them to the opinion poll.

8 A booklet on billing is offered and he agrees it is current.

• • • • 1 • • • • 2 • • • • 3 • • • • 4 • • • • 5 • • • • 6 • • • • 7 • • • • 8 • • • • 9 • • • • 10 • • • • 11 • • • • 12

Number Keying

Rule 4: Numbers with the word "percent" or with decimals should be keyed in figures. *Note:* Percent symbol (%) may be used in tables and statistical keying.
Example:

We received 73 percent on the test covering 0.75 of our course.

Practice

Key each line once, correcting the numbers whenever necessary. Correct lines should end evenly on a 60-space line. The last two lines review rules taken to date. Check your work carefully.

9 The estate was divided: Bob, 0.35; Anne, 0.35 and Al, 0.30.

10 Al's test scores in applied science were: 75% and one hundred percent.

11 26 cheques were sent to the 3 firms before then.

12 Bring four pages, five ball-point pens, and thirteen all-rubber erasers.

Production 2

Key the following personal business letter on plain paper.

500 Jefferson Avenue
New Westminster BC
V3J 3T6

Current Date:

Dasmund Enterprises Ltd.
1025 Granville Street
Vancouver BC
V6P 4X6

Attention: Mr. Fred Baker

Gentlemen:

Today, I received the goods I recently ordered.

When ABC Trucking delivered these goods to my door, the box was in very poor condition. The top was damaged and one side was badly cut and looked as though it had been very roughly handled. I pointed out the condition of the box to the truck driver. He did not seem to feel that it was any of his concern.

Upon opening the carton and checking the goods, I find there was considerable damage. Would you prefer I return the complete shipment or only the damaged items?

Sincerely yours,

Mrs. Isabel Hamatake

Production 3

Key the following letter on the Dasmund Enterprises Vancouver letterhead provided in the Working Papers. Prepare a copy for ABC Trucking Company, 600 Terminal Road, Vancouver, British Columbia V6A 2M8. Key the appropriate envelopes or envelope labels.

Mrs. Isabel Hamatake / 500 Jefferson Avenue / New Westminster, British Columbia / V3J 3T6 / Dear Mrs. Hamatake: / Re: Damaged Goods / I have received your letter of *(use date of letter in Production 2)* and am sorry to hear of the problem you experienced with your recent order. / ¶We have contacted the ABC Trucking Company and they have agreed to pay any damages as a result of their improper handling of this order. Since the goods left our warehouse in good condition, we can assume that any damage is their responsibility. / ¶We have duplicated your order and sent it today by ABC Trucking. They have been instructed to pick up the damaged shipment. We hope this will be satisfactory. / Sincerely yours, / Fred Baker / Manager / c ABC Trucking Company

Production 2

Key the following as a ruled table. Double space the body. Center it horizontally and vertically. Use a half sheet of paper, short edge inserted first. Use automatic options, if available.

CHARITABLE DONATIONS

as ~~of~~ at October 15, 19--

Department	Amount	< #
		< #
Accounting	$1110.50	
Advertising	787.00	
Executive	1320.00	
Personnel	817.28	
Purchasing	714.50	
Sales	~~1405.00~~ 1623.75	
Shipping	1218.00	
TOTAL	$	

Office 317.28

SC

Did you use the underscore key or the underline option for your rulings?

Production 4

Key the following personal business letter on plain paper.

240 Pacific 66 Plaza
700 Sixth Avenue S. W.
Calgary, AB *Alberta*
T2P 0T8
Current Date

Registrar's Office
University of Calgary
2920 - 24 Avenue N. W.
Calgary, AB *Alberta*
T2N 1N4

Gentlemen:

Re: Registration for Douglas C. Geier, I.D. #65138

Enclosed are the necessary registration forms for fall/
winter sessions and a non-refundable deposit fee of $50.

The courses I plan to take are as follows:

Course Number	Section	Year
Biology 417	F	4
Zoology 475	W	4
Geology 201	F	2
Geography 305	F	3
Biology 607	W	6

I plan to graduate in April with one additional course on
my program. Please advise if your records are not in
agreement.

Sincerely yours,

Douglas C. Geier

Enclosure

1 CW 3

Do you have certain jobs which need to be done that you	12	12	4
seem to shelve all the time? Perhaps they are jobs that you	24	24	8
dislike or that you find quite difficult to start. Probably	36	36	12
you have made a habit of avoiding these particular tasks. A	48	48	16
first step to changing any habit is to decide right now that	60	60	20
you are going to change. Begin to act on this decision now.	72	72	24
Do not wait until tomorrow or even this afternoon.	82	82	27

Do you have certain jobs which need to be done that you 12 12 4
seem to shelve all the time? Perhaps they are jobs that you 24 24 8
dislike or that you find quite difficult to start. Probably 36 36 12
you have made a habit of avoiding these particular tasks. A 48 48 16
first step to changing any habit is to decide right now that 60 60 20
you are going to change. Begin to act on this decision now. 72 72 24
Do not wait until tomorrow or even this afternoon. 82 82 27

Once you have made the decision to change, work on only 12 94 31
the single chosen task. It is not a good idea to try to fix 24 106 35
up a lot of bad habits all at once. Make yourself do a kind 36 118 39
of job that you would usually avoid. Do it right now. Pick 48 230 43
the most unpleasant job you have to do tomorrow and do it in 60 142 47
the morning before you begin your usual routine for the day. 72 154 51
This will set a good tone for the rest of the day. 82 164 54

Since you have started to work at some of those jobs it 12 176 58
is very important that you do not make any exceptions to the 24 188 62
new habits you are trying to form. For the first minutes of 36 200 66
each day you will have to be very tough with yourself. As a 48 212 70
few weeks go by you will be pleased to discover that you are 61 224 74
getting your most unpleasant tasks done early in the day and 72 236 78
that your days are going much better than before. 82 246 81

• • • • 1 • • • • 2 • • • • 3 • • • • 4 • • • • 5 • • • • 6 • • • • 7 • • • • 8 • • • • 9 • • • • 10 • • • • 11 • • • • 12 1 min
        1   2   3   4   3 min

Assess Your Improvement

Set spacing at 2. Key at least one 3-min *or* 5-min timing. Circle all errors and calculate gross words per minute. Record the timing on your Progress Chart.

SI   1.30
AWL 3.88

Production Practice

Production 1

Review keying ruled tables in Lesson 29, page 78. Key the following as a ruled table on a full sheet of paper. Use the underscore key or the underline option for rulings. Double space the body. Arrange the names alphabetically. Center it horizontally and vertically. Use automatic options, if available. Know your software.

Title: DASMUND ENTERPRISES LTD.

Subtitle: Employees with at Least Five Years' Service*

Column Headings: Employee / Store / Years of Service

Column Items: Beattie, Jean / Vancouver / 6
Gaudette, John / Montreal / 6
Asmundsen, Kenneth / Toronto / 5
Maclean, Ean / Halifax / 5
Semeniuck, Iris / Edmonton / 5

Footnote: *Regina and Winnipeg stores open less than five years

Assess Your Progress

60-space line
Spacing: 1 and 2

Key two 1-min timings on each line *or* repeat each line three times.

Common-Word Sentences

1 This particular system costs less than those on sale before.

2 We will have the services of a larger staff during the sale.

• • • • 1 • • • • 2 • • • • 3 • • • • 4 • • • • 5 • • • • 6 • • • • 7 • • • • 8 • • • • 9 • • • •10• • • •11• • • •12

Assess Your Speed

Three-Minute Timing

	1	CW	3

Every employee is expected to perform the job at levels | 12 | 12 | 4
which are acceptable to the employer. Of course, these lev- | 24 | 24 | 8
els vary from one job to another but there are some definite | 36 | 36 | 12
expectations for most job classifications. No employer will | 48 | 48 | 16
reward a person with job or salary advancement if the chance | 60 | 60 | 20
to work well is ignored. Schedules must be met and all jobs | 72 | 72 | 24
must be completed as expected. | 78 | 78 | 26

All our employees, both new and experienced, are judged | 12 | 90 | 30
by their productivity. Everyone will be expected to perform | 24 | 102 | 34
a share of this workload, and it is usually the person doing | 36 | 114 | 38
more than that share who gets recognized for further employ- | 48 | 126 | 42
ment opportunities. However, it cannot be stressed too much | 60 | 138 | 46
that producing work cannot be done at the expense of another | 72 | 150 | 50
person and failing to consider his personal needs. | 82 | 160 | 53

• • • • 1 • • • • 2 • • • • 3 • • • • 4 • • • • 5 • • • • 6 • • • • 7 • • • • 8 • • • • 9 • • • •10• • • •11• • • •12   1 min

1   2   3   4   3 min

SI   1.36
AWL 5.97

Did you achieve the unit objective of 30 words per minute with six errors or less?

Production 1

Key the following letter on the Dasmund Enterprises Regina letterhead provided in the Working Papers. Prepare a copy for Thomas Rollins.

Current Date / Ms. E. G. Pineda / 1507 Warner Street / Moose Jaw, Saskatchewan / S6H 7E2 / Dear Ms. Pineda: / Re: Inquiry for Compact Disc Player and Discs / We have received your inquiry of *(use date of one week ago)* regarding the purchase of 36 compact disc players and approximately 500 discs. / ¶We are interested in submitting a bid on this order. As we do not have many disc players in stock, we have forwarded your letter to our head office in Toronto requesting they correspond directly with you. / ¶I am confident that you will receive an excellent price from our Toronto office. If we can be of any further assistance, please do not hesitate to contact us. / Sincerely yours, / Peter Gallin Manager ' c Thomas Rollins / Dasmund Enterprises / Toronto

Assess Your Production Progress

Can you key Production 1 in 10 min?

Ruled Tables

Left-Hand Words

1 ax tar ace tax ware arts raft wave beard fewer batter exacts

2 at tea sad tee wart case rags wear brass freeze straw exceed

Skill Building

Key two 30-s timings on
line 3 of Accuracy Improvement. Circle any errors. If
you have more than one
error for each timing, continue with the Accuracy
Improvement drill. If you
have one error or less on
each timing, key the Speed
Improvement drill and
concentrate on speed.

Accuracy Improvement

3 odd took tall dell looms jeeps wholly offers suggest impress

4 him no lump loop phony lymph holly monopoly in you him union

5 set all 89 with the 76 all the 21 of the 29 but not 37 of 58

Speed Improvement

6 He looked down on the cool pool on the roof outside my room.

7 In my opinion, the staff staged a great Easter show at noon.

8 Please advise us if you are interested in receiving our bid.

• • • • 1 • • • • 2 • • • • 3 • • • • 4 • • • • 5 • • • • 6 • • • • 7 • • • • 8 • • • • 9 • • • •10 • • • •11 • • • •12

Stroking Practice

1. Turn to the Stroking Practice, page 414.
2. Key the lines selected by your instructor or the letter combinations giving you difficulty in the drills just completed.
3. Students on individual progress should select lines from 1 to 15.
4. Key each line twice.

Number Keying

Rule 3: Numbers above ten are usually written in figures.
Example:

There were 18 in the group.

Practice

Key each line once, cor-
correcting the numbers
whenever necessary. Correct
lines should end evenly on a
60-space line. The last two
lines review rules taken to
date. Check your work.

9 Only two hundred nineteen arrived out of the total 420

registered on Tuesday.

10 A lot of thought has been given to the thirty-seven boats

on the lake.

11 We were expecting 3 from the west and 10 from the east.

12 The scores for the bowling were as follows: 219,

two hundred two & 197.

Production 2

Can you complete
Production 2 in 10 min?

Using the Dasmund Enterprises Montreal letterhead provided in the Working Papers, key the following letter. Key an appropriate envelope or envelope label.

Mutual Insurance Company
1094, avenue Fontainebleau
Québec, Québec
G1W 4E8

Attention: Mr. J. A. Renaux

Gentlemen:

Our company is interested in having a complete review of our insurance coverage. We would like to have your representative contact us, at her or his convenience, to assess our insurance needs.

Our existing policies expire January 31, 19--. There is some concern that our present coverage may be inadequate. Insurance would be required for our store, merchandise, and trucks, as well as liability and theft.

We look forward to meeting your representative.

Sincerely yours,

Michelle De Meeres
Manager

oi

Two-line Column Headings

If a column heading is two or more lines, the column heading may be either block centered or each line of the heading may be centered over the column.

Centered column headings are popular.

Underscore all lines of a column heading in the open-style tables.

If the column headings do not have the same number of lines, align the lines horizontally with the last line of the longest heading.

Production Practice

Production 1

Review keying tables with column headings longer than the column in Lesson 24, page 63. Key the following table on a half sheet of paper. Center it horizontally and vertically. Use automatic options, if available.

SC

Did you use two lines for the second column heading?

Title: Number of Employees in Dasmund Enterprises Ltd.

Subtitle: as at September 1, 19--

Column Headings: Branch Stores / Number of Employees

Column Items: Halifax / 167
Montreal / 240
Toronto / 278
Head Office / 249
Winnipeg / 213
Regina / 193
Edmonton / 212
Vancouver / 232
TOTAL / 1 784

SC

Did you align the numbers at the right?

Production 2

Key the following table on a full sheet of paper. Column headings one and three should be two lines. Center the table horizontally and vertically. Use automatic options, if available.

ELECTRIC STOVES

(Current Year's Models)

Model Number	Features	Average List Price
JN-061	Self Clean Deluxe Oven	$ 969
JN-761	Easy Clean Deluxe Oven	759
LN-087	Microwave Oven	399
DL-770	Built-In Easy Clean Side Swing	620
DL-046	Built-In Self Clean Drop Door	950
JN-223	Slide-In Down Draft Grill & Range	1850

Production 3

Can you complete
Production 3 in 15 min?

Key the following letter on Dasmund Enterprises Toronto letterhead provided in the
Working Papers.

Current Date

Ms. Adela Garcia, Department Head
Office Administration Department
Algonquin College of Applied
    Arts & Technology
1385 Woodroffe Avenue
Ottawa, ON
K2G 1V8

Dear Ms. Garcia:

Thank you for your letter requesting our company's price lists on file cabinets, desks, and matching accessories.

We have a large number of our standard line products in stock. They are available in grey, beige, black, red, blue, white, and green. We can also provide you with a custom color of your choice; however, delivery would be three weeks. Wood finishes are available with two weeks required for delivery. Our standard line is available for immediate delivery. Listed below is the specific information.

Catalogue Number	Item Description	Price FOB Toronto
836-60L	Lateral file - 5 high	$830
836-48L	Lateral file - 4 high	690
836-24L	Lateral file - 2 high	420
3360-AB	Double Pedestal desk	627
3360-OB	Single Pedestal desk with secretarial return	888
21	Waste basket	36
421-312	Swivel tilt armchair	350

I hope you will find these prices satisfactory.

Sincerely yours,

Thomas Rollins
Manager
oi

Enclosure

Open Tables

60-space line
Spacing: 1 and 2
Key two 30-s timings on
each line *or* repeat each line
three times.

Sp
neighbor or *neighbour*

Alternate-Hand Words

1 or fit pens foams their handle haughty chairmen burnt flange

2 of fir pays flaps socks formal memento neighbor chair formal

One-Minute Timings

1. Turn to the One-Minute Timings, page 421.
2. Select the paragraph that you think you can complete in one minute.
3. Key the One-Minute Timing as a drill.
4. If you had two or more errors, practice Accuracy Improvement.
   If you had fewer than two errors, practice Speed Improvement.

Skill Building

Key two 30-s timings on
line 3 of Accuracy Improvement. Circle any errors. If
you have more than one
error for each timing, continue with the Accuracy
Improvement drill. If you
have one error or less on
each timing, key the Speed
Improvement drill and
concentrate on speed.

Accuracy Improvement

3 gas nil reef hook fact John scarf pupil attest mill grafters

4 drew greet verge eaters regard estates arrested retreats car

5 egg seen fell yell cooks seeds floors lessee locally passing

Speed Improvement

6 You and Jim can join him in the garage while I pump the gas.

7 However, we will not need to see them when they arrive here.

8 Did you call on the lass who took ill and appears depressed?

• • • • 1 • • • • 2 • • • • 3 • • • • 4 • • • • 5 • • • • 6 • • • • 7 • • • • 8 • • • • 9 • • • •10 • • • •11 • • • •12

Number Keying

Rule 2: Numbers ten and under are spelled out unless used with larger or related numbers or when used for special emphasis. (Be consistent with related numbers – all figures or all spelled out.)
Examples:

There were only seven members at the meeting.

We bought 2 flowers, 12 shrubs, and 14 trees.

Key each line once, cor-
recting the numbers when-
ever necessary. Correct lines
should end evenly on a
60-space line. The last two
lines review rules taken to
date. Check your work
carefully.

Practice

9 For the trip, we packed 4 sleeping bags and 6 blankets.

10 33 of them came but only 7 wanted to camp out.

11 41 youths played: nine with trumpets and twelve with drums.

Unit IV

Objectives

1 The student will learn to recognize and understand all commonly-used editors' marks.

2 The student will learn to format bound reports.

3 The student will learn to format unbound reports.

4 The student will learn to format an outline.

5 The student will learn to format a title page, table of contents, and bibliography.

6 The student will learn how to use and format references.

7 The student will work toward improving keyboard control by the use of selected speed and accuracy drills.

8 The student will work toward developing a minimum speed of 30 words per minute with four or fewer errors on a five-minute timing; *or* 35 words per minute with three or fewer errors on a three-minute timing.

Number Keying

Rule 1: Numbers that begin a sentence are always spelled out.

Example: Twenty-five delegates attended the session.

Practice

7 Ninety-six participants arrived for the fastball tournament.

8 Two hundred and ten were present to vote at the last ballot.

9 86 of the Brownies were chosen for the camping trip.

10 13 employees said that they would work overtime today.

Production 1

Review keying open tables without column headings in Lesson 21, page 54. Key the following table centered horizontally and vertically on a half sheet of paper. Use the automatic horizontal and vertical centering options, if available.

DASMUND ENTERPRISES LTD.

↓ DS

Partial Listing of Merchandise

↓ TS

adapters	camcorders	men's wear
air compressors	cassettes, video	paints
appliances	computers	telephones
barbecues	draperies	typewriters
bedding	filing cabinets	office desks
binoculars	furniture	video recorders

Production 2

Review keying with column headings shorter than the columns in Lesson 23, page 60 and keying footnotes in Lesson 21, page 53. Key the following table on a half sheet of paper. Center it horizontally and vertically. Single space the body in groupings as indicated. Use the automatic horizontal and vertical centering options, if available.

DASMUND ENTERPRISES LTD.

Store Locations and Managers

SC

Did you center the column headings?

SC

Did you use the underscore key or the underline option for the horizontal line?

The underscore key is usually used. Some software will draw a horizontal line with the underline option. Know your software.

Branch	Location	Manager
Edmonton	6817 - 119 Avenue	M. S. Dasmund
Halifax	3729 Bright Street	Edward Grinley
Montreal	300, rue Lepailleur	Michelle De Meeres
Regina	1248 Pasqua Street	Peter Gallin
*Toronto	25 York Mills Road	Thomas Rollins
Vancouver	7025 Granville Street	Fred Baker
Winnipeg	560 Main Street	Joan Deoming

*Head Office

(/) / Reports

60-space line
Spacing: 1 and 2

Key two 1-min timings on each line *or* repeat each line three times.

Use the **L** finger and the left shift to key the **(**. Use the **;** finger and left shift to key the **)**. Key lines 3 and 4 once.

Key lines 5 and 6 twice each.

Skill Building

Set spacing at 2. Key a 2-min timing. Circle all errors. If you had three errors or less, go to line 12 for your next drill. If you had more than three errors, proceed to line 8.

Key 1-min timings as time permits *or* repeat each line twice. Try to concentrate on individual letter stroking as you key.

Key 1-min timings as time permits *or* repeat each line twice. Key each drill as quickly as you can.

Alternate-Hand Words

1 by dot row die clay idle risk girl fight towns embody panels

2 go due rug dig coal jams rock goal firms turns enamel height

Reach to the (and) Keys

3 111 191 1(1 1(1 111 (((191 1(1 1((1 1((1 (1(1((1

4 ;;; ;0; ;); ;); ;;;))) ;0; ;); ;)); ;)););) ;));

5 We need: (1) milk, (2) fruit, and (3) vegetables.

6 Fred Fox (our company manager) will be there, too.

Analyze Your Progress

7   Peter came bounding across the sandy beach. He trotted
confidently along the wooden dock to the end that jutted the
farthest out into the quiet lake. He stood for a moment, to
gaze at the peaceful blue-green water. Carefully, he dipped
one toe in the water. Shivering slightly, he braced himself
and let his body drop into the chilly water. Spring had now
officially arrived.

Accuracy Improvement

8 gas nil rag ply reef hook base plum fare join wears onion ax

9 ax war tar ads dare arts ever sets tease dress access degree

10 odd mitt full book issue error attach street discuss letters

11 Rex is selling quiet vacuum cleaners just to make some money
    for this week's planned trip with the boys to the Grant Zoo.

Speed Improvement

12 Please try to arrange to be there before the meeting begins.

13 Notice was given to the employer but it was not transferred.

14 Donna took coffee and cookies and sat down to read her book.

15 You imply that Jim and Jill are the only ones who know John.

• • • • 1 • • • • 2 • • • • 3 • • • • 4 • • • • 5 • • • 6 • • • • 7 • • • • 8 • • • • 9 • • • • 10 • • • • 11 • • • • 12

101

60-space line
Spacing: 1 and 2
Key two 30-s timings on
each line *or* repeat each line
three times.

One-Hand Words

1 eat pin east null fade jump refer knoll affect John caterers

2 ear nip deaf loom cede link rests Jimmy agrees hill decrease

One-Minute Timings

1. Turn to the One-Minute Timings, page 421.
2. Select the paragraph that you think you can complete in one minute.
3. Key the One-Minute Timing as a drill.
4. If you had two or more errors, practice Accuracy Improvement.
   If you had fewer than two errors, practice Speed Improvement.

Skill Building

Key two 30-s timings on
line 3 of Accuracy Improvement. Circle any errors. If
you have more than one
error for each timing, continue with the Accuracy
Improvement drill. If you
have one error or less on
each timing, key the Speed
Improvement drill and
concentrate on speed.

Accuracy Improvement

3 by dog name eight shale eighth visible chairmen field social

4 bee sell doll coon hoods seeks agrees commit schools filling

Speed Improvement

5 After the flood passes, drill two metres with a steel auger.

6 By 1871 total population of Prince Edward Island was 94 021.

• • • • 1 • • • • 2 • • • • 3 • • • • 4 • • • • 5 • • • • 6 • • • • 7 • • • • 8 • • • • 9 • • • • 10 • • • • 11 • • • • 12

Cylinder Method of Vertical Centering Using a Typewriter

The starting line for vertical centering can be calculated by the Counting Method as explained in Lesson 18, page 45.

An alternate method is the Cylinder Method.

1. Insert a sheet of paper so that the top and bottom edge meet. The paper bail should be closed.
2. Have your machine set on a single spacing. Return the carriage three times. For a full sheet of paper, the keying line is now set for line 33 (the vertical center of the paper).
3. Turn the cylinder toward you (*counter-clockwise*) **one** full line for every **two** lines and spaces to be vertically centered.

Example: Turn the cylinder

        Vertically
        center   )   1

    #> this   )   1

        line*   *Ignore the last line
                                    if it is only one line.

Note: Machines with vertical half spacing will require two "clicks" for one full line.

Note: Some word processing software has an automatic vertical centering option.

Capitalization – Rule 1

Capitalize the first word of a:
- sentence   *That is correct.*
- direct quotation   *He said, "Yes, of course, I can!"*
- complimentary close   *Yours very truly,*

Key each line once, using capital letters as required. Check your work carefully.

16 sincerely yours, your best friend, yours truly, respectfully

17 the lady with the pink hat said, "when are you going north?"

18 "i am going," said the tall man, "to leave for the forests."

19 "son," said the older man, "try to remember the advice now."

Three- or Five-Minute Timing

	1	CW	3

Everyone who is hunting for a job should be shown how a data sheet can be drawn up to present a good word picture of himself or herself. You need to show at a glance the reason that you should be hired for a particular job. Refer to the sample data sheets you can find and use them as a guide when preparing your own. You cannot spend too much time planning your work to end up with a good finished project.

This outline of the details about you may play a significant role in landing the job you hope to get. Do not feel that the sample format needs to be followed rigidly. What a person should see is something special about you and the way you can organize material. All data should be concise while giving enough detail to be meaningful to a reader.

Place your name, address and phone number at the top of your page where they can be seen most easily. If you have a previous work record, give the details in a separate section of the page. If not, then it would be wise to expand information about the training which will help you to succeed. A list of special skills and courses would help to give a picture of you at your best.

Column markings:
- 12 12 4
- 24 24 8
- 36 36 12
- 48 48 16
- 60 60 20
- 72 72 24
- 82 82 27
- 12 94 31
- 24 106 35
- 36 118 39
- 48 130 43
- 60 142 47
- 70 150 50
- 12 162 54
- 24 174 58
- 36 186 62
- 48 198 66
- 60 210 70
- 72 222 74
- 75 227 76

• • • • 1 • • • • 2 • • • • 3 • • • • 4 • • • • 5 • • • • 6 • • • • 7 • • • • 8 • • • • 9 • • • • 10 • • • • 11 • • • • 12   **1 min**

1   2   3   4   **3 min**

Assess Your Improvement
Set spacing at 2. Key at least one 3-min *or* 5-min timing. Circle all errors and calculate gross words per minute. Record the timing on your Progress Chart.

For a 5-min timing divide the cumulative words (CW) by five to calculate gross words per minute.

SI   1.33
AWL 4.09

Unit VI

Objectives

1 The student will review and format open and ruled tables and other related material learned in Unit II.

2 The student will learn to format boxed tables.

3 The student will learn to format tables with braced headings.

4 The student will learn to format tables which are wider or longer than standard paper.

5 The student will learn to format financial statements.

6 The student will learn to format open and closed leader lines.

7 The student will learn to fill in business forms.

8 The student will work toward improving keyboard control.

9 The student will work toward developing a minimum speed of 45 words per minute with three or fewer errors on a three-minute timing; *or* 40 words per minute with four or fewer errors on a five-minute timing.

Note: Students are encouraged to use the automatic options, (e.g. Centering) if they are available on their typewriters or computers.

Reports

A formal report is keyed according to a specified and consistent format.

Prepare Your Machine

1. Set the line length for a 70-space line (elite — 12-pitch) or a 60-space line (pica — 10-pitch) or use the line-length default.
2. Clear all previously set tab stops.
3. Reset a new tab stop at the center and a tab stop for a five-space paragraph indentation, if necessary.
4. Set the line spacing for double spacing.

Keying the Report

1. Read the material in the report carefully before beginning to key.
2. Insert the paper with the backing sheet as a guide if you are using a typewriter.
3. Space down to line 13 or the appropriate line if there is a top margin default for page one.
4. Tab to the center.
5. Center and capitalize the report title.
6. Triple space after the title and key the first page of the report.
7. Space down to line 7 or the appropriate line if there is a top margin default for page two and all subsequent pages.

SC

Did you find the backing sheet supplied with the Working Papers if you are using a typewriter?

Summary of Editors' Marks

¶	new paragraph	¶Make a paragraph	Make a paragraph
⊂	close up space	no s⌒pace here	no space here
∧	insert space	leave aspace here	leave a space here
∧	insert words	this ∧belongs here (word)	this word belongs here
⌐	move left	⌐move to margin	move to margin
⌐	move right	⑤indent five spaces	indent five spaces
∪	transpose	this is out of ordre	this is out of order
ℓ	delete	remove this word	remove word
=	put in capitals	all capital letters	all CAPITAL letters
/	lower case	do not Capitalize	do not capitalize
STET	leave in	do not remove this word (STET)	do not remove this word
∧	insert period	end of this sentence∧	end of this sentence.
#	extra space	this should be double spaced	this should be double spaced

Benefit Changes

1. Health Care - we will now pay 50% of the premium for this.

2. Extended Health Care - we will now pay 50% of the premium for this.

3. Dental Plan - we will now pay 50% of the premium for this.

4. Long-term disability - this is compulsary for all full time employees and optional for employees working less than full time. Premiums are the total responsibility of the employee.

5. Life Insurance - this is optional for all employees. Premiums are the total responsibility of the employee.

6. Pension plan - this is compulsary for all full-time employees and optional for employees working less than full time. We match the employees contribution to this plan.

SC

Did you allow for the top margin default if you are using a computer?

SC

If you are using a computer, did you use word wrap for the body of the report?

Production

Read the information presented in the following one-page report and then key the report on plain paper. If you need a balance line, key the current date in the right hand corner approximately 6-10 lines from the bottom of the page.

13

REPORTS

TS

Reports consist of organized materials prepared for business presentations, speeches, lectures, copy for printing, etc. This sample report is keyed in an unbound form and illustrates one way in which reports may be keyed. You should realize that there is more than one way to key a report. The person for whom you are doing the work will often specify how the report is to be set up.

STET Reports, like letters, need to be arranged attractively on the page. They must also be easy to read. They are normally keyed on standard letter size papper, double spaced, and on a 70 space line of 12-pitch (elite) type (60 spaces if 10-pitch or Pica type). If a report is bound on the side, margins need to be adjusted to allow for this. There are also special ways to display quotations, listings, and tables.

The first page of your report begins on line 13 and the second and succeeding pages begin on line 7. The bottom margin should be 6-10 blank lines. If a one-page report is very short so that the bottom margin is too deep, this can be easily corrected by keying a balance line at the bottom. A balance line is usually a date line keyed in either the lower right or left hand corner and positioned so there will still be 6-10 blank lines remaining at the bottom of the page.

From the desk of James Dasmund

Please prepare a letter for each branch manager (Names and addresses are on Page 272), advising them of changes to our benefit coverage. (attached) Please show the changes in enumerated form. Prepare envelopes also. Advise they should contact Mr. Peter Swanson our Human Resource manager if more detail is required.

I'll sign these when I'm back tomorrow. Thanks.

J.D.

Reports

Skill Building

Set spacing at 2. Key a 2-min timing. Circle all errors. If you had three errors or less, go to line 8 for your next drill. If you had more than three errors, proceed to line 4.

Key 1-min timings as time permits *or* repeat each line twice. Try to concentrate on individual letter stroking as you key.

Key 1-min timings as time permits *or* repeat each line twice. Key each drill as quickly as you can.

Alternate-Hand Words

1 he dye rye dog corn kept rush gown flair usual enrich island
2 if eke she dot dial keys Ruth hair flake visit entity panels

Analyze Your Progress

3   There continues to be good news for people entering the
work force as a secretary. Predictions of employment opportunities in both Canada and the United States show that many
more jobs will be open to college graduates. There is a key
reason for this: more new jobs are being created every day.
Employers are again allocating more of their resources to an
office task force who will help them to have reports exactly
when they need them to make competitive decisions.

Accuracy Improvement

4 rad nip rat ill stew hull beat plop fast hill weave pupil at
5 up ill lip nip pin hull pull null moon hill hulk nylon imply
6 egg doll soon free small allow cannot settle shipped allowed
7 The man held a quiver of arrows in one hand and an ax in the
other; his keen eyes gazed past the birch trees just beyond.

Speed Improvement

8 You agreed to use better verbs and to look at a noun for it.
9 Lee and Gemma shipped the green hull to Fiji free of charge.
10 Whether or not you get a loan will depend upon your capital.
11 You should arrange a time for their question to be answered.

• • • • 1 • • • • 2 • • • • 3 • • • • 4 • • • • 5 • • • • 6 • • • • 7 • • • • 8 • • • • 9 • • • • 10 • • • • 11 • • • • 12

Capitalization – Rule 2

Capitalize proper nouns:
- names of people   *Mr. Harry Ainesley*
- animals   *our pet Duke*
- places and geographic locations   *Yellowknife, Northwest Territories, Canada*
- days of the week and months of the year   *Wednesday, May 10*
- holidays   *Labour Day, Canada Day*

Production 3

Key the following letter on Dasmund letterhead, Toronto office. Use block letter style with paragraph indentations and mixed punctuation. Use the letterhead provided in the Working Papers.

Can you complete Production 3 in 10 min?

Current Date

Wawanesa Mutual Insurance Company
2114 Yonge Street
Toronto, Ontario
M4S 2A5

Gentlemen:

Your company's assistance in helping us review our insurance needs would be welcomed.

As a mail order and retail sales organization with stores in Halifax, Montreal, Toronto, Winnipeg, Regina, Edmonton, and Vancouver, we require various kinds of insurance coverage. We require fire insurance coverage for our buildings and stock, liability insurance coverage, coverage for theft loss, automobile insurance, and life and medical insurance coverage. Our actual dollar needs would have to be discussed in more detail with you.

If you are interested in making a presentation, please submit within two weeks a brief written proposal. Upon receipt of your proposal we will make an appointment to discuss our specific insurance needs.

Sincerely yours,

Thomas Rollins
Manager

oi

P.S. Our existing insurance coverage expires on (use date one month from today)

Key each line once, using capital letters as required. Check your work carefully.

12 mary yuk-wai fung took duke, her big dog, to xian on friday.

13 heinz weissman was born in calgary in the month of february.

14 the fox family always gets together for the christmas break.

15 leon will go to vancouver, british columbia for easter week.

Capitalization – Rule 3

Capitalize nouns showing family relationship when they are used as specific names or when there is no preceding possessive pronoun (mother, father, dad, etc.).
Aunt Mary gave it to her mother.   *Did you give Father his gift?*

Key each line once, using capital letters as required. Check your work carefully.

16 father and mother will bring grandmother with them to hythe.

17 will dad have time to visit uncle fred and aunt clara later?

18 i hope mom will remember to bring the picture of baby peter.

19 has father been able to find a gift for grandmother shannon?

Three- or Five-Minute Timing

Assess Your Improvement
Set spacing at 2. Key at least one 3-min *or* 5-min timing. Circle all errors and calculate gross words per minute. Record the timing on your Progress Chart.

1 CW 3

Computers have had a strong impact on our present style | 12 | 12 | 4
of living. Practically everyone has contact with a computer | 24 | 24 | 8
in some way. This contact might be through bank statements, | 36 | 36 | 12
credit cards, payroll cheques or utility bills. One feature | 48 | 48 | 16
of the computer is the fact that it is able to process great | 60 | 60 | 20
numbers of accounts in a very short time. | 68 | 68 | 23

The earliest computing device was likely a person's ten | 12 | 80 | 27
fingers; hence, our base ten number system. Some time later | 24 | 92 | 31
things like shells, stones and sticks were used as computing | 36 | 104 | 35
devices. Each of these systems was helpful, but likely they | 48 | 116 | 39
were very cumbersome. Soon populations grew and life styles | 60 | 128 | 43
changed, so faster systems were needed. | 68 | 136 | 46

One such system which had been developed by the Chinese | 12 | 148 | 50
is the abacus. This ancient invention is a fairly sophisti- | 24 | 160 | 54
cated calculator which can be used for figuring square roots | 36 | 172 | 58
as well as adding, subtracting, multiplying and dividing. A | 48 | 184 | 62
similar device called a soroban was devised by the Japanese. | 60 | 196 | 66
The abacus is still used in many parts of the world. | 70 | 206 | 69

• • • • 1 • • • • 2 • • • • 3 • • • • 4 • • • • 5 • • • • 6 • • • • 7 • • • • 8 • • • • 9 • • • 10 • • • 11 • • • 12 1 min

1   2   3   4 3 min

SI   1.56
AWL 4.92

Production 1

Key the following letter on City of Red Deer letterhead provided in the Working Papers. Use full block letter style and open punctuation. There should be a "Registered" notation.

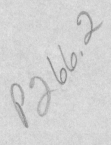

Dasmund Enterprises Ltd. / 6817 – 119 Avenue / Edmonton, Alberta / T5B 4L9 / Attention: Mr. M. S. Dasmund / Gentlemen / Thank you for your land sale application. Your receipt for $1000 is enclosed. Please note the following points: *(Key as enumerations.)*

1. Enclosed is a copy of lots currently available. 2. Please note the easement set backs on all lots. 3. Building and parking regulations are available from the building department. 4. The lot price must be paid in full before a building permit will be issued. 5. Additional electric light and power charges must be paid in full before a building permit will be issued. 6. Sewer and water connection fees are your responsibility. 7. Construction of a building on the lot must begin within nine months of signing the agreement and be completed within fifteen months. /

¶ Please direct any further inquiries to the Land Department, City Hall, Red Deer. / Sincerely yours / C. Hornick, Land Manager / Enclosure

Production 2

Key the following letter on Liberty House letterhead provided in the Working Papers. Use simplified letter style with open punctuation. Prepare a blind copy for the department of Consumer and Corporate Affairs. Key an envelope or an envelope label for Mr. Don Dusik. Fold the copy ready to insert in a No. 8 envelope.

To: Mr. Don J. Dusik 26 Allan Street Red Deer Alberta T4R 1A8

¶ Your letter regarding your account 55115875925 01795 has been received and the contents carefully noted. ¶ Since your last statement was mailed, we have received your payments of $23.15 and $20.80. This pays your account in full at this time. ¶ We look forward to the pleasure of serving you again very soon.

G. Haase

Customer Service Manager

Production

Read the information presented in the following report and then key the report. If you are using a typewriter, use the backing sheet provided in the Working Papers. Leave a bottom margin on page one of 6-10 lines. Start page two on line seven as indicated by the page number in the report.

13↓

BASIC PARTS OF A REPORT

by

(Your Name)

TS↓

To help a report to be easily read and understood, many authors make use of various headings to break their report into small sections.

TS↓

Subheading

DS↓

The subheading is the principal subdivision. It is usually centered and underscored. It is always preceded by a triple space (two blank lines) and followed by a double space. This principal subdivision is often broken down further into smaller sections.

TS↓

Sideheading

↓DS

This is the next most important subdivision. It is always keyed at the side; however, it may be keyed in all capitals or in normal capital and small letters and underscored. Spacing before and after a sideheading is the same as with a subheading--a triple space before the sideheading and a double space following.

DS↓ Paragraph Headings. A paragraph heading is another form of heading used in reports. It identifies the material only within that paragraph. Because it is part of the paragraph, it is keyed at the beginning of the paragraph and is displayed by underscoring the key words.

SC

Did you allow for the top margin default if you are using a computer?

SC

Do you know how to triple space when the line spacing has been set for double spacing?

REPORT 1

Assess Your Progress

60-space line
Spacing: 1 and 2
Key two 30-s timings on
each line *or* repeat each line
three times.

Assess Your Speed

Set spacing at 2. Key at
least one 3-min *or* 5-min
timing. Circle all errors and
calculate gross words per
minute. Record the timing
on your Progress Chart.

SI   1.29
AWL 4.0

Alternate-Hand Words

1 it for rock forks tight island emblems auditory borne enrich
2 me fix risk focus theme height entitle chairman burns entity

Three- or Five-Minute Timing

		1	CW	3
Are you planning to make some changes in a room in your		12	12	4
house or apartment? If you are, some careful planning could		24	24	8
result in a room that is both lovely and functional. Before		36	36	12
you buy anything take stock of what you have in that room as		48	48	16
of today. List the things that you would like to change and		60	60	20
the things that will be staying. Review these lists and add		72	72	24
or delete items to match your budget.		79	79	26
Now that you have decided which things will stay make a		12	91	30
list of the colors that you will be keeping in the room. Do		24	103	34
not overlook any of the colors, even if they are only in the		36	115	38
trim on the woodwork. If possible attach a little swatch of		48	127	42
the colors to your list. This will be helpful when you come		60	139	46
to choose the color scheme for your room.		68	147	49
You are now ready to do a bit of window-shopping. Look		12	159	53
for new ideas in model rooms and magazines. Note how colors		24	171	57
and fabrics are used. Even if a particular room uses things		36	183	61
that are beyond your budget do not despair. Perhaps you can		48	195	65
use one idea from that plan. Once you have done the window-		60	207	69
shopping sit down and see how many good ideas you can put to		72	219	73
use in your own room.		76	223	75

• • • 1 • • • 2 • • • 3 • • • 4 • • • 5 • • • 6 • • • 7 • • • 8 • • • 9 • • • 10 • • • 11 • • • 12   1 min
            1   2   3   4   3 min

Titles. The title of your report is always centered and keyed in all capital letters. If a subtitle is used to further explain the title, it is also centered but is normally not in all capital letters. These two parts - the title and subtitle - are separated from each other by a double space.

By-lines. A by-line is the name of the author of the report. The by-line is centered and keyed following the subtitle (or title if no subtitle is in the report) and separated by a double space. Following the by-line the operator will leave a triple space and then be ready to begin the content section of the report. A by-line is not used when a title page is keyed.

Remember the subject content of the report is always double spaced. Subheadings and side-headings are preceded by a triple space and followed by a double space. Paragraph headings are run in at the beginning of the paragraph and are always underscored to display them. The first page of the report always contains the title and is not numbered. Succeeding pages are numbered consecutively beginning with page two.

SC
Did you begin page two on a new sheet?

SC
Did you allow for the top margin default if you are using a computer?

Production 2

Key the following letter in block style with paragraph indentations on Alberta Air letterhead. Use mixed punctuation and include a special notation that the letter is "Personal." Use the letterhead provided in the Working Papers.

Mr. Thomas Rollins / Dasmund Enterprises Ltd. / 25 York Mills Road / Toronto, Ontario / M2P 1B5 / Dear Mr. Rollins / Re: Air connections, Peace River, Alberta to Edmonton, Alberta / Thank you for your letter of *(last Monday)* inquiring about our airline's flights from Peace River to Edmonton. The information you requested is given below:

1. There is a direct flight every day, departing at 17:25. 2. There are four additional direct flights on Monday through Friday, departing at 7:15, 9:35, 15:45, and 17:30. 3. Approximate flight time is one hour. 4. Air fares change depending on factors such as the day you travel, the length of your stay, and class of service. For further information please contact our ticket office and we will be pleased to quote you the exact fare for your chosen flight. Thank you for your interest in flying with Alberta Air. / Sincerely yours / L. J. Kerry

Key as enumerations.

Production 3

Key the following letter on Dasmund letterhead, Vancouver office. Use the AMS simplified letter style. Use the letterhead provided in the Working Papers.

Mr. Guido D'Angelo 3717 Union Street Burnaby, British Columbia V5C 2W2

CONGRATULATIONS ON YOUR NEW LAWN FURNITURE

You have just won our recent special sales promotion contest: a lawn table, umbrella, and four chairs. Your visit to our store and purchase of our fine quality merchandise allowed us to add your name to the special customers eligible for this lawn furniture ¶ Your new lawn furniture is waiting for you. You have a choice of three colours, and we know there is one just right for your patio. Choose your colour and we will be pleased to deliver your new furniture to your home. ¶ Your family enjoying your new lawn furniture will make a lovely picture. Will you allow us to take your picture and insert it in the local newspaper? Fred Baker, Manager

P.S. Please call soon and make arrangements to receive your new lawn furniture.

64-65

Reports/Listings/ Enumerations

60-space line
Spacing: 1 and 2
Key two 1-min timings on each line *or* repeat each line three times.

Skill Building

Set spacing at 2. Key a 2-min timing. Circle all errors. If you had three errors or less, go to line 8 for your next drill. If you had more than three errors, proceed to line 4.

Key 1-min timings as time permits *or* repeat each line twice. Try to concentrate on individual letter stroking as you key.

Key 1-min timings as time permits *or* repeat each line twice. Key each drill as quickly as you can.

Alternate-Hand Words

1 is end sir due diem laid sick half and lay flame whale flake

2 it eye sit dig dish lake sign hams aid man flaps widow foams

Analyze Your Progress

3   There is a new wave of technology called robotics which is entering our modern offices. Robotics is a term used for any technology which uses a robot or robot-like function for performing controlled actions. It is being used with exact-ing results in the production lines of our factories. Usual factory applications are hooked to a computer control center which allows for decision making based upon input received.

Accuracy Improvement

4 raw no. raw mum draw link beds mill fats jump based union ad

5 at add ace awe daze dart face star taste eager aerate desert

6 nee hill call mill agree seems issued dollar shipped allowed

7 A wacky zebra told queer jokes to a fat pig, a heavy ox, and
   a lazy monkey; a bored old hyena sat in a corner and yawned.

Speed Improvement

8 The hulls are carted east to my pulp mill and then sawed up.

9 The door on the old mill fell off as Garry pressed the edge.

10 We expect the sale to open next week and last for nine days.

11 You should arrange a time for their question to be answered.

• • • • 1 • • • • 2 • • • • 3 • • • • 4 • • • • 5 • • • • 6 • • • • 7 • • • • 8 • • • • 9 • • • • 10 • • • • 11 • • • • 12

Capitalization – Rule 4

Capitalize the first word of a title (book, magazine, article, chapter, etc.) and all other words except joining words (conjunctions, prepositions, or articles).
The Lord of the Flies (book)   *The Globe and Mail* (newspaper)
Learning to Write Effectively (article)

Production Review

60-space line
Spacing: 1 and 2
Key two 30-s timings on
each line *or* repeat each line
three times.

Production Practice

One-Hand Words

1 bag pop bear plum tear pull rafts imply grease link assessed

2 bar pup cafe plop tare pulp rates nylon rarest hoop assesses

Production 1

Key the following on the City of Red Deer letterhead provided in the Working Papers. Use full block letter style and mixed punctuation. Display portions of each paragraph as shown.

Current date

Dasmund Enterprises Ltd.
6817 – 119 Avenue
EDMONTON, Alberta
T5B 4L9

Gentlemen:

Thank you for your recent inquiry re land purchase in our city.

We have a land sale coming up soon ~~next month~~ and the city policy is as follows:

> Only one application can be made per company. Sales are restricted to companies where there are no duplicate shareholders or directors of other companies participating in the sale.

If you submit an application you will also have to include a deposit of $1000.00. This is refundable if you are unsuccessful in obtaining a suitable lot. If you are successful in obtaining a lot, terms of payment are:

¼ of purchase price on signing agreement
½ within 4 months of signing agreement
¼ within 8 months of signing agreement
Full payment must be made before issuing a building permit. [center]

I hope this information will be helpful and look forward to receiving your application for a lot in our upcoming land sale.

Sincerely yours,

C. Hornick, Land Manager

12 there is an article called "splash-down" in the news review.

13 the title of her second book was <u>the shadows of the morning.</u>

14 the feature called "prairie living" is in the calgary times.

15 the book, <u>sand in my shoes,</u> was written by helena g. munden.

Three- or Five-Minute Timing

	1	CW	3
Proofreading skills are important and may be considered	12	12	4
more important than the keyboarding skill itself. To proof-	24	24	8
read, one must develop a skill which is quite different from	36	36	12
that of reading naturally. People often do not realize that	48	48	16
ability as a fluent reader does not transfer directly to the	60	60	20
ability to proofread. Instructions to proofread a page with	72	72	24
care are too often met with resistance.	80	80	27
Proofreading of typewritten copy must be done while the	12	92	31
paper is still in the machine. The most effective way seems	24	104	35
to be to use a pen or pencil to follow line for line along a	36	116	39
line of type just above the paper bail. To help slow up the	48	128	43
reading rate to notice words and word parts, the proofreader	60	140	47
can say the words to himself or herself.	68	148	50
Recent research shows that proofreading is done best in	12	160	54
two readings: the first to analyze each word, comma, period	24	172	58
or other mark to be certain that the language basics are all	36	184	62
correct and the second to read for meaning. A message which	48	196	66
is unclear to the proofreader will likely be unclear to most	60	208	70
other readers as well. Proofreading does take a good amount	72	220	74
of time but it is time well spent in the long run.	82	230	77

SI 1.42
AWL 4.53

• • • 1 • • • 2 • • • 3 • • • 4 • • • 5 • • • 6 • • • 7 • • • 8 • • • 9 • • • 10 • • • 11 • • • 12   1 min

1   2   3   4   3 min

processing position with your company. I am pleased to accept your offer and will report to work on Monday (use next Monday's date) at 08:45. Your office with its pleasant work environment impressed me during the interview. I know I will enjoy working with your staff and for Dasmund. Sincerely yours Shareen Karim

Production 2

Key as a block letter with paragraph indentations. Use mixed punctuation. Key an envelope or an envelope label.

Letter from: 27 Sunnybrae Avenue Halifax Nova Scotia B3N 2G2 To: Mr. James MacDonald Personnel Manager Dasmund Enterprises Ltd. 3729 Bright Street Halifax Nova Scotia B3K 4Z6 Dear Mr. MacDonald Thank you for your letter of (two days ago) and your offer of employment as an information processing specialist. Your interest in my application is appreciated. ¶ I must decline your offer as I had accepted a position with another firm before receiving your letter. ¶ Thank you for the kindness extended to me during my interview. Yours truly Karen W. Hayes

Reference Guide for Reports

Line length   Set a 70-space line (elite — 12-pitch) or a 60-space line (pica — 10-pitch) or use the line-length default.

Right and left margins
- Unbound manuscript – even
- Bound manuscript – move the margins three spaces to the right.

Spacing   Double space the body.

Top margin
- Page one – the title is on line 13.
- Page two – the page number is on line 7.
- Allow for the top margin default if you are using a computer.

Bottom margin   Leave 6-10 lines (usually 6 lines).

Page numbering
- Page one – no page number.
- Page two – pivot at the right margin on line seven followed by a triple space.
- Top bound manuscript – center number at the bottom of the page leaving a bottom margin 6-10 lines.
- Word processing software usually has a page numbering option.

Title   Center and capitalize on line 13 followed by a triple space.

Subtitle   Center. Capitalize principal words. Double space before and triple space after.

By-line   Center. Double space before and triple space after. (Not used if there is a title page.)

Headings in the body
- Subheading – Center and underscore. Triple space before and double space after.
- Sideheading – Place at the left margin, either capitalized or underscored. Triple space before and double space after. When a sideheading follows a subheading, double space between them.
- Paragraph heading – Underscore and place at the beginning of the paragraph. Double space before, which is normal spacing.

Enumerations   Single space if more than one line for the enumeration. Double space between enumerations.

Tables in the body   Triple space before table. Single space the table either centered or within the manuscript margins. Triple space after table.

In-Text References
- In parentheses following the citation in the body of the report.

Bibliography   Key alphabetically on a separate piece of paper. Place the title on line 13, capitalized, centered, and followed by a triple space.
- Single space each bibliographic reference.
- Double space between references.
- Indent the second line of the references 5-10 spaces.

Title page   Center and key attractively. Capitalize the title of the report.

Letters

60-space line
Spacing: 1 and 2
Key two 30-s timings on
each line *or* repeat each line
three times.

Sentences with Double-Letter Words

1 Please arrange the books neatly across the shelf in my room.

2 Bring a vacuum bottle of coffee along with your small lunch.

3 Bill will seek a better supplier of wooden floors and doors.

Speed Building

Key two 30-s timings on
each line concentrating on a
speed goal slightly higher
than your recent speed on
timings. Students on individual progress should key
each line three times with
the increased speed goal in
mind.

Number Practice

4 in all 87 through the 93 but the 45 and all 86 but for 2 563

5 to the 52 give them 74 for all 63 by the 43 so then 24 to 29

Graduated Speed Practice

Turn to the Graduated Alphanumerical Speed Practice, page 403. Select a sentence that you think you can key in the time indicated.

Common-Word Sentences

6 The requests should reach the office three weeks from today.

7 Production should remain more or less constant for one year.

8 She sent the cheque as part payment on the insurance policy.

· · · · 1 · · · · 2 · · · · 3 · · · · 4 · · · · 5 · · · · 6 · · · · 7 · · · · 8 · · · · 9 · · · · 10 · · · · 11 · · · · 12

Skill Building

Key each underlined word
three times. Key each line
once concentrating on the
underlined words.

Concentrate on Correct Spelling

9 The <u>attorneys</u> referred to their <u>calendar</u> in court.

10 The group has <u>benefited</u> from the <u>beginning</u> caveat.

Production Practice

Production 1

Key as a full block letter with open punctuation. Key an envelope or an envelope label.

Letter from: 49 Beaverbrook Avenue Islington Ontario M9B 2N4 *To:* Ms. Jane Isaltis Personnel Director Dasmund Enterprises Ltd. 25 York Mills Road Toronto Ontario M2P 1B5 Dear Ms. Isaltis ¶ Thank you for your letter of (two days ago) offering an information

Production

Read the information in the report and then key the report.

REPORT PREPARATION

Enumerations and Listings

TS ↓

There are some standard rules for displaying material attractively. This report will discuss the normal arrangement for enumerated material and for listing of material.

TS ↓

Enumerations

DS↓

Format

DS↓

Enumerations are really any series of numbered items or steps whose sequence is shown by numbers or letters at the left.

DS↓

1. The numbers are keyed at the margin, followed by a period and
SS↓ two spaces. The text begins after the two spaces.
DS↓

2. Enumerations are single spaced if more than one line is required. A double space separates the numbered enumerations.

3. Run-over lines are indented to align with the beginning of the text. To align the text, a tab stop should be set or an indent option used.

4. If your numerical sequence goes to two-digit numbers (e.g., 10), it is important to align the numbers properly. The periods following the numbers must align.

↑
DS↓   TAB   TS ↓ Listings

Format

DS↓

Listing of material is another way of showing points in a report. To create a centered effect the operator may indent 5

STET

or 10 spaces before beginning the listing, or may exactly center

STET

the longest line in the listing and then block center the others

with it.

Dear Mr. Mac Donald

Please consider my application for the information processing position advertised in today's issue of _The Chronicle Herald_.

I have just completed the Information Processing Diploma Program at Holland College in Charlottetown. A transcript of my grades at Holland College is enclosed. At the end of the program, I received a skill certificate for 80 wpm in keyboarding and certificates to operate both an electronic typewriter with a screen display and an Apple personal computer. I have used a variety of word processing, spreadsheet, database, communications, desktop publishing, and integrated software packages. My work experience includes working as a part-time cashier and sales clerk for the Woolco store in Halifax during high school and as a general office clerk for the Charlottetown Board of Education during my studies at Holland College. My duties as an office clerk included photocopying; faxing; keying letters, routine memorandums, and short reports; and answering the telephone.

The following people have agreed to act as references concerning my academic and work experience: 1. Ms. Danielle Gaudreau, Woolco, Halifax, Nova Scotia B3J 1N9 2. Mr. Stephen Patterson, Board of Education, Charlottetown, Prince Edward Island C1A 1N1. 3. Ms. Shelagh O'Reilly, Secretarial Science Division, Holland College, Charlottetown, Prince Edward Island C1A 4J9.

My work experience in retail sales general office duties together with my recent studies has prepared me for the position you advertised. A personal interview can be arranged at your convenience. I may be contacted during the day at (902) 437-6890.

Sincerely

Karen W. Hayes

5 *Listings are always single spaced with a double
space before and after the listing is completed.
Following is an illustration of a listing.*

10

1. *Enumerations are numbered.*
2. *Enumerations are single spaced.*
3. *Listings are short information points.*
4. *Listings are single spaced.*
⋀DS

*Remember to change the line space
regulator back to double spacing and to return
to the main subject content of your report.*

I have just graduated as an Information Processing major from the Office Administration program at Seneca College. I earned a Keyboarding certificate for 70 wpm and an information processing certificate of proficiency. My experience has included an IBM-compatible computer with a variety of word processing, spreadsheet, and data-base software. I have also used communications, desktop publishing, and integrated software packages.

My work experience has been varied but has convinced me that my future career should be with a retail merchandising company such as Dasmund. Enclosed is my data sheet which summarizes my qualifications.

I am available for a personal interview at your convenience. You may contact me at 416-576-7809 week days after 14:30. Sincerely Shareen Karim

Production 2

Key the following as a block letter with mixed punctuation. Key an envelope or envelope label. This is the type of letter which would be sent without a personal data sheet. Fill in the application form provided in your Workbook.

First Draft

27 Sunnybrae Avenue, Halifax, Nova Scotia B3N 2G2

Mr. James MacDonald, Personnel Manager
Dasmund Enterprises Ltd.
3729 Bright Street
Halifax, Nova Scotia
B3K 4Z6

Outlines

60-space line
Spacing: 1 and 2

Key two 1-min timings on each line *or* repeat each line three times.

Skill Building

Set spacing at 2. Key a 2-min timing. Circle all errors. If you had three errors or less, go to line 8 for your next drill. If you had more than three errors, proceed to line 4.

Alternate-Hand Words

1 me fir six dog disk lamb soak them bib men focus world forks

2 do fit the dot dock land sock then bid map forks right forms

Analyze Your Progress

3 The young child with light blonde hair wore a new shirt covered with light blue and dark blue checks. His old jeans were patched at the knee and threads hung from frayed cuffs. The blue running shoes with faded yellow laces had seen many days tramping through mud and snow and caught on twigs or on rusty nails. His clear blue eyes were dancing with surprise as he announced the big event of the day. He could now ride his new bike.

Accuracy Improvement

4 sad non red ill raze loop beef pill fear link screw jolly aw

5 no ion no. joy you mill pill loom hook milk lump pupil plump

6 tee loll week seem glass speed accept excess install dollars

7 Carl quits his work in the garden before Judy mixes a large, cold, zesty glass of his favorite fresh pink lemonade punch.

Speed Improvement

8 We can join him in a debate on the free use of the ski hill.

9 The letters will arrive weekly at the office on Ross Street.

10 Full details on the question are well explained on page ten.

11 A test on the next unit will be given following the holiday.

· · · · 1 · · · · 2 · · · · 3 · · · · 4 · · · · 5 · · · 6 · · · 7 · · · · 8 · · · · 9 · · · · 10 · · · 11 · · · 12

Capitalization – Rule 5

Capitalize only the first and last words of salutations unless they are titles or proper names.
Dear Sir: My dear Sir: My dear Mrs. Rashad:

12 dear dr. kampmann: dear sir: my dear dr. hill: dear jane:

13 dear mrs. chu: my dear sir: dear madam: dear ms. chirkov:

14 gentlemen: my dear mrs. ali and mr. adler: dear ms. marlo:

15 my dear bob: dear madam: mesdames: dear mr. and mrs. lee:

Set spacing at 2. Key at
least one 3-min *or* 5-min
timing. Circle all errors and
calculate gross words per
minute. Record the timing
on your Progress Chart.

Three- or Five-Minute Timing

	1	CW	3

The microwave oven is becoming more and more popular in `12 | 12 | 4`
this country. The microwave ovens cook food in a short time `24 | 24 | 8`
and use much less electricity than usual cooking methods. A `36 | 36 | 12`
baked potato, for example, will take five minutes with a mi- `48 | 48 | 16`
crowave oven and about an hour in a regular oven. For those `60 | 60 | 20`
in a hurry the microwave oven is designed to put a warm meal `72 | 72 | 24`
on the table in a minimum amount of time. `80 | 80 | 27`

Microwaves are absorbed by the food causing the food to `12 | 92 | 31`
warm. Foods with a high percentage of liquid absorb more of `24 | 104 | 35`
the radiation than those with less liquid. Hence, the foods `36 | 116 | 39`
with more water content will get hotter. However, food that `48 | 128 | 43`
is in a microwave oven is not cooked by just radiation. The `60 | 140 | 47`
radiation does not penetrate the foods very deeply. Much of `72 | 152 | 51`
the cooking is done by conduction. `79 | 159 | 53`

Microwave ovens on the market now seem to be quite safe `12 | 171 | 57`
if care is taken in installing and using them. Proper cook- `24 | 183 | 61`
ing utensils should be used. These could be paper, ceramic, `36 | 195 | 65`
plastic or glass. Metal should be avoided since it reflects `48 | 207 | 69`
heat and can damage the oven. It is a good idea to have the `60 | 219 | 73`
oven checked each year for radiation leakage. `69 | 228 | 76`

• • • • 1 • • • 2 • • • 3 • • • 4 • • • 5 • • • 6 • • • 7 • • • 8 • • • 9 • • • 10 • • • 11 • • • 12   1 min
         1   2   3   4   3 min

SI   1.51
AWL 4.41

Production Practice

Production 1

Key the following as a full block letter with open punctuation. Key an envelope or envelope label. This is the type of letter which could accompany a personal data sheet.

Letter from: 49 Beaverbrook Avenue Islington
                Ontario M9B 2N4

To: Ms. Jane Tsaltis Personnel Director, Dasmund
      Enterprises Ltd. 25 York Mills Road Toronto
      Ontario M2P 1B5

Dear Ms. Tsaltis

Please consider me as an applicant for the information processing position advertised in the February 5, 19-- issue of *The Globe and Mail.*

SC
Do you know the preferred
style for personal business
letters? Refer to page 125 if
you are not certain.

The typewriters in use today have a fairly long history | 12 | 12 | 4
in that the first patent for a typewriter was given to Henry | 24 | 24 | 8
Mill, an English engineer, in 1714. No drawing of his type- | 36 | 36 | 12
writer exists. From 1760 to 1840 other typing machines were | 48 | 48 | 16
invented in several other countries. William Burt devised a | 60 | 60 | 20
typing machine in 1828-1829, the first in North America. | 72 | 72 | 24

Other typewriters soon followed. In 1850 a complicated | 12 | 84 | 28
machine was invented by Oliver Eddy of Baltimore. Having 78 | 24 | 96 | 32
type bars in 13 rows, this machine was similar to the piano. | 36 | 108 | 36
More typing machines were patented. Dr. Samuel Francis from | 48 | 120 | 40
New York devised one that had the appearance and the size of | 60 | 132 | 44
a piano accordion. This was in 1847. | 68 | 140 | 46

Finally in 1867 the man who was to be called "father of | 12 | 152 | 50
the typewriter" sat down and typed, "C. LATHAM SHOLES, SEPT. | 24 | 164 | 54
1867." The words were all in capital letters since Latham's | 36 | 176 | 58
machine had no lower case letters. The idea was there, even | 48 | 188 | 62
though many changes still had to take place. In the time to | 60 | 200 | 66
follow, Sholes produced about 50 different trial models. | 71 | 211 | 70

• • • 1 • • • • 2 • • • • 3 • • • • 4 • • • • 5 • • • • 6 • • • • 7 • • • • 8 • • • • 9 • • • • 10 • • • • 11 • • • 12 | 1 min

1   2   3   4 | 3 min

A:PRD.1

SI 1.77
AWL 4.60

Production Practice

Production 1

Read the following information and then key the report.

PREPARING AN OUTLINE

An outline is used to systematically set up a series of main topics and their subtopics that form the base for the presentation of a subject. An outline can help the writer prepare the subject matter so it is presented in an orderly and logical way. It also aids the readers by allowing them to see the outstanding points to be presented.

97 Application Letters

60-space line
Spacing: 1 and 2
Key two 30-s timings on each line *or* repeat each line three times.

Speed Building

Key two 30-s timings on each line concentrating on a speed goal slightly higher than your recent speed on timings. Students on individual progress should key each line three times with the increased speed goal in mind.

Sentences with One-Hand Words

1 Can you supply us with all the products we need this summer?

2 At noon, Fred, the jolly barber, ate that dessert with milk.

Number Practice

3 There were over 93 fire calls in the first 3 months of 1993.

4 Ambulance calls in 1992 increased to 1 096 from 854 in 1991.

Graduated Speed Practice

Turn to the Graduated Alphanumerical Speed Practice, page 403. Select a sentence that you think you can key in the time indicated.

Sentences with Double-Letter Words

5 Allan said the issue was whether to cool or freeze the food.

6 Take a good look at the message and call toll free tomorrow.

7 She called all the accounting staff into the weekly meeting.

• • • • 1 • • • • 2 • • • • 3 • • • • 4 • • • • 5 • • • • 6 • • • • 7 • • • • 8 • • • • 9 • • • • 10 • • • • 11 • • • • 12

Skill Building

Key each underlined word three times. Key each line once concentrating on the underlined words.

Concentrate on Correct Spelling

8 The recipient of the award will be a reputable person.

9 Separate letters will give the extra reinforcement.

Basic English Skill

raise: means "to lift up" or "to move something upward"
rise: means "to go up" or "to come up"

Key each sentence once, inserting the correct choice from the words in parentheses. Your right margin will not be even.

10 Can we hope to (raise, rise) the standard of living?

11 The cost of food continues to (raise, rise) each year.

For an outline to serve these two purposes, it must be clearly arranged. Following is a standard procedure for keying an outline.

TS ↓
TITLE

TS ↓

   I. First Subheading
      A. Side Heading
      B. Side Heading
         1. Paragraph Heading
         2. Paragraph Heading
            a. Listing
            b. Listing

DS ↓
  II. Second Subheading

TS ↓
Each subtopic is indented in relation to the preceding item. Topics of the same rank are always begun at the same point on the writing scale. A period follows a figure or letter but not a parenthesis.

If a run-over line is needed it is begun under the preceding line. Outlines are usually single spaced with a double space after each important division.

After studying this material try to key the outline illustrated in the following production exercise.

Production 1

Key the personal data sheet for Shareen Karim shown on page 255.

Production 2

Key a personal data sheet for yourself.

Basic English Skill

stationary: without movement
stationery: writing paper

14 We received some new (stationary, stationery) today.

15 The desks will remain (stationary, stationery) throughout

the redecoration of the office.

set: to place
sit: to rest one's body

16 (Sit, Set) the vase of flowers on the credenza.

17 The legislature will (sit, set) for a long session today.

Production 2

Key the following outline centered in a single column using a full sheet of paper.

Choosing the Right Word Processing Software
(Considerations When Buying Your Micro)

↓ TS

I. Performance Criteria
   A. Superior WP capabilities
   B. User friendliness
   C. Productivity
   D. Expandability
   E. Flexibility
II. System Memory Considerations
   A. Video Memory
      1. Foreground operating characteristics
      2. Background operating characteristics
      3. Non-destructive editing
      4. Text manipulation
   B. Instruction Memory
      1. Capacity
      2. Facility of applications
      3. User help features
   C. Data Memory
      1. Multiple simultaneous background functions
      2. Operational flexibility
      3. Back-up capabilities
   D. I/O Module Instruction Memory
   E. Processing Power
      1. RAM available
      2. Expansion considerations
      3. I/O choices and capabilities
III. Integration With Other Software Packages

```
          D A T A    S H E E T


          Shareen Karim
          49 Beaverbrook Avenue
          Islington, Ontario
          M9B 2N4
          Phone:  416-576-7809


EDUCATION RECORD
     1988-89  Seneca College, Toronto, Ontario.  Completed
              two-year Office Administration Program with an
              information processing major.

     1985-86  Graduated from Don Mills High School, university
              entrance.

WORK EXPERIENCE
     1987-88  T. Eaton Company, Toronto.  General office clerk.
              Keyboarding, filing, switchboard, cashiering.

     1986-87  Martin & Stevens Ltd., Toronto.  Receptionist,
              clerk - keyboard operator.

     1985-86  Canada Safeway Ltd., Don Mills.  Part-time cashier.

REFERENCES
     Ms. Lily Chan, Seneca College, Finch Campus,
     1750 Finch Avenue East, Willowdale, Ontario M2J 2X5.
     Phone 416-491-5050.

     Mr. Don Walker, T. Eaton Company, Toronto Eaton Centre,
     Toronto, Ontario M5W 1S2.  Phone 416-591-3111.

     Mrs. Teresa Fauchon, Martin & Fauchon Ltd.
     143 Blackthorne Avenue, Toronto, Ontario M6N 3H7.
     Phone 416-762-8121.


     Mr. Horst Gerhold, Canada Safeway Ltd., Rexdale,
     Ontario M9W 5A5.  Phone 416-241-2631.

OTHER
     Career Goals:  Executive Assistant.  Plan to take evening
     credit courses in Business Administration, Seneca College.

     General Interests:  Sports, Music, Reading.

     Special Abilities:  Enjoy people.  Play piano, sing in
     Community Chorus.  Active in young people's community
     organizations.  Girl Guide leader.
```

Bound Reports

Skill Building

Set spacing at 2. Key a 2-min timing. Circle all errors. If you had three errors or less, go to line 8 for your next drill. If you had more than three errors, proceed to line 4.

Key 1-min timings as time permits *or* repeat each line twice. Try to concentrate on individual letter stroking as you key.

Key 1-min timings as time permits *or* repeat each line twice. Key each drill as quickly as you can.

Key each line once, using capital letters as required. Check your work carefully.

Alternate-Hand Words

1 of fix tie due down lane span they big oak forms girls rigid
2 or for toe end dual lend suck town bit own furor gland risks

Analyze Your Progress

3　　The bright lights of the big city shone in the darkness of the night.　It was a scene of beauty to see the buildings mirrored in the black water of the lake.　The night was calm and there was no shimmer in the portrait of urban progress a short way across the bay.　Each window of the tall buildings was alive with light and the scene of double forms with tiny checks loomed like columns rising up from the water.

Accuracy Improvement

4 sax nun sag him sage lump best hulk feed hoop seats knoll as
5 ad age act art east tart fact teas acres erase refers detect
6 err roll look door added calls agreed differ getting proceed
7 Maizie will fix your jacket pocket very quickly if you would be able to give her a needle and some thread in this basket.

Speed Improvement

8 Look at a few pages of my free verse on sea reefs and water.
9 Attach the needed sheets to the bottom of the school letter.
10 The schedule of events has been planned to include everyone.
11 Give us a hand to arrange the space for the special meeting.
　• • • • 1 • • • • 2 • • • • 3 • • • • 4 • • • • 5 • • • • 6 • • • • 7 • • • • 8 • • • • 9 • • • • 10 • • • • 11 • • • • 12

Capitalization – Rule 6

Capitalize titles or degrees that come before or after proper nouns.
Will Judge Williams be presiding?　　Dean Walter John, Ph.D., will give the address.

12 dr. and mrs. f. r. rowe were in attendance at the last draw.
13 professor laporte, ph.d., will attend our next french class.
14 his eminence, john arnold milman will get an invitation too.

Personal Data Sheet

60-space line
Spacing: 1 and 2
Key two 30-s timings on each line *or* repeat each line three times.

Accuracy Building

Key two 30-s timings on each line concentrating on a speed goal slightly higher than your recent speed on timings. Students on individual progress should key each line three times with the increased speed goal in mind.

One-Hand Words

1 cat hop bars hump wage pink greet plump facade hill arrested
2 bat mop bare poll wars pool radar plunk fester jump asserted

Left-Hand Words

3 be sea act see stag card gets ware bases bears barter evades
4 we set add sex wear care race watt beads feeds evaded savers

Number Practice

5 The score in the football game was Home: 23, Visitors: 15.
6 There are about 67 boys and 49 girls in classroom number 80.

Alphabetic Sentences

7 Quincy plays a five-string banjo, Mike plays his old zither, and Wayne sings with Trixie.

8 Helena hopes to justify her next seven work projects quickly so she can zero in on the first big dam project.

• • • • 1 • • • • 2 • • • • 3 • • • • 4 • • • • 5 • • • • 6 • • • • 7 • • • • 8 • • • • 9 • • • • 10 • • • • 11 • • • • 12

Selected Letter Practice

1. Analyze your errors in the Alphabetic Sentences and Drills.
2. Choose the letters or numbers giving you difficulty or causing errors.
3. Turn to page 405 and select the appropriate Selected Letter and Number Practice.
4. Key each line twice.
5. Practice the drillings for **X**, **Y**, and **Z**.

Skill Building

Key each line once, capitalizing the words to make them correct. Check your work carefully.

Capitalization Practice

9 bring the french text, <u>nos voisins</u>, to the lesson on friday.
10 sincerely yours, my dear mr. sing, aunt susan, sunday, harry
11 rachael's mother, sincerely, prince george, british columbia
12 jacques breau, ph.d., finished the book <u>heritage</u> in October.
13 yours truly, sincerely yours, respectfully, your best friend

Three- or Five-Minute Timing

Assess Your Improvement
Set spacing at 2. Key at least one 3-min or 5-min timing. Circle all errors and calculate gross words per minute. Record the timing on your Progress Chart.

The correct use of the telephone is extremely important | 12 | 12 | 4
in any business. Very often a customer's first contact with | 24 | 24 | 8
a firm is by a telephone call and poor telephone manners can | 36 | 36 | 12
leave a very bad impression with most prospective customers. | 48 | 48 | 16
Even a curt response from the switchboard operator can cause | 60 | 60 | 20
callers to change their minds about dealing with a company. | 72 | 72 | 24

Every office worker must realize that the voices on the | 12 | 84 | 28
telephone are very often being judged by the other people on | 24 | 96 | 32
the line. A good thing to keep in mind is that every time a | 36 | 108 | 36
telephone rings at work, the one who answers represents this | 48 | 120 | 40
company. The impression that the caller is left with is too | 60 | 132 | 44
often ignored by the office worker. | 67 | 139 | 46

Speak pleasantly and use a good clear tone. Answer the | 12 | 151 | 50
telephone each time as if this is the important call you are | 24 | 163 | 54
expecting. Make callers feel that they are special and take | 36 | 175 | 58
time to be helpful. Use callers' names and speak as if they | 48 | 187 | 62
were across the desk from you. Keep any promises of further | 60 | 199 | 66
action and use the basic phrases of courtesy like please and | 72 | 211 | 70
thank you. Such words help to put a smile in your voice. | 84 | 223 | 74

• • • 1 • • • • 2 • • • • 3 • • • • 4 • • • • 5 • • • • 6 • • • • 7 • • • • 8 • • • • 9 • • • • 10 • • • • 11 • • • 12   1 min
                1   2   3   4   3 min

SI   1.43
AWL 4.37

Bound Reports

Prepare Your Machine

Adjust your machine according to one of the following methods:
Paper Guide Method   Move your paper guide three spaces to the left.
Center Point Method   Move the center point three spaces to the right. Reset the margin stops for a 70-space line (elite — 12 pitch) or a 60-space line (pica — 10 pitch), and a 5-space paragraph indentation.
Visual Guide Method   Reset your margin stops and tab stop for a five-space paragraph indentation using the backing sheet as a visual guide.

Keying the Report

1. Read the material in the report carefully before beginning to key.
2. Insert the paper with the backing sheet as a guide if you are using a typewriter.
3. Space down to line 13 or the appropriate line if there is a top margin default for page one.
4. Tab to the center.

Form Letter

Dasmund Enterprises Ltd.

Head Office:
25 York Mills Road   Toronto, Ontario   M2P 1B5

Current Date
Mr. T. Seifert
206 Jarvis Street
Whitehorse, Yukon
Y1A 2H1

Dear *Mr. Seifert*

We are pleased to see that you have used your Dasmund Charge Card for the first time. Congratulations on your purchase of the new *Power-zoom movie camera and multimotion projector.*

Enclosed, for your convenience, is a Dasmund Book to record your payments and to remind you that your payments are $ *30*   due on the *13th* of each month.

If you have any questions regarding the use of your Dasmund card, or your monthly payments, please do not hesitate to contact us.

Sincerely yours

Peter Gallin
Manager

oi
Encl.

Production Practice

Production

Review variable line spacing and the alignment scale for proper alignment on the paper. Use the form letters in the Working Papers to fill in the following information. The amount in parentheses is the monthly payment. Payments begin one month from today. Insert the correct date.

1. *Power-zoom movie camera and multimotion projector ($30) sold to: Mr. T. Seifert, 206 Jarvis Street, Whitehorse, Yukon Y1A 2H1*

2. *Deluxe Upright Vacuum Cleaner ($27) sold to: William Aziz, 2 Bluebird Place, Elmira, Ontario N3B 1W6*

3. *Contemporary 3-piece living room suite ($42) sold to: Ms. G. Ethier, 913 Tremaudan Avenue, The Pas, Manitoba R9A 1P1*

4. *Walking-jogging exerciser ($35) sold to: Gregory Coughlin, 107 Bonaventure Avenue, St. John's, Newfoundland A1B 2X8.*

5. *Steel-belted radial tires ($18) sold to: Mrs. Delores Urquhart, 1201 Second Avenue, Trail, British Columbia V1R 1L7*

5. Center and key the report title.
6. Triple space after the title and key the first page of the report.
7. Space down to line 7 or the appropriate line to allow for the top margin default for page two and all subsequent pages.
8. Triple space after the page numbers and key the text of the report.
   Note: Word processing software usually has a page numbering option.

Keying a Top-Bound Report

Leave extra spaces (two or three lines) at the top of each page. The title on page one would be keyed on line 15 or 16 and the page number for the subsequent pages would be keyed on line 9 or 10.

Production

Read the following report and then key it. Set margins for a side-bound report. If time permits, re-key as a top-bound report.

Dasmund Enterprises Ltd.
A Proposal for Evaluation of Office Systems Equipment

For a meaningful evaluation of office systems equipment to take place, it is imperative that we solicit the help of ALL our employees, especially the primary users at the "grass roots" of our organization. To facilitate such feedback, it is suggested that we gather input in the following areas:

Status of Present Equipment
   It is necessary to take a complete inventory of all existing equipment, listing the capabilities and drawbacks of each piece as it relates to cost effectiveness and office efficiency. Relative to this area, we hope to obtain a complete report of existing equipment servicing together with the cost and effectiveness of that service.

Analysis of Company Needs
   Each employee should be encouraged to review his/her job description with the aim of listing the kind of office services or equipment which would best facilitate that role in the organization. We want everyone to have a part in any planned improvements and to have a definite sense of job security throughout.

Form Letters

Double-Letter Words

1 fee roof dull hull broom creek barrel dinner carrier finally
2 see feel loop cull trill grill coffee assess traffic accrued

Alternate-Hand Words

3 if fur sick furor towns ritual bifocal quantity blame embody
4 is fox rush forms title panels element sorority blend enamel

Number Practice

5 Please order 90 copies of leaflet number 2813 for this room.
6 I have carded 47 of the 56 books in this section of shelves.

Alphabetic Sentences

7 Several farmers planted flax quite soon after the icy rivers broke up, always just hoping it would not freeze.

8 The quilted pyjamas worn by Alexia were crimson, with shades of mauve and azure, making a lovely print.

· · · ·1· · · ·2· · · ·3· · · ·4· · · ·5· · · ·6· · · ·7· · · ·8· · · ·9· · · ·10· · · ·11· · · ·12

Selected Letter Practice

1. Analyze your errors in the Alphabetic Sentences and Drills.
2. Choose the letters or numbers giving you difficulty or causing errors.
3. Turn to page 405 and select the appropriate Selected Letter and Number Practice.
4. Key each line twice.
5. Practice the drill lines for **U**, **V**, and **W**.

Word Division Practice

9 fourteen journal knitting number nutrition obstruction
10 named moves straight plates through friend saved routes salt
11 beauty about smudgy study above able abide ideal enough item
12 zero builder bookkeeper cover darker detail endure recorder
13 hopeful visa ago should omit hitting shopping matter via
14 offset breakfasts useless farewell something sunshines
15 negative nominee odious oculist origin reopens inquire

Objectives for improvements should be listed as they relate to such office information as: turnaround, security, ease of usage, adaptability, cost savings and improved customer service.

Hard Copy Requirements

As an outcome of the needs analysis, it will be necessary to document, in detail, the kinds and quantities of paper or other hard copy reports needed to perform the day-to-day operations of Dasmund. It will be a most useful exercise to try to eliminate any useless copies now being proliferated which provide no useful data for anyone. Related to these concerns is the optimum timing for receipt of information to perform any given task and the frequency for need of reference from any records retention system.

Evaluating New Equipment

In anticipation that some new equipment will be necessary, we are proposing that a complete report be made available to each department in every branch office. The report will list the various vendors, together with a basic comparison of equipment features and back-up service available.

It will be helpful to receive comments or concerns regarding any equipment so listed. It is realized that some local concerns can be of paramount importance in the selection of equipment for any task. At the same time, it is important that we strive for a branch-to-branch interface system which will allow, in turn, cost efficiency, good consumer prices, and job security in a competitive firm.

Choosing Vendors

Since the final task of choosing vendors is a major one for a national company such as ours, it will be necessary to have a committee summarize the data and make a proposal of recommendations for possible

Skill Building

60-space line
Spacing: 1 and 2
Key two 30-s timings on
each line *or* repeat each line
three times.

Right-Hand Words

1 pup oh lily lion hilly pylon jumpy million in hum joy uphill

2 joy no kiln junk lumpy milky plunk monopoly I oh mop him pun

Graduated Speed Practice

Turn to the Graduated Alphanumerical Speed Practice, page 403. Select a sentence that you think you can key in the time indicated.

Accuracy Building

Key two 30-s timings on each line concentrating on accuracy as your goal. Students on individual progress should key each line three times with the accuracy goal in mind.

Alphabetic Sentences

3 They have rejected plans for a quality building complex in a new residential zone in Blackfield.

4 The judge will head the inquiry if he can make those various plans without having to relax the zone blocking.

Number Practice

5 About 124 500 guests registered at our 3 hotels during 1990.

6 By 1997, 63% of our company's exports will be to the Orient.

Selected Letter Practice

1. Analyze your errors in the Alphabetic Sentences and Number Practice.
2. Choose the letters or numbers giving you difficulty or causing errors.
3. Turn to page 405 and select the appropriate Selected Letter and Number Practice.
4. Key each line twice.

Accuracy Improvement

7 wheel carry arrive degree offices matters supplier efficient

8 do air laid ambit towns formal antique endowment work enrich

Speed Improvement

9 Kenn worked the loom in the mill to create fine nylon cloth.

10 The cheque did not quite cover the balance owing on account.

• • • • 1 • • • • 2 • • • • 3 • • • • 4 • • • • 5 • • • • 6 • • • • 7 • • • • 8 • • • 9 • • • 10 • • • • 11 • • • 12

Skill Building

Key two 30-s timings on line 7 of Accuracy Improvement. Circle any errors. If you have more than one error for each timing, continue with the Accuracy Improvement drill. If you have one error or less on each timing, key the Speed Improvement drill and concentrate on speed.

Three- or Five-Minute Timing

Turn to the timing in Unit V of your Working Papers. Students without Working Papers should key the timing in Lesson 92, page 246.

A Proposal cont.

changes by May of next year. This report, circulated to all branches for further staff input, should be finalized for presentation to the Board of Directors by August 15.

<u>A Timeline for Implementation</u>

The following timeline was accepted tentatively by the senior executive officers at their meeting on September 3. It was drawn up using the branch office reports available to us at that time.

<u>October to November</u> — employees' needs surveys and inventory analysis.

<u>December</u> — analysis of reports and retention systems.

<u>January to March</u> — equipment demonstrations and evaluation meetings.

<u>April</u> — consolidating branch office surveys and reports.

<u>May</u> — Administrative Committee to collect branch data and prepare a summary report for distribution to branch offices.

<u>June 30</u> — deadline for additional employee feedback.

<u>July 15</u> — final report to printing office.

<u>July 30</u> — reports mailed: full reports to members of the Board of Directors and a summary to each shareholder.

<u>August 15</u> — Annual Meeting special session report and possible acceptance.

<u>September to December</u> — equipment installation and procedures implementation.

Key the letter to Mr. J. R. Sarai on a half sheet of letter-size paper with the short edge inserted first. Insert the following paragraph before the last paragraph in the letter. This will give you a two-page letter. Use the letterhead provided in the Working Papers.

I am sure that Mr. Baker has explained our personnel policies to you. If you have any questions, please be sure to discuss them with Mr. Baker. We hope that Dasmund will be able to offer you the employment opportunities you are seeking and that you will continue to be our employee for many years to come.

Basic English Skill

sure: use as an adjective
surely: use as an adverb

13 We (sure, surely) can agree with his statement.

14 It is a (sure, surely) thing that we will be present.

there: adverb; statement of place; expletive
their: possessive pronoun
they're: contraction for "they are"

15 (There, Their, They're) holiday will begin on July 15.

16 (There, Their, They're) hoping to travel across Canada.

17 (There, Their, They're) is a good chance that we can travel with them.

Analytical Practice

60-space line
Spacing: 1
Key two 30-s timings on
each line *or* repeat each line
three times.

**Analyze Your
Practice Needs**
Key three 1-min timings on
each sentence *or* repeat each
sentence five times. Every
alphabetic character is
included in each sentence.

Circle all errors.

After Selected Letter
Practice, key two 1-min
timings on each sentence
and determine if you have
improved your accuracy.

If you have practised the
necessary lines before your
instructor calls time, begin
keying at line **A** and key
each line once.

One-Hand Words

1 are him car hip bade hill cede Jill draw hump tread knoll ax

2 cab hop beg hum bags hump seed pump dead lump treat Jimmy at

Alphabetic Sentences

3 The oxen and the sheep graze in placid contentment by a very
tiny jewel-like fish pond that nestles quietly by this hill.

4 Just don't forget to take a box of gauze along with you when
you go for a picnic as many accidents visit in quiet places.

• • • • 1 • • • • 2 • • • • 3 • • • • 4 • • • • 5 • • • • 6 • • • • 7 • • • • 8 • • • • 9 • • • • 10 • • • 11 • • • • 12

Selected Letter Practice

1. Analyze your errors in the Alphabetic Sentences.
2. Choose the letter or letters giving you difficulty or causing errors.
3. Select the appropriate Selected Letter Practice.
4. Key each line twice.
5. Assess your improvement.

A at has all made years same plan tax call ask manner gas near
Carla and Alice can walk as far as the bank if they have to.

B by able bug about board best based better benefits bill book
Brent bought a big box of brown bread but forgot the butter.

C cut price copy service complete case credit price lack costs
Cut a piece of cake in the cabin and carry it to Cal or Cam.

D had paid aid dish down duty dock add mind held round awarded
David washed the dirty dishes and Donna dried the odd plate.

E he end each eager early effort edges evade earn else engines
Every envelope of letters is opened and on Peter's big desk.

F few if safe fed fork flair staff refer effort fade fox safer
Fear of a forest fire forced fifty careful families to flee.

G dog goal gases stage grade barges eight gag geared gave sage
The group of gracious guests guard the gates to the grounds.

• • • • 1 • • • • 2 • • • • 3 • • • • 4 • • • • 5 • • • • 6 • • • • 7 • • • • 8 • • • • 9 • • • • 10 • • • 11 • • • • 12

Different Paper Sizes

Businesses use letterhead paper of various sizes. Use the alignment scale to measure the number of horizontal spaces on the paper. Determine the center point and adjust for left and right margin of 10–15 spaces.

One of the common paper sizes is 14 cm × 22 cm, which is a half-sheet of letter-size paper with the short edge inserted first. To prepare to key a letter on such stationery, set margins for a 50-space line (elite) or a 40-space line (pica).

Production 1

Key the letter to Mr. J. R. Sarai on a half-sheet of letter-size paper with the short edge inserted first. Use the letterhead provided in the Working Papers. Key an envelope or an envelope label.

Production Practice

---

10 or DS below letterhead

Current Date

4↓

Mr. J. R. Sarai
1781 Delta Avenue
Burnaby, British Columbia
V5B 3G6

Dear Mr. Sarai

You are now an employee of Dasmund and I would like to take this opportunity to welcome you personally.

As a condition of employment with Dasmund, every new employee must join the company group insurance plan. The company pays 50 percent of the premiums. This provides you with disability insurance, as well as life insurance payable to your beneficiary. A copy of your specific policy is enclosed. You will find this a very worthwhile policy.

The next time I am in Vancouver I hope to meet you and wish you success in your new job.

                    Sincerely yours

                    Thomas Rollins
                    Manager

oi

Enclosure

H hi wish hay than eight shake tight that has them help height
He has a habit of heading for help if he hears a horse jump.

I in bit rig iron wish six risks signal hip into nip it height
Invite the intelligent librarian to inform us on this issue.

J jump jar just jeans jaws job jute junior justify joys jammed
The judge will join James to jointly study the law journals.

K kept knives bake known kit kick park knack yolk kilts kidded
A kind widow kept the keen knives in a black kitchen kettle.

L lad lake tail land ball halt lawyer league logic lots loving
Lazy Leon loafed in the last language lesson; Lola listened.

M maker map march marine mean same meters minds modern moulded
Sam and Mel came to the matinee to see the same music movie.

N link mink nail on nerve noble notes null down nurses nothing
The nine new neighbors phoned nearly everyone about a party.

O oat once only come odious opens off outing outward oven hoop
The officer objected to the odor of onions from the old box.

P hop loop imply pays nip flops prevent panels protest pursuit
Philip planned to play water polo at our private pool party.

Q query quarrel sequin quickest quality quote quotations quiet
Quentin is quite quiet but he can quote the quarterly paper.

R rail rapid enrich recent recourse rich room ore rust rid red
Rory ran across the railroad tracks trying to trap his bird.

S said scrap secure rests skid snug forms sock spare she signs
This side scored the first goal but several players sat out.

T at cut city totals truck typist twice slant averts hat treat
My train will travel on this track, then switch to that one.

U fun upset up umpire units turkey usually urban utmost furors
Una could jump just as high as Uta but she stubbed her foot.

• • • • 1 • • • • 2 • • • • 3 • • • • 4 • • • • 5 • • • 6 • • • • 7 • • • • 8 • • • • 9 • • • • 10 • • • • 11 • • • 12

Different Paper Sizes

60-space line
Spacing: 1 and 2
Key two 30-s timings on
each line *or* repeat each line
three times.

Sentences with Double-Letter Words

1 He is selling green and yellow coordinated outdoor supplies.

2 Those tall fellows will arrive at school tomorrow afternoon.

3 I need three eggs to make cinnamon cookies for the meetings.

Number Practice

4 In 1888 a woman working in a shop earned about $6 each week.

5 We hope that 24 of the 39 students will return for test 426.

Graduated Speed Practice

Turn to the Graduated Alphanumerical Speed Practice, page 403. Select a sentence that you think you can key in the time indicated.

Sentences with One-Hand Words

6 In the opinion of Phillip, a few rewards wouldn't deter him.

7 The onion bread tasted milky; add some poppy seed to it now.

8 Jill saw a hare hop up the west hill to feed on the cabbage.

· · · · 1 · · · · 2 · · · · 3 · · · · 4 · · · · 5 · · · · 6 · · · · 7 · · · · 8 · · · · 9 · · · · 10 · · · · 11 · · · · 12

Concentrate on Correct Spelling

9 It is often beneficial to shop for extra bargains.

10 We are believing that the bulletin is now correct.

Metric Usage

Rule 9: Numeric dating consists of the year, month, and day in descending order with a space between each component.
Example:

We sent the letter on 1991 03 21.

Rule 10: All numeric time is expressed in terms of the 24-hour clock; a colon divides hours from minutes. Add zeroes as necessary for times less than ten hours.
Examples:

We arose at 06:30 to reach the meeting by 10:05.
We returned home at 17:05.

11 That concert should start at 20:30 on Wednesday, 1990 08 23.

12 The new house has 109.5 m^2 and they will move in 1991 12 06.

Speed Building

Key two 30-s timings on each line concentrating on a speed goal slightly higher than your recent speed on timings. Students on individual progress should key each line three times with the increased speed goal in mind.

Skill Building

Key each underlined word three times. Key each line once concentrating on the underlined words.

Key each line twice, concentrating on the correct metric format.

v visor voters give never vitally visa vacate valley van visas
   Vince will view this very village from this vital viewpoint.

w work wed draw yellow wise widow works wage were waded sewers
   Where are those wide wheels for this workman's white wagons?

x xerox fox ox mix taxes phlox taxi wax fix toxic boxes Trixie
   Rex and Roxy will relax in the taxi before paying their tax.

y yarn yet your youth yields yearn try slay my cry every sixty
   Yes, you may try your hand at this year's yearbook, Shirley.

z zinc zing zeal size zither zinnia fuzz zippers prize zoology
   This dazed zebra won a fuzzy peach as its prize in this zoo.

• • • • 1 • • • • 2 • • • • 3 • • • • 4 • • • • 5 • • • • 6 • • • • 7 • • • • 8 • • • • 9 • • • •10 • • • •11 • • • •12

Sentence with Numbers

There are 23 new cars on lot 106, 37 on lot 215, 8 on lot 7,
19 on lot 29, 14 on lot 435, 4 on lot 86, 9 on lot 87, 91 on
lot 45, and 201 on lot 190.

• • • • 1 • • • • 2 • • • • 3 • • • • 4 • • • • 5 • • • • 6 • • • • 7 • • • • 8 • • • • 9 • • • •10 • • • •11 • • • •12

Selected Number Practice

1. Analyze your errors in the Sentence with Numbers.
2. Choose the number or numbers giving you difficulty or causing errors.
3. Select the appropriate Selected Number Practice.
4. Key the line twice.

1 a 1 and a 1 or an 11 or 111 and 12 for a 31 by 1 among 1 121
2 a 2 or 22 by 12 since 212 by 2 and a 2 or 21 and 2 122 or 12
3 the 3 or 13 and 33 by 313 yet 3 131 or 3 323 by 3 but 3 or 3
4 or 4 and 41 but 14 and 4 141 by 44 among 41 for 4 424 and 14
5 a 5 and a 55 or 515 by 51 but 25 at least 5 251 for 51 and 5
6 the 6 or 16 since 616 then 61 but 16 626 for 16 or 66 but 62
7 a 7 and a 7 or a 71 or 7 171 and 7 for a 72 by 7 among 7 737
8 the 8 or 18 and 88 by 818 yet 8 181 or 8 828 by 8 but 8 or 8
9 or 9 and 92 but 19 and 9 191 by 9 among 949 for 9 929 and 19
0 a 0 and a 03 or 040 by 30 but 20 at least 1 040 for 20 and 0

• • • • 1 • • • • 2 • • • • 3 • • • • 4 • • • • 5 • • • • 6 • • • • 7 • • • • 8 • • • • 9 • • • •10 • • • •11 • • • •12

Key three 2-min timings on the sentence *or* repeat the sentence five times. All numbers are included in the sentence.

Circle all number errors.

After Selected Number Practice, key two 2-min timings on the sentence and determine if you have improved your number accuracy.

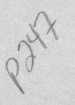

Production 1

Key the following letter on Dasmund letterhead, Winnipeg office. Use block style with paragraph indentations. Use open punctuation. Use the letterhead provided in the Working Papers. Key an envelope or envelope label.

Apple Canada Inc. / 7495 Birchmount Road / Markham, Ontario / L3R 5E2 / Attention: Consumer Products Division / Gentlemen / We are considering expanding our line of office equipment and would appreciate receiving information on the Apple Computer line. / ¶ It is our understanding Apple has many unique computer lines and software packages for both business and personal use. Our store is interested in adding a computer line to our present offerings and we would appreciate receiving your product information as soon as possible. Please include the current price list and information concerning your computers with the catalogue. / Sincerely yours / Rosemary McGraw / Office Equipment Manager / P.S. Any brochures or literature featuring the computers would be appreciated.

Production 2

Key the following on Dasmund letterhead, Vancouver office. Use simplified style. The letter should be confidential. Use the letterhead provided in the Working Papers. Key an envelope or envelope label.

Mr. B. C. Wong / 13415 Vine Maple Drive / Surrey, British Columbia / V4A 2X7 / Dear Mr. Wong

Credit is a very valuable asset in today's business world and we feel you value your credit rating.

Credit ratings are available on every business and individual who has used credit. Until now, you have always had a very good credit rating.

Please make arrangements to bring your account to its proper 30-day credit status. Your cheque for $375.25 would clear the over-due balance and leave a current balance of $113.75. If some unexpected financial burden has created a problem for you, please inform us as we may be able to work together to the mutual benefit of both you and Dasmund.

Your business is valued by us, and we know your credit is valued by you. See me, at your earliest convenience, to make arrangements to pay your account.

Sincerely yours

Herman Schultz
Credit Manager

P.S. Your cheque for $375.25 would be welcomed!

SC
Did you omit the salutation and the complimentary closing?

Title Page / In-text References

60-space line
Spacing: 1 and 2

Key two 1-min timings on each line *or* repeat each line three times.

Skill Building

Set spacing at 2. Key a 2-min timing. Circle all errors. If you had three errors or less, go to line 8 for your next drill. If you had more than three errors, proceed to line 4.

Key 1-min timings as time permits *or* repeat each line twice. Try to concentrate on individual letter stroking as you key.

Key 1-min timings as time permits *or* repeat each line twice. Key each drill as quickly as you can.

Alternate-Hand Words

1 so fox tow eye duty lens than turn bow pan gowns handy panel

2 to fur tug fir firm lent them when box pay proxy rifle works

Analyze Your Progress

3   In a brief analysis of advertisements for secretaries, you will find that the demand is high, the requirements are more professional, and the salaries are generally getting a great deal higher. National surveys of newspaper ads indicate there is an increasing call for skills in microcomputer usage, with nearly 50 per cent of the ads making some reference to word processing, spreadsheets, or databases.

Accuracy Improvement

4 wax ohm sat hip stab milk bred pull fees oily seeds plump re

5 in joy oil Lou ion link mink mono pool pull pump nylon Jimmy

6 lee zoom feet fall annum bills better passed arrived express

7 I will give Max a flask of quince jelly if there is time for me to prepare it as well as glaze my large baked picnic ham.

Speed Improvement

8 The yolk in an egg rates high in vitamin A and tastes great.

9 Keep a copy of the tariff bill in your office accounts file.

10 The facilities have been designed with the customer in mind.

11 A high premium has been paid to everyone with quality stock.

• • • • 1 • • • • 2 • • • • 3 • • • • 4 • • • • 5 • • • • 6 • • • • 7 • • • • 8 • • • • 9 • • • • 10 • • • • 11 • • • • 12

Capitalization – Rule 7

Capitalize the names of departments, organizations, historical events or documents, and specific courses in schools or colleges.

Send it directly to the Credit Department of William Bros. Ltd.
That happened before the signing of the British North America Act.
We hoped to learn more accounting so we registered in Accounting 201.

Double-Letter Words

9 all call bell cook looks shell seeing billed planned assumed

10 add hill eggs heel loops dolls school afford attempt officer

**Assess Your
Improvement**

Set spacing at 2. Key at
least one 3-min *or* 5-min
timing. Circle all errors and
calculate gross words per
minute. Record the timing
on your Progress Chart.

Three- or Five-Minute Timing

	1	CW	3
A young worker should not underestimate the chance that	12	12	4
experience can be gained on that very first job. Many young	24	24	8
people are fearful of seeking their first employment and the	36	36	12
many newspaper ads asking for experience seem to justify the	48	48	16
fear. However, students who have learned the job skills for	60	60	20
the task, and who are ambitious about pursuing a career will	72	72	24
always find their own niche in the world of work.	82	82	28
Use every opportunity to learn from people in the firm.	12	94	32
There are many fine experienced men and women in every busi-	24	106	36
ness who love to help a young worker to get started out on a	36	118	40
good career footing. Give these people the respect they de-	48	130	44
serve and you will be rewarded many times over. Any lack of	60	142	48
experience can be balanced off by the potential you can show	72	154	52
by being polite and always ready to go the extra mile learn-	84	166	56
ing from the employees with experience.	92	174	58

CW means cumulative word
count.

For a 5-min timing divide
the cumulative words (CW)
by five to calculate gross
words per minute.

SI   1.49
AWL 4.52

• • • • 1 • • • • 2 • • • • 3 • • • • 4 • • • • 5 • • • • 6 • • • • 7 • • • • 8 • • • • 9 • • • • 10 • • • • 11 • • • • 12   1 min

1   2   3   4   3 min

Postscript

A postscript should either emphasize something important left out of the letter or indicate
an afterthought. It should not reflect a poorly written letter. A postscript notation is
usually keyed a double space below the last notation of the letter. A postscript should be
blocked or indented to match the style used.
Example:

DS↓

    oi
DS↓
P.S. Any brochures or literature featuring the new computers
would be appreciated.

Key each line once, using capital letters as required. Check your work carefully.

12 roald lee of the department of agriculture will give a talk.

13 the manager of dasmund enterprises will come to economics i.

14 the history since confederation will be tested in history 2.

15 gail tried to recall the date of the statute of westminster.

Capitalization – Rule 8

Capitalize adjectives derived from proper nouns unless such words have developed meanings as common nouns.

The Chinese do not manufacture all of the chinaware sold in Hong Kong.

Key each line once, using capital letters as required. Check your work carefully.

16 i took two courses in french in high school but i need more.

17 register in subjects like english, german, italian and arts.

18 the china was not made by the factories in northern england.

19 he grows chinese snow peas because they are early and tasty.

Three- or Five-Minute Timing

Assess Your Improvement
Set spacing at 2. Key at least one 3-min *or* 5-min timing. Circle all errors and calculate gross words per minute. Record the timing on your Progress Chart.

	1	CW	3
One step in your hunt for a job should be to go through	12	12	4
the local newspapers and choose the ads which seem to give a	24	24	8
picture of a firm for which you would like to work. Plan an	36	36	12
answer to each of these ads depending upon the kind and type	48	48	16
of information given. Most ads give telephone numbers or an	60	60	20
address. Others give a box number. Some give all three.	71	71	24
If you tend to be a little nervous on the phone, it may	12	83	28
be best to plan out your response and practise by doing some	24	95	32
role playing before you make the important call. Speak with	36	107	36
your natural tone of voice, clearly and firmly. Remember to	48	119	40
give the reason for your call and be ready with all informa-	60	131	44
tion of your ability, school record, and work experience.	71	142	48
Ads may not say that a data sheet is necessary but most	12	154	52
of the time, you will find that it has been worth your extra	24	166	56
time to prepare a data sheet which presents you in your most	36	178	60
favorable light. In addition to enclosing one with all let-	48	190	64
ters it is a good idea to file one with an employment agency	60	202	68
as well as have one with you at each interview. Sometimes a	72	214	72
data sheet in the hands of a job hunter comes in very handy.	84	226	76

SI 1.33
AWL 4.20

• • • • 1 • • • • 2 • • • • 3 • • • • 4 • • • • 5 • • • • 6 • • • • 7 • • • • 8 • • • • 9 • • • • 10 • • • • 11 • • • • 12   1 min

1　　　　　　2　　　　　　3　　　　　4   3 min

Postscripts

Alternate-Hand Words

1 go ham soak gland usual social augment ornament cosign augur

2 he got sign girls turns signal bicycle problems bible emblem

Number Practice

3 There are 489 people on board; there is room for 501 people.

4 We hope that 37 of the 62 members will come for the meeting.

Alphabetic Sentences

5 That jet pilot will spend this vacation making quantities of

prize gadgets and trying to buy a saxophone.

6 Quickly, the wily fox broke through a maze of nervous people

and jumped over the picket fence.

• • • • 1 • • • • 2 • • • • 3 • • • • 4 • • • • 5 • • • • 6 • • • • 7 • • • • 8 • • • • 9 • • • • 10 • • • • 11 • • • • 12

Selected Letter Practice

1. Analyze your errors in the Alphabetic Sentences and Drills.
2. Choose the letters or numbers giving you difficulty or causing errors.
3. Turn to page 405 and select the appropriate Selected Letter and Number Practice.
4. Key each line twice.
5. Practice the drill lines for **R**, **S**, **T**, **9**, and **0**.

Metric Usage

Rule 7: Exponents are always used to express square and cubic units.
Example:

The volume of the case was 8 m^3 while its area was 2 m^2.

Rule 8: Always key metric symbols in lower case unless the symbol refers to a proper name, the exception being the capital L for litre to prevent confusion with the number 1.
Examples:

The 100 W bulb had a length of 15 cm.

We asked for 4 L but received 8 L.

7 6.3 m^3, 4 m^2, 4 L, 1980 09 26, 03:30, 7.9 m^2, 3 cm^3, 171 mm^2

8 14:08, 1981 11 04, 36 L, 5.86 m^3, 24 L, 50 W, 13:35, 145 cm^3

Title Page

A title page is used to identify a report. It usually states the report title, author's name, purpose of the report, and the date. The information is attractively centered, both horizontally and vertically, on a full sheet of paper.

```
                TITLE PAGE

               Author's Name

               Current Date
```

In-text References

Whenever the author of a report quotes a reference source, the reference must be properly acknowledged. One increasingly popular method, in-text referencing, is introduced in this lesson. Formal footnoting will be introduced in Lessons 121-122 of the *Career Course*.

Reference Guide for In-text References

1. Reference to one author (Author's name, year of publication, page number)
   Example: . . . as stated in one report (Cameron, 1990, p. 123).

2. Author's name already mentioned in the text (year, page number).
   Example: . . . as stated by Cameron in Montreal (1990, p. 123).

3. More than one author and only one work being referenced by these authors (Authors' surnames, page number). Note: the year of publication may be omitted because the other information clearly identifies the source.
   Example: . . . in Keyboarding for Canadian Colleges (Ubelacker, Delaney, and Allan, p. 34).

4. More than three authors (First author's name et al., year of publication, page number).
   Example: . . . referred to recently (Kowalsky et al., 1990, p. 17).

5. More than one author with same surname (First and last names, page number).
   Example: . . . stated recently (Ernest Wolsey, pp. 13-18).

Production 1

Key a title page for each of the reports keyed in Lessons 61, 64-65, and 68-69.

suit was sent to our Halifax store and sold to one of our customers, Mrs. J. Doret, who purchased it as a gift for her son. ¶ Mrs. Doret recently returned this suit to our Halifax store and explained to our manager, Mr. Grinley, that her son was very unhappy with the suit. When discussing this problem with Mrs. Doret, Mr. Grinley was advised that the suit had been worn only once. ¶ You will be able to see, upon examination, the seams have split. It would seem that the quality of the work must have been inferior. Therefore, we are returning it to you for credit. ¶ Mrs. Doret has received another suit from our Halifax store as your company always guarantees its products. Please credit our account. Sincerely yours Thomas Rollins Manager cc Mrs. Doret

Production 2

Key the following letter on Dasmund letterhead, Regina office. Use block letter style with paragraph indentations. Use open punctuation. This letter should be sent Registered Mail and have a blind copy notation for Dennis Duhamel. Use the letterhead provided in the Working Papers.

Claims Department / Wawanesa Mutual Insurance Company / 2114 Yonge Street / Toronto, Ontario / M4S 2A5 / Ladies and Gentlemen / Re: Insurance Policy A8564 A34, Dasmund Enterprises Ltd. / Enclosed is a Statement of Claim for injury received by our customer, Mr. L. E. Galati, when he tripped over an extension cord in the aisle of our store in Regina, Saskatchewan. / ¶ Mr. Galati required hospitalization for one day. Attached are his bills for medical attention. Mr. Galati is not interested in initiating any further claims although he realizes that he may be entitled to further compensation as a result of this accident. /
¶ Fortunately, Mr. Galati was not seriously hurt. Please process this claim and reimburse him as quickly as possible. / Very truly yours / Peter Gallin / Manager / c L. E. Galati

SC

Did you read the body of the letter to see if there are any enclosures?

Production 2

Read the report carefully before beginning to key it; then prepare the material as a side-bound report. The report will be completed in Lessons 74-75.

FORMAL REPORTS
Including In-text References

Whenever the author of a report quotes from or uses an idea gleaned from another source, the reference must be properly acknowledged by a reference note. The referencing of published material can be effectively shown in one of three ways:

1. As footnotes at the bottom of the page where the reference is being made. This method is the most challenging for the operator unless a special word processing software package is available. The instructions for this formal method of referencing source materials will be left to a separate report. A brief presentation of this method can be found elsewhere in your keyboarding textbook (Ubelacker, Delaney, and Allan, pp. 331) or in Canadian Secretary's Handbook (pp. 233-243).

2. As endnotes at the end of the text. These are typically found in the same format as footnotes but are keyed on a separate page under the title "References" or "Notes." This places the reference material in the supplementary part of the report but does not replace the separate bibliography page. A concise and clear presentation of the endnote style is presented in Brief Handbook for Writers (pp. 351-352) and Pitman Office Handbook (Smith and Hay-Ellis, pp. 303-304).

3. As in-text references or citations. More than one format is in use today. In-text references or citations are becoming increasingly popular because they are easy

Concentrate on Correct Spelling

13 I hope there is no <u>argument</u> about the <u>arrangement</u>.

14 The usual deeds should be <u>available</u> <u>automatically</u>.

Blind copy notation (bc)

A blind copy notation indicates that a copy of the letter was sent to one or more persons without the knowledge of the recipient of the letter. This notation is keyed a double space below the copy notation (c). The bc notation will appear on the copy but not on the original letter.

Example:

```
c Mrs. Doret
DS↓
bc E. Grinley
```

An alternative method is to key the blind copy notation (bc) between the date and inside address at the left margin on the copy.

Special Notations

If a letter is sent by Registered Mail, Special Delivery, Priority Post, or courier, or considered Personal and Confidential, these notations may be keyed a double space below the date at the left margin. The notation can either be capitalized or underscored and should also be keyed on the envelope as shown on page 119.

Example:

```
August 17, 19--
DS↓
REGISTERED
DS↓
Mr. M. S. Dasmund
```

Production Practice

Production 1

Key the following letter on Dasmund letterhead, Edmonton office. Use block letter style with mixed punctuation. This letter should have a blind copy notation for E. Grinley, 3729 Bright Street, Halifax, Nova Scotia B3K 4Z6. Key an envelope or envelope label. Use the letterhead provided in the Working Papers.

Smith-Ryan Textiles Ltd. 1526 Peoria Avenue Wilmette, IL 60091-5984 Gentlemen and Ladies We are returning, under separate cover, one men's red two-piece ski suit Model #507 purchased on invoice 64294 on January 17, 19--. This particular for the writer to use. They enable the writer to produce a professional looking business or academic report. If the report has very few references, the reference data can be contained within parentheses and inserted within the text of the report as textnotes. This method usually replaces a bibliography and is used only when there are very few references in the report (Sabin and O'Neill, p. 338).

You are no doubt aware that you have already been using in-text referencing so far in this report. The method presented here is the "APA style" (documented first by the American Psychological Association and used widely in many business training institutions). A very similar style is called the "MLA style" and was documented in 1984 by the Modern Language Association. If you are interested in this latter style, you will find clear presentations in either _Brief Handbook for Writers_ (Howell and Memering, pp. 332-343) or _Harbrace College Handbook For Canadian Writers_ (Hodges, Whitten, and Lundgren, 1986, pp. 456-459).

Notice that it is "common sense rather than hard and fast rules which determines the information that must be included in a parenthetical citation" (Hodges, Whitten, and Lundgren, p. 460). These abbreviated references depend on the fact that details of each source are provided in the bibliography at the end of the report. Make sure that you include any necessary information to help the reader to find the original published material.

Special Notations

60-space line
Spacing: 1 and 2
Key two 30-s timings on
each line *or* repeat each line
three times.

Common-Word Sentences

1 We are interested in knowing which payment plans you prefer.
2 He will obtain any current information on the firm's policy.
3 The application for the additional space should be approved.

Number Practice

4 Plan to attend the next meeting, to be held June 7 at 19:30.
5 All 42 members were present at the meeting held December 31.

Graduated Speed Practice

Turn to the Graduated Alphanumerical Speed Practice, page 403. Select a sentence that you think you can key in the time indicated.

Speed Building

Key two 30-s timings on
each line concentrating on a
speed goal slightly higher
than your recent speed on
timings. Students on individual progress should key
each line three times with
the increased speed goal in
mind.

Sentences with Double-Letter Words

6 It looks like the staff needs the summer to assess the room.
7 Choo will follow across the bottom according to arrangement.
8 The classroom will accommodate the press if they need space.

· · · ·1· · · ·2· · · ·3· · · ·4· · · ·5· · · ·6· · · ·7· · · ·8· · · ·9· · ·10· · ·11· · ·12

Skill Building

Metric Usage

Rule 4: Numbers less than one should be expressed in decimals, with a zero preceding the decimal marker.
Examples:
The cherries had a mass of 0.75 kg when purchased.
We will arrive 0.5 h from now.

Rule 5: No period is used after metric symbols unless the symbol appears at the end of a sentence.
Example:
Luigi has a mass of 83 kg while Jay's is only 78 kg.

Rule 6: Metric symbols are unchanged to denote singular or plural.
Example:
We asked for 1 kg but we received 3 kg.

9 0.75 kg of fruit, 0.25 h, 12 kg of cheese, 0.36 cm, 23.051 m
10 0.86 km/h, 37 m, 2.55 h, 73.9 km, 83.6 kg, 26.47 cm, 27 km/h
11 The meeting will last 1.75 h; then we will break for 0.25 h.
12 A bag with 1 kg of apples costs the same as the 2.24 kg bag.

Key each line once, con-
centrating on the correct
metric format.

The information keyed into the text (in parentheses) is the author's name, year of publication, and the page number. If some of this information is easily identifiable in the text, it may be omitted from the parenthetical information. For example, if only one work by one author or group of authors is being referenced, the date of publication is not necessary in the in-text reference. The reason for this is that the year will appear in the bibliographical entry for that work.

One of the main advantages of the APA method is that it "eliminates the footnoting process entirely, yet delivers the information required for appropriate acknowledgment" (Huseman, et al., p 276). Huseman and his colleagues also point out that the same format of citation or reference is used whether the item is a book, article, or an interview (p. 276).

You will notice that the APA style of referencing does not use the title of the work in the citation. However, the reader can easily look up the title in the bibliography at the end of the report which is alphabetized by first author. It is also important to note that if more than one work by the same author is being referenced, the date must be included in the parenthetical information and the works will be included in the bibliography in order of date, starting with the earliest publication (Hodges and Whitten, p. 468).

Production 1

Key the following envelopes or envelope labels on the forms provided in the Working Papers.

No. 8 1. Ms. Kelly Szabo
74 Shakespeare Street
Stratford, Ontario
N5A 3W4

2. <u>Registered</u>

Ms. H. Toohey
5165, rue Sherbrooke Ouest
Montreal, Quebec
H4A 1T6

3. Mr. Leon Murray
Murray Architects
1235 Edward Street
Halifax, Nova Scotia
B3H 3H3

No. 10 4. Mr. W. R. Schroeder
Schroeder Computer Services Ltd.
8103 - 133 Street
Edmonton, Alberta
T5R 0A9

Production 2

Key the following letter on Dasmund letterhead, Edmonton office, in block style with open punctuation. Prepare a copy for Lynda Fletcher, 13012-115 Street, Edmonton, Alberta T5E 5G3. Fold the original letter for a No. 10 envelope and the copy for a No. 8 envelope. Use the letterhead provided in the Working Papers.

Current date Mr. W. R. Schroeder Schroeder Computer Services Ltd. 8103-133 Street Edmonton, Alberta T5R 0A9 Dear Mr. Wilson Re: Lynda Fletcher ¶ This is in reply to your letter of (last Wednesday) requesting a reference for a previous employee, Lynda Fletcher. ¶ Lynda was my personal secretary for three years, and I was extremely pleased with her work. She was very dependable, reliable, friendly, and helpful. Her keyboarding and computer skills were excellent. She had a strong sense of duty and was a great asset to our business. ¶ During her employment with us, Lynda took business courses at the University of Alberta to further her career. These studies enabled her to accept a position as an executive assistant with a large firm in Edmonton. At that time, there was no opportunity for advancement in our organization. ¶ I do not hesitate to recommend Lynda on the basis of her qualifications, training, and experience. Sincerely yours M. S. Dasmund General Manager

Bibliography / Table of Contents

60-space line
Spacing: 1 and 2

Key two 30-s timings on each line *or* repeat each line three times.

Skill Building

Set spacing at 2. Key a 2-min timing. Circle all errors. If you had three errors or less, go to line 8 for your next drill. If you had more than three errors, proceed to line 4.

Key 1-min timings as time permits *or* repeat each line twice. Try to concentrate on individual letter stroking as you key.

Key 1-min timings as time permits *or* repeat each line twice. Key each drill as quickly as you can.

Alternate-Hand Words

1 us got urn fit fish maid then wish but rid chair signs rocks
2 am did end got flap fuel sick with sir the towns forms proxy

Analyze Your Progress

Choosing the right new typewriter for your office is a task that is becoming more and more complex in the world of new office technology. Electronic typewriters are becoming available in such variety that it can be difficult to match the machine with the need to solve particular revision problems. It is important to put into priority all of the office needs and choose a machine that will best match this.

Accuracy Improvement

4 wad ply saw hop stag mink brew null feet holy sewer plunk be
5 aw bad wax bed deaf swat fade tear acted erect agrees drafts
6 ebb gall room foot gross needs commit arrive assured success
7 Try to buy a jacket with the new flex zipper; this zipper is
  very dependable and will quite likely give much longer wear.

Speed Improvement

8 It gives him much joy as we hum a jolly tune and look happy.
9 The first issue of that book will appear within three weeks.
10 It will be our pleasure to report to you at the monthly tea.
11 That section of the new building will be open to them today.
• • • • 1 • • • • 2 • • • • 3 • • • • 4 • • • • 5 • • • • 6 • • • • 7 • • • • 8 • • • • 9 • • • • 10 • • • • 11 • • • • 12

Capitalization – Rule 9

Capitalize the principal words designating sums of money in business and legal documents.

Three months after date I promise to pay Andrew C. Mathews One Thousand One Hundred Twenty-Five Dollars ($1125).

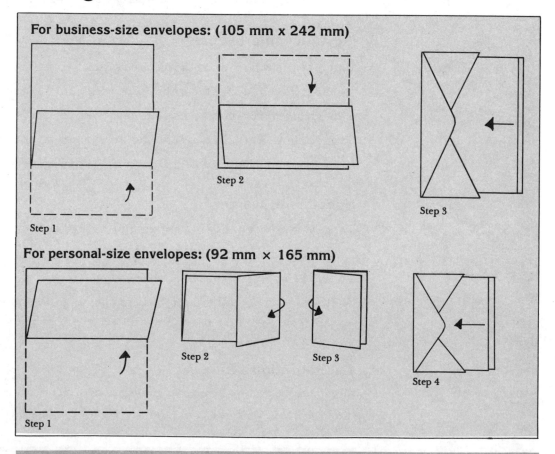

Skill Building
Key each underlined word
three times. Key each line
once concentrating on the
underlined words.   ·

Concentrate on Correct Spelling

13 It is <u>advisable</u> to send an <u>acknowledgment</u> at once.

14 Did the <u>announcement</u> give an <u>allowance</u> for replies?

Envelopes

Review the keying of business-size envelopes (size 10) in Lesson 44 page 120. The address on the envelope should be identical to the inside address of the letter; however, the city is keyed in capital letters.

	Business-size (No. 10 – 105 mm x 242 mm)	**Personal-size (No. 8 – 92 mm × 165 mm)**
Address	50 spaces (elite) or 42 spaces (pica) from the left edge	30 spaces (elite) or 25 spaces (pica) from the left edge
Return Address	starts on line 3 3 spaces from the left edge	starts on line 3 3 spaces from the left edge
Special Instructions	start on line 10 3 spaces from the left edge	start on line 8 3 spaces from the left edge

Folding Letters

For business-size envelopes: (105 mm x 242 mm)

Step 1

Step 2

Step 3

For personal-size envelopes: (92 mm × 165 mm)

Step 1

Step 2

Step 3

Step 4

12 the invoices totalled two hundred twenty-six dollars ($226).

13 the cheque is for one thousand two hundred dollars ($1 200).

14 titles will be transferred for the sum of ten dollars ($10).

15 five hundred ninety-six dollars ($596) was paid to an agent.

Assess Your Improvement
Set spacing at 2. Key at least one 3-min or 5-min timing. Circle all errors and calculate gross words per minute. Record the timing on your Progress Chart.

Three- or Five-Minute Timing

	1	CW	3
Shorthand is making another comeback in the office pro-	12	12	4
cedures of the 1990's but the vehicle for recording is not a	24	24	8
pen or a pencil! Electronic typewriters have been developed	36	36	12
to utilize specially designed software to automatically take	48	48	16
short forms and transcribe them into full English text. The	60	60	20
operator types a few letters on the typewriter keyboard when	72	72	24
a common word or phrase is desired. The software program in	84	84	42
the typewriter recognizes the "short form" and types out the	96	96	48
corresponding "long form" as the appropriate word or phrase.	108	108	54
It has been reported that an operator's new keyboarding	12	120	40
speed can be increased by 50 percent when the short forms in	24	132	44
the word list have been mastered. For example, a short form	36	144	48
such as "asap" can be translated immediately into the phrase	48	156	52
"as soon as possible." Operators who have studied shorthand	60	168	56
previously have an advantage in the learning stages, but one	72	180	60
can learn the shorthand short forms in from 12 to 25 hours.	84	192	64
The word lists used for the shorthand software programs	12	204	68
usually consist of the most commonly used words of more than	24	216	72
four characters, common business phrases, words which always	36	228	76
find themselves on the commonly misspelled lists, city names	48	240	80
and province names, letter salutations and closings, and the	60	252	84
names of months and days of the week. In addition to prede-	72	264	88
termined word lists, a glossary of characters is provided so	84	276	92
that the operator can create an individualized word list. A	96	288	96
higher speed of data entry is a real breakthrough for a key-	108	300	100
board operator.	111	303	101

· · · · 1 · · · · 2 · · · · 3 · · · · 4 · · · · 5 · · · · 6 · · · · 7 · · · · 8 · · · · 9 · · · · 10 · · · · 11 · · · · 12   1 min

1   2   3   4   3 min

SI 1.55
AWL 4.91

Envelopes

Common-Word Sentences

1 This investment company issued a mortgage for program costs.

2 Kindly forward this invoice along with a cheque for the car.

3 The charge for the telephone conversation is on the invoice.

Speed Building

Key two 30-s timings on each line concentrating on a speed goal slightly higher than your recent speed on timings. Students on individual progress should key each line three times with the increased speed goal in mind.

Number Practice

4 To see this beautiful 3-bedroom house drive by 49 - 105 Ave.

5 The 2-door hardtop, which sells for $6 747.23, is on my lot.

Graduated Speed Practice

Turn to the Graduated Alphanumerical Speed Practice, page 403. Select a sentence that you think you can key in the time indicated.

Sentences with One-Hand Words

6 Jill and Jim imply that we are better served by union wages.

7 No, my debts to you are added up and an extra fee is stated.

8 A jolly puppy fed on beef hip after being awarded top breed.

. . . . 1 . . . . 2 . . . . 3 . . . . 4 . . . . 5 . . . . 6 . . . . 7 . . . . 8 . . . . 9 . . . . 10 . . . . 11 12

Skill Building

Metric Usage

Rule 1: When a metric symbol is expressed as an alphabetic character leave one space between the quantity and the symbol. *Note:* always use numerals with symbols. *Example:*

We had driven 748 km at an average of 90 km/h.

Rule 2: When a metric symbol starts with other than an alphabetic character, no space is left between the quantity and the symbol. *Example:*

The temperature was 23.7°C yesterday.

Rule 3: Numerals are grouped by threes to the left and right of the decimal marker. *Note:* whole numbers below 10 000 may be keyed without the space. *Examples:*

The calculator gave an answer of 13 746.271 38 m.
At least 4 000 people came. **OR** At least 4000 people came.

The preferred practice is to leave one space between groups of three numerals.

Key each line once, concentrating on the correct metric format.

9 39 km, 62 m, 63 mm, 47 km/h, 15 cm, 37.9°C, 24 069, 239 km/h

10 69 725.246 31, 5 mm, 2 346 km/h, 19.4 C, 4 629, 24 cm, 17 kg

11 The new airplane traveled 1 150 km at a speed of 821.2 km/h.

12 Over 10 500 stood in temperatures of 32°C to view that show.

Reference Guide for a Bibliography

Book Title:

Author's Surname first. Book Title. City of Publication:⌃##‖55
5to10 Publisher,# Date of Publication.

Example:

Melanson, Marg. Time It! Toronto: Copp Clark Pitman Ltd., 1983.

Journal Article:

Author's Surname. "Journal Article Title," Journal Title,
    Month, Year, Page numbers for total article.

Example:

Lithgow, Terry and Judith McCutcheon. "Student-Centred Learning
    in Keyboarding," Memo, June, 1988, pp. 14 - 15.

Production Practice

Production 1

Read the contents of the following report before keying it in a left-bound report format.

COMPLETING A FORMAL REPORT

Bibliography

A bibliography at the end of a report lists all the works consulted in the preparation of the report as well as works cited in the references. A bibliography should begin on a new page under the centered heading, BIBLIOGRAPHY. It may be vertically centered on the page or begin on line 13. The same margins and placement of page numbers used in the report are continued in the bibliography.

Each entry is single spaced with a double space between the entries. A triple space is left between the title and the first entry. Each entry is started at the left margin and run-over lines are indented 5 to 10 spaces. The indentations must be consistent for all entries.

The following should be noted when keying bibliographical entries:

1. entries are not numbered

2. first author's name in each entry is transposed

Production 2

Key the following letter on Chapman, Duhamel & Hawthorne letterhead using legal letter style. Refer to file no. 2379DMD. Use the letterhead provided in the Working Papers.

Mr. A. and Mrs. B. J. Clayton / 3340 - 44A Avenue / Red Deer, Alberta / T4N 3J9/

Dear Mr. and Mrs. Clayton:

            Re: Your sale to Bell
                 Lot 9, Block 6, Plan 762 0630
                 31 Nyberg Avenue, Red Deer, Alberta

            Further to our correspondence of March 19, 19--, we are now enclosing the following, namely:

            1. Photocopy of correspondence dated March 30, 19--, from Messrs. Hunter, Lyle and Manning;

            2. Amended Statement of Adjustments; and

            3. Photocopy of statement of account.

            As we expected, there was an error in the Trust Company Mortgage Statement and there was an overpayment by the purchasers in the sum of $1,289.78. We would request that you pay the same to our office in order that we may refund it to the solicitors for the purchasers in accordance with their correspondence.

            We trust the following meets with your approval; however, should you have any questions please feel free to contact our office.

Yours very truly, / CHAPMAN, DUHAMEL & HAWTHORNE / Per: / D. M. Duhamel / oi / Enclosures

3. page numbers are not cited except for journals

4. entries are listed alphabetically by author

Even though there may be a number of footnotes for one particular reference source, the reference source is only listed once when setting up the bibliography.

Attach your bibliography to the back of your formal report.

Table of Contents

The table of contents is always at the beginning of the report and it is normally prepared on a new sheet of paper. It follows the title page and precedes the introduction. The table of contents is a listing of the material which is covered in the report and the page number where the material may be found. It is best to compile the table of contents after the body of the report has been keyed.

The sample table of contents in this report is set up as a table, so the title must be set apart from the rest of the report by three blank lines (four returns). The body may be centered under the title writing line or keyed or planned to fit the 70-space line used for keying the report. A short table is usually centered on the writing line.

The heading of the table of contents should be keyed leaving a two-inch top margin (start on line 13) unless it is desirable to center the table of contents vertically.

A sample table of contents follows:

TS ↓ TABLE OF CONTENTS

		Page
I.	Introduction	1
II.	Headings	2
	Subheadings	4
	Sideheadings	6
	Paragraph Headings	7
III.	Enumerations and Listings	9
IV.	Bound Reports	12
V.	Bibliography	15

Legal Letters

Legal letters usually have 10-space indentations for any material that is indented. In the closing lines of the letter, key the name of the law firm in capital letters. Legal keying usually includes the comma in money.

Production 1

Key the following letter on Hunter, Lyle & Manning letterhead using legal letter style. Use the letterhead provided in the Working Papers.

```
Messrs. Chapman, Duhamel & Hawthorne
Barristers and Solicitors
Suite 201, 4909 Gaetz Avenue
Red Deer, Alberta
T4N 4A7

Attention D. M. Duhamel, Esq.

Gentlemen:

               Re:  Sale - Clayton to Bell
                    31 Nyberg Avenue, Red Deer
                    Our File RO45 GLF/lw
```

SC

Did you indent 10 spaces?

LEG.1

We wish to confirm our telephone advice of March 28, in which we advised that proper title to the above property had issued into the names of our clients and you were at liberty to release the funds being held by you, subject to the trust conditions set forth in our letter of March 13, 19--.

We have now received a statement of account from Commerce Capital Trust, a copy of which is enclosed, and we have prepared and enclose herewith an amended Statement of Adjustments based on that statement of account.

SC

Did you include commas when keying amounts of money? Commas are inserted in numbers appearing in legal documents.

Since we forwarded to you the sum of $22,812.26 with our letter of March 13, and the balance due to your clients pursuant to the enclosed amended Statement of Adjustments is $22,522.48 (being the cash to close, less the holdback of $3,000.00), we would appreciate receiving your cheque in the amount of $1,289.78 being the refund due to our clients, at your earliest convenience.

We trust you will find the enclosed to be in order.

SC

Use of the word "Per" is optional.

```
                         Yours very truly,

                         HUNTER, LYLE & MANNING
                           ↓3
               4-5  │  Per:
                         ↓↓2
oi
                         L. G. Manning
Enclosures
```

The table of contents is usually double spaced; however, if it is quite long, it may be single spaced with a double space left only between the major sections.

Production 2

Key a bibliography for the report in Lessons 71-73 using the following entries. If necessary, refer to the instructions in Production 1 of this Lesson.

Howell, James F. and Memering, Dean (1986). <u>Brief Handbook for Writers</u>. Englewood Cliffs: Prentice-Hall.

Hodges, J. C. and Whitten, M. E. (1986). <u>Harbrace College Handbook For Canadian Writers</u> (2nd ed.). Don Mills: Harcourt Brace Jovanovich Canada Inc.

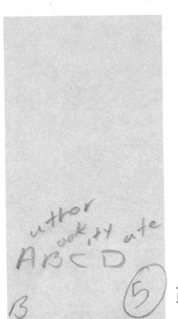

Line 13

⑩ Ubelacker, S.D., Delaney, M.R., and Allan, D.J. (1990). <u>Keyboarding for Canadian Colleges</u> (3rd ed., Toronto: Copp Clark Pitman Ltd.

⑩ Huseman, R. et al. (1988). <u>Business Communication Strategies and Skills</u> (2nd Canadian ed.), Toronto: Holt, Rinehart and Winston of Canada, Limited.

⑩ Sabin, W.A. and O'Neill, S.A. (1986). <u>The GREGG Reference Manual</u> (3rd Canadian ed.), Toronto: McGraw-Hill Ryerson Limited.

⑩ Smith, P. and Hay-Ellis, P.J. (1988). <u>Pitman Office Handbook</u>. Toronto: Copp Clark Pitman.

⑩ Collier Macmillan Canada, Inc. (1983). <u>Canadian Secretary's Handbook</u> (2nd ed.), Don Mills : CMCI.

Production 3

Key a Table of Contents and a Title Page for the report, <u>Formal Reports</u>, which begins in Lesson 71.

Basic English Skill

principal: main or primary
principle: rule or law

12 The (principle, principal) reason for changing plans was the abrupt change in the weather.

13 What is the main (principal, principle) behind changing the format of the meeting?

quiet: silent
quite: entirely or completely

14 The songs of birds fill the otherwise (quiet, quite) woodland.

15 The walk through the field is (quiet, quite) refreshing.

Timing

Set spacing at 2. Key at least one 3-min timing. Circle all errors and calculate gross words per minute. Record the timing on your Progress Chart.

SI   1.03
AWL 3.25

Three-Minute Timing

	1	3
Pack up your new boots and the rest of your gear and we	12	4
will go on a hike through the hills. The feel of spring and	24	8
the need for a good break from work adds up to the need that	36	12
can be met by a good long hike in the woods. Since we could	48	16
start this day, why don't we get our back packs ready now so	60	20
we can go by noon? Would you like to phone Steve and see if	72	24
he would like to go with us? We can pack our tents along so	84	28
we can camp at Ram River Falls. We might even catch a fresh	96	32
trout for a meal.	99	33

• • • • 1 • • • • 2 • • • • 3 • • • • 4 • • • • 5 • • • • 6 • • • • 7 • • • • 8 • • • • 9 • • • • 10 • • • • 11 • • • • 12 1 min
              1   2   3   4 3 min

Skill Building

60-space line
Spacing: 1 and 2
Key two 1-min timings on
each line *or* repeat each line
three times.

One-Hand Words

1 art pup tee pin rate pool car hull rags mill taxes plump bee

2 bad joy vat nip rear pull data link rare pill taxed plunk we

Skill Building

Key two 1-min timings on
each line *or* repeat each line
three times. Circle all
errors. If most of your
attempts have two errors or
less, proceed to line 7. If not
repeat this drill.

Accuracy Improvement

3 we err red far fade beds feed vast agree exert assess Easter

4 egg seem ball reef wells holly indeed attach million appoint

5 inn good cool hall green steer dollar copper arrears calling

6 in pup him Lou nip milk join mink only pool pull pupil nylon

Key two 1-min timings on
each line *or* repeat each line
three times. Key each drill
as quickly as you can. Try to
increase your speed slightly
on each attempt.

Speed Improvement

7 The board learned the real meaning of bull and bear markets.

8 The market is quite good now for buying used cars and buses.

9 He has applied for the new position advertised in the paper.

10 He agrees that berry spoon sales seem to be about a billion.

· · · · 1 · · · · 2 · · · · 3 · · · · 4 · · · · 5 · · · · 6 · · · · 7 · · · · 8 · · · · 9 · · · · 10 · · · · 11 · · · · 12

Key each underlined word
three times. Key each line
once concentrating on the
underlined words.

Concentrate on Correct Spelling

11 Collecting dated stamps is not an <u>unusual</u> <u>pastime</u>.

12 It is <u>desirable</u> to show all <u>disbursements</u> to date.

Basic English Skill

Key each sentence once,
inserting the correct choice
from the words in
parentheses. Your right
margin will not be even.

in: denotes location   *into:* denotes action

13 Did you drive the car (in, into) the garage?

14 Is your new car (in, into) the driveway?

Capitalization – Summary of Basic Rules

1. Capitalize the first word of a sentence, a direct quotation, a complimentary close.
2. Capitalize proper nouns: names of people, animals, places, geographic locations, days of the week, months of the year, holidays.
3. Capitalize nouns showing family relationship when they are used as specific names or when there is no preceding possessive pronoun (mother, father, dad, etc.).
4. Capitalize the first word of a title (book, magazine, article, chapter, etc.) and all other words except joining words: conjunctions, prepositions, or articles.
5. Capitalize only the first and last words of salutations unless they are titles or proper names.
6. Capitalize titles or degrees that come before or after proper nouns.

Legal Letters

60-space line
Spacing: 1 and 2
Key two 30-s timings on
each line *or* repeat each line
three times.

Accuracy Building

Key two 30-s timings on
each line concentrating on
accuracy as your goal.
Students on individual
progress should key each
line three times with the
accuracy goal in mind.

Right-Hand Words

1 in lip ink nip non hoop jump poll plop null moon knoll imply

2 my oil ion nil ohm noon only pool pulp pump jump nylon pupil

Left-Hand Words

3 as raw sag red sage cafe gave wars award faded badges eraser

4 re sat wax saw stab cage gear ward barge fared barges estate

Number Practice

5 All 24 students went to the 3 plays presented on October 15.

6 We need 76 pencils, 3 note pads, and 89 sheets of art paper.

Alphabetic Sentences

7 The quarrels started before Izzy called the taxis which just
arrived in time to take the protesting men home.

8 The answers to the quiz might be posted on the board next to
the vacant room on the left of your jumbled locker.

• • • • 1 • • • • 2 • • • • 3 • • • • 4 • • • • 5 • • • • 6 • • • • 7 • • • • 8 • • • • 9 • • • •10• • • •11• • • •12

Selected Letter Practice

1. Analyze your errors in the Alphabetic Sentences and Drills.
2. Choose the letters or numbers giving you difficulty or causing errors.
3. Turn to page 405 and select the appropriate Selected Letter and Number Practice.
4. Key each line twice.
5. Practice the drill lines for **O**, **P**, **Q**, **7**, and **8**.

Skill Building

Capitalization

Rule 7: Capitalize the names of departments, organizations, historical events or documents, and specific courses in school or college.
Rule 8: Capitalize adjectives derived from proper nouns unless such words have developed meanings as common nouns.
Rule 9: Capitalize the principal words designating sums of money in business and legal documents.

Key each line once, cap-
italizing the words to make
them correct. Check your
work carefully.

9 send it to the education department at medicine hat college.

10 he hopes to study french and german for the next four years.

11 this car will cost ten thousand four hundred twenty dollars.

7. Capitalize the names of departments, organizations, historical events or documents, or specific courses in school or college.
8. Capitalize adjectives derived from proper nouns unless such words have developed new meanings as common nouns.
9. Capitalize the principal words designating sums of money in business and legal documents.

Key each line once, capitalizing the words to make them correct. Check your work carefully.

15 give this copy of <u>robinson crusoe</u> to dad or to dr. hendersy.

16 we were told, "go directly to the sweet shoppe on third st."

17 he will go with lars to edmonton on the first sunday in may.

18 since she entered the business division jo likes accounting.

19 i would use the college french text. say "yours sincerely."

Three- or Five-Minute Timing

Assess Your Improvement
Set spacing at 2. Key at least one 3-min or 5-min timing. Circle all errors and calculate gross words per minute. Record the timing on your Progress Chart.

	1	CW	3
The tarsands of Alberta retain the largest known source	12	12	4
of hydrocarbons in the world. However, until recently these	24	24	8
oil rich sands have successfully defied any attempts to part	36	36	12
them from their liquid gold. Years of research and many man	48	48	16
hours have brought a measure of success; the tarsands are at	60	60	20
last yielding their rich cargo of oil.	68	68	23
In areas where the tarsands are close to the surface it	12	80	27
has been possible to use conventional mining methods. Those	24	92	31
deposits are uncovered and removed with huge machines. Then	36	104	35
the material is taken to a plant where the bitumen will then	48	116	39
be separated from the sand. This method is useful only near	60	128	43
Fort MacMurray along the Athabasca River where the river has	72	140	47
carved its valley into the layer of tarsand.	81	149	50
The tarsands in other parts of the province are too far	12	161	54
from the surface to be mined so other methods are being used	24	173	58
to remove the oil. At Cold Lake, for example, steam is sent	36	185	62
down a well to melt the bitumen. The steam is turned off so	48	197	66
that the liquid bitumen, mixed with thinners, can be removed	60	209	70
from the same well.	64	213	71

• • • • 1 • • • • 2 • • • • 3 • • • • 4 • • • • 5 • • • • 6 • • • • 7 • • • • 8 • • • • 9 • • • 10 • • • 11 • • • 12   1 min

1   2   3   4   3 min

SI   1.45
AWL 4.67

AMS (Administrative Management Society) Simplified Letter

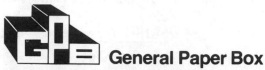 **General Paper Box**

Box 1159, Station A, Montréal, Québec   H3C 2Y5

Current Date

Dasmund Enterprises Ltd.
25 York Mills Road
Toronto, Ontario
M2P 1B5
TS ↓

CORRUGATED PRODUCTS
TS ↓

Due to the increase in the costs of containerboard and supplies, and increased taxes, we are obliged to increase our
prices. Effective with shipments after November 1, 19--,
there will be a general minimum increase of 5 percent on
our basic selling prices.

Our sales representative will continue to assist you with
your requirements in an effort to minimize the effect of
these increased prices.

Your business is appreciated and we will endeavor to supply
you with quality products at reasonable prices.
4 ↓

C. M. COISON, PRESIDENT AND GENERAL MANAGER
DS ↓
oi

Production 1

Key the letter on page 233 using simplified letter style.
Use the letterhead provided in your Working Papers. Key an envelope.

Production 2

Key the letter on this page using AMS simplified letter style.
Use the letterhead provided in your Working Papers.

Skill Building

Select a sentence that you think you can key in the time indicated by your instructor. If you complete the line within the time limit, try the next line. If not, try again or adjust your goal.

Students on individual progress should begin at the top and key each line twice, as quickly as possible.

Graduated Speed Practice

20 s 15 s 12 s

#	Sentence	20s	15s	12s
1	Trees line the roads in towns.	18	24	30
2	Houses are getting hard to buy.	19	25	31
3	That is not a sure thing at all.	19	26	32
4	This is the last chance to do it.	20	26	33
5	The boys were wearing old clothes.	20	27	34
6	The horse can jump that high fence.	21	28	35
7	Menh scored many points at the game.	22	29	36
8	A new bus line wants to move to town.	22	30	30
9	He could read the map while she drove.	23	30	38
10	Cy will have to pay his bill by cheque.	23	31	39
11	A tug boat has just come into the locks.	24	32	40
12	The firm gave their final bid on the job.	25	33	41
13	Sean bought a science book for me to read.	25	34	42
14	We hope to get the right blend in one week.	26	34	43
15	Sales of knives and forks are low this year.	26	35	44
16	Rocks began to fall just in front of the car.	27	36	45
17	The flames leaped high from the tall building.	28	37	46
18	She tried to show them how interest rates vary.	28	38	47
19	The fuel was well down in the tank of the truck.	29	38	48
20	The lease on the building will expire next month.	29	39	49
21	World travel has increased during the last decade.	30	40	50
22	Six new keys were made for the doors of our office.	31	41	51
23	The theme of the show seemed hard to grasp at first.	31	42	52
24	Fresh corn and cabbage is on sale at the city market.	32	42	53
25	The boy risks his life when he races the bike in snow.	32	43	54
26	She can't blame them for trying to get there very fast.	33	44	55
27	He made a major move towards solving the current crisis.	34	45	56
28	We hope to work with you on the next project they handle.	34	46	57
29	They wish to get our tickets before they go to shop again.	35	46	58
30	The big air show will be held for two great days this year.	35	47	59
31	A new neon sign has been hung above their shop's front door.	36	48	60

• • • • 1 • • • • 2 • • • • 3 • • • • 4 • • • • 5 • • • • 6 • • • • 7 • • • • 8 • • • • 9 • • • • 10 • • • • 11 • • • • 12

Basic English Skill

nor: use with "neither"
or: use with "either" or alone in sentences

12 Neither you (or, nor) your friend was invited to the party.

13 Either car (or, nor) bus could be used for the trip.

Simplified Letter Style

General Paper Box

Box 1159, Station A, Montréal, Québec   H3C 2Y5

Current Date

Dasmund Enterprises Ltd.
25 York Mills Road
Toronto, Ontario
M2P 1B5
DS↓

No Salutation
No Subject Line

Due to the increase in the costs of containerboard and supplies, and increased taxes, we are obliged to increase our
prices. Effective with shipments after November 1, 19--,
there will be a general minimum increase of 5 percent on
our basic selling prices.

Sp

percent or *per cent*
Know the preference in your part of Canada and be consistent.

Our sales representative will continue to assist you with
your requirements in an effort to minimize the effect of
these increased prices.

Sp

endeavor or *endeavour*
Know the preference in your part of Canada and be consistent.

Your business is appreciated and we will endeavor to supply
you with quality products at reasonable prices.

4↓

No Closing

C. M. Coison
President and General Manager
DS↓
oi

Use two lines.

Alternate-Hand Words

Key two 1-min timings on each line *or* repeat each line three times.

20 do and ham dug both flap male dish blend shape entity height

21 of cub pep but both hems pant fork fight turns enrich panels

Analyze Your Progress

Set spacing at 2. Key a 2-min timing. Circle all errors. If you had three errors or less, go to line 29 for your next drill. If you had more than three errors, proceed to line 25.

22   Many senior secretaries point to their shorthand skills as the key to their advancement from junior to senior secretarial positions. Expert shorthand ability still commands a high place in the requirements of the high-level secretarial position, even where the secretary dictates to others rather than takes dictation. It is still worth the time and effort to learn this skill to advance to senior positions.

Accuracy Improvement

Key 1-min timings as time permits *or* repeat each line twice. Try to concentrate on individual letter stroking as you key.

23 war ill sea mop wear mink cage loom free polo staff imply we

24 my you mop him ink pill hull hook ploy look pool onion knoll

all boot tell wall books doors unless recall offered meeting

25 What size is that jug of vinegar? I would like to mix up my

26 batch of pickles quite soon and I might need a large amount.

Speed Improvement

Key 1-min timings as time permits *or* repeat each line twice. Key each drill as quickly as you can.

27 Can Jill join him by the east pool by the pulp mill at noon?

28 You can see that the debt created no look of joy on my face.

29 They regret to say that the whole group cannot attend today.

30 You should telephone them about their requirements for that.

• • • • 1 • • • • 2 • • • • 3 • • • • 4 • • • 5 • • • • 6 • • • • 7 • • • • 8 • • • • 9 • • • • 10 • • • • 11 • • • • 12

Graduated Speed Practice

Turn back to page 204 and drill on the Graduated Speed Practice.

Three- or Five-Minute Timing

Assess Your Improvement

Turn back to page 203. Set spacing at 2. Key at least one 3-min or 5-min timing. Circle all errors. Assess your improvement by comparing your score (speed and accuracy) with your first timing.

88

Simplified Letters

60-space line
Spacing: 1 and 2
Key two 30-s timings on each line *or* repeat each line three times.

Accuracy Building

Key two 30-s timings on each line concentrating on accuracy as your goal. Students on individual progress should key each line three times with the accuracy goal in mind.

Sp

colour or *color*
Know the preference in your part of Canada and be consistent.

Skill Building

Key each line once, capitalizing the words to make them correct. Check your work carefully.

One-Hand Words

1 are him bade hill wart noun great knoll bearer upon abstract
2 cab hip bags Jill wade only greed Jimmy freeze join affected

Left-Hand Words

3 ad few gas get draw bred free wads swede facts screws averts
4 aw rag far rat raze brew gate wage avert fades awards erases

Number Practice

5 I canvassed 742 households during the first 6 weeks of 1990.
6 My company hopes to win 3 of the 5 awards offered this year.

Alphabetic Sentences

7 The exit from the prize fighter's quarters was jammed by the several fans who kept hoping to see the champ.

8 The <u>colors</u> in the quilted blazer are an excellent match with the pretty mauve flocking on that jumper.

• • • • 1 • • • • 2 • • • • 3 • • • • 4 • • • • 5 • • • • 6 • • • • 7 • • • • 8 • • • • 9 • • • •10 • • • •11 • • • •12

Selected Letter Practice

1. Analyze your errors in the Alphabetic Sentences and Drills.
2. Choose the letters or numbers giving you difficulty or causing errors.
3. Turn to page 405 and select the appropriate Selected Letter and Number Practice.
4. Key each line twice.
5. Practice the drill lines for **K, L, M, N,** and **6**.

Capitalization

Rule 4: Capitalize the first word of a title (book, magazine, article, chapter, etc.) and all other words except joining words: conjunctions, prepositions, or articles.
Rule 5: Capitalize only the first and last words in salutations unless they are titles or proper names.
Rule 6: Capitalize titles or degrees that come before or after proper nouns.

9 read the first article in news monthly and write a synopsis.
10 dear sue, my dear friend, dear sir, gentlemen, dear ms. grey
11 dr. barbeau will assist dr. helen leung in surgery tomorrow.

Production Review

60-space line
Spacing: 1

Key two 1-min timings on each line *or* repeat each line three times.

One-Hand Words

1 age mop tax ill wars only cast ploy race plum straw jolly as

2 act pop tea ply tear pink craw hook raft plop taste knoll re

• • • • 1 • • • • 2 • • • • 3 • • • • 4 • • • • 5 • • • • 6 • • • • 7 • • • • 8 • • • • 9 • • • • 10 • • • 11 • • • 12

Production Practice

Production 1

Key the following letter on the Dasmund Enterprises Toronto letterhead provided in the Working Papers. Key an appropriate envelope.

Current Date / Copp Clark Pitman / 2775 Matheson Blvd East / Mississauga, Ontario / L4W 4P7 / Gentlemen: / Re: Paper Stocks / Thank you for your letter of (use date of one week ago) and the information on postal rates in Canada. / ¶ Enclosed is a list of paper stocks which we carry in all our stores. We can provide special order stocks if you require a size not in our regular stocks. / ¶ Please do not hesitate to contact me if I can be of further assistance. / Sincerely yours, / Thomas Rollins / Manager

SC

Did you remember to provide operator's initials and enclosure notation?

Production 2

Key the following table in open style, centred on a full sheet of paper. Use double spacing. Make any necessary corrections.

DASMUND ENTERPRISES LTD.
List of
STANDARD PAPER STOCKS

SC

Did you remember to align the numbers?

Stock Number	Standard Sheet Size in Centimetres	Standard Sheet Size in Inches
J1185	56 x 86	22 x 34
J1186	43 x 56	17 x 22
J1187	28 x 43	11 x 17
J1188	*21.5 x 28	*$8\frac{1}{2}$ x 11
J1189	14 x 21.5	$5\frac{1}{2}$ x $8\frac{1}{2}$
J1190	10.7 x 14	$4\frac{1}{2}$ x $5\frac{1}{2}$

*Common letter size of paper.

6. Internal Servicing: Cost of providing the actual installation of Point Five above.

7. Administration and Co-ordination: Cost of hiring yourself or some other person to provide the services of administrator if deemed advisable by the investor - developers.

8. Landscaping: The expense is self-explanatory and will depend upon the personal preference of each investor - developer.

9. Legal: Costs of preparing the necessary co-ownership agreements, registering mortgages, interim and long-term finance documents would be under this heading.

10. Cost of Interim Financing: Actual cost of interim financing incurred and is dependent upon the nature and duration of such financing instruments as may be entered into by the investor - developers.

If you have any further questions, please do not hesitate to contact us. / Yours very truly / CAPITAL COMMERCE TRUST / G. L. Gwozd

SC
Did you use the indent option or the tab?

Production 3

Key the following material as an unbound report.

THE METRIC SYSTEM

As published by the Metric Commission of Canada

Introduction

Once you understand metric, it is easier to use than the old Imperial system. Someone has said: "Metric makes it 10 times easier, 100 times faster, and 1 000 times better." Money is based on the same system of tens, hundreds, and thousands and most people have no problem calculating the number of dimes in a dollar.

Thinking metric is a matter of getting used to the measurements and knowing whether they refer to distance, area, volume, pressure, temperature, or mass.

Metric Units

Length

A millimetre (mm) is about the thickness of a dime. A stack of 10 dimes is 10 mm or 1 cm high.

A centimetre (cm) is about the width of your little fingernail.

A metre (m) is easily illustrated by looking at the handle on a door. It is about 1 m from the floor. The door is about 2 m high (100 cm = 1 m).

A kilometre (km) is 1 000 m. The distance from St. John's, Newfoundland to Victoria, British Columbia is 7 605 km.

Temperature

Temperature is measured on the Celsius scale. Water freezes at 0°C and boils at 100°C. Normal human body temperature is 37°C, and room temperature is 20°C.

Production

Key the following two-page letter using the letterhead in the Working Papers. Key it in either block style or full block style with open punctuation.

Dasmund Enterprises Ltd. / 25 York Mills Road / Toronto, Ontario / M2P 1B5 / Attention: Mr. Thomas Rollins / Gentlemen /

In response to your telephone call this afternoon, we are listing a brief outline of the expenses usually considered to be the development expenses or first-time costs which a person in the business of developing can write off as a business expense.

1.   Search and Find:

Includes all out-of-pocket expenses incurred in negotiating the acquisition of a suitable parcel of land on which to build a specific type of development.

2.   Off-Site Servicing: / Cost of bringing to the lands, main trunk lines for sewer, water, gas, electricity, cable, T.V., etc. Cost of roads, sidewalks, boulevards, etc. all of which are dedicated to the municipality.

3.   Site Investigation: / Costs of surveying, soil testing, architect's and/or engineer's reports on substrata, water levels, and the like. Fees or other expenses incurred in establishing the relevant municipal by-laws and other regulations governing the permitted use of the site, including building restrictions or requirements. Fees to ascertain the limitations on use of the land created by registered instruments. Costs of conducting a financial feasibility study in respect of the planned use of the building or other structure, including estimates of revenue potential, probable competition, etc.

4.   Development Permit: / Specific application, pursuing and discussing the application with the relevant authority.

5.   Engineering: / Cost of designing the sewer, water, gas, electrical, and cable T.V. service systems between the boundary line of property and individual units, which is the investor-developer's place of business.

Production 4

Key the following report in unbound form.

TELEPHONE INFORMATION

By (Your Name)

Telephones are a modern convenience which we take for granted. It is well worth while to remember Alexander Graham Bell, who invented the telephone, # and the immense effect this had on communications, both in everyday life and certainly in the business world.

Some of the films on telephone companies' services available through Alberta Government Telephones in Edmonton, Alberta are listed below.

FILMS
Provided by Alberta Government Telephones

Film Title	Length	Black & White or Color
The First Hundred Years with the Telephone	18 min	color
Ferromagnetic Domains	22 min	color
Growing Together	28 min	color
Here is Tomorrow	28 min	color
Anatomy of an Accident	27 min	color

There are many other films available. If you would like further information, write to the Audio-Visual Services division of Alberta Government Telephones, 10020 - 100 Street, Edmonton, Alberta T5J 0N5, or phone 1-403-425-3679.

Basic English Skill

lie: present tense, to rest
lay: present tense, to put

12 I hope to (lie, lay) down for a while this afternoon.

13 Did you (lie, lay) the pen on the desk?

Two-Page Letters

If the body of a letter requires more than one page, the following rules should be applied:
1. Page one should have a bottom margin of six to ten lines.
2. The last paragraph of page one should have at least two lines of text. The paragraph carried over to the top of page two should have at least two lines of text. A hyphenated word should not be carried over to the next page.
3. Page two and subsequent pages should be keyed on quality plain paper or continuation stationery (not letterhead).
4. The heading of page two should begin on line seven.
5. Triple space after the heading on page two.
6. The heading should include the name of the addressee, page number, and date.

Note: Allow for top and bottom margin defaults if you are using a computer.

Common with Full Block Style

```
7

Dasmund Enterprises Ltd.
Page 2
August 16, 19--

   TS

4.  Development Permit

    Specific application, pursuing and discussing the
    application with the relevant authority.
```

Common with Block Style

```
7

Dasmund Enterprises Ltd.    -2-           August 16, 19--

   TS

4.  Development Permit

    Specific application, pursuing and discussing the
    application with the relevant authority.
```

80

Assess Your Progress

60-space line
Spacing: 1
Key the sentence twice.
Every alphabetic character
is included in the sentence.

Alphabetic Sentence

I had planned to view the oxen grazing beside the first calm
jewel of a lake, but a flighty quarter horse was running by.

• • • • 1 • • • • 2 • • • • 3 • • • • 4 • • • • 5 • • • 6 • • • • 7 • • • • 8 • • • • 9 • • • •10• • • •11• • • •12

**Assess Your
Speed**

Set spacing at 2. Key at
least one 3-min or 5-min
timing. Circle all errors and
calculate gross words per
minute. Record the timing
on your Progress Chart.

Three- or Five-Minute Timing

1 CW 3

	When answering the telephone, make sure that you ident-	12	12	4
	ify who is answering the call. All too often the caller has	24	24	8
	to ask for the name of the person at the other end. This is	36	36	12
	a real waste of time. Similarly, when you place a call make	48	48	16
	sure that you are very clear about who is calling. Business	60	60	20
	telephone calls are most effective when both the callers and	72	72	24
	receivers know the names of the other parties on the line.	84	84	28
	Even though the business call can be answered with some	12	96	32
	routine information, this is not an excuse for saying that a	24	108	36
	caller like this doesn't need to know the name of the person	36	120	40
	giving the information. At times telephone calls disconnect	48	132	44
	or it may be necessary at a later time to get other informa-	60	144	46
	tion. Without the name of the party on the other end of the	72	156	50
	line it can be next to impossible to get the right person.	84	168	54
	Once you get the name of the person on the other end of	12	180	60
	the call, it is advisable to jot down the name on a memo pad	24	192	64
	printed for the purpose of recording telephone messages. It	36	204	70
	is important to jot down the name of the person calling, the	48	216	74
	name of the person called, the date and time of the call and	60	228	78
	the message. If this procedure becomes a habit, it will set	72	240	82
	you apart as one who cares for people and for your firm.	84	252	86

**SI   1.38
AWL 4.19**

Did you achieve the unit
objective of 30 words per
minute with four errors or
less on a five-minute
timing; or 35 words per
minute with three errors or
less on a three-minute
timing?

• • • • 1 • • • • 2 • • • • 3 • • • • 4 • • • • 5 • • • • 6 • • • • 7 • • • • 8 • • • • 9 • • • •10• • • •11• • • •12 1 min

                    1   2   3   4 3 min

Two-Page Letters

60-space line
Spacing: 1 and 2
Key two 30-s timings on
each line *or* repeat each line
three times.
Sp
neighbor or *neighbour*

Accuracy Building

Key two 30-s timings on
each line concentrating on
accuracy as your goal.
Students on individual
progress should key each
line three times with the
accuracy goal in mind.

Alternate-Hand Words

1 by hen span handy shale turkey audible chairmen angle handle

2 do hay sock gowns visit theory auditor neighbor audit eighth

Double-Letter Words

3 goo wall pull seed blood feels exceed yellow running smaller

4 too door seek wool spoon flood issues really bottles payroll

Number Practice

5 Only 42 of a possible 65 members were present on January 30.

6 The 17 yellow daffodils stood out among the 98 black tulips.

Alphabetic Sentences

7 The sixty guests at the banquet will be provided with formal

prizes just as soon as the speaker comes to dinner.

8 The service depot will transfer sixty jumbo-sized golf clubs

to the back of the quiet club house.

• • • • 1 • • • • 2 • • • • 3 • • • • 4 • • • • 5 • • • • 6 • • • • 7 • • • • 8 • • • • 9 • • • • 10 • • • • 11 • • • • 12

Selected Letter Practice

1. Analyze your errors in the Alphabetic Sentences and Drills.
2. Choose the letters or numbers giving you difficulty or causing errors.
3. Turn to page 405 and select the appropriate Selected Letter and Number Practice.
4. Key each line twice.
5. If you finish before the time limit, practice the drill lines for **G, H, I, J,** and **5**.

Skill Building

Key each line once, cap-
italizing the words to make
them correct. Check your
work carefully.

Capitalization

Rule 1: Capitalize the first word in a sentence, of a direct quotation, in complimentary closes.
Rule 2: Capitalize proper nouns: names of people, animals, places, geographic locations,
days of the week, months of the year, holidays.
Rule 3: Capitalize nouns showing family relationship when they are used as specific
names or when there is no possessive pronoun preceding (mother, father, dad, etc.).

9 The tall boy said, "we will be leaving as soon as possible."

10 sean, russel and peter will go to swift current on Saturday.

11 eric went with father, mother, aunt alice and uncle william.

Production 1

Key the following report in bound form.

P U N C T U A T I O N

MAJOR MARKS

By (Your Name)

Punctuation marks are the mechanical means for making the meaning of a sentence easily understood. They indicate the proper relationships between words, phrases, and clauses when word order alone is not sufficient to make these relationships clear. (Sabin and O'Neill, 1986, p. 3)

Using punctuation marks should come easily but if you are finding it very difficult to punctuate your work, a good reference manual is an excellent reference to check on the proper punctuation marks and their usage.

The Period

A period is used at the end of a sentence. It is also used to end an expression that represents a complete statement or command and to separate a whole number from a decimal fraction. Enumerations also use periods after the numbers or letters in an outline or displayed list.

The Question Mark

A question mark is used to end a sentence when a direct question has been asked. Sabin and O'Neill also mention the fact that a question mark is used "in parentheses when there is doubt or uncertainty about a word or phrase within a sentence" (p. 7).

Skill Building

60-space line
Spacing: 1 and 2
Key two 30-s timings on
each line *or* repeat each line
three times.

Alternate-Hand Words

1 am bid lamb angle usual height paucity amendment wish embody

2 by bib lake amend turns handle problem authentic with enamel

Graduated Speed Practice

Turn to the Graduated Alphanumerical Speed Practice, page 403. Select a sentence that you think you can key in the time indicated.

Alphabetic Sentences

3 That giraffe lives in the zoo next to the big aquarium which
is enjoyed by many people every week.

4 The quiet boy wore striped pyjamas while he dozed next to my
package that held five cakes.

Number Practice

5 then the 13 signed up 19 to the 44 when all 50 still have 52

6 through the 29 but the 20 in all 87 give them 7 103 then 604

Selected Letter Practice

1. Analyze your errors in the Alphabetic Sentences and Number Practice.
2. Choose the letters or numbers giving you difficulty or causing errors.
3. Turn to page 405 and select the appropriate Selected Letter and Number Practice.
4. Key each line twice.

Accuracy Building

Key two 30-s timings on
each line concentrating on
accuracy as your goal.
Students on individual
progress should key each
line three times with the
accuracy goal in mind.

Accuracy Improvement

7 you in kill John pulpy kinky pully uphill ohm yon pulp nylon

8 press proof vessel assume keeping summary offering occasions

Speed Improvement

9 Kindly pay the balance upon receiving the service equipment.

10 They agreed to accept the offer issued by the food business.

· · · · 1 · · · · 2 · · · · 3 · · · · 4 · · · · 5 · · · · 6 · · · · 7 · · · · 8 · · · · 9 · · · ·10 · · · ·11 · · · ·12

Skill Building

Key two 30-s timings on
line 7 of Accuracy Improvement. Circle any errors. If
you have more than one
error for each timing, continue with the Accuracy
Improvement drill. If you
have one error or less on
each timing, key the Speed
Improvement drill and
concentrate on speed.

Three-Minute Timing

Turn to the Three-Minute Timing in Unit V of your Workbook. Students without a Workbook should key the Three-Minute Timing in Lesson 84, page 222.

Key the following material as page 2 of an unbound report.

THE METRIC SYSTEM   page 2

<u>Mass</u>

To measure mass (or weight) the basis metric unit is the gram. Prescription drugs and household medicines are measured in milligrams (mg). A headache tablet has a mass of 300 mg (1000 mg = 1g). Small packaged goods are measured in grams (g); for example, you can buy a 500 g bag of potato chips (1000 g = 1 kg).

Heavier products are packaged by kilograms (kg). Sugar is sold in 2 kg and 4 kg bags. A small truck has a 1 t (tonne) mass. To measure larger masses, it may help to remember that 1000 kg = 1 t.

<u>Volume</u>

<u>The litre</u> (L) is the standard unit of volume measurement. The millilitre (mL) is used to measure fluids and products such as toothpaste. Kitchen measures are in 250 mL, 500 mL, and 1000 mL sizes (1000 mL = 1 L). You buy milk, ice cream, and other liquid products in litres. Your car's fuel consumption is measured in litres per hundred kilometres.

<u>Summary</u>

SI stands for Système international d'unités, the simplest and most up-to-date version of the metric system. By referring to SI-metric measurements you can ensure that not only will your calculations be simpler, but that over 98 percent of the world will be able to understand them.

Can you key Production 2 in 15 min?

Sp

percent or *per cent*
Know the preference in your part of Canada and be consistent.

Production 2

Key the following letter on Caty, Kierans, Turnbull & Company letterhead. Use full block style with mixed punctuation. Use the letterhead provided in the Working Papers.

Dasmund Enterprises Ltd. 3729 Bright Street Halifax, Nova Scotia B3K 4Z6 Attention: Edward Grinley Gentlemen ¶ Have you ever thought of the possibility of reducing your company's annual income tax? This can be done by a perfectly legal manoeuvre known as Deferred Profit Sharing. ¶ Deferred Profit Sharing is a type of pension plan where you can deduct, as a business expense, that portion of your firm's earnings which you and your partners decide to set aside to reward certain key employees. Unlike straight cash bonuses, there is no income tax liability which creates a real incentive for employees to remain with the company. ¶ The most important factor affecting the future success of any pension plan is the sound long-term investment of the plan's assets. Since we are qualified in this field, we would like to pursue this matter on a more personal basis. ¶ Our Halifax area agent, Mr. William Newman, will call on you early next week to learn when you may wish to have him visit you and discuss our Deferred Profit Sharing Plan. If there is any assistance that he can provide, you may be sure he will be happy to be of service to you. Yours very truly CATY, KIERANS, TURNBULL & COMPANY M.V. Vimfield Registered Representative

SC

Did you use the current date for these letters?

Unit V

Objectives

1 The student will review business letters in full block style with mixed punctuation and other related material learned in Unit III.

2 The student will learn to format block letters with open punctuation.

3 The student will learn to format display letters.

4 The student will learn to format simplified letters.

5 The student will learn to format legal letters.

6 The student will learn to format business letters on different paper sizes and envelopes of different sizes.

7 The student will learn to format form letters and special notations on letters.

8 The student will learn to format personal data sheets.

9 The student will work toward improving keyboard control by the use of selected speed and accuracy drills.

10 The student will work toward developing a minimum speed of 40 words per minute with three or fewer errors on a three-minute timing; *or* 35 words per minute with four or fewer errors on a five-minute timing.

> The following information was discussed and agreed upon:
>
> 5 → 1. Mall and Steinberg generators to be installed ← 5
>   by an electrical contractor as per...
>   ↑
>   TAB

Production 1

Review Subject Lines in Lesson 48, page 131, and Attention Lines in Lesson 50, page 136.

Key the following letter on Dasmund letterhead, Montreal office. Use full block letter style with open punctuation. Use the letterhead provided in the Working Papers.

SC

Did you use the indent option or the tab?

Blom, Kobayashi & Associates, Consulting Engineers, P.O. Box 199, Devon PA 19333-0199 Attention: Mr. A. Hirsch Gentlemen Re: Gatineau Shopping Centre, Our File Number 6705 ¶ This is to confirm our telephone conversation concerning emergency generators at the above project. The following information was discussed and agreed upon: ¶ 1. Mall and Steinberg generators to be supplied and installed by an electrical contractor as per preliminary electrical specifications issued to Zain & Lakuzta. 2. Steinberg generator to be oil fired diesel and air cooled using supply louvers to cool compressors. 3. Mall generator to be approximately 45 KV. ¶ Cooling details for the Mall generator are needed urgently so that our plan may be finalized. Yours truly Jack McAllister Consulting Engineer

81

Full Block Letter — Review

60-space line
Spacing: 1 and 2
Key two 30-s timings on
each line *or* repeat each line
three times.

Accuracy Building

Key two 30-s timings on
each line concentrating on
accuracy as your goal.
Students on individual
progress should key each
line three times with the
accuracy goal in mind.

Alternate-Hand Words

1 am key than proxy works rotary ambient auditory ambit burial

2 am jam suck panel widow visual antique chairman amend burlap

Left-Hand Words

3 ax fat sat fed reef beef fees vats areas extra assets eaters

4 at fee far war stew best feet vest swear faces attest effect

Postal Code Drill

Set tab stops 12, 24, and 36 spaces from the left margin.

5 G8B 2M5   K7S 1T8   L4G 1M1   J2G 7N3

6 J6J 2H1   H9R 2G5   G8T 4C8   H2C 2G2

7 N9V 1L2   P8N 2W1   M5R 1E1   K9H 4G7

Alphabetic Sentences

8 We will try to utilize the maximum numbers of local students
on every equipment project we are undertaking.

9 Trix played a crazy joke on the croquet field when she moved
a glass ball in with the wooden ones.

· · · · 1 · · · · 2 · · · · 3 · · · · 4 · · · · 5 · · · · 6 · · · · 7 · · · · 8 · · · · 9 · · · · 10 · · · · 11 · · · · 12

Selected Letter Practice

1. Analyze your errors in the Alphabetic Sentences and the Postal Code Drill.
2. Choose the letters or numbers giving you difficulty or causing errors.
3. Turn to page 405 and select the appropriate Selected Letter and Number Practice.
4. Key each line twice.
5. Practice the drill lines for **A**, **B**, **C**, **1**, and **2**.

Enumerations in Letters

Spacing: 1 and 2
Key two 30-s timings on
each line *or* repeat each line
three times.

Sentences with Double-Letter Words

1 The rooms were assessed by the lessee who seemed to approve.

2 Letters supporting the process were dropped off at the mill.

3 It took a week to sell all the wooden doors and odd barrels.

Speed Building

Key two 30-s timings on
each line concentrating on a
speed goal slightly higher
than your recent speed on
timings. Students on individual progress should key
each line three times with
the increased speed goal in
mind.

Postal Code Drill
Set tab stops 12, 24, and 36 spaces from the left margin.

4	A2H 6J6	B2G 2M3	N8X 2E2	C1A 6S2
5	E1N 2L6	R8A 0M2	T1Y 1K3	L6W 1M9
6	V0E 2E0	J6A 1X7	H3L 2E9	T4N 5E1

Graduated Speed Practice
Turn to the Graduated Alphanumerical Speed Practice, page 403. Select a sentence that
you think you can key in the time indicated.

Common-Word Sentences

7 The board will suggest we purchase the additional equipment.

8 We would appreciate a statement covering the above contract.

9 The letter has been sent regarding the proposed tax program.

• • • • 1 • • • • 2 • • • • 3 • • • • 4 • • • • 5 • • • 6 • • • • 7 • • • • 8 • • • 9 • • • •10• • • •11• • • •12

Skill Building

Key each underlined word
three times. Key each line
once concentrating on the
underlined words.

Concentrate on Correct Spelling

10 The prevalent attitude is less stress on quantity.

11 We hope to receive the questionnaire by next week.

Enumerations in the Body of a Letter
There are two ways of keying enumerated material in the body of a letter.
1. Align the enumerated material with the left and right margins. This style is always used with
full block letters. **OR**
2. Indent the enumerated material five spaces from the left and right margins. The second line
of an enumeration should be aligned with the beginning of the sentence not the number.
Single space each enumeration but double space between enumerations.
Example 1:

```
        The following information was discussed and agreed upon:

        1.   Mall and Steinberg generators to be installed by an
left         electrical contractor as per preliminary...
margin↑
```

Three-Minute Timing

Timing

Set spacing at 2. Key at least one 3-min timing. Circle all errors and calculate gross words per minute. Record the timing on your Progress Chart.

SI   1.23
AWL 3.66

Have you read a good book in the last week? If not, it   `12 | 4`
will seem like it is time to take a break and come to browse   `24 | 8`
through our shelves of new and used books. We have many new   `36 | 12`
titles in our shop since you last came to see us. In total,   `48 | 16`
we have put 389 titles on the shelves that we have never had   `60 | 20`
stocked before. I know that you tend to like accounts about   `72 | 24`
life on the prairies and 13 new authors have published books   `84 | 28`
along this theme. Phone me if you would like to have a book   `96 | 32`
put aside until you can come in to see it.   `104 | 35`

```
• • • • 1 • • • • 2 • • • • 3 • • • • 4 • • • • 5 • • • 6 • • • 7 • • • • 8 • • • • 9 • • • 10 • • • 11 • • • 12   1 min
                    1                    2                    3                    4   3 min
```

Production Practice

SC

Did you key the current *numeric* date?

SC

Can you use an automatic date option?

Production 1

Review full block letter style with mixed punctuation in Lesson 41, page 108. Key the following letter on Dasmund letterhead, Toronto office. Use the letterhead provided in the Working Papers.

Ms. Kelly Szabo
74 Shakespeare Street
Stratford, Ontario
N5A 3W4

Dear Ms. Szabo:

You have been recommended as someone who possesses the necessary qualities to fill a position currently open in our Executive Sales Training Program.

I have no way of knowing whether this would be of interest to you, but based on what I have been told, I believe it could be of mutual benefit for us to meet personally to discuss this matter further.

Please call me at (416) 363-5133 so that a mutually satisfactory time can be arranged for an interview.

Sincerely,

Catherine McInnis
Assistant Manager

oi

SC

Did you key the current date?

SC

Did you use the indent option or the tab?

SC

Do you know the Editors' Marks? If not refer to page 168 (Lesson 61).

Production 1

Key the following letter on Dasmund letterhead, Montreal office. Use hanging indented letter style with mixed punctuation. Emphasize the word YOU. Use the letterhead provided in the Working Papers.

```
Mr. G. Desjardins
2339 Belgrave Street
Montreal, Quebec
H4A 2L9

Dear Mr. Desjardins:

YOU are now one of our customers who will receive preferred
     treatment from Dasmund Enterprises.

YOU as a preferred customer of Dasmund have credit privileges
     in not only our Montreal store, but in Dasmund stores
     across Canada.
```

¶ YOU will receive special mailings of the latest in savings in all the various departments of our stores. These specials are only available to our credit card customers. / ¶ You can always take advantage of our daily low prices as you will only have to pay for your purchases when you receive our billing, once every month. / ¶ You will always have a listing of your purchases to refer to as our customer card statement will list every item for you. / ¶ You will be able to take advantage of our regular sales items as you can use your charge account. Simply sign the back of your new card and present it to the cashier at any of our stores across Canada when you wish to make a purchase. / Sincerely yours / Michelle De Meeres / Manager / Enclosure : Credit Card

Production 2

Key the following letter on Dasmund letterhead, Vancouver office. Display the beginning of each paragraph as capitalized and centered. Use mixed punctuation. Use the letterhead provided in the Working Papers.

Mr. J. S. Damji / 1615 – West 11th Avenue / Vancouver, British Columbia / V6J 2B8 / Dear Mr. Damji /

OUR GRAND OPENING

is finally here! We have moved into our new and modern premises at 7025 Granville Street.

09 : 00 to 21 : 00

will be our hours for the first week in our new premises. We want to be sure all of our old customers, as well as any new customers, will have the opportunity to see our new building and take advantage of our opening specials. / ¶ JUICE, COFFEE, AND DOUGHNUTS will be available all week for your enjoyment while you are browsing and perhaps purchasing some of our fine specials. / ¶ FREE PARKING is another fine feature of our new premises. No longer do you have to spend your valuable time looking for a place to park your car. Parking will be available for all our patrons, at no charge to you, our customer. / ¶ WE HOPE TO SEE YOU SOON! / Fred Baker /Manager

Production 2

Key the following letter in full block style with mixed punctuation. Use the letterhead provided in the Working Papers.

Mr. J. R. Chang
Chang's Appliance Store
1212 Main Street South
Dauphin, Manitoba
R7N 1M8

Dear Mr. Chang:

Thank you for your letter of December 18, 19-- and your order for two Compline Systems mobile computer workstations. These have been shipped to you today via Canapak.

In answer to your enquiry, we do have a compact laser/fax stand with slots for individual fax messages and a roll-out shelf for manuals and log books. Stand No. 5501 in light oak retails for $249.

We hope you will be pleased with your shipment and look forward to doing business with you in the near future.

Sincerely yours,

Joan Deoming
Manager

oi

SI   1.06
AWL 3.46

YOU is the displayed word.

Three-Minute Timing

	1	3
Have you felt the call of the cool blue water since the	12	4
days have become so hot? There are lots of people who leave	24	8
their chores in town and head for the beach on such days. A	36	12
week from now the beach will be too crowded but if you leave	48	16
right now, you will find lots of room. A few more hot hours	60	20
should cause the water to be warm enough to go in for a swim.	72	24
A walk along the beach can also be a lot of fun if you start	84	28
at the north end and go right around the lake. There is one	96	32
part of the walk where you will have to go on a worn path at	108	36
the edge of the bank above the water.	115	38

• • • • 1 • • • • 2 • • • • 3 • • • • 4 • • • • 5 • • • • 6 • • • • 7 • • • • 8 • • • • 9 • • • • 10 • • • • 11 • • • • 12   **1 min**

1   2   3   4   **3 min**

Display Letters

Display letters are popular for company promotion. They are used to attract the eye of the reader by displaying the first word or words of the paragraph.

In the hanging-indented letter style, the other lines of the paragraph are blocked to the right of the displayed word or words. Usually each paragraph of the letter begins with the same word.

Example:

Dear Mr. Desjardins:

YOU are now one of our customers who will receive preferred

      treatment from Dasmund Enterprises.

↑
TAB

Another style of display is to center and capitalize the beginning word or words of the paragraph.

Example:

Dear Mr. Damji:

DS↓

        OUR GRAND OPENING

DS↓

is finally here! We have moved into our new and modern
premises at 7025 Granville Street.

82

60-space line
Spacing: 1 and 2
Key two 30-s timings on
each line *or* repeat each line
three times.

Speed Building

Key two 30-s timings on
each line concentrating on a
speed goal slightly higher
than your recent speed on
timings. Students on individual progress should key
each line three times with
the increased speed goal in
mind.

Skill Building
Key each underlined word
three times. Key each line
once concentrating on the
underlined words.

Production Practice

SC

Did you use the current date
for these letters?

SC

Can you use an automatic
date option?

Block Letter

Common-Word Sentences

1 Some of the enclosed information should please your company.

2 We require a meeting of the complete department every month.

3 I would appreciate a copy of the following insurance policy.

Postal Code Drill
Set tab stops 12, 24, and 36 spaces from the left margin.

4 B4H 2B2   H3Z 2L8   C1A 8A4   R2M 3K4

5 R7N 2C9   T0B 1J0   K8N 3A5   V9N 5M9

6 J7R 4A6   E3N 1V7   P9N 2J4   H8R 3L3

Graduated Speed Practice
Turn to the Graduated Alphanumerical Speed Practice, page 403. Select a sentence that
you think you can key in the time indicated.

Sentences with One-Hand Words

7 In my opinion, this test seems to be too hard in some areas.

8 The cases of fresh bread sat in the corner of the mill cafe.

9 There was a sag in the roof of the garage on John's acreage.

• • • • 1 • • • • 2 • • • • 3 • • • • 4 • • • • 5 • • • • 6 • • • • 7 • • • • 8 • • • • 9 • • • •10 • • • •11 • • • •12

Concentrate on Correct Spelling

10 This procedure was predictable from the beginning.

11 It was a privilege to be preparing for this event.

Production 1

Read the letter on page 217 and key it as a block letter with open punctuation. Use the
letterhead provided in the Working Papers.

Production 2

Key the following letter on Dasmund letterhead, Vancouver office. Use block letter style
and mixed punctuation. Use the letterhead provided in the Working Papers.
Mr. Bruce Clendinning / 3329 Monmouth Street / Vancouver, British Columbia / V5R
3R7 / Dear Mr. Clendinning / ¶ We wish to thank you for the time you have taken
recently to discuss employment opportunities with us. Your interest in our Company is very
much appreciated. / ¶ After careful consideration of our requirements, however, we
regret to advise that we are not in a position to make you an offer of employment. / ¶ We
trust you will be successful in exploring other employment possibilities and wish you every
success in your chosen field. / Yours very truly / P.J. Vanderwerf / Employee Relations
Manager.

Display Letters

60-space line
Spacing: 1 and 2
Key two 30-s timings on
each line *or* repeat each line
three times.

Sentences with One-Hand Words

1 Lou, the fattest pupil, ate a raw onion with many sad tears.

2 Jimmy was too ill to mop the ink stain from the waxed stage.

3 Kim will clean a pool if she is paid the minimum union wage.

Speed Building

Key two 30-s timings on
each line concentrating on a
speed goal slightly higher
than your recent speed on
timings. Students on individual progress should key
each line three times with
the increased speed goal in
mind.

Number Practice

4 This Shaftmobile 5-84 has 31 500 km and it sells for $3 495.

5 The 3 people have 19 or 20 new machines to sell for only $5.

Graduated Speed Practice

Turn to the Graduated Alphanumerical Speed Practice, page 403. Select a sentence that you think you can key in the time indicated.

Sentences with Double-Letter Words

6 I agree to press the issue if we cannot carry all the goods.

7 He attends summer school during the middle of the afternoon.

8 See the full moon across the channel as it follows the hill.

· · · · 1 · · · · 2 · · · · 3 · · · · 4 · · · · 5 · · · 6 · · · 7 · · · · 8 · · · · 9 · · · ·10 · · · ·11 · · · ·12

Skill Building
Key each underlined word
three times. Key each line
once concentrating on the
underlined words.

Concentrate on Correct Spelling

9 You can <u>precede</u> your speech with <u>pleasant</u> remarks.

10 The <u>preceding</u> events were truly a <u>surprise</u> to all.

Word Division
Rule 5: Divide words between double letters of speech syllables.
Rule 6: Divide only between complete words of a compound word.
Rule 7: A single syllable in the middle of a word should be left on the first line of keying. If there are two single syllables, divide between them.

Key each line once, inserting a hyphen between each
speech syllable. Correct
lines should end evenly on a
60-space line. Check your
work carefully.

11 blotter butter knitting kitten raccoon vaccine matter

12 found busy sometimes painting alone sunning mower summer

13 neglect namesake mover mould neon nipple orator picnics

Basic English Skill
its: possessive pronoun
it's: contraction for "it is"

Key each sentence once,
inserting the correct choice
from the words in
parentheses. Your right
margin will not be even.

14 (Its, It's) the best news I have heard so far.

15 The tree had (its, it's) branches broken by the wind.

Block Letter Style

Open punctuation is also known as *no-point punctuation*.

 Dasmund Enterprises Ltd.

300, rue Lepailleur Montréal, Québec H1L 6J1
(514) 863-7932

                                        Current Date

Ms. H. Toohey
5165, rue Sherbrooke Ouest
Montreal, Quebec
H4A 1T6

Dear Ms. Toohey

Thank you for your letter requesting information on the letter
styles used in our office. This is an example of block letter
style with open punctuation.

You will notice that the date line and the closing lines are
blocked at the center. The other letter parts are blocked at the
left margin. In other words, this letter has been blocked around
two points. Therefore, it is commonly referred to as the block
letter style. It is common to find this style with no paragraph
indentations.

The style of punctuation in this example is open punctuation.
This means there is no punctuation after any of the letter parts.

The block letter style is the second most popular letter style
used in business. This letter style is used with either open or
mixed punctuation. I hope this information will be helpful in
your survey.

                            Yours truly

                            Michelle De Meeres
                            Manager

oi

Production 2

Key the following letter in block style. Use mixed punctuation with paragraph indentations. Use the letterhead provided in your Working Papers.

Current Date   Mr. T. Rollins   Dasmund Enterprises Ltd. 25 York Mills Road   Toronto, Ontario   M2P 1B5   Dear Mr. Rollins   ¶ Our contract with the Printing Specialties & Paper Productions Union Number 323 has expired. We were negotiating with the union before the contract expired.   ¶ On September 6, 19--, a Memorandum of Agreement was agreed upon through conciliation. This agreement was presented to the union membership on September 16 with the union committee's unanimous recommendation that the offer be ratified. The membership did not ratify the offer.   ¶ We have now entered mediation in a continuing effort to reach an agreement which could be accepted by both the company and the union. It is possible that a legal work stoppage could occur on or about October 10. We will be unable to ship your packaging materials from our inventories in the Leaside plants or any other warehouse should a work stoppage occur. Therefore, we recommend that you carefully examine your present supplies of packaging materials and provide us with your shipping instructions at the earliest possible date.   ¶ Please be assured that we are doing everything possible to supply materials to you. We feel it is important that you be informed of our current situation.   Yours very truly   E.S. & A. SAUVE (CANADA) LTD.   J.R. Pitsakis   Vice-President

Block Letter with Paragraph Indentations

Right-Hand Words

1 my pup pin nip oil pulp pump holy jump join mill jolly imply

2 on hum you him pin moon holy oily jump hill upon plunk plump

Double-Letter Words

3 boo toot noon adds cross upper cotton rubber college settled

4 coo week beef keen tools drill tariff bottle efforts pattern

Postal Code Drill

Set tab stops 12, 24, and 36 spaces from the left margin.

5 E2A 4B4   A2H 2C4   E2H 1V5   V2X 7B5

6 T0A 0L0   S6H 4R5   R7N 1W5   V2P 4N8

7 T3A 1H9   M2H 1K2   S6H 3X7   T1C 1L2

Alphabetic Sentences

8 Liza quit her work on the tax journal because she forgot the value of the very demanding project.

9 We hope to obtain the extra grazing land in question if this move can be quickly justified.

· · · · 1 · · · · 2 · · · · 3 · · · · 4 · · · · 5 · · · · 6 · · · · 7 · · · · 8 · · · · 9 · · · · 10 · · · · 11 · · · · 12

Selected Letter Practice
1. Analyze your errors in the Alphabetic Sentences and the Postal Code Drill.
2. Choose the letters or numbers giving you difficulty or causing errors.
3. Turn to page 405 and select the appropriate Selected Letter and Number Practice.
4. Key each line twice.
5. Practice the drill lines for **D, E, F, 3,** and **4**.

Word Division
Rule 1: Divide words between speech syllables.
Rule 2: Never divide words of one syllable.
Rule 3: Do not divide off syllables with one letter.
Rule 4: Avoid dividing off two-letter syllables if possible.

10 blooming standard seldom central censorship fountains

11 role scales sawing scheme scratched sector service screen

12 rejects since sludge truthful wrapped aboard idea usurp say

13 happily bookstore cooled over racy service shall simpler

Basic English Skill

latest: refers to something still in effect
last: that which comes after all others

14 The (latest, last) news is that nobody was hurt in the accident.

15 The (latest, last) news yesterday gave no new facts in the case.

less: refers to money or things which cannot be counted
fewer: refers to things which can be counted

16 We hope to have (less, fewer) complaints this year.

17 The cost of these articles is (less, fewer) than before.

18 She thinks of her old friends (less, fewer) than she did

when she first arrived in the new town.

Block Letter Style with Paragraph Indentations

In block letters, the first line of each paragraph may be indented five spaces, ten spaces, or aligned with the last character of the salutation. A five-space paragraph indentation is commonly used.

Production 1

Review letters with tables in the body in Lesson 53, page 145.
Key the following letter in block letter style with paragraph indentations. Use mixed punctuation. Use the letterhead provided in your Working Papers.

Current date / Mr. M. S. Dasmund / 6817 – 119 Avenue / Edmonton, Alberta / T5B 4L9 / Dear Mr. Dasmund / ¶ We are pleased to enclose your membership in the Alberta Motor Association. As a member, you are entitled to services from all motor clubs affiliated with the Canadian Automobile Association and the American Automobile Association. Some of these direct services are as follows: (Set up the next paragraph as a two-column table.)

¶ Expert Travel Planning / Driver Education / Credit Card Protection / Passport Photos / Legal Advice / Reservation Service / Arrest Bond Certificate (USA) / Legal Reimbursement / Game Licence Service / Licence Plates / Road Reports / Consumer Information / Westworld Magazine / Personal Accident Insurance / Travel Agency / Emergency Road Service / ¶ In welcoming you as a new member, it is hoped you will take advantage of these services. Please do not hesitate to call upon your club at any time we may be of service. / Yours truly / B. H. Hartley / Manager